CULTURAL DIFFERENCES BETWEEN THE MILITARY AND PARENT SOCIETY IN DEMOCRATIC COUNTRIES

Contributions to

CONFLICT MANAGEMENT, PEACE ECONOMICS AND DEVELOPMENT VOLUME 4

SERIES EDITOR

MANAS CHATTERJI

Contributions to
CONFLICT MANAGEMENT, PEACE ECONOMICS
AND DEVELOPMENT VOLUME 4

CULTURAL DIFFERENCES BETWEEN THE MILITARY AND PARENT SOCIETY IN DEMOCRATIC COUNTRIES

EDITED BY
GUISEPPE CAFORIO
Italian Interuniversity Centre of Historical and Military Studies, Italy

Emerald

United Kingdom – North America – Japan – India – Malaysia – China – Australasia

Emerald Group Publishing Limited
Howard House, Wagon Lane, Bingley BD16 1WA, UK

Reprints and permission service
Contact: booksandseries@emeraldinsight.com

British Library Cataloguing in Publication Data
A catalogue record for this book is available from the British Library

ISBN: 978-0-444-53024-0

Transferred to Digital Printing 2007

CONTENTS

INTRODUCTION

Giuseppe Caforio

ABSTRACT

This book is a report of cross-national research on the civil–military cultural differences in democratic societies, particularly centred on the attitudes of national elites, here considered as being mainly composed of professionals.

Our research is limited to the democratic countries: This limit is grounded in the consideration that the cultural dynamics, especially in civil–military relations, of countries with non-democratic regimes are completely different.

The initial project, written up and published in the ERGOMAS and RC01 newsletters, was later discussed at several conferences, and subsequently elaborated in a restricted working group.

Researchers investigated a sample of cadets at military academies and their generational peers at civilian universities ("future elites"). An expert survey was also employed to sample "present elites", both civilian and military.

The book is therefore a report of the cross-national research on the civil–military cultural gap in democratic societies. It is divided into three parts: the first is devoted to describing the project's theoretical framework and the methodology used in the field research. The second part, deals with the results of the research on the main survey themes. The third part is aimed at illustrating the national specificities to the reader for better understanding of the results of the cross-national comparison. Finally, the last chapter presents a comparison between the responses of the two interviewed elites, present and future, and an attempt to draw a few conclusions.

The idea of a comparative survey on the thoughts, attitudes and values of cadets at military academies and those of their generational peers at civilian universities had been rattling around in my head for several years, probably since I had the opportunity of conducting the first empirical researches on the attitudes and values of officers in Europe back in 1991–1992 (see Caforio, 1994). The question that I asked myself was: "What are the differences between the values, opinions and attitudes of officers and those of professionals belonging to other categories? What is the incidence of these differences on group life in each country, and on the national security sector in democratic countries in particular?"

But what gave the decisive push towards carrying out this idea and expanded and sharpened its outlines was reading the work of Feaver and Kohn in *Armed Forces and Society* (Feaver & Kohn, 2001b), completed by a subsequent reading of *Soldiers and Civilians* by the same authors (Feaver & Kohn, 2001a).

Could a research like that of Feaver and Kohn be applied to realities different from the American one? This was naturally the first question, together with a few methodological reservations on the procedures used in the TISS research,[1] that led me to study the problem independently and to seek a more European solution, but one also suited to countries comparable to European ones. Having the good fortune (and the burden) of directing both an ERGOMAS working group and being president-elect of the International Sociological Association's Research Committee on Armed Forces and Conflict Resolution, I immediately involved the two groups of researchers in my idea and right away had numerous acceptances[2] and a fundamental contribution in terms of thought.

From the start I thought of this research as cross-national because there are so many reasons nowadays that make researches that transcend national boundaries meaningful and forward-looking. In the first place that fact that medium-sized and small countries are no longer, and can no longer be, the leading players in the international arena is increasingly leading to large regional aggregations[3] whose dimensions and economic and political power allow them to compete with those that are already, so to speak, *continent-countries*, like the United States, Russia, China and India. Secondly, the realisation of the "global village" (McLuhan, Fiore, & co-ordinated by Jerome Agel, 1968; McLuhan & Powers, 1988), particularly accentuated for the countries of the Western area, has led to strong mutual influence between the respective cultures and to the formation of opinion attitudes that extend beyond national confines. Finally, but without any claim to exhaustiveness, the ever more frequent recourse to multinational military missions means civil–military relations in the participating countries have common, shared aspects.

As indicated in the title, the theme of the research is limited to the democratic countries. This limit is grounded in the consideration that the cultural dynamics, especially in civil–military relations, of countries with non-democratic regimes are completely different, and it would be arduous, and perhaps even improper, to survey those dynamics together with those of the democratic countries.

My initial project, written up and published in the ERGOMAS and RC01 newsletters, was later discussed at the Budapest (September 2001) and Portorose (September 2002) conferences, where we had contributions in criticism and thought from all the participants. But after these extremely useful plenary discussions, it was clear that the multiple ideas and proposals that had emerged on those occasions would have to be elaborated in a restricted working group. So, with the agreement of all the project participants, a restricted group was created, comprising Ljubiça Jelusic, Karl Haltiner, René Moelker, Tibor Szvircsev Tresch and myself. By the end of 2002, with continuous e-mail exchanges, the group rewrote and modified the theoretical framework for the research I had initially set in motion as it now appears in the chapter of this volume titled "Theoretical Framework of the Research". It was decided and specified in the framework that the research would be a survey of elites, conducted on present and future civilian and military elites of the participating countries.

Immediately thereafter, the restricted group met in Morschach (Switzerland) from 7 to 9 February 2003, to discuss and set down a first concrete plan for the empirical phase of the research (determination of the samples of elites, empirical research methods and related tools: see the chapter devoted to methodology in this volume).

The questionnaire drawn up for the survey of future elites and the general plan for the interviews with current elites were then presented at a meeting of the entire research group and discussed in detail on the occasion of the International Conference in Breda (Netherlands, May 2003), called for this purpose. After Breda, the restricted group wrote the definitive version of the questionnaire to administer to the cadets and their generational peers in civilian universities (future elites), as well as the outline for the semi-structured interviews to be conducted among current leaders and opinion-makers (current elites) on the basis of the indications received from the colleagues of the countries participating in the research. The questionnaire was pre-tested on a group of Italian Army cadets (June 2003) and a few subsequent modifications were made.

After three years of work, the framework and the research tools were ready. So, starting in the autumn of 2003 and continuing throughout 2004, the empirical phase of the research got under way, conducted by means of the two planned surveys (survey of future elites and interviews with current elites) in each of the 13 countries whose researchers, overcoming all the difficulties internal to each country, succeeded in carrying out and completing the field research. The countries involved in the research were therefore the following:

Country	Researchers
Bulgaria	Yantsislav Yanakiev
France	Axel Augé and Claude Weber
Germany	Gerhard Kümmel and Sabine Collmer
Italy	Giuseppe Caforio and Marina Nuciari
The Netherlands	René Moelker and Joseph Soeters
Poland	Adam Kołodziejczyk
Romania	Marian Zulean
Slovenia	Ljubica Jelušič and Maja Garb
South Africa	Lindy Heinecken
Spain	Rafael Martínez Martínez and Antonio M. Díaz Fernández
Switzerland	Karl W. Haltiner and Tibor Szvircsev Tresch
Sweden	Alise Weibull
Turkey	Kadir Varoğlu, Sibel Kalaycıoğlu, Bahattin Akşit, Mehmet Çakar

During the empirical survey another two working meetings were held (Chicago, USA, October 2003, and Pisa, Italy, April 2004), aimed at monitoring the progress of the survey and making appropriate corrections where necessary.

After the empirical phase of the survey, in three well-attended work sessions at the International Conference in Ankara (Turkey, July 2004) we began the analysis of the national results and their international comparison; the plan of this book was also laid down and the tasks were divided among the various researchers who expressed a willingness to participate in drawing up the report.

The book that I am presenting is therefore a report of the cross-national research on the civil–military cultural gap in democratic societies. It is divided into three parts: the first is devoted to describing the project's theoretical framework and the methodology used in the field research. It therefore comprises two chapters: the first is "Theoretical Framework of the

Research", which had constituted the point of departure and the guideline for the whole research. In the second, three researchers, Tibor Szvircsev Tresch, René Moelker and Giuseppe Caforia, explain the methodology followed by the team in conducting the research, thus making it easily repeatable and extendable – there is no one who does not see an interest in a repetition of the research at a later date.

The second part, in a comparative international dimension, deals with the results of the research on the survey themes that appeared most important for the purposes of the questions that the research was intended to answer. They were identified on the basis of the indicators deemed significant in the approach to the research (see Chapter 1); the development of the comparative analysis of each topic of investigation was entrusted to a restricted group of the same researchers who carried out the empirical phase of the research; each group had an international makeup and was led by a coordinator, as shown in the book's index.

The third part is aimed at briefly illustrating the national specificities to the reader for better understanding of the results of the cross-national comparison developed in the preceding part. It was written by the individual national researchers and thus reflects, in the different expository methodologies, also the scientific approach of the individual national writers.

Finally, the last chapter presents a comparison between the responses of the two interviewed elites and an attempt to draw a few conclusions (but many others have been left to the reader).

It is a sensation shared by the entire research group that this is a pioneering work, carried forward amid many difficulties and with a few approximations. More interrogatives than certainties are often present in the analysis and comparison of the data, but the scientific contribution of the work is not less for this, we feel.

NOTES

1. Reservations already expressed in the literature: see, for example, James Burk (1998) and Thomas Sowers (2005). The research conducted by us avoids the principal critique that the above authors make regarding the approach of Feaver's research, i.e., not having taken into account the internationalisation of today's military operations and hence the influence of individual nationalities on civil–military relations. Sowers, for example, referring to the works of Avant (1994), writes: "*Deborah Avant makes a powerful argument that nationality, a factor exogenous to Feaver's framework, explains why soldiers from different nations may perceive their relationship with the state differently*" (op. cit., p. 386).

2. Colleagues from 19 countries initially expressed their intention of participating concretely in the research. Later, difficulties encountered in the individual national contexts (problems of research authorisation, financial support, etc.) reduced the group to 13 countries, whose researchers carried out the surveys in their respective countries. One of them, in the Netherlands, wasn't able to complete the expert survey in due time.

3. The first and most immediate example is the European Union, but the trend is certainly also seen in the increasingly widespread military and economic alliances that take in multiple countries in the same region of the world, such as SEATO and ASEAN for Southeast Asia, SATO for South America, CAEMC for Central Africa, ECOWAS for West Africa, and the Treaty of Izmir for the countries connected to Turkey. Many others could be cited.

REFERENCES

Avant, D. (1994). *Political institutions and military changes: Lessons from peripheral wars*. Ithaca: Cornell University Press.

Burk, J. (1998). The logic of crisis and civil military relations theory: A comment on Desch, Feaver and Dauber. *Armed Forces & Society*, *24*(3), 455–462.

Caforio, G. (Ed.) (1994). The military profession in Europe [special issue]. *Current Sociology*, 42(3).

Feaver, P. D., & Kohn, R. H. (Eds). (2001a). *Soldiers and civilians. The civil–military gap and American national security*. Cambridge: MIT Press.

Feaver, P. D., & Kohn, R. H. (2001b). Media and education in the U.S. civil–military gap: Overview. *Armed Forces & Society*, *27*(2), 177–182.

McLuhan, M., & Fiore, Q., co-ordinated by Agel, J. (1968). *War and Peace in the Global Village: An Inventory of Some of the Current Spastic Situations That Could Be Eliminated by More Feedforward*. Bantam Books Random House.

McLuhan, M., & Powers, B. (1988). *The global village: Transformations in world life and media in the 21st century*. Oxford University Press.

Sowers, S. T. (2005). Beyond the soldier and the state: Contemporary operations and variance in the principal–agent relationship. *Armed Forces & Society*, *31*(3), 385–409.

PART I: GENERAL FEATURES OF THE RESEARCH

THEORETICAL FRAMEWORK OF THE RESEARCH

Giuseppe Caforio, Karl W. Haltiner, Ljubica Jelušič, René Moelker and Tibor Szvircsev Tresch

ABSTRACT

The aim of this chapter is to present and discuss the theoretical framework that the group has set up for the research presented here. We deal here with the following topics:

- *a clarification of the general concept of culture adopted by us, and especially of culture of democratic countries*
- *the concept of military culture, along with its subcultures, and the process of change in its dimensions of de-militarisation of societies and re-militarisation of the militaries*
- *a discussion on the possibility of a cross-national research on the subject.*

Discussion leads us to realise the possibility and the convenience of a research as such. Therefore, we materialise our intent to carry on an empirical research on the civil–military cultural differences in Europe in comparison with results already obtained for the U.S. (but it can be employed in non-European countries too, where living conditions can be assumed to be that of all modern democratic societies).

Cultural Differences between the Military and Parent Society in Democratic Countries
Contributions to Conflict Management, Peace Economics and Development, Volume 4, 3–19

ISSN: 1572-8323/doi:10.1016/S1572-8323(07)04001-5

In order to do that, we agreed with several guidelines for our research project, i.e., one basic assumption and three working hypothesis.

1. INTRODUCTION

If it is true that today "the boundaries between military and civilian ... have blurred," in face of this change the comparison and the relationship between the two cultures has taken on greater importance now than in the past.[1]

The main reason for this change is the fact that, as Antony Forster observes (Forster, 2006, p. 1), "In the post-Cold War era, militaries across the world are engaged in an ongoing re-definition of their roles, organisation and financing. This adaptation is dramatically changing the relationship between armed forces and the societies they serve."

This observation, as well as recognition that an empirical research on this subject has never been carried out outside the U.S., has led to the initiative of our research group to promote a cross-national survey on the cultural differences between the military and the parent society.

Our choice is borne out by statements that we find in sociological literature on these differences also called civil–military gap.

For instance, Antony Forster writes in a recent collective book (Forster, Edmonds, & Cottey, 2003, p. 36), "Is the military a separate or unique institution – with its own imperatives, culture and demands or does it reflect society? If the former, then to what extent is 'the military' inherently shaped by societal change?" This question "has long been debated in the civil–military relations literature. One argument is that the military's 'right to be different' results from the twin pressures of the need for fighting effectiveness which necessitates particularly 'military' forms of organisation (what has been labelled the 'functional imperative'), and the need to preserve its domestic sources of legitimacy by remaining close to the society of which it is a part (its so-called 'socio-political' imperative)."

To summarise, we can in fact say that two main positions are present in the literature, one is that there is a necessary cultural gap between the military and the civilian, and that particular gap is not negative, on the contrary "the functional imperative of war ensures that the military will always stand apart from civilian society" (Dandeker, 2000).[2] Another side also accepts the idea that the military has a different culture from the civilian society, but argues that traditional military culture now serves a less essential purpose; according to them the military has no functional imperative to retain a culture contrary to the prevailing civilian values.

On this situation, we can cite what John Hillen writes for the States (Hillen, 1999, p. 54), "the cultural gap between the two entities is not necessarily dangerous to American democracy in and of itself, but can and should exist so the military can accommodate both the society it protects and the battlefield on which it must perform… To many observers, the values and social mores of 1990s America – narcissistic, morally relativist, self-indulgent, hedonistic, consumerist, individualistic, victim-centered, nihilistic, and soft – seem hopelessly at odds with those of traditional military culture."

Despite that, "Whether politically motivated by the agenda pushers or not, there is now (in the States) an inexorable momentum to 'close the gap' between the military and society without clearly identifying the nature of the gap, the extent to which it might in fact be healthy and desirable, or how such a gap might be narrowed."

A similar opinion is expressed by Hew Strachan (Strachan, 2000, p. 5) for the U.K., who writes, "In the U.K. the gap can be seen as the product of continuity" and "If the price of political utility is armed forces that make a virtue of their separation from civilian society, then it may be worth paying," and in the end, "In Britain the civil–military gap should be recognised for what it is, rather than wished away."

Moving away from this set of considerations, our working group decided to set up a broad cross-national empirical research on the subject, taking its cue from the research performed by Feaver and Kohn (2001) in the U.S. but completely revising both the theoretical framework and the empirical methodology (for this, see Chapter 2 in Part I of this book) of the research. The aim of this chapter is to present and discuss the theoretical framework that the group has set up for the purpose.

Therefore, we deal here with the following topics:

- a clarification of the general concept of culture adopted by us, and especially of culture of democratic countries
- the concept of military culture along with its subcultures, and the process of change
- a discussion on the possibility of a cross-national research on the subject

2. DEFINITION OF CULTURE

There are many definitions of culture, but for the purpose of our study we are going to refer to those that are placing the phenomenon of culture within the context of national security policy and international relations.

Hofstede, for instance, gives us a very synthetic definition, writing that, "culture is the collective programming of the mind, which distinguishes the members of one group or category of people from another" (Hofstede, 1991, p. 5).

A more articulated definition is provided by Soeters, Winslow, and Weibull (2003, p. 238) who state, "Culture refers to common ways of seeing the environment, it relates to values and priorities in life, as well as to subconscious convictions, ideas, interpretations and norms that are taken for granted. Culture is shared by collectivities of people: nations, regions, organisations, schools, churches and families. Culture is a group phenomenon, hence leaving the impact of personality structures outside."

And a third and last definition (last, in order to avoid boring the reader) is by Edgar Schein, i.e., "Culture can now be defined as

(a) a pattern of basic assumptions,
(b) invented, discovered, or developed by a given group,
(c) as it learns to cope with its problems of external adaptation and internal integration,
(d) that has worked well enough to be considered valid, and therefore, is to taught to new members as the
(e) correct way to perceive, think, or feel in relation to these problems" (Schein, 1990, p. 110).

We find some common elements in these definitions that should be summarised as follows:

Culture:

1. is the pertinence to a group of people and, particularly, to an organised group
2. it constitutes a pattern of basic assumptions that become a collective programming of the mind
3. as such, it has to be learned by newcomers
4. it indicates a particular way to cope with problems of internal integration and external adaptation
5. this particular way needs to have worked in the past well enough to be considered valid.

If we limit our assessment to democratic societies, as our societies are, we realise that the military culture is a subculture of the culture of the national society as a whole, i.e., of the civil society that, in a democracy, is clearly predominant over the military. Therefore, our comparison is between the culture of the democratic society in general and its military subculture.

We should, first of all, try to characterise and define the culture of a modern democratic society.

2.1. Modern Democratic Society and its Culture

To define the culture of a democratic society means to find – following our theoretical scheme – the pattern of basic assumptions that constitutes the collective programming of the mind of the members of the society and that determines their behaviour, as well as values, way of thinking and the like.

The concept of culture helps us to explain the changes in civil–military relations, which we are facing after the end of the Cold War. More precisely, it is the concept of political culture, which has become one of the most important theoretical explanation of citizens' behaviour and legitimacy of national security systems in past decade. The history of the political culture as theoretical framework began in 1960s, when Almond and Verba developed the civic culture concept as subset of beliefs and values of society that relate to the political system (Almond & Verba, 1963, pp. 11–14). Political culture includes a commitment to the values like democratic principles and institutions, ideas about morality and the use of force, the rights of individuals or collectivities, or predispositions towards the role of a country in global politics (Lantis, 2002, p. 90). Duffield (according to Almond and Verba's proposal) operationalised the concept of political culture on at least three levels "the cognitive, which includes empirical and causal beliefs; the evaluative, which consists of values, norms and moral judgments, and the expressive or affective, which encompasses emotional attachments, patterns of identity and loyalty, and feelings of affinity, aversion, or indifference" (Duffield, 1998, p. 23).

Going closer to our topic of survey, civil–military relations, we should review the political culture as a whole and especially the military culture. Military culture as the component of political culture is, therefore, the subset of beliefs, values, orientations and behaviour of society that relate to the national security system and its military subsystem.

3. MILITARY CULTURE

Organisations are – from a sociological point of view – goal-oriented cultural systems. The task of an organisation is the key to the understanding of its specific structure and culture (Etzioni, 1975). Military organisations, unlike other coercive organisations, such as the police, are specialised on threatening and making use of collective violence. In other words, they are focused on inter-social macro-violence or on "hard power". War fighting "determines the central beliefs, values and complex symbolic formations that define military culture" (Burk, 1999). Functionally, the use of focused and massive macro-violence calls for a high degree of coordination. The organisational culture of the military is therefore based on a leadership strictly structured from top to bottom with a closed chain of command organised according to the principle of centralisation. This assures that the central forming of willpower and planning processes can develop into the actions of the organisation as a whole. The information relevant for action moves from the top down, the competence to initiate action is strongly limited at the bottom of the hierarchic structure (Feld, 1959; Snider, 1999).

The borderline case of a war, in other words the management of an anomic phenomenon such as war is, constitutes a measure of the quality of the military culture not only in times of war but also in times of peace.[3] The organisation culture and structure in all its details is imprinted by the capability for massive force application and the risk of macro-violence. The expectancy of violence is therefore constantly prevalent in the organisational rationale. The military is probably the only organisation that is ready to risk its partial destruction and to put the lives of its members will fully at risk when aiming to reach its goals. Consequently, the preparation of force operations is aimed at including as many uncertainties as possible. An extreme degree of formalisation, ritualisation and standards of procedure are supposed to guarantee calculable and coordinated behaviour of the members of the organisation under conditions of extreme stress and in case of the destruction of parts of the organisation.

In democratic societies, military operations including violence on a large scale, on which the military culture remains focused, have become rather rare (Moskos, Williams, & Segal, 2000, p. 3). However, if they do occur, they normally demand the use of a great number of people and resources. Therefore, military culture is Janus-faced: in times of peace it tends towards routine and bureaucracy; in case of emergencies it is to face the utmost turbulence (Geser, 1994; Soeters et al., 2003, p. 238). This promotes a tendency towards ritualisation of behaviour. Functionally, ritualisation serves to "guide individual conduct" and to "provide a semblance of order to the harsh reality of death and destruction that often threatens to be overwhelming" (Snider, 1999, p. 838).

As a rule, armed forces are accommodated in barracks and garrisons separated from the civilian world. Members are taken care of in a totalitarian fashion. Soldiers generally live in "total institutions" (Goffman, 1961). For functional needs the community is valued higher than the individual, there is a clear primacy of the collective. In military culture the individual is instrumentalised and de-individualised in favour of the group, i.e., it is expected that the soldier sacrifices his individual freedom and, if inevitable, his life for a collective goal he may not be able to enjoy anymore. This "Social Dilemma" (Olson, 1965) is solved by a specific socialisation oriented at a professional ethos, a high corps spirit and discipline (Soeters et. al., 2003, p. 242). The professional ethos implies a "set of normative self-understandings which for the members define the profession's corporate identity, its code of conduct and, for the officers in particular, the professional work" (Burk, 1999). Morale and cohesion are vital ingredients for combat motivation and are part of the soldier's education and training. Discipline means that the organisation members can be forced to set back their individual interests in favour of the collective goal. It serves as an instrument of control in extreme risk exposures and "to minimise the confusion and disintegrative consequences of battle by imposing order on it with a repertoire of patterned actions" (Burk, 1999). Therefore, extrinsic motivational instruments, such as money, are usually insufficient incentives. As a rule, intrinsic motivational elements play a role as well (Lang, 1965; Geser, 1994). The military culture, while highly bureaucratic, has therefore strongly communitarian and even authoritarian features (Soeters et al., 2003, p. 240). This only reinforces the tendency towards inward orientation, or even "castellation" (Huntington, 1964).

To sum up, military organisations are, according to their internal rationale and culture, top-down organisations. In order to be capable to apply collective force they are structured along the principles of centralisation and formalisation, and they traditionally rely on socialisation procedures based on moral and repressive means of behaviour control. Consequently, military cultures are based inherently on anti-individualistic and anti-market ideologies and differ therefore in a principal way from the civilian democratic culture and the social organisation of modern societies.

3.1. Changing Military Subcultures

However, on the inside, the military is not something unique and homogeneous. If you go down from the macro to the micro level, little by little you shall discover that armed forces themselves are a mosaic of subcultures (Soeters et al., 2003).

We find, in fact, internal subdivisions of a structural as well as geographical nature.

Structural subdivisions appear to be of two different kinds: vertical among services and horizontal among different categories of personnel, such as the classic one among officers, non commissioned officers (NCOs) and the rank and file (where the officers' culture is dominant). Some scholars add other structural subdivisions, such as the distinction between the *soldier on the battlefield* and the one in *the garrison*, between *the military professionals working at the MoD* and the *commanders in the field*, between the "*corporate*" and the "*muddy boots*" army, so to speak (McCormick, 1998: cited by Soeters et al., 2003, p. 238).

Subcultures due to the geographical location are overall the national ones, because what influences "the culture of military organisations are factors such as history, the professional ethos, geography, the milieu within that organisation operates, recent military experience, and the Weltanschauung of the external society" (Murray, 1999, p. 28), so that you can talk about "national military styles" (Soeters et al., 2003; see also Bland, 1999).

In our study we consider the particular subculture of officers, because it appears to be predominant inside the military, it shapes the relationship among the military and its parent society, and it appears to be the only one that belongs to a professional group. Therefore, we are trying to draw here a general scheme of the professional officer culture, adapting the Feaver and Kohn (2001) scheme to non-U.S. realities.

Professional officer culture:

1. is a culture that considers the officership as a service to the country, in order to provide the security to the national community
2. is a culture that stresses the group cohesion and the professional ethical code
3. determines a group that considers individual leadership as a duty and responsibility
4. determines a group strongly motivated by their social obligation of a pursuit of excellence
5. determines a group submitted to the political leadership and characterised by a strong loyalty to the country basic law
6. determines a group characterised by duty, honour, self-abnegation, for example, communal character, hierarchy, discipline and control

7. determines a group passed through an accurate selection and a deep professional education.

Furthermore, we cannot consider the military culture as something of constant and identical over the times, on the contrary "Change is characteristic of military culture because of the many influences that constantly affect the values, behavior, and beliefs that together define it." (Hillen, 1999, p. 43).

From ever, the process of change is characteristic of the military culture that needs to adapt both to cultural changes of the parent society and to the changing face of war. In fact, armed forces tend to reflect the predominant cultural characteristics of their societies as well as the societal change. Summing up, as Martin Edmonds (1988, p. 87) writes, the military "is influenced by three key variables; first, levels of technology and their associated prerequisites education, industrialisation and the strength of the economy; second, the particular culture of a society including connotations of history, tradition and political ideology; and third, the socio-economic structure of society, and particularly the existence, nature and influence of elites."

As far as the changing face of the war is concerned, nowadays we seem to be witnessing a return to the Hobbesian world in which (Mearsheimer, 1990) ethnic, religious, national and/or regional antagonisms, kept in check for over 40 years by the balance of power between the superpowers, are being unleashed (Caforio, 2001).

This is the reason for the extraordinary growth from the 1990s of the operations generically called peace support operations (PSOs); this is why the military instruments of most countries are called on today to place side by side the traditional function of making war to the quite different one of ensuring peace.

This set of changes brought about several important development inside the military culture of many countries.

Substantially, following the statement by Soeters, Winslow and Weibull, nowadays, "various developments point at the emergence of a more contemporary civilian or businesslike culture in the military. This new culture will most probably consist of a general tendency towards occupationalism and team-based, self-steering practices relying on general, 'enabling' frameworks of rules and operating procedures. Obviously, there are national culture-related variations on this axis, and not every branch or unit within the military – not even within one nation – will be the same in this respect. Differentiation pervades the military; that is for sure. In these macro-developments the Janusian character of the military plays a role as well.

In the current era of 'New Wars' it looks like the organisation-in-action – the 'hot' organisation – becomes more dominant in the design and command philosophies of military organisations, at least compared to earlier Cold War times when the 'cold' military organisation provided the model for organising activities (Vogelaar & Kramer, 1997). These general developments will induce changes in the uniformed organisations' cultures which merit further research" (Soeters et al., 2003, p. 252). Where, as "cold" organisation you have to intend the bureaucratic one (the military working at the MoD and in garrison) and as "hot" organisation, the soldier on the battlefield.

3.2. De-militarisation of Societies and Re-militarisation of the Militaries.

The question to what degree military culture should be considered as unique and to what extent it should be given the status of an ethical and organisational special case, whether and to what degree the military is and should be an institution "sui generis" has been a concern of sociologists for a long-time, both from a macro (Comte, 1853; Spencer, 1896; Tocqueville, 1835/1840; Weber, 1972) as well as from micro-perspective (Huntington, 1964; Boëne, 1990). Thus, Comte and Spencer assumed that the principles of modern market societies were opposed to those of the military and that the former and latter would be increasingly incompatible. They inferred from this an increasing incompatibility between the organisational culture of modern societies and that of the military. In a certain sense, they predicted a rise of a civil–military gap concurrent with the further differentiation of labour-divided societies (see Caforio, 2003, p. 10).

Huntington and Boëne thoroughly analysed the organisational dilemmas of armed forces. If military organisations are to be effective, strong in combat and successful, they have to observe the functional imperatives outlined above. As institutions of democratic societies, on the other hand, they have to meet the socio-political requirements of integration and legitimisation of modern societies and to accept a certain degree of civilianisation and adaptation to the democratic way of life.

With the rise of citizen–soldier system and the "nation in arms" based mass armies in the United States and Europe, in the 18th and 19th century, a historically unique phase of civil–military relations began. It seems as though – with reference to the mentioned dilemma concerning the integration of the military – the soldier–citizenry was a kind of workable compromise between the demands of both, the functional and the social imperatives, which reconciled the civil–military cultural differences. Conscription promoted the militarisation of societies but it did this at the cost of a certain civilianisation of the military. Thus, up to the present day, the predictions of incompatibility made by the sociologists of the 19th century proved to be incorrect.

Now, however, due to social and geo-strategic changes, the period of the citizen–soldier and the mass armies is coming to an end (Haltiner, 2003; Tresch, 2005). Among the driving forces of these processes we find technological progress and the market penetration into all spheres of life and society. This development implies an increasing degree of individualisation and normative pluralisation as well as a decreasing importance of traditional values and an erosion of community-based life styles in modern societies. The development of military systems – technically, economically and socio-politically – follows the same logic of change based on differentiation and economisation. The deeper the division of labour in the military cuts, the greater is the tendency to rely on highly trained professional soldiers (Burk, 1994, p. 45). This means that the armed forces of modern societies are fully professionalised and become leaner in personnel size. After Great Britain and the USA, continental Europe is also now shifting to small all-volunteer systems.

The thesis can be put forward that, after a two hundred years tradition of soldier-citizenry, with the suspension of the draft and the downsizing of the mass armies a de-militarisation of societies and a re-militarisation of the militaries is taking place and, as a consequence of this process, a civil–military gap is developing in Europe the same way as it can be observed in the U.S.

In our context, the term "militarisation" refers to the fact that the spread of the draft on the European continent made quantitatively representative parts of the population mobilisable for military ends and thus familiar with military norms and behaviours. The term "civilianisation," on the other hand, implies that the strong presence of civil societal norms and behaviours in a system of conscription strongly limited the cultivation of classic military virtues and the stressing of solely functional imperatives. There are indicators that with the end of the reciprocal process of militarisation of society on the one hand and civilianisation of the military on the other the civil–military divergences predicted by Comte and Spencer have started to grow.

The decline of conscription is reducing the share of society involved in the defence sector and the military. The sheer quantity of people having the chance to experience the military personally is shrinking considerably.

The formerly close relation between the citizenship and the military is getting looser on a quantitative level and with the growing social distance very probably also in a qualitative sense. Simultaneously to the reduction and professionalisation, support parts of the armed forces are removed organisationally from the forces. Increasingly, some of the logistical charges and areas without immediate combat function are civilianised and even transferred to private enterprises through outsourcing-measures (private security companies are often hired, nowadays, for the guarding of barracks and military bases, private catering companies take over the sustenance of entire brigades, the civilian flight-control controls the mission of the air force up to the point of combat-like events, etc; Singer, 2003). The actual military combat capability is concentrated in a downsized organisational nucleus. This creates the paradox that with the increasing civilianisation and economisation of the military an actual re-militarisation is taking place in the core area dealing with combat tasks. The soldier's own role-definition is newly discussed and promoted, military professionalism becomes the borderline of all thinking and acting in military culture, and the importance of military functional imperatives, as opposed to socio-economic ones, is again stressed and traditional military virtues are revitalised. The social homogeneity that was a typical feature of the mass armies (van Doorn, 1975) is disappearing. Consequently, a return to the elitist warrior ethos as a military subculture is encouraged.

Obviously, this opens a historically new divide between the democratic culture of modern, highly differentiated societies on the one hand and the military culture of tradition on the other. The pluralizing value and norm orientations of the individualised civil market societies and the normative and behavioural profiles of the functionally orientated military seem to be drifting apart.

4. THE POSSIBILITY OF A CROSS-NATIONAL RESEARCH AS SUCH

As the reference for our project is the Triangle Institute for Security Studies (TISS) research already carried out in the U.S., we have of course to ask ourselves if it is possible to compare the American reality with the one of Europe and that of other democratic countries. The U.S. situation with regard to the civil–military gap is in fact quite different from what we face in other countries for many reasons: difference in state size, difference in the function of the military in foreign and security policy, differences in political and social culture, difference in the history of civil–military relations, and the like.

Not only, but referring to Europe, according to several analysts, "the U.S. revolution in military affairs (RMA) will, in turn, widen the gap between American and European military strategies and capabilities. In addition, a so-called value-gap seems to be opening … Politically, strategically and culturally the U.S. and Europe appear to be slowly drifting apart" (van Ham, 2002, p. 1).

Besides that, this is not the only difference we can find in a cross-national analysis. If we look, for instance, at post-communist states, Jones and Mychajlyszyn (2002) found a set of common (inside the post-communist states) differences from these countries and the western ones in civil–military relations, as for instance:

1. the difficulties of developing cultures of democratic civil–military relations
2. the lack of development of a cadre of civilian defence experts as members of legislatures or as high-level officials in ministries of defence or other key national bureaucracies
3. the lack of experts on military-security issues in the media
4. no complains about military officers intruding into civilian politics
5. the high ratio of paramilitary forces in respect to the regular forces.

In order to face this issue – the possibility of a cross-national analysis – in a more concrete way, we analysed the main research findings as written in the TISS report (Feaver & Kohn, 2001), i.e.,

1. Our first finding was that there are many "gaps" to be explored, reflecting multiple dimensions and between different segments of the military and civilian populations.
2. The gap between the U.S. military and civilian society is growing.
3. As we leave the 20th century, the number of people have served in the military or have other personal connections with the military is declining. This "experience gap" is an artefact of the shrinking all-volunteer force.
4. The elite military is fairly critical about the quality of leadership in the political institutions.
5. The elite military posseses a pervasive hostility towards the media.
6. Military (and the mass military) have more trust and confidence in government institutions than in civilians.

7. On social values, elite military officers diverge from both elite and mass civilians.
8. By a very large margin (76%), elite military officers oppose gays and lesbians openly serving in the military. But a majority of civilian elites (55%) and the mass public (57%) support gays and lesbians openly serving.
9. The civilian population, both elite and especially mass, has very little understanding of civil–military relations and civilian control of the military.
10. The popular media through fiction and film reinforces a diverse set of stereotypes about the military and civilian society.

But, if we think of the European reality, as it emerges from recent surveys on civil–military relations, we find that most of these findings apply to most European and non-European civil–military relationships too. If we look, for instance, at the country papers presented at Portorose[4] and referring to several countries, we find that these conclusions are true for these countries too. Therefore, we can consider that a good working hypothesis can be that there are several common features of the civil–military gap everywhere, in the post-modern democracies at least. Probably other features are regional, continental (East European/West European, for instance), and other ones characteristic of a single country only. But this fact is, and was, common to every cross-national research.

To conclude, in our discussions during several meetings (see the introductory chapter), we realised the possibility and the convenience of a research as such and intended to carry on an empirical research on the civil–military cultural differences in Europe in comparison with results already given for the U.S. (but it can be employed in non-European countries too, where living conditions can be assumed to be that of all modern democratic societies).

In order to do that we agreed with the following guidelines for our research project, i.e., one basic assumption and three working hypothesis.

The basic assumption is that several indicators show the existence in democratic countries of a gap between the military culture and that one of its parent society, generally speaking. We have several indicators of this fact; some of them are already cited, while others are present in literature.

First working hypothesis is that we can consider officers as opinion-leaders/ opinion-makers in the armed forces, as well as civil professionals (in broad sense), among the most significant opinion-leaders in the civil society, so that it seems convenient to carry on an elite research among these categories.

Second working hypothesis is some kind of uniqueness of the military profession (Boëne, 1990) in respect to the other professions. To be clear, we are making the hypothesis that officer's profession is culturally more distant from the medium mindset of civil professions than single civil professions are among them. Therefore, it makes sense to compare the professional culture of officers with the culture of other civil professions.

Third working hypothesis is that there are several common features of the cultural civil–military gap in democratic countries, so that it makes sense to do a cross-national research.

Having said that we can conclude that our purpose was to get from that research some answer to the following main questions:

1. Is the gap confirmed, what is its nature and what are its national dimensions?
2. What shapes the gap?
3. Does that gap affect the military effectiveness and civil–military relations?
4. Is there some difference between the attitude of present and future elites (changes over time)?

In the following chapters (Part II and Part III) of the book we try to describe what kind of answer to these questions we were able to draw from the empirical data of the research carried out.

NOTES

1. See the foreword to the 1st Cranfield international conference on defence management, "Post-modern military: Rethinking the future" Cranfield University, U.K., April 24–25, 2003.
2. This position is shared by several authors, such as Edmonds (1988), Forster et al. (2003).
3. The fact that since the end of the Cold War armed forces have mainly been used for Military Operations Other Than War (MOOTW) and, particularly, for PSOs (Peace Support Operations) has no influence on that but is a source of organisational dilemmas (Caforio, 2001; Haltiner, 2000).
4. The reference is to the ERGOMAS VIIII Biennial Conference, held in Portorose, Slovenia, September 18–22, 2002.

REFERENCES

Almond, G. A., & Verba, S. (1963). *The civic culture: Political attitudes and democracy in five nations*. Princeton: Princeton University Press.

Bland, D. L. (1999). A unified theory of civil–military relations. *Armed Forces and Society*, *26*(1).
Boëne, B. (1990). How unique should the military be? A review of representative literature and outline of a synthetic formulation. *Archives Europeennes de Sociologie*, *31*(1).
Burk, J. (Ed.) (1994). *The military in new times: Adapting armed forces to a turbulent world.* Boulder, CO: Westview Press.
Burk, J. (1999). Military culture. In: L. Kurtz (Ed.), *Encyclopedia of violence, peace and conflict.* San Diego: Academica Press.
Caforio, G. (2001). *The flexible officer*. Gaeta: Artistic & Publishing Company.
Caforio, G. (2003). Introduction. In: G. Caforio (Ed.), *Handbook of the sociology of the military*. New York/Boston/London: Kluwer Academic/Plenum Publishers.
Comte, A. (1853). *The cours de philosophie positive (1830–1842)*. English translation & condensation. *The Positive Philosophy of August Comte*, by Harriet Martineau.
Dandeker, C. (2000). 'On "The need to be different": Recent trends in military culture'. In: H. Strachan (Ed.), *The British army, manpower and society into the twenty-first century.* London: Frank Cass.
Duffield, J. S. (1998). *World power forsaken: Political culture, international institutions, and german security policy after unification.* Stanford: Stanford University Press.
Edmonds, M. (1988). *Armed services and society*. Leicester: Leicester University Press.
Etzioni, A. (1975). *A comparative analysis of complex organizations.* New York: Free Press.
Feaver, P. D., & Kohn, R. H. (Eds). (2001). *Soldiers and civilians. The civil–military gap and American national security*. Cambridge: MIT Press.
Feld, M. D. (1959). Information and authority: The structure of military organization. *American Sociological Review*, *24*, 1522.
Forster, A. (2006). *Armed forces and society in Europe*. Basingstoke: Palgrave-Macmillan.
Forster, A., Edmonds, T., & Cottey, A. (2003). *Soldiers and societies in postcommunist Europe: Legitimacy and change*. Basingstoke: Palgrave-Macmillan.
Geser, H. (1994). *The New Challenge of Global Policing: An Organizational Perspective*. Paper presented at the Coinference Professione militare e problematiche sociali emergenti nel nuovo contesto navale e geopolitico, Livorno, 15–16 April.
Goffman, E. (1961). *Asylums: Essays on the social situation of mental patients & other inmates.* New York: Doubleday.
Haltiner, K. W. (2000). Policemen or soldiers? – Organizational dilemmas in the donstabularization of armed forces. In: M. Marjan (Ed.), *International security, mass media and public opinion* (pp. 17–31). Ljubljana: University of Ljubljana.
Haltiner, K. W. (2003). The decline of the European mass armies. In: G. Caforio (Ed.), *Handbook of the sociology of the military* (pp. 361–384). New York/Boston/London: Kluwer Academic/Plenum Publishers.
Hillen, J. (1999). Must U.S. military culture reform? *Orbis*, *43*(1), 43–58.
Hofstede, G. (1991). *Culture and organizations: Software of the mind.* London: McGraw-Hill.
Huntington, S. P. (1964). *The Soldier and the state* (2nd ed.). Cambridge: Harvard University Press.
Jones, C., & Mychajlyszyn, N. (2002). Overview: Civil–military relations in central and eastern Europe in former communist societies. *Armed Forces and Society*, *28*(3), 375–384.
Lang, K. (1965). Military organizations. In: J. G. March (Ed.), *Handbook of organizations* (pp. 836–878). Chicago: Rand McNelly.

Lantis, J. S. (2002). Strategic culture and national security policy. *International Studies Review*, *4*(3), 87–113.

McCormick, D. (1998). *The downsized warrior. America's army in transition*. New York: New York University Press.

Mearsheimer, J. J. (1990). Back to the future. Instability in Europe after the cold war. *International Security*, *15*(1), 5–56.

Moskos, C. C., Williams, J. A., & Segal, D. R. (Eds). (2000). *The postmodern military: Armed forces after the cold war*. New York & Oxford: Oxford University Press.

Murray, W. (1999). Does military culture matter? *Orbis*, *45*, 27–42.

Olson, M. (1965). *The logic of collective action*. Cambridge, MA: Havard University Press.

Schein, E. (1990). Organizational culture. *American Psychologist*, *45*(February), 110.

Singer, P. W. (2003). *Corporate warriors, the rise of the privatised military industry*. New York: Cornell University Press.

Snider, D. (1999). An uninformed debate on military culture. *Orbis*, *43*(1), 11–26.

Soeters, J., Winslow, D., & Weibull, A. (2003). Military culture. In: G. Caforio (Ed.), *Handbook of the sociology of the military*. New York/Boston/London: Kluwer Academic/Plenum Publishers.

Spencer, H. (1896). *The priciples of sociology* (2 Vol.). New York: D. Appleton.

Strachan, H. (2000). The civil military gap in Britain. Paper presented at international conference on civil–military relations, Ecole de Saint Cyr Coetquidan, France.

Tresch, T. S. (2005). Europas Streitkräfte im Wandel: Von der Wehrpflichtarmee zur Freiwilligenstreitkraft. Eine empirische Untersuchung europäischer Streitkräfte 1975 bis 2003. Dissertation, Universität Zürich, Zürich.

Tocqueville, A. de (1835/1840). De la démocracie en Amerique. Paris: Lévy.

van Doorn, J. (1975). *The soldier and social change*. Beverly Hills: Sage.

van Ham, P. (2002). *Western unity and transatlantic security challenge*. Marshal Center Papers, No. 4.

Vogelaar, A., & Kramer, F. J. (1997). Mission-oriented command in ambiguous situations. *Netherlands Annual Review of Military Studies*, pp. 74–94.

Weber, M. (1972). *Wirtschaft und Gesellschaft. Grundriss der verstehenden Soziologie*. Tübingen: Mohr.

THE METHODOLOGICAL APPROACH OF THE STUDY ON THE DIFFERENCES BETWEEN CIVILIAN STUDENTS AND MILITARY CADETS

Tibor Szvircsev Tresch, René Moelker and Giuseppe Caforio

ABSTRACT

The researchers' first contact for the project on civil–military relations began in 2001. The empirical phase of the research started in autumn of 2003 and ended in 2005. The study was carried out on two levels of empirical investigation: The first was constituted by future elites, represented by civilian students and military cadets. The research among civilian students was limited to three faculties in order making an empirical examination manageable. All in all 3,015 persons from 13 countries have been interviewed. The second level of investigation was constituted by interviewing a sample of current elites through an expert questionnaire.

The questionnaire employed for the survey of future elites is reported in Annex 1.

Cultural Differences between the Military and Parent Society in Democratic Countries
Contributions to Conflict Management, Peace Economics and Development, Volume 4, 21–48

ISSN: 1572-8323/doi:10.1016/S1572-8323(07)04002-7

1. INTRODUCTION

Realizing a cross-national study requires time and a research design which resolves cultural differences between the involved researchers. International military research projects about civil–military relations, like our civil–military gap project, face at least two difficulties. First, in order to study in the armed forces, authorization is needed from the political and/or military leadership in most countries. In some countries, data gathering is restricted because of, e.g., ethical codes, security reasons, intelligence needs, and laws. The publication of research results can be subject to state control. This means that only approved parts of the research results can be published. A next point is that the access to the research object, in our case the military cadets, is not easily obtained in all countries.

Secondly, the difference in knowledge about the military between civilian students and military cadets is considerable. For example, the meaning of the term "peace operations" could be different for cadets and civilian students. The former probably focus more on the operational components. They can better point out the word "operations". On the other hand, civilian students most likely connect the word "peace" with "peace operations" and are more often thinking in ideological–political categories.[1] We have to keep in mind these differences if we survey civilian students and military students. In other words: The military can be seen sometimes as a segment that differs from the social, political, and economic natural spheres of life in a society. The second point can be connected to the basic assumption of our research project and frames the introduction to the methodological chapter.

2. HISTORY OF THE RESEARCH

Initially, colleagues from 19 countries intended to participate in the study in civil–military relations. Later, difficulties encountered in the individual national contexts (problems of research authorization, financial support, etc.) reduced the group to 13 countries, whose researchers carried out the surveys in their respective countries (see the table in the introduction of this book with the names and affiliations of the researchers and the countries).

The researchers' first contacts for the project on civil–military relations were at the Budapest (September 2001) and Portorose (September 2002) conferences (see for more details the introduction of this book). With the agreement of all the project participants, a restricted group was created, comprising Giuseppe Caforio, Ljubiça Jelusic, Karl W. Haltiner, René Moelker, and Tibor Szvircsev Tresch. The restricted group met in Morschach (Switzerland) from 7 to 9 February 2003, to discuss and produce a first concrete plan for the empirical phase of the research. The questionnaire for the survey of future elites and the general plan for the interviews with current elites were presented at a meeting of the entire research group and discussed in detail on the occasion of the International Conference in Breda (Netherlands, May 2003). The revised questionnaire was pre-tested on a group of Italian Army cadets (ten interviewees, June 2003) and a few subsequent modifications were made (see the questionnaire in the Annex 1).

The empirical phase of the research started in autumn of 2003 and continued throughout 2005 in each of the 13 participating countries. According to the planning of the research project the following research steps were carried on in the participating countries:

1. Investigation of the political culture of future (civilian and military) elites by simultaneously surveying cadets at military academies and students at civilian universities on three levels:
   (a) cognitive – beliefs, attitudes, opinions
   (b) evaluative – values, norms, moral judgements
   (c) expressive or affective – emotions (identity, loyalty), feelings (affinity, aversion, indifference)
2. Carrying out semi-structured interviews with present elites (an expert survey) in order to assess changes in civil–military relations over time.
3. Elaborating and comparing results at cross-national level and comparing and contrasting them with data from the American TISS survey research (Feaver & Kohn, 2001).

3. RESEARCH PROCEDURE AND METHODS

The research has been carried out on two levels of empirical investigation: The first is constituted by future elites, represented here by students and military cadets. This context was identified in the educational institutions that provide professional training, e.g., civilian universities and military academies. The second level of investigation is constituted by a sample of current elites.

3.1. Common Research Plan

According to the research plan each participating country had to sample at least 30 cadets at the military academies (15 in their first year and 15 in their fourth year) and compare them with samples of at least 30 university students in each of the following faculties: economics, law, and political science. The approach was a class room situation.[2] The research among university students is limited to three faculties in order to make an empirical examination manageable. The choice of the economics, law, and political science faculties was based on the assumption that they are major producers of civil elites.[3] The responsibility of organization was in the hand of the individual researchers in the participating countries.

Simultaneously to the cadet and student surveys, each participating country had to interview experts in order to assess changes in both civil and military culture, from the past to the present. These interviews served as a methodological tool to handle the longitudinal dimension of the research issue. The idea was to select at least 10 experts on civil–military relations in every country.

3.2. Future Elites Survey

3.2.1. Questionnaire

The research instrument for the civil–military-gap project was an 18-page questionnaire with 47 questions. Many of them included multiple items. For example, as a part of the first question the students were asked to rate the importance of 12 possible foreign-policy goals.[4] The third question asked the respondents to evaluate the likelihood of 16 threats to national security. The investigation is subdivided into four different parts: (1) "civil–military relations", (2) "military and public opinion", (3) "main security issues", and (4) "military and politics".

Besides this subject matter the questionnaire included questions for demographic items like age, gender, military service, religion, education, occupation, political orientation (left–right scale), and parent's professions. One of the biggest difficulties in the research project was to translate the questions from English into different languages (e.g., Bulgarian, French Italian, Swedish) and respect the research group's first intentions.

For the purpose of preparing a questionnaire suitable to our goal, we drew the following list of significant indicators:

List of Indicators

1. Trust to institutions (how central is military still?)
2. Gender roles (machismo, combat masculine warrior versus feminization of military)

3. Democracy index
4. Threat perception
5. New/Old missions of the military
6. Patriotism
7. Existence of the armed forces (right to exist, way of existing, being proud of armed forces)
8. Democratic control of the armed forces
9. Values (values to educate children, values within the military)
10. Globalism/localism
11. Warriorism
12. Sources of information on military
13. Evaluation of the media–military relations
14. Social prestige of the military occupation (among other occupations)
15. Professional qualifications
16. Recommendation to peers, children to enlist in military
17. Role of father in socialization on military issues
18. Foreign-policy goals
19. Format and size of the military (conscription)
20. Military lagging behind in social modernization
21. Religion
22. Conservativism
23. Materialism/post-materialism

Based on this list of indicators a questionnaire has been created (Annex 1). The construction of the questionnaire was inspired on the research in the U.S. by Feaver and Kohn (2001). For reasons of comparison we used a part of the Feaver and Kohn questionnaire (see Table 1).

Three thousand one hundred and fifteen persons from 13 countries have been interviewed. Table 2 provides information about the distribution of the cross-national sample. Bulgaria provided the smallest sample (121 persons: 4% of the whole sample); Germany ranks number one with 368 interviewees (12.2% of the whole sample), followed by Switzerland, Sweden, and the Netherlands.

In South Africa, the first interviews were administered in July 2003, whilst Turkey started data collection in January 2004 and closed it in June 2004. The duration of collecting the data in all participating countries runs from July 2003 to June 2004, which is one year. From a methodological critical point of view, we have to be aware that interceding events have influenced the answers of the interviewees. It cannot be precluded that threat perceptions of the respondents during the war in Iraq have changed or at least have

Table 1. Comparative Questions from Feaver and Kohn Questionnaire and Civil–Military Gap Questionnaire.

Feaver and Kohn Questionnaire	Civil–Military Gap Questionnaire
1a	1a
1b	1b
1c	1c
1d	1d
1e	1e
1g	1g
1h	1h
1i	1i
2k	2a
2h	2c
2b	2e
3g	3c
3i	3e
3l	3i
3b	3m
7d	4e
7f	4g
7h	4h
20 (similar)	7
21	9
24	10
27	11
25	12
32 (similar)	14
47a	17a
47b	17b
47c	17c
47d	17d
47e	17e
63	18
64	19
68	21x
18 (similar)	26
19 (similar)	27
52 (similar)	42
33c	44a
33d	44b
33e	45f

Table 2. Sample of the Civil–Military Gap Survey.

	Frequency	Percent of the Whole Sample	Time and Locations of Survey
Bulgaria	121	4.0	March to June 2004 Students: University of Sofia, New Bulgarian University, University for National and World Economy Cadets: National Defense University
France	137	4.5	October to December 2003 Students: Institut d'Etudes Politiques de Paris (political science), University of Rennes (economy and law) Cadets: Military Academy of St-Cyr
Slovenia	164	5.4	January to June 2004 Students: University of Ljubljana Cadets: Military Officers School
Romania	180	6.0	September to December 2003 Students: University of Bucharest Cadets: Military Academies of Land-Sibiu, Air-Brasov, and Navy-Constanta
South Africa	190	6.3	July 2003 to March 2004 Students: Universities of Cape Town, Western Cape, and Stellenbosch Cadets: SA Military Academy
Poland	224	7.4	November to December 2003 Students: Economic Academy in Wrocław, University in Toruń, Catholic University in Lublin and University in Wrocław Cadets: Navy Academy in Gdynia and High Oficer Air School in Dęblin
Italy	226	7.5	November 2003 to February 2004 Students: Universities of Turin, Pisa, and Salerno Cadets: all Military Academies
Turkey	253	8.4	January to June 2004 Students: Middle East Technical University, Ankara Cadets: Military Academy, Ankara
Spain	270	9.0	April 2004 Students: Universities of Granada, Burgos, and Madrid Cadets: Academia General Militar del Ejército de Tierra in Zaragoza, Academica General del Naval en Marín in Pontevedra, Academica General del Aire in San Javier

Table 2. (*Continued*)

	Frequency	Percent of the Whole Sample	Time and Locations of Survey
Netherlands	287	9.5	April 2004 Students: Tilburg University Cadets: Military Academy in Breda
Sweden	295	9.8	February to June 2004 Students: University of Uppsala, University College in Östersund Cadets: Military Academy in Östersund; Military Academy in Halmstad
Switzerland	300	10.0	mid-October to mid-December 2003 Students: Universities of Fribourg, Zurich, Bern, Lausanne, St. Gallen Cadets: Military Academy at the ETH Zurich
Germany	368	12.2	January to May 2004 Students: University of Potsdam Cadets: Bundeswehr University, Munich
Total	3015	100.0	

been influenced. Between September and October 2003 the number of attacks in Iraq escalated of over 40 per day. From this point in time we can speak about a guerrilla war against the U.S. led coalition. Further the assaults in Riad (8 November 2003) and Istanbul (15 November 2003) could have influenced the appraisal of the security situation in the world. The terrorist attack in Madrid (11 March 2004) with around 200 victims and 1,200 injured people has of course had an effect on the given answers of the interviewees. How strong the ascendances of Estonia, Lithuania, Latvia, Poland, Czech Republic, Slovakia, Hungary, Slovenia, Cyprus (Greek part), and Malta to the EU have changed the security–political opinion is difficult to answer.[5] To sum up it can not be excluded that our data have a temporary bias. But we have not the opportunity to produce evidence because the appropriate questions were not asked.

All countries have fulfiled the preconditions of the empirical research, e.g., to interview at least 30 cadets and 90 civilian students with the exception of France. In France too few students have been selected (see Table 3).[6] The number of interviewed cadets are in Bulgaria (30) and Slovenia (35) the lowest.[7] As for the experts survey, our Dutch colleague was not able to conclude it in the Netherlands in due time, so that in the present elites' comparison that country is absent.

Table 3. Distribution of the Sample by Cadets and Students and Gender.

	Cadets	Students	Male	Female	Male Cadets	Male Students	Female Students	Female Cadets
Bulgaria	30	91	54	65	20	34	55	10
France	88	48	100	35	83	16	30	5
Germany	136	229	320	42	116	202	24	17
Italy	125	97	144	79	94	48	48	31
Netherlands	191	95	206	80	159	47	48	32
Poland	89	134	141	83	81	59	75	8
Romania	89	91	103	75	78	25	64	11
Slovenia	35	129	80	84	31	49	80	4
South Africa	59	130	127	63	51	76	54	8
Spain	91	179	156	112	82	74	104	8
Sweden	188	107	219	74	170	49	58	16
Switzerland	109	191	217	83	107	110	81	2
Turkey	97	155	142	108	93	49	106	1
Total	1327	1676	2009	983	1165	838	827	153

The variation in gender ratios among the single countries is large. In the German sample we can find a ratio of 7.6 men to 1 woman, so in the German sample males are over-represented. On the other side, in the sub samples of Bulgaria and Slovenia women are in the majority. It makes sense to inspect our cross-national data for the variables "military or not military" and "male versus female". Except the Netherlands and Italy, we learn from Table 3 that in all countries "female cadets" are under-represented. A detailed analysis of the data on this level makes no sense. Secondly, females are over-represented in the student sample. In eight countries (Bulgaria, France, Romania,[8] Poland, Slovenia, Spain, Sweden, and Turkey) women are disproportionately represented.

If we examine the sub sampling of the students we can see that several countries have not fulfiled the prerequisites of the research. It was intended to select at least 30 students of economy, law, and political science. Slovenia, Spain, and Switzerland surveyed in each student's category at least 30 persons (see Table 4). Italy, Romania, and South Africa reached almost the given number. In the Netherlands we had enough students who participated but can not be related to one of the three branches of study (economy, law, and political science).[9]

Regarding the distribution of the age the data can not be called homogeneous. The youngest interviewee is 17 years old and the oldest is 43 years

Table 4. Distribution of the Sample by Study.

	Military Academy	Economy	Law	Political Science	Other
Bulgaria	30	27	19	28	17
France	88	1	23	19	5
Germany	136	125	88	5	11
Italy	125	41	23	29	4
Netherlands	191	11	6	2	76
Poland	89	55	34	16	29
Romania	89	32	28	31	
Slovenia	35	32	66	31	
South Africa	59	22	33	31	44
Spain	91	60	48	54	17
Sweden	188	74		33	
Switzerland	109	39	84	59	9
Turkey	97	80		43	32
Total	1,327	599	452	381	244

old (both in Sweden, see Table 5). On average the cadets are the older respondent. But there are large differences among nations. We can distinguish between three groups:

1. Cadets are clearly older than the average of the students (South Africa, France, Turkey, Switzerland, and Slovenia). The reason is that in some countries (e.g., Slovenia and Switzerland) future professional officers have first completed their civil study, and this is a precondition for admission to a military academy. In Switzerland cadets had been at first officers in the militia for some years before gaining access to the military academy.
2. Students and cadets have similar age. This is true for Romania, Spain, Poland, Italy, and Germany.
3. Students are older than cadets (Bulgaria, Netherlands, Sweden).[10]

To sum up: Our two populations, students and cadets, do not have the same profile in terms of age, gender, military experience, etc. These factors could have an influence of the results of the analysis in the next chapters. Also, the return rates of the questionnaire are different. In some countries like Germany or Switzerland sample return rates for military sample are 99%. On the other side, in Germany just 25% of the civil sample filled in the questionnaire.

Table 5. Distribution of the Sample by Age.

	Cadets			Students		
	Mean Age	Minimum Age	Maximum Age	Mean Age	Minimum Age	Maximum Age
Bulgaria	20.87	20	23	23.48	19	36
Romania	21.75	19	25	21.49	19	25
Netherlands	22.40	19	34	23.99	19	34
Poland	22.82	20	25	23.49	20	32
Sweden	22.95	17	32	27.53	18	43
Italy	22.98	19	29	22.52	19	34
Spain	24.31	19	37	22.09	19	30
Germany	24.54	19	37	24.15	20	36
South Africa	25.27	20	38	22.53	19	36
France	25.41	18	30	20.96	18	30
Turkey	27.69	19	33	20.63	17	28
Switzerland	28.30	23	41	23.76	19	41
Slovenia	32.49	25	42	21.91	19	37

3.3. Expert Interviews

While the first part of the study investigates, through a questionnaire, the values, attitudes, opinions, norms, emotions, and feelings of the military and civilian respondents, the second part is a qualitative analysis of the actual elites to show the evolution of the civil–military culture over time and to use similar indicators as control variables. We intend to interview experts, in order to assess changes in civil–military relations. The idea is to select 10 experts on civil–military relations in every country. Ideally, sampling should be balanced, meaning that it is preferred to interview both women and men, young and old(er), left and right. Composition of experts should comprise

- Two expert top-military (colonel or higher)
- Two journalists on military affairs (from different nation-wide newspapers, television, or other media)
- Two parliamentarians specialized in the political–military decision-making (different political affiliation: preferably one from the right and one from the left)
- Two scientists (a political scientist, historian, international relations, etc.)
- Two managers
- Option: opinion leaders like military union chairpersons, peace movement, etc.

Table 6. Matrix for the Expert-Interviews in Each Country.

	Bulgaria	Germany	France	Italy	Netherlands	Poland[a]	Romania
Military	4	1	2	2			3
Politicians	1	2	1	2		1	2
Managers		3	1	2			1
Journalists	1	1	4	2			2
Academics	7	2	2	2		1	2
Others							
Time of interviews	Between March and June 2004	Between January and May 2004	Between October and December 2003	Between February and May 2004	Data don't collected	Between November and December 2003	Between November 2003 and February 2004

	Slovenia	South Africa	Spain	Sweden	Switzerland	Turkey
Military	2	2	3	2	2	2
Politicians	1	2	2	1	3	2
Managers					2	2
Journalists		2	1	2	2	2
Academics		2	1		2	2
Others	1	1		1		
Time of interviews	Between May and June 2004	Between August and September 2003	June 2004	Between September 2004 and January 2005	Between December 2003 and March 2004	Between January and June 2004

[a]Because problems of realising enough interviews in Poland existed, the Polish researcher elaborated his expertise on civil–military relations on interviews with two scientific experts in this field, representative from two political parties (left and right oriented) and on his own expertise ripened in 13 years as director WIBS/WBBS and observator of the events in the field of civil–military relations.

Table 6 shows the number and the distribution of the questioned experts in our research. Most interviews were taken in the beginning of 2004 till June 2004. However, for the most countries it was not easy to catch enough experts in each category. Just Italy, Switzerland, and Turkey were able to interview for each sphere at least two persons. The data from Slovenia, Bulgaria, Poland, Spain, and Sweden were gathered according to the guidelines.

4. CONCLUSION

We have to keep in mind that our research sample does not have the claim for representation. On the one side we have interviewed a selected sample of students mainly from three branches: economics, law, and political science. We assume that the future civilian elites will arise from these students. On the other side we asked military cadets as representatives of the next generation of leaders in the officer's corps. To do civil–military research is very difficult: Only few countries have fulfiled the preconditions of the sampling, e.g., to get at least 30 cadets or students for all branches. Besides this, it was much more difficult to interview enough experts. A third problem of the research was the time required to collect the data. It took more than one year. During this time span, we have had different assaults in Europe and in the Middle East which can change opinion related to security questions. We can sum up that our investigation on civil–military differences is a first attempt to structure this field for future research projects and to make our data comparable on the time axis.

NOTES

1. For example the remarks of the French studies in our project: "We noted that the answers given by the students were extremely logical and full of prejudgement while the answers of their counterparts military students were more open, because they have a better experience of the military profession. Almost all of them had military work experience before joining Coëtquidan military school".

2. This means the cadets and students were questioned during a lecture at their institution.

3. We gave the possibility to single country researchers to investigate students from other faculties, if he/she thought that country elites were coming from these faculties. These civilian students were labelled as 'various'.

4. In the TISS survey there were ten possible items to rate (see Feaver & Kohn, 2001, p. 19).

5. Also few country situations can have influenced the validity of the data like the one in Sweden: "At the time of the data gathering the situation for cadets was difficult. It was a rumour that it might be meaningless for them to complete their education to become an officer, as a position in the military could not be guaranteed. This turbulent situation might at least in part explain some of the results of the Swedish results. It seems that among the cadets there was a tendency toward a reduced feeling of professional identity, motivation and legitimacy".

6. The cadets were students from the French military Academy of St-Cyr. The civil population came from Law students in public and private institutes and from students in Politics mainly from one of the top Institute of Political Studies school in Paris called IEP (Institut d'Etudes Politiques).

7. Slovenia has a specific military education system, in which there is no military academy. The candidates for officers must as a precondition hold a university degree or high college degree before entering the so-called Military Officers School. The cadets are first employed by Slovenian Army and then sent to a one-year course at the Officers School.

8. The Romanian system of education has been changed, after 1997, so the military cadets would pursue only brief military training, during their four years of study, but they will professionalize in the fifth year in a training course.

9. In the Netherlands the bulk of civilian students came from "policy and organization studies" from Tilburg University.

10. As a result of sampling Netherlands has more second and third years students in the sample and the Dutch sample does not have sufficient first year students (civilians) in the sample.

REFERENCE

Feaver, P. D., Kohn, R. H., (Eds). (2001). *Soldiers and civilians. The civil–military gap and American national security*. MIT Press, Cambridge

ANNEX 1. QUESTIONNAIRE FOR THE FUTURE ELITES SURVEY

ERGOMAS

Research Committee 01 "*Armed Forces & Conflict Resolution*"
European Research Group on Military and Society
Working group "The Military Profession"

CULTURAL DIMENSIONS OF CIVIL-MILITARY RELATIONS IN DEMOCRATIC SOCIETY:

country code !__!__!

ID !__!__!__!

Premise

Dear Student, as you certainly know, military culture presents some particular characters different from the civilian culture of the parent society. The purpose of this poll is to investigate what are the differences and what the similarities in these two cultures: this is an important topic to improve and make easier civil/ military relations in democratic countries. We trust your support in answering to the following questions in a very frank and open way. This questionnaire will remain completely anonymous, of course, as we are interested in numbers and percentages only. Please skip all questions to which you do not want to respond; with regard to all other questions, please just tick off the answer which best meets your personal opinion/ situation. Thank you.

The Working Group Co-ordinator
Dr. Giuseppe Caforio

1ST SET OF QUESTIONS

1.	**Here is a list of possible foreign policy goals that our country might have.** Please indicate **how important** these goals are!					
		very important	rather important	rather unimportant	very unimportant	DK, NA
1a.	Helping to improve the standard of living in less developed countries	1	2	3	4	5
1b.	Worldwide arms control	1	2	3	4	5
1c.	Combating world hunger	1	2	3	4	5
1d.	Strengthening the United Nations	1	2	3	4	5
1e.	Fostering international cooperation to solve common problems, such as food, inflation, and energy	1	2	3	4	5
1f.	Preserve world peace	1	2	3	4	5
1g.	Preventing the spread of weapons of mass destruction	1	2	3	4	5
1h.	Promoting and defending human rights in other countries	1	2	3	4	5
1i.	Helping to bring a democratic form of government to other nations	1	2	3	4	5
1j.	Strengthening regional security alliances or agreements (NATO, for example)	1	2	3	4	5
1k.	Maintaining the external security of our country	1	2	3	4	5

1l.	Fighting terrorism	1	2	3	4	5
2.	**What is your opinion on the following statements?**					
		agree strongly	agree some-what	disagree some-what	disagree strongly	no opinion
2a.	When force is used, military rather than political goals should determine its application.	1	2	3	4	5
2b.	Public opinion of my country will not tolerate large numbers of casualties in military operations.	1	2	3	4	5
2c.	We shouldn't think so much in international terms but concentrate more on our own national problems.	1	2	3	4	5
2d.	The national security of my country depends more on international trade and a strong domestic economy than on our military strength.	1	2	3	4	5
2e.	It is vital to enlist the cooperation of the U.N. in settling international disputes.	1	2	3	4	5
3.	**This question asks you to evaluate the <u>likelihood of each of the following threats to national security</u> of our country.** Please use the scale below.					
		very likely	rather likely	rather not likely	not likely at all	DK, NA
3a.	Mass immigration from foreign countries	1	2	3	4	5
3b.	Terrorism in our countries	1	2	3	4	5
3c.	International drug trafficking	1	2	3	4	5
3d.	Organised crime	1	2	3	4	5
3e.	Environmental problems like air pollution and water contamination	1	2	3	4	5
3f.	A possible indirect involvement in a civil war	1	2	3	4	5
3g.	An armed conflict between African countries with which we have co-operation relations	1	2	3	4	5
3h.	An armed conflict in the Middle East	1	2	3	4	5
3i.	Attacks on computer networks	1	2	3	4	5
3j.	Nuclear blackmail by Third World countries	1	2	3	4	5
3k.	Nuclear war between Third World countries with global consequences	1	2	3	4	5
3l.	An armed conflict between Asia countries.	1	2	3	4	5
3m.	Proliferation of weapons of mass destruction	1	2	3	4	5
3n.	An accidental nuclear war	1	2	3	4	5
3o.	An armed conflict over the control of vital raw materials (water, oil, etc.)	1	2	3	4	5
3p.	Military attack by foreign state	1	2	3	4	5
4.	**The following are some possible uses of the military.** Please indicate how much **you approve of the <u>military being used</u> for the each of the following missions.**					
		approve very strongly	rather approve	rather dis-appro ve	strongly disappro-ve	DK, NA
4a.	To defend our country	1	2	3	4	5
4b.	To participate in peace-keeping missions	1	2	3	4	5
4c.	To participate in peace-enforcing missions (missions against the will of local parties)	1	2	3	4	5
4d.	To participate in combat missions	1	2	3	4	5
4e.	To provide disaster relief	1	2	3	4	5
4f.	To provide humanitarian relief abroad	1	2	3	4	5
4g.	To deal with domestic disorder within our country	1	2	3	4	5
4h.	To combat drug trafficking	1	2	3	4	5
4i.	To prevent the proliferation of weapons of mass destruction	1	2	3	4	5
4j.	To control mass immigration from foreign countries	1	2	3	4	5

4k.	To fight terrorism	1	2	3	4	5
4l.	To contribute to the protection of the environment	1	2	3	4	5
5.	**The % of the GDP of our country spent for defence is** __INSERT THE %___. **According to your opinion should the defence budget of our country:**					
	1 - raise considerably					
	2 - raise somewhat					
	3 - remain as it is					
	4 - lower somewhat					
	5 - lower considerably					
6.	**How much interested are you in defence related security issues?**					
	1 - very much					
	2 - somewhat					
	3 - a little					
	4 - not at all					
7.	**How important are the following sources of information on military matters to you?**					
		very impor-tant	rather impor-tant	rather unim-portant	very unim-portant	DK, NA
7a.	newspapers	1	2	3	4	5
7b.	television network news	1	2	3	4	5
7c.	radio news	1	2	3	4	5
7d.	general news newspapers	1	2	3	4	5
7e.	general news magazines	1	2	3	4	5
7f.	special military newspapers or magazines	1	2	3	4	5
7g.	political newspapers or magazines	1	2	3	4	5
7h.	movies	1	2	3	4	5
7i.	military trade/professional publications	1	2	3	4	5
7j.	internet	1	2	3	4	5
7k.	other	1	2	3	4	5
8.	**How do you judge the level of information that media of our country give you on the military issues?**					
	1 - very good					
	2 - somewhat good					
	3 - not good					
	4 - no opinion					
9.	**In general, mass media depictions of the military in our country are:**					
	1 - very supportive					
	2 - somewhat supportive					
	3 – neutral					
	4 - somewhat hostile					
	5 - very hostile					
	6 - no opinion					

10.	**How knowledgeable do you think our political leaders are about the modern military?**					
	1 - very knowledgeable					
	2 - somewhat knowledgeable					
	3 - somewhat ignorant					
	4 - very ignorant					
	5 - no opinion					
11.	**Do you think military leaders, in general, share the same values as our country people?**					
	1 – yes					
	2 – no					
	3 – not sure					
	4 – no opinion					
12.	**Do you think political leaders, in general, share the same values as our countrypeople?**					
	1 – yes					
	2 – no					
	3 – not sure					
	4 – no opinion					
13.	**According to your opinion, what is the public image of armed forces in our society?**					
	1 - very good					
	2 - rather good					
	3 - not very good					
	4 - not good at all					
	5 - no opinion					
14.	**The following is a list of some institutions in our country.** How much of **confidence** do you have in each of them? And how much **knowledge** do you have about each of them? Please use a scale from 1 to 10, **where 1** means **no confidence/knowledge at all and 10** means **complete confidence/knowledge.**					

		CONFIDENCE	KNOWLEDGE			
14a.	The church	!___!	!___!			
14b.	President	!___!	!___!			
14c.	Media	!___!	!___!			
14d.	Justice	!___!	!___!			
14e.	Parliament	!___!	!___!			
14f.	Government	!___!	!___!			
14g.	Banks	!___!	!___!			
14h.	Companies	!___!	!___!			
14i.	Trade unions	!___!	!___!			
14j.	Universities	!___!	!___!			
14k.	Organized political parties	!___!	!___!			
14l.	The military	!___!	!___!			
14m.	The police	!___!	!___!			
14n.	Voluntary organizations	!___!	!___!			

15.	**According to your opinion, how important would be each of the following qualities for education of your children?**					
		very important	rather important	rather unimportant	very unimportant	DK, NA
15a.	Discipline	1	2	3	4	5
15b.	Responsibility	1	2	3	4	5
15c.	Tolerance	1	2	3	4	5
15d.	Patriotism	1	2	3	4	5
15e.	Comradeship	1	2	3	4	5
15f.	Orderliness	1	2	3	4	5
15g.	Traditionalism	1	2	3	4	5
15h.	Obedience	1	2	3	4	5
15i.	Creativity	1	2	3	4	5
15j.	Loyalty	1	2	3	4	5
15k.	Spirit of equality	1	2	3	4	5
15l.	Generosity	1	2	3	4	5
15m.	Initiative	1	2	3	4	5
15n.	Self-control	1	2	3	4	5
15o.	Determination	1	2	3	4	5
15p.	Open-mindedness	1	2	3	4	5
15q.	Team spirit	1	2	3	4	5
15r.	Honesty	1	2	3	4	5
15s.	Honor	1	2	3	4	5

16.	**According to your opinion, how important is each of the following qualities for the military?**					
		very important	rather important	rather unimportant	very unimportant	DK, NA
16a.	Discipline	1	2	3	4	5
16b.	Responsibility	1	2	3	4	5
16c.	Tolerance	1	2	3	4	5
16d.	Patriotism	1	2	3	4	5
16e.	Comradeship	1	2	3	4	5
16f.	Orderliness	1	2	3	4	5
16g.	Traditionalism	1	2	3	4	5
16h.	Obedience	1	2	3	4	5
16i.	Creativity	1	2	3	4	5
16j.	Loyalty	1	2	3	4	5
16k.	Spirit of equality	1	2	3	4	5
16l.	Generosity	1	2	3	4	5
16m.	Initiative	1	2	3	4	5
16n.	Self-control	1	2	3	4	5
16o.	Determination	1	2	3	4	5
16p.	Open-mindedness	1	2	3	4	5
16q.	Team spirit	1	2	3	4	5
16r.	Honesty	1	2	3	4	5
16s.	Honor	1	2	3	4	5

17.	**What is your opinion on the following statements concerning the military's role in civil society?**					
		agree strongly	agree some-what	disagree some-what	disagree strongly	no opinion
17a.	Members of the military should not publicly criticize members of the government.	1	2	3	4	5
17b.	Members of the military should not publicly criticize their parent civil society.	1	2	3	4	5
17c.	Members of the military should be allowed to publicly express their political views just like any other citizen.	1	2	3	4	5
17d.	It is proper for the military to explain and defend in public the policies of the government.	1	2	3	4	5
17e.	It is proper for the military to advocate publicly the military policies it believes are in the best interests of the country.	1	2	3	4	5
17f.	It is proper for the military to have direct political influence in the society.	1	2	3	4	5
	2nd SET - SOCIODEMOGRAPHIC QUESTIONS **Here are a few questions for background information**					
18.	**Are you**					
	1 – male					
	2 – female					
19.	**Year of birth** (last 2 digits) !___!___!					
20.	**What are you studying (university course)?**					
	1 – military academy					
	2 – economy					
	3 – law					
	4 – political science					
	5 – other					
21.	**In which year of course are you?** !___!					
	ONLY COUNTRIES THAT KEEP THE CONSCRIPTION SYSTEM AND WHERE PEOPLE ARE DRAFTED BEFORE OR DURING THE UNIVERSITY STUDIES SHALL BE ASKED THE FOLLOWING 3 QUESTIONS!!! (***Instructions for coding:*** if the following 3 questions are not asked, insert **code 66** ("not applicable") for all 3 questions in database!!!)					
21x.	**Have you ever served in the military?**					
	01 – yes					
	02 - no **GO TO QUESTION 22**	***Instructions for coding, if the answer is "no":*** *use* ***code 99*** *("not applicable") for questions* ***21y and 21z****, and* ***code NA*** *for question* ***21w*** *in database!!!*				
21y.	**How would you generally characterize your experience in the military?**					
	01 – very positive					

	02 – somewhat positive					
	03 – mixed					
	04 – somewhat negative					
	05 – very negative					
	06 – no opinion					
21z.	**What rank did you reach?**					
	01 – private					
	02 – NCO					
	03 – officer					
21w.	**How long had you served?**					
	!___!___! months					
22.	**What are your parents' professions?** Please, circle number on the left in each column.					

	22a. Mother's profession		**22b. Father's profession**	
11	Legislators and senior officials	11	Legislators and senior officials	
12	Corporate managers	12	Corporate managers	
13	General managers	13	General managers	
21	Physical, mathematical and engineering science professionals , architects	21	Physical, mathematical and engineering science professionals , architects	
22	Life science and health professionals, nursing and midwifery profs .	22	Life science and health professionals, nursing and midwifery profs .	
23	Teaching professionals (all levels from university to primary education)	23	Teaching professionals (all levels from university to primary education)	
24	Other professionals (legal, business, social sciences, writers, religious professionals	24	Other professionals (legal, business, social sciences, writers, religious professionals	
31	Physical and engineering science associate professionals, Computer prof, optical and electronic equipment operatores, ship and aircraft controllers, safety inspectors	31	Physical and engineering science associate professionals , Computer prof, optical and electronic equipment operatores, ship and aircraft controllers, safety inspectors	
32	Life science and health **associate** professionals	32	Life science and health **associate** professionals	
33	Teaching associate professionals	33	Teaching associate professionals	
34	Other associate professionals (i.e. Finance and sales associate professionals,Business services agents and trade brokers, Administrative associate professionals, Customs, tax and related government associate professionals, Police inspectors and detectives , Social work associate professionals, Artistic, entertainment and sports associate professionals, Religious associate professionals)	34	Other associate professionals (i.e. Finance and sales associate professionals,Business services agents and trade brokers, Administrative associate professionals, Customs, tax and related government associate professionals, Police inspectors and detectives , Social work associate professionals, Artistic, entertainment and sports associate professionals, Religious associate professionals)	
41	Office clerks	41	Office clerks	
42	Customer service clerks	42	Customer service clerks	
51	Personal and protective services workers (i.e. Travel attendants and related workers, Housekeeping and restaurant services workers, Personal care and related workers, Other personal service workers)	51	Personal and protective services workers (i.e. Travel attendants and related workers, Housekeeping and restaurant services workers, Personal care and related workers, Other personal service workers)	
52	Models, salespersons and demonstrators	52	Models, salespersons and demonstrators	

	61	Market-oriented skilled agricultural and fishery workers	61	Market-oriented skilled agricultural and fishery workers
	62	Subsistence agricultural and fishery workers	62	Subsistence agricultural and fishery workers
	71	Extraction and building trade workers (Miners, stonecutters, building frame, building finishers, painters, structrue cleaners)	71	Extraction and building trade workers (Miners, stonecutters, building frame, building finishers, painters, structrue cleaners)
	72	Metal, machinery and related trades workers	72	Metal, machinery and related trades workers
	73	Precision, handicraft, printing and related trades workers	73	Precision, handicraft, printing and related trades workers
	74	Other craft and related trades workers (Food processing and related trades workers, Wood treaters, cabinet-makers and related trades workers , Textile, garment and related trades workers, Felt, leather and shoemaking trades workers	74	Other craft and related trades workers (Food processing and related trades workers, Wood treaters, cabinet-makers and related trades workers , Textile, garment and related trades workers, Felt, leather and shoemaking trades workers
	81	Stationary plant and related operators (operators in mining, metal, glass, wood, chemical products, papermaking, food, assemblers)	81	Stationary plant and related operators (operators in mining, metal, glass, wood, chemical products, papermaking, food, assemblers)
	83	Drivers and mobile plant operators (train, motor vehicles, agriculture, ships' deck crews)	83	Drivers and mobile plant operators (train, motor vehicles, agriculture, ships' deck crews)
	91	Sales and services elementary occupations (Street vendors, Shoe cleaning and other street services' elementary occupations, Domestic and related helpers, cleaners and launderers, Building caretakers, window and related cleaners, Messengers, porters, doorkeepers and related workers, Garbage collectors and related labourers)	91	Sales and services elementary occupations (Street vendors, Shoe cleaning and other street services' elementary occupations, Domestic and related helpers, cleaners and launderers, Building caretakers, window and related cleaners, Messengers, porters, doorkeepers and related workers, Garbage collectors and related labourers)
	92	Agricultural, fishery and related labourers	92	Agricultural, fishery and related labourers
	93	Labourers in mining, construction, manufacturing and transport	93	Labourers in mining, construction, manufacturing and transport
	01	Armed forces	01	Armed forces

23.	**Has your father ever served in the military?**					
	01 – yes					
	02 - no **GO TO QUESTION 23x** *(in the case, that women could have military experiences in the country)* ***or 26***	***Instructions for coding, if the answer is "no":*** *use code* ***99*** *("not applicable") for questions 24 and 25 in database!!!*				
24.	**If yes, what was/is his primary service?**					
	01 - Army					
	02 – Navy					
	03 - Air Force					
	04 – Marines					
	05 - Coast Guard					
	06 - Border Guard					
	07 - *Carabinieri/ Gendarmerie* or other military police 08 - Other paramilitary force					
	09 - Other					
25.	**If yes, what is the highest rank/rate hereached?**					
	01 – private					
	02 – NCO					
	03 – lieutenant					

	04 – captain					
	05 - major					
	06 – lt. colonel					
	07 – colonel					
	08 – general					
The following 3 questions about mother's military experiences are OPTIONAL FOR COUNTRIES! ***Instructions for coding**: if the questions **are not asked**, please use the **code 66** ("not applicable") for questions 23x, 24x and 25x in database!!!*						
23x.	**Has your mother ever served in the military?**					
	01 – yes					
	02 - no **GO TO QUESTION 26**	***Instructions for coding, if the answer is "no":*** *use code **99** ("not applicable")for questions 24x and 25x in database!!!*				
24x.	**If yes, what was/is her primary service?**					
	01 - Army					
	02 – Navy					
	03 - Air Force					
	04 – Marines					
	05 - Coast Guard					
	06 - Border Guard					
	07 - *Carabinieri/ Gendarmerie* or other military police 08 - Other paramilitary force					
	09 - Other					
25x.	**If yes, what is the highest rank/rate she reached?**					
	01 – private					
	02 – NCO					
	03 – lieutenant					
	04 – captain					
	05 - major					
	06 – lt. colonel					
	07 – colonel					
	08 – general					
26.	**Would you tell us, if you are religious and how regularly do you attend religious services?** (please circle one)					
	1- am religious and I regularly (every week) attend religious services					
	2 - am religious and I attend once per month religious services					
	3 - am religious, but I attend religious services only for the biggest fests					
	4 - I can't tell if I am religious or not					
	5 - am not religious					
	6 - no answer					
27.	**Would you tell us, to what religion/ confession do you belong?**					
	1 – Roma catholic					

	2 – Protestant
	3 – Christian orthodox
	4 – Muslim
	5 – other, please specify___________
	6 – I do not belong to any confession, am atheist
	7 – no answer
28.	**How would you describe your political position?** Please use the following scale and circle:

1	2	3	4	5	6	7	8	9	10
extreme left									extreme right

29.	**When you get into an argument do you usually get your own way or do you often give in?**	
	1	never give in
	2	usually not give in
	3	usually give in
	4	always give in
	5	cannot say
30.	**People have a range of opinions about many things. Which best describes you? I have:**	
	1	strong opinions
	2	moderate opinion
	3	uncertain opinion
	4	no opinion
	5	cannot say
31.	**When you make up your mind about something is it pretty hard to argue you out of it or do you change your mind pretty easily?**	
	1	very hard to change my mind
	2	hard to change my mind
	3	easy to change my mind
	4	very easy to change my mind
	5	cannot say

3rd SET OF QUESTIONS

32. **Listed below are persons and groups: how much attachment do you feel to each of them?** Please indicate your degree of attachment by ranking the importance of the following items, where **10** means your strongest attachment and <u>**1** your weakest attachment.</u>

	rank		***Instructions for coding**: use the codes **01, 02.....10**!!!*
32a.	!___!	world community	
32b.	!___!	Europe	
32c.	!___!	your country (Italy, Germany, etc.)	
32d.	!___!	natural environment	

32e.	!___!	your profession, your colleagues				
32f.	!___!	your friends				
32g.	!___!	your family				
32h.	!___!	your religious community				
32i.	!___!	your native city				
32j.	!___!	Yourself				

33. According to your opinion, what should be the most important goal of our government in domestic policy for the next ten years? Please indicate what is the most important in the following list.

	1 - Maintaining order in the nation
	2 - Giving the people more say in important government decisions
	3 - Fighting rising prices
	4 - Protecting freedom of speech

34. And what would be your second choice?

	1 - Maintaining order in the nation
	2 - Giving the people more say in important government decisions
	3 - Fighting rising prices
	4 - Protecting freedom of speech

35. Please indicate how important are the following principles for you?

		very important	rather important	rather unimportant	very unimportant	DK, NA
35a.	equality of people, regardless of gender, race, religion etc.	1	2	3	4	5
35b.	respect for individuals	1	2	3	4	5
35c.	basic freedoms of the individuals (freedoms of assembly, ideas, speech, press, etc)	1	2	3	4	5
35d.	respect for the national basic law (constitution and the like)	1	2	3	4	5
35e.	safeguard of individual opportunities and responsibilities	1	2	3	4	5
35f.	defense of the societal system and the way of life of the country	1	2	3	4	5
35g.	peaceful relationship with the other societies in the world	1	2	3	4	5
35h.	subordination of the military to the political leadership	1	2	3	4	5
35i.	integration of the military in the parent society	1	2	3	4	5

36. How well do you consider that each of these principles is realised in our country?

		completely realised	rather realised	rather unrealised	unrealised at all	DK, NA
36a.	equality of people, regardless of gender, race, religion etc	1	2	3	4	5
36b.	respect for individuals	1	2	3	4	5
36c.	basic freedoms of the individuals (freedoms of assembly, ideas, speech, press, etc)	1	2	3	4	5
36d.	respect for the national basic law (constitution and the like)	1	2	3	4	5
36e.	safeguard of individual opportunities and responsibilities	1	2	3	4	5
36f.	defense of the societal system and the way of life of the country	1	2	3	4	5
36g.	peaceful relationship with the other societies in the world	1	2	3	4	5
36h.	subordination of the military to the political leadership	1	2	3	4	5
36i.	integration of the military in the parent society	1	2	3	4	5

37.	**How far do you agree with the following statements?**					
		agree strongly	agree some-what	disagree some-what	disagree strongly	no opinion
37a.	The military exists for the defence of the country and its interests.	1	2	3	4	5
37b.	The military job implies to guarantee a peaceful and free trade international arena.	1	2	3	4	5
37c.	The military profession is subordinate to the political leadership.	1	2	3	4	5
37d.	Civilians and military must share the same basic values.	1	2	3	4	5
37e.	Politicians must give professional autonomy to the military.	1	2	3	4	5
37f.	The military should be abolished.	1	2	3	4	5
37g.	The military is necessary evil.	1	2	3	4	5
37h.	The military is the most important part of the public life.	1	2	3	4	5
37i.	The military should represent the parent civil society with regard to social and ethnic groups and classes.	1	2	3	4	5

38. **What image do you think the military profession has in the public eye in our country?** Please rate using the following scale and circle!

very positive image								very negative image	
1	2	3	4	5	6	7	8	9	10

39. **How do you rate military officer education?** Please rate using the following scale and circle!

very positive								very negative	
1	2	3	4	5	6	7	8	9	10

40. **Listed below are 16 professions. Would you please put them into what you consider to be their order of prestige.** Please enter a »**1**« for the most prestigeous profession, a »**2**« for the second one, etc.

	rank		***Instructions for coding**: use the codes **01, 02.....16**!!!*
40a.	!___!	Medical doctor	
40b.	!___!	Priest, clergy man	
40c.	!___!	University professor	
40d.	!___!	Lawyer	
40e.	!___!	Diplomat	
40f.	!___!	Military officer	
40g.	!___!	Manager of a company	
40h.	!___!	Civil airline pilot	
40i.	!___!	Pharmacist	
40j.	!___!	Entrepreneur	
40k.	!___!	Journalist	
40l.	!___!	Artist	
40m.	!___!	Teacher at secondary school	
40n.	!___!	Civil servant	
40o.	!___!	Police inspector	
40p.	!___!	Engineer	

41. **Do you support the full integration of women into the armed forces?** Please, circle in each column.

41a. On an optional basis?	**41b. On a compulsory basis?**

	1– yes, in all (also combat) roles	1– yes, in all (also combat) roles				
	2 – yes, but not in combat roles	2 – yes, but not in combat roles				
	3 – no	3 – no				
	4 – no opinion	4 – no opinion				

42.	**If you oppose women serving in all military occupations and roles, how <u>important are the following factors in shaping your opinion?</u>**					
	9 - I do not oppose women serving in all military roles	***Instructions for coding:*** *if the anwer is "do not oppose...", use the* ***code 9*** *for questions from* ***42a to 42h!!!***				
		very important	rather important	rather unimportant	very unimportant	DK, NA
42a.	religious/moral convictions	1	2	3	4	5
42b.	the presence of women disrupts small unit cohesion	1	2	3	4	5
42c.	women could be taken prisoner and abused	1	2	3	4	5
42d.	women are not fully deployable as men because of pregnancy	1	2	3	4	5
42e.	there is too little privacy for men and women in military jobs	1	2	3	4	5
42f.	men will not fight as effectively with women present in combat units	1	2	3	4	5
42g.	the deaths of female soldiers will demoralize male soldiers and public	1	2	3	4	5
42h.	the women in the military take jobs away from men	1	2	3	4	5

43.	**And here are some statements on our society, world situation, problems of war and peace.** Using the scale provided, please indicate the <u>degree to which you agree/disagree with each statement.</u>					
		agree strongly	agree somewhat	disagree somewhat	disagree strongly	DK,NA
43a.	The INSERT NATIONALITY! should always feel that his or her primary allegiance is to his/her own country.	1	2	3	4	5
43b.	The strongest indicator of good citizenship is performance of military service in defense of our country.	1	2	3	4	5
43c.	The promotion of the patriotism should be an important aim of citizenship education.	1	2	3	4	5
43d.	All INSERT NATIONALITY! should be willing to fight for our country.	1	2	3	4	5
43e.	We should strive for loyalty to our country before we can afford to consider world brotherhood.	1	2	3	4	5
43f.	Today, peacekeeping and other non-combat activities should be central military function.	1	2	3	4	5
43g.	The military should be prepared to cover the whole spectrum of possible missions (from war to aid to the civil power)	1	2	3	4	5
43h.	The most important role of the military is preparation for and conduct of war.	1	2	3	4	5
43i.	Sometimes war is necessary to protect the national interest.	1	2	3	4	5
43j.	Human nature being what it is, there will always be war.	1	2	3	4	5
43k.	Strong armed forces improve our image throughout world.	1	2	3	4	5
43l.	The increasing multinational character of military missions shows the need for stronger United Nations.	1	2	3	4	5
43m.	The United Nations should have more control of the armed forces of all members.	1	2	3	4	5
43n.	The Security Council of the United Nations should be the only power to verify military actions against sovereign states.	1	2	3	4	5
43o.	NATO should have freedom to intervene on its own initiative.	1	2	3	4	5
43p.	The USA should have freedom to intervene on its own initiative.	1	2	3	4	5

43r.	The EU should have freedom to intervene on its own initiative.	1	2	3	4	5
44.	**Here are two statements about national service.** Using the scale provided, please indicate the degree to which you agree/disagree with each statement					
		agree strongly	agree some-what	disagree some-what	disagree strongly	DK,NA
44a.	All male citizens should be required to do some national service (military or civil service).	1	2	3	4	5
44b.	All female citizens should be required to do some national service (military or civil service).	1	2	3	4	5
45.	**Here are some statements about the military.** Using the scale provided, please indicate the degree to which you agree/disagree with each statement.					
		agree strongly	agree some-what	disagree some-what	disagree strongly	DK,NA
45a.	There is a natural link between democracies and conscription	1	2	3	4	5
45b.	The general military draft should include women too	1	2	3	4	5
45c.	The draft guarantees a steady exchange of values, opinions and perceptions between society and armed forces	1	2	3	4	5
45d.	An all-volunteer force (AVF) fits better than conscription the requirements of new missions	1	2	3	4	5
45e.	Looking at the whole national economy, conscription causes more costs then AVF, because of the waste of human resources	1	2	3	4	5
45f.	I am proud of women and men who serve in the military	1	2	3	4	5
45g.	The INSERT NATIONALITY! Armed Forces are attracting high-quality, motivated recruits.	1	2	3	4	5
46.	**These questions concern some of your more general types of attitudes about other matter.** Please circle the words that most nearly reflect your feelings about each.					
		agree strongly	agree some-what	disagree some-what	disagree strongly	no opinion
46a.	What young people need most of all is firm discipline by their parents	1	2	3	4	5
46b.	Most people who don't get ahead just don't have enough will power	1	2	3	4	5
46c.	A few strong leaders could make this country better than all the laws and talk	1	2	3	4	5
46d.	An insult to your personal honor should not be forgotten	1	2	3	4	5
47.	**To what extent do you agree with the following statements?**					
		agree strongly	agree some-what	disagree some-what	disagree strongly	no opinion
47a.	I usually favour group consensus	1	2	3	4	5
47b.	I do not hesitate to disagree with the group	1	2	3	4	5
47c.	I like to beat the system	1	2	3	4	5
47d.	I always listen to my leaders	1	2	3	4	5
Thank you for your participation! Your opinion is important to us.						

PART II:
CROSS-NATIONAL ANALYSIS

VALUE ORIENTATIONS AND POLITICAL ATTITUDES AMONG FUTURE MILITARY AND CIVILIAN ELITES

Karl W. Haltiner and Alise Weibull

ABSTRACT

In this article the basic value orientations of future officers and civilian students are compared. It is found that the variance between the 13 countries included in the survey is mostly larger than the one between civilian and military students when it comes to the basic value dimensions such as tradition vs. modernity, left vs. right, cosmopolitan vs. localistic, materialistic vs. post-materialistic and civilian vs. military values. Thus, the military are not consistently in all countries more religious, more right oriented and more materialistic than their civil fellow students, even if there exists a tendency for such a trend.

INTRODUCTION

The past 10 years have seen a resurgence in interest in the relationship between civilian society and the military, and there is a high probability that

Cultural Differences between the Military and Parent Society in Democratic Countries
Contributions to Conflict Management, Peace Economics and Development, Volume 4, 51–81

ISSN: 1572-8323/doi:10.1016/S1572-8323(07)04003-9

this interest will increase in the years to come (Kümmel, 2003; Born, Haltiner, & Malesic, 2004). Nevertheless, in western European research this relationship has long been viewed as a peripheral matter, a problem that on the whole has been resolved. Opinion polls in most countries show politically satisfactory levels of acceptance of the armed forces, and these levels tend to be quite stable. The fact that these levels have risen in many countries since the end of the Cold War is considered to be due to the fact that the broadened nature of the assignments (humanitarian and other) has given the military, in the publics' view, a new and more positive role. Does this mean that, mainly and foremost in post-Cold War Europe, civil–military relations are intact? This issue is of interest since there seems to be a widening civil–military gap with regard to basic values, political ideology and the social role of the military in the US – a gap that seems to have grown steadily since the abolition of conscription there (Holsti, 2001).

THE US STUDY

In their study on the existence of a civil–military gap in the US, Feaver and Kohn (2001) argue that emerging norms and values within the officer corps promise more friction in civil–military relations. Military officers tend to express an increasing pessimism about the moral health of the country. Political preferences of the average American officer have become more conservative, politicised and right-wing oriented over the past two decades. Many tend to believe that society should adopt more of the military's values and behaviour. The interviewed civilian group seems to share this pessimism about civilian society but disagree strongly that the military has a role in changing this.

Many of the findings in the American study are ambiguous. Even if the military and the civilian group both harbour strong stereotypes about each other, there are also expressions of mutual respect and confidence. While the officers criticise the quality of political leadership and are hostile towards the media, at the same time they express more confidence in government institutions than the civilians do. Correspondingly, we cannot consider military culture as something constant and identical over time. On the contrary, "change is characteristic of military culture because of the many influences that constantly affect the values, beliefs, and behaviours that together define it" (Hillen, 1999). Some of these influences can be attributed to the military adjusting to changes in civilian society while other changes are related to the new faces of war. Within this context the soldier's identity is changing too.

Even if many are impressed by the American study, which aimed at scientifically investigating what thus far had been a combination of myths and rumours concerning civil–military relations, there are also critics. The critics reason that even if there is something of a "gap", does this really matter? Many of them (Segal, 2003; Garp, 2005) point at the fact that differences in values and perspectives between soldiers and civilians have historical roots. Others (Roman & Tarr, 2001; Snider, Priest, & Lewis, 2001) feel that there are more urgent challenges to address, such as recruitment, retention, and a shrinking budget, and that the "gap" has very little to do with all this. Still others argue that civilian and military roles are so blurred in policymaking nowadays that any possible "gap" is well concealed in any case. Some others (for example Segal, Freedman-Doan, Bachman, & O'Malley, 2001; Huntington, 1957; Janowitz, 1960) view a cultural divide between the armed forces and civilian society as more or less natural. In this view the existence of a civil–military gap is due to the differences between the inherent character of democratic societies and the functional requirements of organisations whose scope is the management of violence.

VALUES IN THIS STUDY

In this paper we limit ourselves to the value aspects of a potential gap between future military and civilian elites. We will first analyse and compare the basic value orientation of future officers and civilian students from 13 different countries. Second, we will look at the importance attributed by the two groups to their own values in the daily life, indicated by values for the education of children, and the core values attributed to the military as an institution. Third, we will focus to the relative value position given by the two groups to the individual rights and duties in democratic societies on one hand and the interests of the collective (state, nation) on the other.

A general assumption which underlies most of the research on values has been that shared values, as expressed at the collective level on the one hand, and individual values as operating in daily occupational behaviour on the other, are somehow interrelated, although the causality of this interrelation is still a debated issue (Roe & Ester, 1999). The literature gives a large number of definitions of values (see for example Ashkanasy, Wilderom, & Peterson, 2000; Roe & Ester, 1999). Much cited in military sociology is Hofstede's definition, where values are defined as "a broad tendency to prefer certain states of affairs over others" (Hofstede, 1984, p. 18).

For the purpose of this study we refer to Hofstede and define values as norms of a principle character, which help to rank preferences. We see values as being measurable on a scale of importance (very important to very unimportant).

FINDINGS

Basic Value Dimensions

"Traditional vs. modern", "left vs. right" and "local vs. global" are among the most significant value dimensions in the social sciences. Since the late 1970s, Inglehart's index of post-materialism belongs to the standard repertoire of value research. Inglehart (1977, 1990) believes that the change of values in modern societies can be witnessed in the simple form of changes from material values, i.e. values stressing peace and order, welfare and security, to post-material values, which mainly emphasise active participation in politics and freedom of thought.

Referring to these four dimensions we will use the term "basic value orientations" in this article. They will be indexed as follows: a high church attendance usually indicates a more traditional-conservative social orientation. We follow traditional usage by measuring the political value dimension along the interviewees' self-assessment on a left–right scale. A rather global–cosmopolitan orientation vs. a rather nationalistic–localistic one will be indicated by the prioritisation of reference groups that range from "family" to "nation" to "world community". In order to verify the thesis of materialism–post-materialism, we rely on the most widely used short index by Inglehart (1977, 1990), which contains four items.

Church Attendance and Religiosity

In 4 out of 13 countries, the future military elites see themselves as more religious and more close to the church and in 5 out of 13 countries less religious and less close to the church than their civilian academic counterparts. There are huge differences between countries, as Table 1 shows. There is no general trend in the manner of military personnel being more religious and closer to the church than their fellow civilian students. The figures rather seem to reflect the general degree of religiosity in a particular society and not so much the differences between cadets and civilian students. Hence, the self-assessments of both military and civilian interviewees indicate a high degree of religiosity in South Africa, Poland and Italy. In

Table 1. Church Attendance and Religiosity.

	Regular Church Attendance[a]			Not Religious At All[b]			
	Cadets (%)	Students (%)	Difference (%)	Cadets (%)	Students (%)	Difference (%)	(*N*)
Bulgaria	7	8	−1	22	24	−2	(111)
France	35	9	+26	20	36	−16	(124)
Germany	15	11	+4	52	52	0	(307)
Italy	35	46	−11	14	4	+10	(213)
Netherlands	16	13	+3	55	39	+16	(271)
Poland	45	58	−13	8	4	+4	(209)
Romania	23	30	−7	8	14	−6	(175)
Slovenia	13	28	−15	25	28	−3	(152)
South Africa	61	70	−9	16	11	+5	(167)
Spain	31	16	+15	20	42	−22	(257)
Sweden	1	4	−3	49	45	+4	(285)
Switzerland	14	10	+4	34	40	−6	(290)
Turkey	7	25	−18	27	30	−3	(225)

Agreement in % for church attendance: once a week & once a month & self-assessment as being "religious".
Items not counted in the table: "I am religious, but I attend religious services only during the big festivals"/"I don't know if I am religious or not"/"no answer".
[a]I am religious and I regularly (once a week) attend religious services & I am religious and I attend a religious service once a month.
[b]I am not religious.

Germany, Bulgaria, the Netherlands, Sweden, Switzerland and Turkey however, secularity seems to dominate equally in both groups. The cross-country variance exceeds the intra-national variance.

Nevertheless, there are also some interesting findings for each country in the civilian–military comparison. In the former communist countries like Poland, Romania and Slovenia but also in Catholic Italy, church attendance of civilian students is higher than that of their military counterparts. The communist–atheist party line has obviously left marks in the eastern European military elites. The same is true for South Africa and Muslim Turkey. In the latter, as is generally known, the armed forces have served as a guarantor of the separation of church and state (and hence of a secular nation) since Ataturk. The quota of self-assessed high religious affiliation among Turkish military cadets is very low at just 7%, as is the case with Sweden and Bulgaria. Italian cadets declare themselves significantly less religious than their civilian comparison group. In France and Spain we find the contrary situation. Therefore, it is wrong to assume a kind of pattern of higher religious affiliation of the military in Latin countries. Frequently, military personnel are less religious in absolute figures than the civilian students (the Netherlands, Sweden, South Africa). Sweden and Germany are typical examples of countries particular characterised by relatively low religious affiliation of both officers and civilians.

Apart from Italy and Sweden, the western European cadets tend to show a slightly higher degree of church attendance and thus a more traditional behaviour than their civilian counterparts. This is especially true for France, Spain and Switzerland (arranged in order of decreasing intensity). However, it has to be said that apart from France, areligiosity is widespread among both groups. A country's religious propensity seems a better explanation of the respondents' religious affiliation than the civil–military differences.

Left–Right Orientation

Cadets in 4 out of 13 countries assess themselves as more left than right oriented, while in 9 countries, they see themselves as more right oriented (Table 2). The often-heard hypothesis whereby military personnel are said to be more right oriented than civilian students is supported with the present data. However, due to the fact that in 4 out of these 9 countries the civilian students also declare themselves as predominantly right oriented (France, Germany, the Netherlands, Sweden), the hypothesis must be relativised at the same time. Obviously it is worthwhile to differentiate:

Table 2. Self-Declared Political Left–Right Orientation.

	Cadets		Students		Difference	
	Left (%)	Right (%)	Left (%)	Right (%)	Left (%)	Right (%)
Bulgaria	27	20	21	32	+6	−12
France	6	74	14	44	−8	+30
Germany	33	39	21	29	+12	+10
Italy	13	55	39	32	−26	+23
Netherlands	18	53	30	42	−12	+11
Poland	35	21	21	29	+14	−8
Romania	38	15	19	25	+19	−10
Slovenia	15	24	40	23	−25	+1
South Africa	23	19	35	18	−12	+1
Spain	8	52	62	20	−54	+32
Sweden	15	54	21	40	−6	+14
Switzerland	5	66	53	22	−48	+44
Turkey	16	16	53	15	−37	+1

Note: Basis: Scale ranging from 1 (extremely left) to 10 (extremely right): "left": 1/2/3, "right": 8,9,10.

- With the exception of Slovenia, there is a predominant left orientation of cadets in the post-communist countries Bulgaria, Poland, Romania, while students there are predominantly right oriented. As was the case with religiosity, the former communist socialisation might serve as an explanation here. In other words, in these countries, the cadets are less prone to the capitalistic-liberal market thinking than the civilian students.
- In South Africa and Turkey, the political orientation is less polarised and more balanced within the military while it is more accentuated among civilian students.
- The issue of the degree of political polarisation in both groups interviewed might be just as interesting as the question of a left or right dominance in the political orientation. A situation can be defined as polarised if two-thirds or more of the military or civilian students self-situate themselves on the poles of the tripartite scale. This is the case with the military students in the following countries (arranged in order of decreasing intensity): France (80%), Germany (72%), the Netherlands (71%), Switzerland (71%), Sweden (69%) and Italy (68%). If the fact that more than 50% of the military assess themselves as politically right is taken as a further criterion, Spain (52% right) belongs to this group. In all these countries, with the exception of Switzerland and Italy, the degree of polarisation is smaller among civilian students than among the cadets. Among western European counties the degree of political polarisation tends to be comparatively high. In contrast the post-communist countries feature a clearly lower degree of polarisation of both military and civilian students.

Put simply, it can be concluded that the division between left and right orientation, a remnant of the Cold War, has to a large extent been maintained. In the former communist East, the cadets are predominantly left oriented, while western European cadets are predominantly right oriented. Feaver and Kohn (2001) have argued that one of the main reasons for the widening civil–military gap was the end of conscription in the US. Following this argument we would expect cadets of those countries that have abolished conscription and moved to an all-volunteer force in our sample to be more right-wing oriented than of countries maintaining the citizen-soldiering system. In fact, cadets of France, Italy, the Netherlands and Spain reveal a quite high proportion of right-wing oriented military students. However, that is also the case with countries with a long-standing tradition of citizen soldiers such as Sweden and Switzerland. Our database is obviously too small for a significant conclusion.

Local vs. Global Reference Groups

Are the military students more cosmopolitan or more nationally and locally oriented than their civilian counterparts?[1] Overall, the ranking in the 13 countries is similar concerning the importance of the individual reference groups (Table 3). The family is seen as the most important reference group, world community and religious community as the least important compared to the other reference groups listed.

The interviewee's own country, the national society, generally ranks high; in second position after family for the military students in 10 out of 13 countries, while for the civilian students this is only the case in 7 out of 13 countries. Italy is noteworthy, as both cadets and civilian students rank their mother country first. In Spain (1.82), France (1.49), Switzerland (1.48), Turkey (1.21), Romania (0.99) and Italy (0.96) (arranged in order of decreasing intensity), military students attribute significantly higher importance to the nation than do their civilian counterparts. Bulgaria is an exception inasmuch as its cadets ascribe less importance to their country than their civilian colleagues. Thus, for the future officers of most countries in our survey, their own nation plays a more important role as a reference group than for civilian students. This supports the thesis of Janowitz that in the US a feeling of national identity among officers was above average (1960, p. 82). It hints at a finding that will be analysed in detail later on.

Only in 6 countries does the item "profession/colleagues" precedes "own country" in importance, according to the civilian students. It is considered to be less important according to the officers. The Netherlands deviate from the average insofar as both military and civilian students rank the item "profession/colleagues" immediately after "family".

It is a matter of particular interest that "Europe" as a reference group is more important to cadets than to civilian students in 7 countries, which is more than the half of all the European nations in our sample (France, Germany, Italy, the Netherlands, Romania, Slovenia and Turkey). Hence, it seems that the European identity is more important to a majority of Europe's future officers than to their civil fellow students. These nations are all either EU members or are striving for membership. There is a striking civil–military difference in Switzerland and Bulgaria, where Europe is significantly more important for the civilian students than it is for cadets. Considering the partially small size of the differences these findings must, however, be taken with caution.

Table 3. Reference Groups (Global–Local Scale).

	Bulgaria			France			Germany			Italy			Netherlands			Poland			Romania		
	C	S	Δ	C	S	Δ	C	S	Δ	C	S	Δ	C	S	Δ	C	S	Δ	C	S	Δ
World community	4.53	5.53	1.00	3.84	4.44	0.60	3.60	3.41	0.19	5.55	5.61	0.06	4.97	4.98	0.01	4.96	5.03	0.07	5.54	5.11	0.43
Europe	5.13	6.23	1.10	5.51	5.35	0.16	5.46	5.10	0.36	6.55	6.07	0.48	5.87	5.66	0.21	5.32	5.40	0.08	6.54	6.30	0.24
Own country	7.53	7.65	0.12	8.34	6.85	1.49	7.02	6.89	0.13	7.98	7.02	0.96	7.21	6.64	0.57	6.11	6.05	0.06	8.69	7.70	0.99
Profession/Colleagues	7.60	7.26	0.34	7.32	6.29	1.03	6.90	7.04	0.14	7.50	6.64	0.86	7.88	7.09	0.79	6.00	6.08	0.08	8.08	7.71	0.37
Family	7.77	8.22	0.45	8.89	9.00	0.11	8.63	9.12	0.49	7.92	7.00	0.92	9.21	8.82	0.39	6.30	6.85	0.55	9.38	9.53	0.15
Religious community	5.45	4.96	0.49	4.76	3.29	1.47	3.09	2.75	0.34	5.38	5.69	0.31	3.07	3.27	0.20	5.47	5.71	0.24	6.42	5.91	0.51

	Slovenia			South Africa			Spain			Sweden			Switzerland			Turkey		
	C	S	Δ	C	S	Δ	C	S	Δ	C	S	Δ	C	S	Δ	C	S	Δ
World community	4.35	4.23	0.12	4.98	4.76	0.22	4.70	5.74	1.04	5.43	6.00	0.57	4.17	6.03	1.86	5.53	5.83	0.30
Europe	6.27	6.08	0.19	3.66	3.98	0.32	6.30	6.77	0.47	6.14	6.44	0.30	5.26	6.36	1.10	5.32	4.91	0.41
Own country	8.42	7.91	0.51	8.30	7.95	0.35	8.63	6.81	1.82	8.49	7.81	0.68	8.76	7.28	1.48	9.16	7.95	1.21
Profession/Colleagues	8.19	8.13	0.06	7.71	7.70	0.01	8.08	7.42	0.66	8.64	7.54	1.10	8.00	7.13	0.87	8.27	7.51	0.76
Family	9.88	9.10	0.78	9.43	9.13	0.30	9.00	8.95	0.05	9.61	9.67	0.06	9.16	9.24	0.08	9.23	9.11	0.12
Religious community	3.12	3.82	0.70	6.52	6.73	0.21	4.72	3.41	1.31	2.84	3.31	0.47	3.08	2.98	0.10	5.66	5.34	0.32

Note: How much attachment do you feel for the following persons and groups? 10: means strongest attachment, 1: weakest attachment. The table shows means for cadets (C) and students (S) and differences (Δ) between the means.

Inglehart Index of Materialism vs. Post-materialism
The Inglehart items of our survey refer to the primacy of law and order and financial security (fighting rising costs) vs. the primacy of political say and protection of freedom of speech (1977, 1990). If the former are clearly favoured, this indicates a materialistic value orientation, whereas if the latter are favoured, this indicates a post-materialistic value orientation.

Table 4 shows the distribution of the degree of materialists and post-materialists, omitting the mixed type. The share of cadets and civilian students who cannot be assigned to either of the two value types totals more than 50% in most countries. This means that only minorities can clearly be assigned to a pure value type. Inglehart's index is therefore of limited explanatory power.

Generally speaking, there are clearly more materialistic oriented cadets than non-materialistic ones; their share lies above a third (33%) in 7 out of 13 countries. The share of post-materialists among military students is generally low, usually below 10% (exceptions: Germany, the Netherlands and Slovenia). The differences with civilian students are quantitatively significant (Table 4, column differences). There is, however, no dominance of either one of the two value types among the civilian students. Here too, the mixed types (not listed in the table) dominate quantitatively. In 7 out of 13 countries, the number of materialists among students is equal to the

Table 4. Index of Materialistic versus Post-Materialistic Values.

	Cadets		Students		Difference Cadets – Students	
	Material (%)	Post-mat (%)	Material (%)	Post-mat (%)	Material (%)	Post-mat (%)
Bulgaria	41	0	21	6	+20	−6
France	30	6	13	24	+17	−18
Germany	26	18	16	14	+10	+4
Italy	37	4	25	22	+12	−18
Netherlands	27	12	15	15	+12	−3
Poland	48	4	36	7	+12	−3
Romania	35	6	18	19	+17	−12
Slovenia	23	11	18	10	+5	+1
South Africa	40	4	8	50	+32	−46
Spain	28	8	9	37	+19	−29
Sweden	15	8	13	32	+2	−24
Switzerland	40	2	15	21	+25	−19
Turkey	45	9	20	17	+25	−8

Note: The "mixed" type is not included in the table.

post-materialists or even outnumbers them (arranged in order of decreasing intensity: Poland, Italy, Bulgaria, Turkey, Slovenia, Germany, and the Netherlands). In the remaining 6 countries, we find relatively more post-materialistic than materialistic civilian students. A polarisation of the type "materialistic oriented cadets vs. post-materialistic civilians" is especially distinct in South Africa (40 vs. 50), Spain (28 vs. 37), France (30 vs. 24), Sweden (15 vs. 32) and Switzerland (40 vs. 21).

All in all, military cadets tend to be more materialistic (which probably means more "law and order" oriented) than their civilian counterparts. Among the latter there is no dominant mindset, and hence, there is no general materialism–post-materialism gap between the military and civilian students.

Values Attributed to the Education of Children and to the Military

What values are important to the interviewees when it comes to the education of their children and what values do they find important for the military as an institution? It is to be expected that the interviewees' personal values will be mirrored in the answers given to the question of the most important values for their children's education. The questions referring to the importance of values in the military gives us an indication of the officers' as well as the civilian students' views of the military as a social institution. A profile of basic values for the military on the one hand, and for civilians on the other hand has been determined by 19 pre-given value items which could be rated as "important" or "less important" by the interviewees for both spheres.

The figures below show the average results of the importance attributed by military and civilian students to a set of specific values. In Figs. 1(a) and (b), an expected profile can be identified: the classical values of heteronomy, i.e. discipline, orderliness, obedience and loyalty are seen as of major importance for the military by both groups, cadets and students. However, for the education of children, which ultimately means for one's own daily life, those values are widely rated as less important. This is also true for values such as comradeship and team spirit.

The values patriotism and tradition are rated as more important for the military than for one's own life, but these generally rank low.

In contrast, typical values of autonomy such as creativity, generosity, honesty, initiative and open-mindedness are usually rated as more important for children's education and thus for one's own private life in a modern

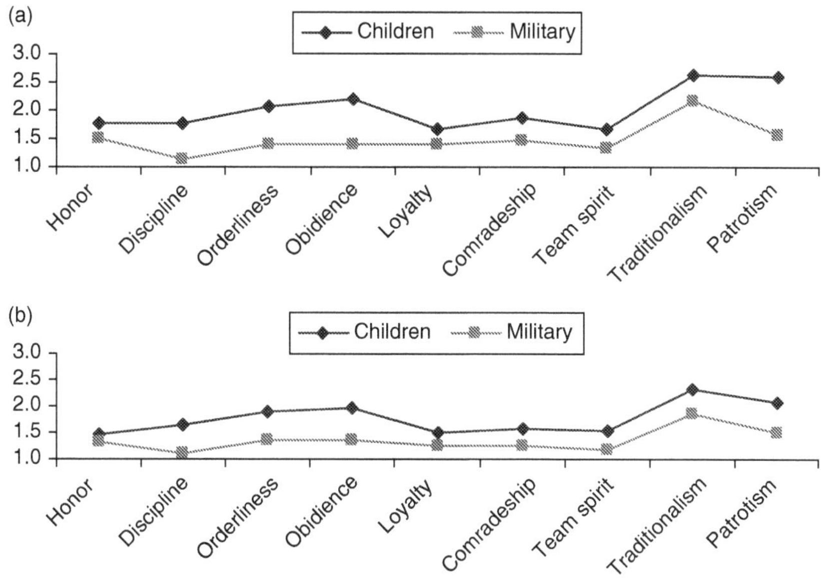

Fig. 1. (a) Civilian Students' View of the Importance of Values in the Education of Children and in the Military (1 = Very Important, 2 = Rather Important, 3 = Rather Unimportant, 4 = Very Unimportant). (b) Cadets' View of the Importance of Values in the Education of Children and in the Military (1 = Very Important, 2 = Rather Important, 3 = Rather Unimportant, 4 = Very Unimportant).

society than for the satisfactory functioning of the military as an institution. This, however, is not the case with the values self-control, determination and responsibility, as all are considered to be of about equal importance in both spheres of life.

As a provisional conclusion, it can be said that the general picture of the military as a centralised and hierarchical institution, where values of subordination are of major importance, dominates in both young elites of the 13 countries examined here. In contrast, the value profile of the importance of children's education mirrors a trend towards increasing importance of individualistic values in modern civil societies. This can be seen most clearly in the importance commonly ascribed to the value "responsibility", presumably the most significant value of autonomy. It is of importance to note that civilians as well as the military are aware of the major importance of this value both for the military and civil life (children's education), i.e. there is no gap between the two groups, cadets and civilian students.

However, Figs. 2(a) and (b) also show marked and interesting differences between the two groups. Civilian students tend to assess the classical values of autonomy (creativity, equality, generosity, initiative, open-mindedness, tolerance), as being of great importance for children's education, hence for one's own life in civil society, but much less of importance for the military (Fig. 2(a)). The future officers view this quite differently. For them, values such as tolerance, open-mindedness and initiative are also important values in the military, even if they are considered to be of somewhat less importance there than in child education (Fig. 2(b)). That means that civilian students tend to draw a much more sharp distinction between the value profiles for the daily life (children's education) and the military life than cadets.

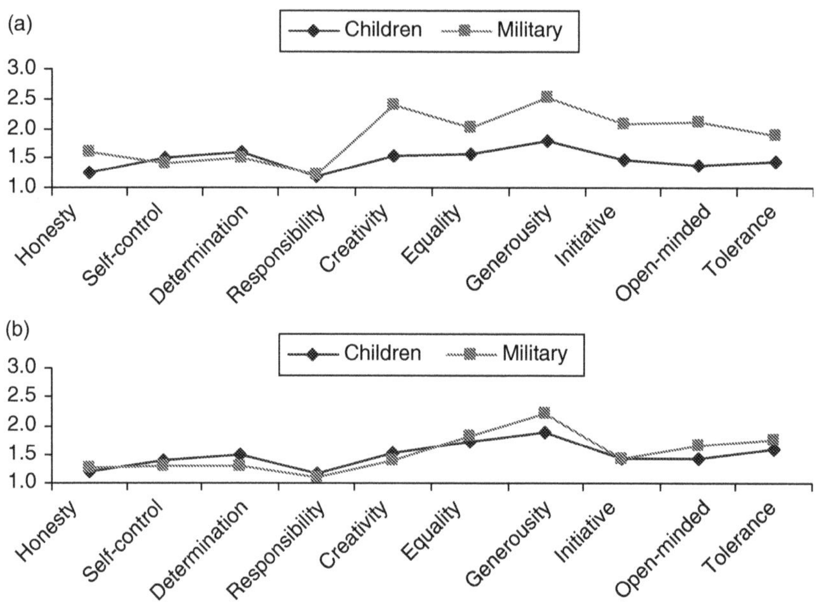

Fig. 2. (a) Civilian Students' View of The Importance of Values in the Education of Children and in the Military (Continued) (1 = Very Important, 2 = Rather important, 3 = Rather Unimportant, 4 = Very Unimportant). (b) Cadets' View of the Importance of Values in the Education of Children and in the Military (Continued) (1 = Very Important, 2 = Rather Important, 3 = Rather Unimportant, 4 = Very Unimportant).

Where do we find differences between cadets and civilian students in different countries and, if they exist, how great are they? Due to the fact that the amount of data referring to the various values is very large, it is hardly possible to present all the values in detail, by country and cadets vs. students. Therefore, we will limit ourselves to giving an overview of the average values of all nations for cadets and civilian students on selected values for both groups per nation (Table 5).

Generally speaking, the value's variance in the comparison between military and child education in all 13 countries is usually higher than the variance between cadets and civilian students. This can be witnessed in Table 5, where the delta values (difference per value child education minus military) of the civilian students not only outweigh the delta values of the cadets, but that they, with few exceptions, are also higher in all 13 countries. The value "initiative" is a matter of particular interest, as it features the highest civil–military differences between the countries. In Bulgaria, France, the Netherlands, Romania, Sweden and Switzerland, the cadets ascribe a higher importance of this value to the military than to child education, while the civilian students see it the other way around. For them, the value "initiative" is predominantly a civil, and not a military value. Both cadets and civilian students in Germany, Italy, Poland, South Africa, Spain, Slovenia and Turkey agree with this view.

To sum up: Concerning the values that are important for military on one hand and civil life on the other, there is a remarkably high degree of agreement between cadets and students. There is consensus that the classical values of heteronomy, but also patriotism and tradition, are classical military values, and hence less important for one's own life in civil society. On the other hand, values of autonomy are seen as more important for civil life. While, concerning the values of heteronomy, both groups' value profiles widely match, there is a difference in the assessment of values of autonomy, inasmuch as the cadets rate these as important also for the military. This means that the distinction made by students between what is important in modern daily life and in the military is more contrasting than the one made by cadets. Or in other words, the cadets view military values more close to their own civil values than students. If this is due to a more conservative value socialisation of cadets, which led them to choose the military as a profession, or if it is rather an effect of professional socialisation remains an open question, which cannot be answered on the basis of our data.

Table 5. Perception of Selected Values for the Military and for Children's Education.

		Bulgaria		France		Germany		Italy		Netherlands		Poland		Romania		Slovenia		South Africa		Spain		Sweden		Switzerland		Turkey	
		ΔC	ΔS	ΔC	ΔS	ΔC	ΔS	ΔC	ΔS	ΔC	ΔS	ΔC	ΔS	ΔC	ΔS	ΔC	ΔS	ΔC	ΔS	ΔC	ΔS	ΔC	ΔS	ΔC	ΔS	ΔC	ΔS
Heteronomity	Discipline	0.27	0.43	0.42	0.62	0.65	0.65	0.42	0.51	0.59	0.52	0.46	0.56	0.27	0.53	0.47	0.75	0.02	0.17	0.69	0.74	0.71	0.85	0.46	0.82	0.65	0.72
	Obedience	0.28	0.72	0.23	0.35	0.89	0.98	0.47	0.53	0.74	0.73	0.38	0.62	0.51	1.27	0.62	0.99	0.16	0.22	0.52	0.72	0.70	0.82	0.59	1.01	1.19	1.36
	Tradition	0.17	0.11	0.47	0.40	0.28	0.27	0.37	0.35	0.67	0.47	0.26	0.03	0.62	1.18	0.41	0.26	0.19	0.15	1.88	1.80	0.54	−.03	0.15	0.68	0.16	0.48
	Patriotism	0.57	0.56	0.37	1.20	0.68	0.63	0.64	0.89	0.74	1.27	0.39	0.59	0.69	1.04	0.59	1.33	0.29	0.72	1.12	1.88	0.62	0.99	0.28	1.40	0.23	0.64
Autonomy	Creativity	0.17	0.31	−.49	1.00	−.84	−.80	−.56	−.54	0.21	−.71	−.09	−.25	−.33	−1.10	−.44	1.42	−.24	−.32	−.76	1.33	0.05	−.41	−0.40	−1.66	−.24	−0.92
	Initiative	0.14	−.64	0.14	−.46	−.22	−.36	−.03	−.26	0.22	−0.57	−.17	−.34	0.12	−0.73	−.03	−.82	−.10	−.19	−.31	−.96	0.14	−.27	0.12	−1.02	−.20	−0.64
	Open-mindedness	0.03	−.38	−.20	−.77	−.69	−.62	−.23	−.46	−.22	−.82	−.24	−.38	−.03	−.68	−.48	1.00	−.12	−.20	−.39	1.12	−.01	−.44	−.23	−1.28	−.33	−0.61
	Tolerance	−.03	−.07	−.15	−.64	−.50	−.43	0.00	−.17	0.02	−.31	−.33	−.31	−.13	−.42	0.00	−.18	0.09	0.05	−.58	−.96	0.21	−.07	−.38	−1.10	−.41	−0.67

Note: Δ = Difference between the ranking of the value for the education of children and the ranking for the military, example: "discipline" for the cadets of Bulgaria: importance given to children's education 1.30 ÷ importance for the military 1.03 = 0.27; (*positive* delta: the value is considered more important for the military; *negative* delta: the value is considered more important for the education of children); (1 = very important, 2 = rather important, 3 = rather unimportant, 4 = very unimportant).

Values Referring to State, Nation and the Individual

Many hypotheses concerning civil–military relations claim that soldiers tend to have a closer relationship to the national community, compared to the civilian students (prominently Huntington, 1957). Our data referring to the relevant reference groups seem to corroborate this assumption. Moreover, these hypotheses usually claim that the soldiers tend to have a general view of life that is closer to realistic thinking in categories of power than to idealistic notions of a peaceful world. However, it often remains unclear as to what the causal relationships are. Do soldiers tend to be more loyal and more patriotic in their moral concepts because they serve their country and thus might have to protect and execute its interests, and do thus the normative values influence their view of the world and their country? In other words, are those value inclinations the result of military socialisation? Or have they chosen their profession because their early socialisation made them prone to hierarchical and conservative political views or because they originate from conservative social groups? In that case, we would speak of a selection effect.

These questions cannot be answered with a statistical analysis of correlation of our data. Moreover, the findings of basic value orientations for cadets and students of 13 nations presented in the previous sections should make us beware of thinking in simple stereotypes. Despite the inclination of cadets towards a more conservative "Weltanschauung" in all countries, the differences between the surveyed nations mostly outbalance the "gaps" between the future military and civil elites. The political cultures and military traditions of the different nations obviously influence the existence and size of possible civil–military gaps. The national cultures might even better explain the imprint of soldiers' moral concepts than universal trend typologies. Despite these facts, or maybe because of them, the following section will deal with the issue as to whether there are significant civil–military differences in the 13 nations regarding moral concepts concerning war and peace, the citizens' attitudes towards rights and duties as well as the function of the armed forces.

Ideal and Reality of Individual, State, and Civil–Military Relations Related Values

How important are values like equality, respect for the individual, safeguard of individual opportunities and responsibilities and individual freedom to the future military and civilian elites? How important are the respect of the basic laws of a country and the maintenance of its social welfare institutions to them? Are peaceful relations with other societies, social integration of the military and its subordination under the sphere of politics of importance? Furthermore, how do they judge the realisation of these values in their countries society? Are there differences between the two groups?

Taking the hypothesis that value orientations of the military students are more national conservative and conformist compared to the civilian students (Huntington, 1957), as a starting point, the following is to be expected: Compared to the civilian students, cadets attach less importance to individual than to collective related values, and see the former as being more positive and granted with regard to the degree of their implementation. At the same time, we would expect cadets to rate state-oriented values as more important but less granted in their implementation than civilian students do. Over all, this hypothesis is confirmed to a great extent (Table 6).

According to the figures in Table 6 the following holds for the *individual* related values:

- They are consistently rated highly by both groups (i.e. between very important and quite important). The only exception is Turkey when it comes to safeguard of individual opportunities and responsibilities. (This exception might be due to an error in the translation of the questionnaire.)
- They are, however, almost consistently rated as more important by the civilian students than by the military students. Germany is partially an exception, as it features an astonishingly high congruency between both groups interviewed.
- The cadets rate the deficits in implementation (differences between ideal and reality, second row in italics in Table 6) generally, and partially even significantly, lower than the civilian students do. That is to say that the military students, compared to the civilian students, consider the individual basic values to be implemented and granted in their nations to a larger extent. Bulgaria and Germany are partial exceptions here.

The following holds for the *state-oriented* values in Table 6:

- These values are usually seen as being of great importance, whereby the value "respect for law" is almost consistently rated as more important by cadets (with the exception of Bulgaria and France). This also holds for the importance of the maintenance of the welfare state, even if only to a lesser extent.
- Cadets perceive more deficits in the implementation of the value "respect of the law" than civilian students.

Table 6. Principles and Values in Politics (Norms) and their Realisation in One's Own Country.

	Bulgaria		France		Germany		Italy		Netherlands		Poland		Romania	
	C	S	C	S	C	S	C	S	C	S	C	S	C	S
Individual related values														
a. Equality of people, regardless of gender, race, religion	1.63	1.62	1.91	1.53	1.43	1.45	1.52	1.31	1.51	1.33	1.63	1.35	1.61	1.40
	−1.37	*−1.15*	*−.45*	*−1.26*	*0.15*	*0.10*	*−.35*	*−1.01*	*−.35*	*−.76*	*−.76*	*−1.32*	*−1.06*	*−1.32*
b. Respect for individuals	1.37	1.24	1.38	1.19	1.47	1.47	1.30	1.28	1.43	1.25	1.49	1.47	1.38	1.36
	−1.55	*−1.62*	*−.97*	*−1.31*	*−.97*	*−.95*	*−1.01*	*−1.00*	*−.61*	*−1.00*	*−.99*	*−1.11*	*−1.44*	*−1.52*
c. Basic freedoms for the individuals	1.76	1.55	1.81	1.35	1.38	1.42	1.46	1.30	1.43	1.33	1.60	1.57	1.40	1.15
(freedom of assembly and ideas, speech and press)	*−.79*	*−.83*	*0.3*	*−.52*	*0.33*	*.31*	*−.30*	*−.82*	*−.16*	*−.43*	*−.51*	*−.73*	*−.93*	*−1.14*
d. Safeguard of individual opportunities and responsibilities	1.50	1.32	1.72	1.65	1.73	1.77	1.65	1.54	1.79	1.67	1.49	1.52	1.29	1.30
	−1.00	*−1.55*	*−.52*	*−.68*	*−.62*	*−.65*	*−.69*	*−.97*	*−.36*	*−.57*	*−1.22*	*−1.43*	*−1.33*	*−1.33*
State related values														
e. Respect for the national basic law	1.40	1.31	1.49	1.46	1.44	1.56	1.40	1.56	1.59	1.69	1.36	1.67	1.47	1.37
	−1.34	*−1.55*	*−.88*	*−.81*	*−.73*	*−.60*	*−.63*	*−.62*	*−.58*	*−.68*	*−.82*	*−.75*	*−1.26*	*−1.14*
f. Defence of the societal system and the way of life	1.70	1.48	1.58	1.67	1.78	1.96	1.80	1.80	1.75	1.88	1.61	1.67	1.57	1.44
of the country	*−1.07*	*−1.54*	*−.70*	*−.50*	*.26*	*.40*	*−.42*	*−.58*	*−.37*	*−.29*	*−.93*	*−.97*	*−1.36*	*−1.54*
Values related to civil–military relations														
g. Peaceful relationship with other societies in the world	1.50	1.34	1.88	1.48	1.63	1.77	1.70	1.65	1.64	1.68	1.59	1.68	1.65	1.67
	−.32	*−.53*	*0.11*	*−.42*	*0.57*	*0.70*	*−.42*	*−.59*	*−.18*	*−.19*	*−.22*	*−.34*	*−.27*	*−.43*
h. Subordination of the military to the political leadership	2.54	2.28	2.01	2.27	1.76	1.97	2.31	2.22	1.96	2.27	2.77	2.66	2.46	2.20
	0.77	*0.23*	*0.50*	*0.47*	*.42*	*.51*	*.51*	*.05*	*0.01*	*0.02*	*.83*	*.55*	*0.27*	*−.33*
i. Integration of the military in the parent society	1.41	1.85	1.63	2.45	1.67	1.75	1.52	2.05	2.04	2.59	2.06	2.29	1.42	1.99
	−1.63	*−.87*	*−.77*	*−.21*	*−.91*	*−.96*	*−.89*	*−.27*	*−.48*	*−.09*	*−.44*	*−.33*	*−1.01*	*−.53*

	Slovenia		South Africa		Spain		Sweden		Switzerland		Turkey	
	C	S	C	S	C	S	C	S	C	S	C	S
Individual related value												
a. Equality of people, regardless of gender, race, religion	1.51	1.33	1.47	1.27	1.33	1.19	1.41	1.21	1.75	1.25	1.32	1.17
	–.65	*–1.29*	*–.75*	*–.84*	*–1.11*	*–1.43*	*–.62*	*–1.13*	*–.14*	*–.92*	*–1.02*	*–1.74*
b. Respect for individuals	1.43	1.26	1.30	1.16	1.21	1.14	1.33	1.19	1.49	1.21	1.31	1.14
	–1.09	*–1.26*	*–.91*	*–1.13*	*–1.13*	*–1.35*	*–.70*	*–1.02*	*–.30*	*–.69*	*–1.41*	*–1.86*
c. Basic freedoms for the individuals (freedom of assembly ideas,	1.40	1.25	1.45	1.31	1.40	1.21	1.33	1.21	1.61	1.29	1.42	1.20
speech, press)	*–.63*	*–.97*	*–.52*	*–.73*	*–.44*	*–.84*	*–.29*	*–.49*	*.28*	*–.31*	*–1.10*	*–1.73*
d. Safeguard of individual opportunities and responsibilities	1.83	1.67	1.45	1.44	1.69	1.62	1.48	1.45	1.91	1.64	2.53	2.72
	–.56	*–.84*	*–.96*	*–.99*	*–.78*	*–.90*	*–.56*	*–.77*	*.05*	*–.37*	*–1.02*	*–1.22*
State related values												
e. Respect for the national basic law	1.38	1.55	1.14	1.39	1.60	1.81	1.28	1.63	1.62	1.63	1.28	1.54
	–.97	*–.94*	*–1.29*	*–1.13*	*–.70*	*–.40*	*–.74*	*–.31*	*.02*	*–.07*	*–1.24*	*–.93*
f. Defence of the societal system and the way of life of the country	1.60	1.87	1.44	1.73	2.13	2.30	1.45	1.90	1.92	1.88	1.37	1.64
	–.86	*–.66*	*–.65*	*–.63*	*–.01*	*.08*	*–.73*	*–.36*	*–.04*	*–.24*	*–1.02*	–.60
Values related to civil–military relations												
g. Peaceful relationship with other societies in the world	1.46	1.77	1.48	1.56	1.64	1.52	1.46	1.50	1.95	1.45	1.59	1.43
	–.49	*–.16*	*–.32*	*–.36*	*–.52*	*–.98*	*–.35*	*–.21*	*.28*	*–.24*	*–.45*	*–.73*
h. Subordination of the military to the political leadership	2.00	2.41	1.88	1.98	2.18	2.43	1.96	1.72	1.99	1.70	2.32	2.45
	0.21	*0.41*	*–.11*	*–.21*	*.17*	*.29*	*0.25*	*–.06*	*.54*	*–.21*	*–.20*	*–.21*
i. Integration of the military in the parent society	1.74	2.55	1.70	2.04	1.95	2.69	1.85	2.55	1.64	2.65	1.72	2.46
	–.84	*–.17*	*–.56*	*–.46*	*–.56*	*–.03*	*–.80*	*–.21*	*–.61*	*.22*	*–.74*	*–.11*

Note: First line: means of how important the principle is considered (1 = very important; 2 = rather important; 3 = rather unimportant; 4 = very unimportant). Second line: difference between how important the principle should be minus the perceived realisation (1 = compl. realised, 2 = fairly well realised, 3 = not particularly realised, 4 = compl. unrealised.

- There is a country-to-country variation between the civil and military groups when it comes to the rating of the deficits in implementation concerning the maintenance of both the welfare state and one's own way of life.

The following holds for the *civil–military* related values in Table 6:

- The maintenance of peaceful relations with other societies is rated generally high by cadets and civilian students. Civilian students tend to perceive the implementation of peaceful relations as more deficient than cadets. Germany, Slovenia and Sweden are exceptions here.
- The integration of the military and its subordination under the primacy of the civil political leadership are on average seen by both groups as of slightly less important than the individual and state-related value categories.
- The principle of the subordination of the military to the civilian leadership ranks on the average between "rather important" and "rather unimportant" which indicates certain indifference. In 7 out of 13 countries it is considered more important by cadets than by students (France, Germany, Netherlands, Slovenia, South Africa, Spain and Turkey). The elites of both groups do not rank the item very highly in Bulgaria, Poland, Romania and Turkey. The primacy of politics over the military is seen as a given by cadets of the western European nations, but not by those of Turkey (2.32/2.52 = −0.20). Turkish interviewees of both groups and Romanian students perceive civilian control of the military in their countries as not implemented to a satisfactory degree. South Africans attribute comparatively high relevance to civilian control but see deficits in its fulfilling. That is, interestingly, also the case with civilian students in Switzerland. Students tend generally to assess the realisation of the subordination of the military to the political leadership more critically than cadets.
- The integration of the military into society is considered to be of a comparatively high importance. Its realisation is seen consistently in 11 out of 13 countries as more deficient by the cadets than by the civilian students (exception: Germany, Switzerland).

All in all, the future officers are obviously more state compliant and less critical concerning the implementation of basic values and the primacy of civilian control of the forces than the civilian students. However, more than their civilian counterparts they perceive the integration of the military into today's society as a problem.

Patriotism and Perceived Obligations towards One's Own Country

How patriotic are future officers and the future civilian elites? What duties are expected from citizens concerning their country? Are there significant differences in the value dimensions between military and civilian students regarding these?

Table 7 shows the degree of approval of five requirements, ranging from the primacy of loyalty to the country, to demands of national education to requirements whereby the willingness to fight for one's own country is seen as the strongest indicator of high civic duty. The indicated intensity of national cohesion tends to increase from the top to the bottom item in Table 7. The first row shows the strong agreement (agree strongly) and the second the total agreement (agree strongly and partially agree). The gamma coefficient indicates the degree of difference between military and civil interviewees. The higher the γ-value, the greater the difference between military and civilian students.

As shown in Table 7, cadets agree much stronger to all requirements compared to the civilian students (with the exception of Germany). For them, all forms of national cohesion, from the primacy of nationality to the willingness to fight for the nation, are clearly higher compared to the civilians, both in relative as well as in absolute figures. The strength of the correlation coefficient, a sign of difference, increases from top to bottom for most countries.

However, there are differences when it comes to the intensity of agreement. Not surprisingly, on average the biggest difference concerns the demand to be willing to fight for one's nation. This demand is consistently higher for the cadets than for the civilian students. Huge differences between the two groups we find mainly in France, Romania, Slovenia, Spain, Switzerland and Turkey, moderate differences between the two groups in Italy, South Africa and Sweden, and only small differences in Poland, the Netherlands, Bulgaria and Germany.

When it comes to the civic duties, cadets pledge significantly more allegiance to the state than civilian students. Generally cadets give primacy of the collective over the individual. Here we find a civil–military gap of a principle dimension.

Role of National Interests, War and the Armed Forces

Is war related to human nature? Can war still be justified as a means of securing national interests, even today? Furthermore, what role do the armed forces play, in general, when it comes to protecting national interests? Do cadets differ from students in these respects and if so to what extent? The

Table 7. Patriotism and Perceived Obligations Towards One's Own Country.

	Bulgaria			France			Germany			Italy			Netherlands			Poland			Romania		
	C (%)	S (%)	γ (%)	C (%)	S (%)	γ (%)	C (%)	S (%)	γ (%)	C (%)	S (%)	γ (%)	C (%)	S (%)	γ (%)	C (%)	S (%)	γ (%)	C (%)	S (%)	γ (%)
A citizen should always feel that his/her primary allegiance is to his/her own country	73 (97)	49 (86)	.11	33 (73)	15 (34)	.61	22 (71)	23 (71)	.01*	46 (89)	28 (67)	.40	34 (88)	20 (64)	.35	65 (94)	47 (86)	.34	56 (94)	23 (65)	.65
We should strive for loyalty to our country before we can afford to consider world brotherhood	45 (96)	52 (91)	.07*	40 (69)	12 (24)	.64	20 (56)	19 (61)	.04*	42 (86)	25 (66)	.40	17 (62)	11 (55)	.18	55 (95)	37 (84)	.37	34 (93)	23 (61)	.47
The promotion of patriotism should be an important aim of citizenship education	45 (79)	39 (80)	.08*	25 (83)	13 (38)	.60	11 (73)	6 (75)	.19	37 (81)	16 (55)	.50	5 (34)	0 (18)	.43	45 (94)	27 (75)	.43	44 (91)	18 (65)	.58
All citizens should be willing to fight for their country	60 (87)	24 (62)	.59	56 (94)	11 (41)	.82	27 (64)	19 (62)	.06*	46 (85)	13 (51)	.65	22 (67)	4 (28)	.64	64 (94)	29 (78)	.60	46 (93)	9 (44)	.80
The strongest indicator of a good citizen is to perform military service in defence of the country	37 (77)	10 (39)	.65	10 (38)	0 (11)	.67	15 (44)	6 (32)	.16*	11 (42)	9 (36)	.24	8 (42)	3 (17)	.50	24 (70)	13 (37)	.47	20 (65)	3 (27)	.65

	Slovenia			South Africa			Spain			Sweden			Switzerland			Turkey		
	C (%)	S (%)	γ (%)	C (%)	S (%)	γ (%)	C (%)	S (%)	γ (%)	C (%)	S (%)	γ (%)	C (%)	S (%)	γ (%)	C (%)	S (%)	γ (%)
A citizen should always feel that his/her primary allegiance is to his/her own country	60 (97)	25 (75)	.66	69 (92)	46 (84)	.41	48 (78)	12 (39)	.62	35 (82)	14 (49)	.55	48 (94)	13 (49)	.45	60 (94)	25 (79)	.58
We should strive for loyalty to our country before we can afford to consider world brotherhood	38 (97)	25 (80)	.41	75 (92)	44 (78)	.50	30 (61)	9 (29)	.51	21 (69)	9 (45)	.44	25 (78)	7 (37)	.65	55 (89)	19 (75)	.56
The promotion of patriotism should be an important aim of citizenship education	40 (87)	10 (46)	.73	56 (87)	26 (66)	.50	33 (64)	3 (15)	.70	12 (74)	1 (55)	.69	14 (56)	3 (16)	.79	49 (84)	19 (60)	.54
All citizens should be willing to fight for their country	54 (83)	12 (43)	.66	75 (93)	23 (54)	.76	27 (52)	4 (14)	.63	46 (71)	16 (33)	.66	33 (90)	7 (29)	.83	60 (91)	31 (50)	.55
The strongest indicator of a good citizen is to perform military service in defence of the country	23 (68)	6 (17)	.79	41 (80)	15 (39)	.62	6 (37)	3 (12)	.53	16 (60)	7 (16)	.69	6 (41)	4 (33)	.76	13 (56)	6 (37)	.33

Note: First row: strong agreement in %, second row: total agreement in %, γ: correlation cadets (C)/students (S). *not significant $p \geqslant 0.05$; C = cadets, S = civilian students.

answers to such questions should provide an indication of the values that shape civil–military relationships in a given country.

The list of requirements in Table 8 shows the future elites' opinion concerning these issues. The "strong" agreement is listed in the topmost row, while the row below gives the total agreement in brackets. The strong agreement discriminates more than the total agreement. Therefore, we refer primarily to the first category. The items in Table 8 first deal with the relation between war and human nature and the question of what national purpose the armed forces serve. Second, the issue of the function of the armed forces will be addressed. Do they still serve the purpose of war, or should they be used increasingly for new non-combat operations?

Both future elites, military and civilian, agree that war is ultimately unavoidable, as it is rooted deeply in human nature. Yet, across the 13 countries, both groups differ in the degree of agreement. The military view of man's nature is significantly more pessimistic, as Huntington (1957) notably alleged.

- The degrees of agreement as well as differences between the two groups are rather small in Bulgaria, Germany and Slovenia. Variations in agreement become stronger and the difference between military and civilian students more distinct in Italy, the Netherlands, Romania, Spain, Sweden and Switzerland. In France, Poland, South Africa and Turkey, roughly 6 out of 10 interviewed cadets agree with the statement that war is unavoidable, while the students' agreement with this statement is considerably lower. In the latter 4 countries, we note a substantial civil–military gap when it comes to the basic image of human nature.
- The results are similar when it comes to war as a means to defend national interests (second item in Table 8). The total degree of agreement is more moderate for students than for cadets, and it is not always a majority that agrees with this statement (Germany, Slovenia, Spain and Switzerland). Again, the cadets in France, South Africa and Turkey reveal the highest degree of approval. There is hardly a majority of their civil counterparts that agree as intensively any more. Even if there is a slightly higher degree of agreement in the military group of interviewees (less than 35% strong agreement), the issue is not strongly agreed with in Germany, Slovenia, Switzerland, Bulgaria, Italy, Poland, Romania, Spain and Sweden, i.e. in 9 out of 13 countries.
- Even though total agreement also outweighs the third item in Table 8, which postulates an image benefit of powerful armed forces and of national projection of power, the intensity of strong and total agreement

Table 8. Perceived Role and Missions of the Armed Forces.

	Bulgaria		France		Germany		Italy		Netherlands		Poland		Romania		Slovenia		South Africa		Spain		Sweden		Switzerland		Turkey	
	C (%)	S (%)	C (%)	S (%)	C (%)	S (%)	C (%)	S (%)	C (%)	S (%)	C (%)	S (%)	C (%)	S (%)	C (%)	S (%)	C (%)	S (%)	C (%)	S (%)	C (%)	S (%)	C (%)	S (%)	C (%)	S (%)
Function of the military																										
Human nature being what it is, there will always be war	37 (70)	32 (63)	65 (92)	42 (69)	38 (74)	34 (81)	35 (73)	25 (62)	35 (81)	24 (56)	61 (91)	34 (79)	41 (79)	26 (63)	40 (91)	35 (84)	58 (88)	37 (73)	39 (73)	22 (57)	38 (80)	17 (54)	43 (88)	25 (63)	59 (88)	18 (53)
Sometimes war is necessary to protect national interests	27 (80)	31 (61)	73 (94)	37 (74)	11 (49)	11 (47)	28 (76)	14 (54)	36 (85)	16 (58)	28 (61)	11 (50)	25 (72)	20 (62)	14 (60)	9 (48)	73 (94)	36 (72)	34 (66)	11 (32)	34 (76)	19 (53)	26 (73)	10 (34)	73 (90)	30 (67)
Strong forces improve our image throughout the world	24 (83)	27 (65)	35 (87)	42 (79)	14 (46)	7 (41)	29 (72)	9 (39)	18 (53)	8 (39)	48 (93)	25 (66)	32 (87)	21 (64)	6 (52)	3 (24)	58 (87)	24 (57)	31 (71)	11 (34)	13 (53)	8 (33)	3 (43)	4 (13)	40 (79)	41 (70)
War and peace and national interests																										
The most important role of the military is the preparation for and the conduct of war	24 (79)	32 (72)	77 (100)	29 (73)	8 (24)	4 (18)	24 (54)	11 (38)	20 (60)	9 (35)	26 (64)	12 (43)	30 (82)	18 (51)	6 (40)	3 (18)	85 (94)	36 (69)	37 (64)	5 (27)	23 (56)	5 (20)	20 (61)	6 (18)	62 (91)	27 (66)
The military should be prepared to cover the whole spectrum of possible missions	48 (93)	40 (82)	42 (81)	54 (88)	54 (87)	44 (82)	54 (87)	34 (75)	49 (87)	31 (86)	51 (91)	39 (86)	75 (97)	59 (92)	23 (71)	40 (92)	67 (90)	46 (81)	58 (88)	42 (84)	63 (91)	49 (94)	50 (86)	23 (63)	51 (81)	22 (64)
Today peacekeeping and non-combatant activities should be the central military function	27 (73)	35 (76)	23 (66)	42 (81)	20 (74)	23 (81)	16 (69)	25 (76)	23 (78)	31 (80)	33 (81)	33 (85)	53 (91)	47 (96)	29 (60)	38 (92)	33 (69)	32 (80)	33 (68)	52 (85)	39 (86)	42 (86)	6 (42)	41 (87)	19 (69)	31 (69)

is even more moderate compared to the use of armed forces for national interests. Yet, the total agreement of the officers is again higher than 50% in 11 out of 13 countries, while this is only the case in 6 countries if one looks at the civilian students. Their intensity of agreement is again considerably lower here. Hence again, the cadets' thinking in categories of military power is much more pronounced than that of the civil equivalent.

- There are interesting variations in the functions that are ascribed to the military (Table 8, three bottom rows). If the primary role of the military is seen as preparing for and waging war, the agreement of the cadets outweighs that of the civilian students both in total as well as in the intensity of agreement. However strong agreement is usually low, with the exception of the cadets in South Africa (85%), France (77%) and Turkey (62%).
- The issue referring to the military as a multifunctional rather than a war-waging institution, already features balanced approval rates in both groups. There is an inverted approval-ratio between military and civilian students concerning the demand that the military should primarily have peacekeeping and non-combatant functions.

Apparently, the future officers in our 13 countries feel very insecure about the identity of the military and the soldiers' profession in a post-Cold War world. Inter-state war has become obsolete, whereas military operations other than war (MOOTW) have become the rule. Compared to the cadets, the civilian students show a significantly higher willingness to give the armed forces a new identity as the main means for peacekeeping and political stabilisation. With regard to the military identity we might speak here of a civil–military gap.

Comparing Identities of the Military Leaders and the Country's People

Do the military leaders share the common values of the country's population? The perception of convergence or divergence by young officers and civilian students may serve as a reliable indicator of the quality of future civil–military relations in a given country and ultimately of the degree of mutual trust. Perceived consonance by both groups might mean fewer tensions, considerable differences however a possible potential of future tensions in the civil–military relations of the future elites of a country.

As Table 9 shows, there is a common trend insofar as cadets assess the situation more positively in general than the civilian students do. There are however significant differences between the countries.

Table 9. Perceived Value Identity Between the People and the Military Leaders.

	Cadets		Students		Difference Cadets – Students	
	Yes (%)	No (%)	Yes (%)	No (%)	Yes (%)	No (%)
Bulgaria	25	46	27	28	−2	+18
France	44	35	22	35	+22	0
Germany	44	34	47	32	−3	+2
Italy	54	16	38	20	+16	−4
Netherlands	29	32	15	45	+14	−13
Poland	44	20	22	29	+22	−9
Romania	35	41	14	57	+21	−16
Slovenia	56	21	18	39	+38	−18
South Africa	33	37	26	36	+7	+1
Spain	28	44	13	47	+15	−3
Sweden	45	21	25	40	+20	−19
Switzerland	45	38	12	53	+33	−15
Turkey	64	17	34	25	+30	−8

"Do you think military leaders in general share the same values as people?" (yes / no / not sure / no opinion).

- There is a remarkable consonance in the answers given to this question in Germany, where strong relative majorities both among the officers and among the students answer this question positively. To a smaller degree cadets and civilian students in Italy and Turkey have largely the same opinions.
- A negative consonance is found in Romania, Spain, South Africa, Switzerland and Bulgaria, where many in both groups doubt that there is such an identity of values of the population and the military command. The civilian students' doubts are usually stronger than the military students'. Bulgaria is a remarkable exception, where almost every second cadet utters mistrust (46%), whereas the civilian students are rather insecure and more balanced (28% "no").
- Considerable civil–military perception differences (yes >20%) are to be found in 6 of the 13 countries. (Slovenia, Switzerland, Turkey, France, Poland, Romania, arranged in order of decreasing intensity)

Whereas absolute or relative majorities of military students affirm an identity of values of the military command, absolute or relative majorities of civilian students doubt that this is the case. In Switzerland, Spain and Romania, almost or sometimes more than every second civilian student doubts this. While cadets assess the civil–military relations as intact, students see problems with them.

CONCLUSIONS

The variance between the 13 countries included in our survey is mostly larger than the one between civilian and military students when it comes to the basic value dimensions such as tradition vs. modernity, left vs. right, cosmopolitan vs. localistic, materialistic vs. post-materialistic and civilian vs. military values. Thus, the military are not consistently more religious, more right oriented and more materialistic than their civil fellow students, even if, simply put, there is a tendency for such a trend. It is equally correct that the nation as a point of reference – and Europe for the future military elites in countries of the EU in particular – tends to be more significant for the cadets of some countries than for the civilian students. We could therefore conclude that those cadets tend to have a more cosmopolitan view than their civilian counterparts. On the other hand cadets are more prone to radical political ideologies, they are more law and order oriented and show a somewhat higher inclination towards materialistic values than civilian students. Our data do not allow us to conclude that cadets in countries, which have replaced conscription by all-volunteer forces, tend to have a more pronounced right-wing orientation than cadets in countries, which have maintained conscription.

Even if we have to conclude that there are underlying differences between cadets and students, the former being basically more conservative than the latter, according to our data the patterns and the intensity of a potential gap vary across the 13 countries, sometimes considerably. For instance, the fact that cadets in the post-communist countries assess themselves as more left and less religious than their civil counterparts indicates that the division of Europe has left ideological marks that remain today. Or, the secular tradition cultivated by Turkey's military – the heritage of Ataturk – seems to influence the fundamental value dimensions of Turkish cadets and Turkish civil–military relations in general much more strongly than simply the role affiliation to the military profession does per se. The high convergence of cadets and students in Germany can be considered as an outcome of the newly founded post-World War military culture based on the concept of the "citizen in uniform" and an officer socialisation in civilian stamped military universities there. Obviously the political culture and tradition of a nation shape civil–military relations as much or even more than stereotypical culture models of the professional military establishment as a special subculture one the one hand and democratic society on the other. And, despite the demonstrated underlying differences in values and attitudes between the two groups, there is remarkable consensus between the military and the civilian students about which values are relevant for military and for civil life. Concerning the basic value orientations, there are gradual differences between the future military and civil elites but there is not a consistent value gap of a notable size.

This picture changes significantly when it comes to moral concepts that concern the rights of the individuals and their relation to national community, the assessment of war and the socio-political function of the armed forces. Apart from some exceptions and partially remarkable differences between the 13 national groups, here civil–military differences of a more principle character are visible. It seems that the closer the values and attitudes are related to the military as a national institution, the higher the probability of civil–military differences and the less an issue is related to the military, the lower the probability of differences between students and military cadets. The future military elite is generally inclined to identify itself more with the interests of the national community and to defend more strongly the interests of the collective than civilian students. The state and its role as a guarantor of civil rights are less critically assessed by the cadets than by the civilian students. The former generally see values concerning state and national community as more important than values concerning individuals. The "we" loyalty is given more often priority to the citizen's rights by cadets while the students tend to rank the priorities the other way around. In other words, cadets are more ready and willing to accept the primacy of the community before that of the individual than civilian students.

Something that might be a disappointment for the military elite with regard to civil society is that cadets in the US expect civilians to think the same way (Feaver & Kohn, 2001). Here we might locate the potential for a civil–military gap. The presently dominant culture of "individualisation" in modern democratic societies clashes with the still communitarian-based military subculture. More precisely, the cadets project the communitarian ideal that is still inherent in the military institution onto the parent society, and this creates expectations among young officers which can no longer be fulfilled and which can therefore lead to disappointment and mistrust. Consequently, the military students see shortcomings in implementation mainly in the military's integration into society and much less in the rights of the individuals. Compared to students, cadets are generally more prone to assess international politics in categories of national power and interests and to assign the military the function of defending these interests by force if necessary. It is probably also due to this fact that the military seems to find it more difficult than students to accept the role change of the armed forces from an instrument of national defence to a means of international stability, from a means of waging national war to new missions of non-combatant and policing character.

To sum up, it is mainly with regard to the attitudes towards the nation, the assessment of the relation between the citizens and the state, and the social and political role of the armed forces in today's democratic societies that the future military elites in the 13 countries of our survey differ from their civilian counterparts. And they differ on these points more than they differ on basic value orientations. It is an open question whether we would maintain that this indicates a deplorable "gap". We might simply interpret this fact as a difference between the dominant social culture and a group subculture, which is more or less common in modern pluralistic societies. The size of the differences varies strongly between the nations. As measured by our data, the differences in culture, if we want to stay with this term, are assessed as: extraordinarily small or even inexistent in Germany; visible to a moderate extent in Italy, the Netherlands, Poland and Slovenia; rather large in France, Spain, Sweden and Switzerland; and varying in degree or inconsistent in Bulgaria, Romania, South Africa and Turkey. Our data do not give us any ground for the assumption that these differences in culture are new, nor that they have increased in recent years.

NOTE

1. Only those items of question 32 have been tabulated which measure along that dimension. The items "natural environment", "friends" and "native city", "yourself", which were also part of the question battery, have been omitted.

REFERENCES

Ashkanasy, N. M., Wilderom, C. P. M., & Peterson, M. F. (Eds). (2000). *Handbook of organizational culture and climate*. Thousand Oaks: Sage Publications, Inc.

Born, H., Haltiner, K., & Malesic, M. (Eds). (2004). *Renaissance of democratic control of armed forces in contemporary societies*. Baden-Baden: Nomos.

Feaver, P. D., & Kohn, R. H. (Eds). (2001). *Soldiers and civilians. The civil-military gap and American national security*. Cambridge: MIT Press.

Garp, M. (2005). Civil-military gap issues and dilemmas: A short review. In: G. Caforio & G. Kümmel (Eds), *Military missions and their implications reconsidered: The aftermath of September 11th* (pp. 83–92). Amsterdam: Elsevier.
Hillen, J. (1999). Must U.S. military culture reform? *Orbis*, *43*(1), 43–58.
Hofstede, G. (1984). The cultural relativity of the quality of life concept. *Academy of Management Review*, *9*, 389–398.
Holsti, O. R. (2001). Of chasms and convergences: Attitudes and beliefs of civilian and military elites at the start of a new millennium. In: P. D. Feaver & R. H. Kohn (Eds), *Soldiers and civilians. The civil-military gap and American national security* (pp. 16–99). Cambridge: MIT Press.
Huntington, S. (1957). *The soldier and the state: The theory and practise of civil–military relations*. Cambridge: Harvard University Press.
Inglehart, R. (1977). *The silent revolution: Changing values and political styles among Western publics*. Princeton: Princeton University Press.
Inglehart, R. (1990). *Culture shift in advanced industrial society*. Princeton: Princeton University Press.
Janowitz, M. (1960). *The professional soldier: A social and political portrait*. New York: Free Press.
Kümmel, G. (2003). A soldier is a soldier is a soldier? The military and its soldiers in an era of globalisation. In: G. Caforio (Ed.), *Handbook of the sociology of the military* (pp. 417–433). New York: Kluwer Academic.
Roe, R. A., & Ester, P. (1999). Values and work: Empirical findings and theoretical perspective. *Applied Psychology: An International Review*, *48*(1), 1–21.
Roman, P. J., & Tarr, D. W. (2001). Military professionalism and policymaking: Is there a civil-military gap at the top? If so, does it matter? In: P. D. Feaver & R. H. Kohn (Eds), *Soldiers and civilians* (pp. 403–428). Cambridge: MIT Press.
Segal, D. R. (2003). The study of military and society in the United States: Recent trends. In: J. Callaghan & F. Kernic (Eds), *Armed forces and international security. Global trends and issues* (pp. 59–64). Münster: LIT Verlag.
Segal, D. R., Freedman-Doan, P., Bachman, J. G., & O'Malley, P. M. (2001). Attitudes of entry-level enlisted personnel: Pro-military and politically mainstreamed. In: P. D. Feaver & R. H. Kohn (Eds), *Soldiers and civilians. The civil-military gap and American national security* (pp. 163–212). Cambridge: MIT Press.
Snider, D. M., Priest, R. F., & Lewis, F. (2001). The civilian-military gap and professional military education at the precommissioning level. *Armed Forces and Society*, *27*(2), 249–272.

EFFECTS OF THE SOCIALISATION PROCESS ON THE CULTURAL ATTITUDES OF FUTURE ELITES

Giuseppe Caforio and Maja Garb

ABSTRACT

This chapter deals with the effects that the socialisation process, both primary and professional, has on the cultural attitudes of young people interviewed with regard to national security.

The data show the great importance of primary socialisation, especially among cadets, who form a military mindset already before entering the training academies. The process is less accentuated for youths who attend civilian universities.

Professional socialisation then operates in both environments, at times in contradictory ways with respect to the aims of the profession for cadets, and with respect to greater awareness of security issues for university students.

1. INTRODUCTION

This chapter examines the influence that the socialisation process has on the values, opinions and attitudes toward the military of the two groups of future elites looked at here.

Cultural Differences between the Military and Parent Society in Democratic Countries
Contributions to Conflict Management, Peace Economics and Development, Volume 4, 83–106

ISSN: 1572-8323/doi:10.1016/S1572-8323(07)04004-0

As is well known, a primary socialisation process is distinguished which consists in individual learning of cultural models, rules and behaviours characteristic of a given society which this society imparts to its members. It takes place in the family, in school, through friends, youth and sports associations, churches and so forth.

There is also a later socialisation, termed secondary or professional (Merton, Reader, & Kendall, 1957), that takes place through the preparation for a specific professional activity (called also re-socialisation) and continues at the workplace, in the group where the individual finds himself carrying out his professional life.

The hypothesis on an existing value gap (major value differences) between the military and civilian populations brings to the surface the question of what could cause that gap. Sociology usually finds answers in the processes of socialisation. Some socialisation concepts have been brought into debate and also taken as the theoretical background for empirical surveys in the framework of studies of military values and military culture. Let us briefly mention some of those concepts and theories.

The first concept that usually comes to mind when discussing socialisation in the military is the concept of secondary socialisation or re-socialisation. After entry into the armed forces the process of abolishing previous, civilian values and an old lifestyle and forging new ones begins. Ricks (1997) describes some experiences from American military boot camps and some differences that appear between civilians and those who completed basic military training in those camps. It seems that basic military training aims not only to provide military knowledge but also to re-socialise the candidates for military service. In some cases, the military re-socialisation is very intense and leads to complete substitution of previous civilian values with new, military ones. Goffman calls such complete change "mortification" (Jelušič, 1997, p. 110).[1]

However, re-socialisation is not needed as much when the candidates for military service have already socialised the military values. We could put such cases under the concept of primary or anticipatory socialisation.

Since more and more countries abolish conscription and accept volunteer armed forces, it is expected that the armed forces would be comprised of highly motivated military personnel who volunteer for military service mostly in order to be soldiers, experience military life, serve their country, etc. The value scheme of such military personnel is expected to be congruent with the values of the military organisation they are entering. It could be said that they are socialised for military values before entering military service. It could be said that they are socialised for military service through their primary socialisation. After entering the armed forces such personnel are not re-socialised; on the contrary, their previous pro-military values are further strengthened (see De Fleur & Warner, 1987; on self-selection see also Bachman, Sigelman, & Diamond, 1987; Franke, 2001).

One important factor in shaping the pro-military orientation of a child or youth in a primary socialisation process is parents' values and occupations. Empirical surveys show that a family military tradition is an important factor for recruitment into military service. However, some authors have established that candidates from military families are not more pro-military oriented than other candidates for the military profession, they are only represented far above average among candidates (McAllister & Smith, 1989; McAllister, 1995; De Fleur & Warner, 1987, p. 519).

And, when we talk about candidates for commissioned officer and their education at military academies, it could also be expected that the professional socialisation at those academies has effects as a re-socialising factor for the cadets. It is interesting that an American longitudinal empirical survey among military cadets and civilian students shows that there are significant differences among cadets and students, but these differences are the result of their primary socialisation, not the result of professional education and socialisation at military academies and civilian universities. The changes during four years of schooling were similar in both groups of respondents, military cadets and civilian students (see Priest & Beach, 1998, pp. 93–96; Priest, Fullerton, & Bridges, 1982).

Last but not least, the selection processes should also be mentioned here. The military organisation (and also other organisations) tries to choose as its members candidates whose values are rather congruent with the organisational values. So, among other things, the selection process has the function of strengthening the organisational culture. Consequently, the selection results in greater organisational efficiency and greater allegiance of members to the organisation (see Etzioni, 1964, p. 69). One might say that selection differentiates between properly and not properly socialised (primary socialisation) candidates for the organisation.

It thus seems meaningful, in this chapter, to distinguish between the two socialisations (primary and professional) and to see how much the data of this research can tell us about each of them.

One significant indicator of primary socialisation can be gleaned here by comparing the cadets' attitudes toward the military upon entering the training institutes with those of the average for the university students of other faculties. If we limit this comparison to the two groups in their first year of study, their attitudes clearly cannot yet be considered to be influenced by the professional socialisation they receive at those educational institutions but go back to each person's primary socialisation. The comparison is more specific for the cadets, because for them there is a precise term of comparison with the average of the university students, who constitute a more heterogeneous set: however, in the comparison between the two cultures, civilian and military, it appears particularly meaningful, for the purposes of this research, to evaluate how the primary socialisation of the cadets differs from that of the other young people pursuing leadership careers.

Professional socialisation seems to be just as important, however, particularly for the military, as we have already observed in another study (Caforio & Nuciari, 1998):

> Professional socialisation deserves special emphasis for those roles where the value pattern is institutionalised not only as far as general goals at the level of the social system are concerned, but even with reference to values, behaviours, norms and performances which are defined by an institutional authority within codes delimiting that role's scope of action and specifying its competence. (p. 7)

Professional socialisation, in its reflections on attitudes toward the military, will be examined here by comparing the values, opinions and attitudes of interviewees in their first two years of study with those in their later years. This type of research would require a diachronic procedure, i.e., analysis of the same group of subjects in their first year and then at the end of the professional training process; however, previous experiences in the field (see Caforio & Nuciari, 1998) have shown that the results of a synchronic investigation like the one presented here do not differ greatly from those of a cohort analysis.

The first part of the chapter will thus be devoted to analysing the extent to which the primary socialisation of the cadets may have differed from that of their generational peers of like condition, with particular reference to attitudes toward military security issues. The second part will examine, by comparing interviewees from different class years, what changes the professional socialisation at work in the training institutes may have made in the attitudes and values of the two elite groups examined here.

The analysis regards the sample in its entirety, i.e., it is aimed at sketching the ideal-type of the cadet and, more approximately, that of his university student peer, without regard to their nationality or gender. Such breakdowns are delegated to two other chapters in this part of the book: the eighth, which analyses national differences as well as those of broader geographic areas identified from the political (East European countries,

Western countries, etc.) or cultural standpoint (such as by areas of religious culture: Catholic, Orthodox Christian, Islamic, Protestant) and the seventh, where the gender gap is studied on a sample made up of approximately 2,000 males and 1,000 females.

2. PRIMARY SOCIALISATION

This section on primary socialisation analyses the differences that the newest members of the two cultures, military and civilian, display from two points of view: attitudes toward values in general, and attitudes toward the military. From the differences in attitude of the two surveyed groups one can then infer what that specific primary socialisation leads to that brings a young person to embrace the officer's career or, in other words, what is the ideal-type of young person who is recruited for that career.

The section will therefore be divided up as follows: attitudes toward values and attitudes toward the military.

2.1. Attitudes Toward Basic Values

To sketch the ideal-type of the young person attracted by a career in the military ("cadet") in comparison with the average for their age peers pursuing higher education in universities ("students") we shall first examine some basic values like religion, democratic ideals (since we are talking about the social context of democratic countries) and political leanings. We shall then go on to analyse other, complementary aspects to such values.

For what regards religiosity, the cadets show themselves to be less religious on average than the students: those who attend religious services even only occasionally represent 46.4% of the total for the cadets, compared to 52.9% of the students. Although with different percentages, this datum is common for the four great religions of the young people included in the sample, namely Catholic, Orthodox Christian, Islamic and Protestant. The breakdown by frequency of attendance, as well as the percentage of non-believers, are indicated in Table 1.

Democratic ideals appear to be widely shared by all the young people in the sample, both cadets and students. The differences on some fundamental principles are slight (see Table 2) and can be summed up as follows: the cadets seem to attach more importance to respect for the national basic law, safeguarding individual opportunities, defence of the societal system and the

Table 1. Religiosity of the Beginners.

	Cadets (%)[a]	Students (%)
Religious and attend religious services regularly (every week)	8.8	12.6
Religious and attend religious services once a month	9.3	13.0
Religious but attend religious services only for the most important holidays	28.3	27.3
Can't say whether religious or not	15.3	11.7
Not religious	34.0	30.6
No answer	4.3	4.8

[a]The terms "cadets" and "students" in this section refer to those who are in their first year of study.

Table 2. How Important are the Following Principles?

	Cadets (%)	Students (%)
Equality of people	91.8	96.2
Respect for individuals	98.4	98.4
Basic freedom	96.2	97.7
Respect constitution	97.1	94.6
Safeguarding individual opportunities	94.7	92.3
Defence of my country's way of life	90.3	86.6
Peaceful relationship with nations	93.6	92.3
Subordination of military to political leadership	67.1	61.2
Integration of military in parent society	81.6	59.6

country's way of life, and, more markedly, the aspects of "military democracy", so to speak, i.e., subordination of the military to politics and integration into the parent society.

The greater importance given to these principles gives shape to an ideal-type of cadet who is more tied to the institutions (constitutional law) than his student peers – this is a characteristic that will be confirmed in other parts of the survey – and also more jealous of his country's national identity. The greater importance given to aspects of "military democracy" is expected, but nonetheless indicative of an anticipatory socialisation that is already oriented toward the chosen profession.

The opinions of the two groups on the level of realisation that these principles have attained in the home country are instead quite different (Table 3).

Table 3. How have these Principles been Realised?

	Cadets (%)	Students (%)
Equality of people	69.9	51.8
Respect for individuals	65.1	50.1
Basic freedom	80.4	66.2
Respect constitution	68.0	62.0
Individual opportunities	65.5	55.8
Defence of way of life	66.2	60.9
Peaceful relationship	84.6	76.2
Subordination of military	77.3	64.8
Integration of military	47.3	40.2

Table 4. Political Position.

Political Position	Cadets (%)	Students (%)
Left	17.3	36.1
Centre	37.4	37.4
Right	43.5	26.5

Here the cadet is considerably more optimistic than the student everywhere, with differences as big as 15 percentage points. The survey does not provide clear interpretive elements for this tendency: the only hypothesis that can be advanced as that of a greater "legalism" on the part of the cadet that leads him to consider what the law provides as having been implemented, and perhaps also a certain conformism that leads him to contest current social structures less than his peers.

A political breakdown of the cadets shows the action of significant anticipatory socialisation as well: in more or less in all studies of the sector,[2] one sees political attitudes among active-duty officers that are more conservative than the average for other national elites, and in this survey cadets clearly put themselves on the same positions (see Table 4).

It appears interesting at this point to investigate further by analysing the attitudes of the two groups on qualities and values which, in the lack of better terminology, I have indicated here with the word "complementary".

The first attitude examined regards the assessment made of individual qualities, investigated here by posing the question "How important is each of the following qualities for education of your children?" The response frequencies are reported in Table 5.

Table 5. Preferred Qualities for Children's Education.

How Important is Each of the Following Qualities for Education of Your Children?	Cadets (%)	Students (%)
Discipline		
1 – very important	41.4	41.7
2 – rather important	52.0	49.6
Responsibility		
1 – very important	82.9	82.2
2 – rather important	16.5	17.6
Tolerance		
1 – very important	47.5	61.4
2 – rather important	46.8	33.4
Patriotism		
1 – very important	24.6	18.2
2 – rather important	39.6	29.8
Comradeship		
1 – very important	61.9	36.8
2 – rather important	29.6	45.9
Orderliness		
1 – very important	29.9	27.3
2 – rather important	53.0	46.1
Traditionalism		
1 – very important	17.7	12.9
2 – rather important	37.2	30.4
Obedience		
1 – very important	25.8	26.8
2 – rather important	52.9	42.5
Creativity		
1 – very important	55.9	59.6
2 – rather important	36.2	32.0
Loyalty		
1 – very important	56.9	46.5
2 – rather important	37.9	39.1
Spirit of equality		
1 – very important	50.0	60.7
2 – rather important	38.6	29.9
Generosity		
1 – very important	34.8	42.7
2 – rather important	50.5	39.8

Table 5. (*Continued*)

How Important is Each of the Following Qualities for Education of Your Children?	Cadets (%)	Students (%)
Initiative		
1 – very important	61.2	61.3
2 – rather important	34.8	32.9
Self-control		
1 – very important	66.1	61.6
2 – rather important	30.4	33.0
Determination		
1 – very important	54.8	56.1
2 – rather important	39.2	36.3
Open-mindedness		
1 – very important	62.6	70.6
2 – rather important	33.3	24.8
Team spirit		
1 – very important	52.8	46.0
2 – rather important	42.5	45.1
Honesty		
1 – very important	85.1	76.9
2 – rather important	13.6	20.6
Honour		
1 – very important	63.8	48.5
2 – rather important	28.7	33.3

From the table we can see that for a fair-sized set of qualities the cadet's appreciation is in line with that of his university peers: these are discipline, responsibility, obedience, initiative, self-control and determination. Others seem to characterise him particularly, such as loyalty, comradeship, honesty, honour, patriotism, orderliness, traditionalism and team spirit, while a certain negative gap is revealed for what regards spirit of equality, open-mindedness, creativity, and tolerance.

It seems to me that a more precise picture of the qualities characteristic of military culture could hardly emerge. At the start of his professional training the cadet is already fully framed in that culture, a clearly significant result of his primary socialisation.

This appears to be further confirmed by the greater confidence the cadet has in the most important social institutions: church, the president, justice, parliament, the government, banks, companies, trade unions and, of course, the military and the police all inspire greater confidence in the cadet than among his university peers. The positions are reversed only for the media – where the traditional distrust of the military towards journalists is confirmed[3] – and universities and voluntary organisations, where we see not so much a lack of confidence by the cadet as much greater closeness on the part of the student to such institutions.

The young people's confidence in political parties appears to be generally low for both categories, with very little difference between them.

As mentioned above, the responses to this question confirm and supplement the more institutional attitude of the cadet than of the student (Table 6).

Like for his university peers, the cadet's affective attachment is chiefly directed toward his family, friends, homeland and profession (Table 7). Both surveyed groups show themselves to be rather localistic in their choices, and the great supranational aggregations – the world community, Europe – are not perceived as belonging to the affective sphere by most. As one might expect in view of the effects, already noted, of his anticipatory socialisation, the cadet displays greater attachment to his native land, but also to his profession, obviously the fruit of a precise choice already made, while the first-year university student generally still has a range of professional options ahead.

Table 6. Confidence in Institutions[a] (Mean Score).

	Cadets	Students
Church	4.9822	4.7096
President	6.0974	5.4912
Media	4.5519	5.0422
Justice	6.2175	5.9452
Parliament	5.5298	4.9870
Government	5.5970	5.3911
Banks	6.2206	5.7300
Companies	5.8175	5.2908
Trade unions	5.2807	5.0765
Universities	6.7789	7.0678
Political parties	4.6863	4.5336
The military	7.9289	5.9448
The police	6.7585	5.4890
Voluntary organisations	5.8956	6.3202

[a]The higher the score, the greater the confidence.

Table 7. Affective Attachments[a] (Mean Score).

	Cadets	Students
World community	4.9583	4.9525
Europe	5.8294	5.6412
My country	8.2341	7.3558
Natural environment	7.0000	6.8864
My profession	8.0341	7.4816
My friends	8.6815	8.4349
My family	9.1728	8.8789
My religious community	4.0311	4.3116
My native city	5.9224	6.1502
Myself	8.4122	8.4571

[a]The higher the score, the greater the confidence.

2.2. Attitudes Toward the Military

Generally speaking the evident primary socialisation toward a military-compatible culture encountered in the cadet leads us to expect a different attitude toward national security and military defence issues from that of his student peers. However, a detailed investigation on some items presents elements of interest and is worthy of further study.

The majority of the youths in the indicated sample concur in believing that the phenomenon of war is not destined to disappear from the panorama of international relations, at least in the medium term, just as a smaller majority feel that the protection of national interests sometimes makes resorting to war necessary.

From his first year of study the young cadet looks to be decidedly more "militaristic" than the average for his peers, however, as can easily be seen in Table 8. In particular, the percentage gap between those who agree strongly appears to be sizeable: nearly 9 percentage points for the first item, almost 18 for the second.

The opinions on the existence of the military are consequential: a strong majority of interviewees feel that the military should exist and that, even though it may be an evil for some, it is a necessary one. Here, too, one must note (see Table 9) that the cadet's attitude is quite different from that of his average peer attending university.

The public image of the military perceived by the sample (graphed in Fig. 1) does not appear to be very differentiated between cadets and students, but is obviously higher in the opinions expressed by the cadets.

Table 8. Opinions on War.

Agreement	Cadets (%)	Students (%)
Human nature being what it is, there will always be war		
1. I agree strongly	38.6	31.0
2. I agree somewhat	40.9	37.1
3. I disagree somewhat	15.1	17.6
4. I disagree strongly	3.7	10.3
5. No opinion	1.6	4.0
Sometimes war is necessary to protect national interests		
1. I agree strongly	35.3	17.6
2. I agree somewhat	40.0	35.4
3. I disagree somewhat	15.5	27.3
4. I disagree strongly	7.2	14.7
5. No opinion	2.0	5.0

Table 9. Opinion on the Military.

Agreement	Cadets (%)	Students (%)
The military should be abolished		
1. I agree strongly	0.7	5.9
2. I agree somewhat	4.0	10.8
3. I disagree somewhat	10.1	21.1
4. I disagree strongly	81.2	57.2
5. No opinion	4.0	5.0
The military is a necessary evil		
1. I agree strongly	9.6	11.4
2. I agree somewhat	14.4	21.7
3. I disagree somewhat	16.5	23.0
4. I disagree strongly	54.6	37.3
5. No opinion	4.9	6.6

The data of these few examples are repeated when one analyses the evaluation that the sample gives of officers' professional training (positive for 75% of the cadets versus 47% of the students), interest in national defence issues (high for 60% of the cadets versus 28% of the students) and the prestige rankings assigned to the various professions by these youths in their first year of higher education, tabulated in Table 10.

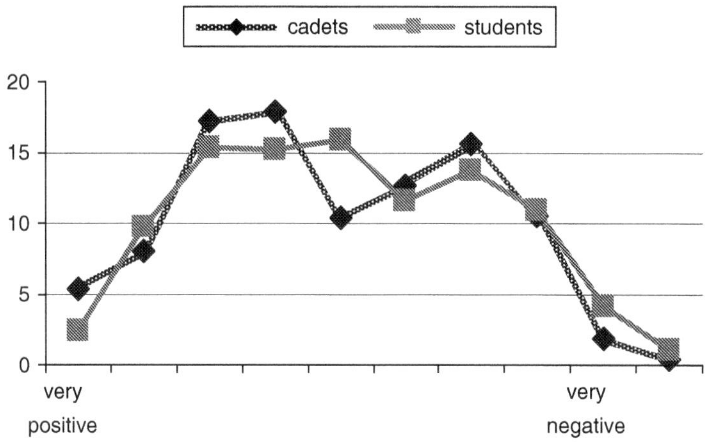

Fig. 1. The Public Image of the Armed Forces: Cadets and Students Compared.

Table 10. Ranking of Professions According to Prestige.

Profession	Cadets	Students
Medical doctor	1	1
Priest, clergyman	12	12
University professor	4	3
Lawyer	5	4
Diplomat	3	2
Military officer	2	8
Company manager	6	5
Civil airline pilot	7	9
Pharmacist	11	11
Entrepreneur	10	7
Journalist	14	10
Artist	15	15
Secondary school teacher	13	14
Civil servant	16	16
Police inspector	9	13
Engineer	8	6

2.3. Some Conclusions on the Primary Socialisation of Cadets

The comparison between first-year cadets and first-year university students shows a series of differences both in values and attitudes that can only be attributed to each group's primary socialisation.

The ideal-type of cadet that emerges is characterised by an accentuated adherence to the national institutions in their various aspects that is not found in his average student peer. He ascribes greater importance to democratic principles of an institutional or nationalistic type, such as respect for the national basic law and defence of the national societal system and his country's way of life, and accords greater confidence to the country's main social institutions.

This "institutionalism" is undoubtedly the outcome of a primary education that is likely inculcated within the family in good part due to the prevalent social origins of cadets, for whom the phenomenon of endorecruitment is significant in all the examined countries.

An institutionalism that goes hand in hand with a political conservatism demonstrated by the interviewees' declared political leanings.

What may surprise, however, because it departs from this picture a little, is the cadet's lower participation in the life of a founding institution of his country's culture, the national church, manifested in less frequent church attendance than his interviewed peers and in the modest ranking (in common, however, with the students) given to the clergy as a profession.

From a more strictly military standpoint the choice that the cadet makes of the most important personal qualities results in a set that is perfectly integrable in military culture, and this, too, differentiates him from the choices of his university peers.

The attitudes toward national defence and the armed forces are entirely consequential for the cadet: he has a greater interest in these issues, is more favourable to recourse to war to protect the national interests (when necessary), has a very positive image of the training received in the officer's profession (to which he assigns a considerably higher prestige ranking than his peers), feels the armed forces are absolutely essential to his country, and so on. One could go on at length listing the numerous more positive attitudes than the sample average toward the various aspects of the activities connected with military security.

3. PROFESSIONAL SOCIALISATION

In view of the strong impact – perhaps stronger than anticipated – that primary socialisation seems to have in shaping the military mindset, it seems meaningful to look at how professional socialisation acts on the cultural attitudes both of cadets and their peers studying at civilian universities.

As already stated, the analysis is made by comparing, for the two groups, the opinions and attitudes of youths in their first two years of higher education with those of young people further along in their studies. This section, too, will be subdivided into analysis of change in basic values and of attitudes toward the military.

3.1. Attitudes Toward Basic Values

Following the same order that we used to look at primary socialisation, we see first of all that the older students, in both the military academies and the universities, display greater religiosity than the younger ones (see Table 11). This phenomenon is more accentuated among the cadets, who move to percentage positions that are close to those of their university peers as they progress in their studies. The percentage of "no answers" also declines, probably the result of greater maturity and awareness.

The nearly unanimous adherence to democratic principles developed during primary socialisation, recorded at the outset of the training process, is confirmed over time both for the cadets and the students, with such low variance indices that it is not worth reporting the data here in detail.

More significant changes are seen in the perception of the extent to which the fundamental principles of democratic coexistence have been realised in

Table 11. Religiosity: Trend During Studies.

	Cadets (%)		Students (%)	
	First and second year	Third and beyond	First and second year	Third and beyond
Religious and attend religious services regularly (every week)	9.2	12.4	11.0	12.7
Religious and attend religious services once a month	9.0	10.1	10.6	12.7
Religious but attend religious services only for the most important holidays	28.1	38.3	28.0	32.9
Can't say whether religious or not	15.0	9.0	14.2	11.9
Not religious	33.9	26.3	31.8	27.0
No answer	4.8	3.9	4.3	2.9

the social context to which the respondents belong. Here the variations appear sizeable – more for the cadets than the students – and go in the direction of lower confidence in the real application of such principles. Life experience seems to have its weight here and some youthful illusions appear to get shed along the way. More than to a professional socialisation process, part of this trend is likely due to what we might call "life socialisation". For the cadets one must also hypothesise some influence of their specific professional socialisation, however, as the variations are larger for them than for their university peers (see Table 12).

Political leanings change for the cadets as the years of training pass: although conservative positions remain prevalent, there is a rebalancing of the various positions, with some increase on the left and a slight decrease on the right. There is almost no variation among the students during their years of study (see Table 13)

The preferences of the future elites for individual personal qualities do not display substantial variations during the professional socialisation: changes are noted only on some of them, indicated in Table 14. In particular, during

Table 12. How Realised are the Following Principles: Trend During Studies.

	Cadets %			Students %		
	First and second year	Third and beyond	Variance	First and second year	Third and beyond	Variance
Equality of people	71.3	69.8	−1.5	54.0	53.8	−0.2
Respect for individuals	66.0	58.4	−7.6	52.5	53.7	+1.2
Basic freedom	80.5	74.6	−5.9	69.4	67.9	−1.5
Respect constitution	68.6	63.0	−4.4	62.9	62.2	−0.7
Safeguarding individual opportunities	65.8	59.2	−6.6	56.2	46.7	−9.5
Defence of my country's way of life	67.4	63.5	−3.9	60.2	58.0	−2.2
Peaceful relationship with nations	84.4	82.3	−2.1	78.2	77.5	−0.7
Subordination of military to political leadership	78.8	79.0	+0.2	65.0	68.7	+3.7
Integration military in parent society	49.2	49.0	−0.2	39.3	40.1	+0.8

Table 13. Political Position: Trend During Studies.

Political Position	Cadets (%)		Students (%)	
	First and second year	Third and beyond	First and second year	Third and beyond
Left	16.7	21.3	35.8	36.1
Centre	36.4	37.4	37.2	37.2
Right	46.9	41.3	26.9	26.7

Table 14. Preferred Qualities: Variations During Studies.

How Important is Each of the Following Qualities for Education of Your Children?	Cadets (%)		Students (%)	
	First and second year	Third and beyond	First and second year	Third and beyond
Patriotism				
1 – very important	25.6	34.5	17.0	15.1
2 – rather important	39.2	37.8	27.5	32.6
Traditionalism				
1 – very important	18.0	22.5	11.8	11.6
2 – rather important	32.8	36.3	30.8	33.3
Spirit of equality				
1 – very important	49.3	39.7	60.9	53.6
2 – rather important	38.5	42.2	29.8	34.8
Determination				
1 – very important	54.4	60.6	52.8	49.9
2 – rather important	39.0	33.4	39.3	41.6
Team spirit				
1 – very important	51.5	54.3	44.4	46.1
2 – rather important	43.6	39.7	46.0	43.7
Honesty				
1 – very important	84.9	75.9	77.7	79.9
2 – rather important	13.9	22.5	19.6	19.0

this socialisation phase the cadet acquires greater awareness of qualities like patriotism, respect for tradition, determination and team spirit. These first two qualities are connected to the values, and certainly to the ethics, of the specific profession, while the remaining two are operational as they are more linked to the exercise of the profession itself. Honesty and the spirit of equality, although remaining important, lose a little of their prominence.

For what regards the university students, the range of the changes is more modest: in the same direction as the cadets for patriotism and traditionalism, in the opposite direction for honesty.

One of the connotations of the ideal-type of cadet evidenced by the investigation of primary socialisation was its "institutionalism", that is, confidence in and attachment to the main social institutions. The socialisation process during the studies has divergent effects on this attitude: as shown graphically in Table 15, confidence grows in the cadet for the national church and the media, which was rather low, and in the head of state. For all the other institutions we see a falloff in confidence except for two cases where it stays the same. This negative trend is common to the whole future elite, however, since it is repeated, without even the exceptions of the national church and the media, for the university students as well.

The same phenomenon of decline occurs for affective attachments, toward groups, people and entities, here too with the partial exception of one's religious community; in addition, we see a growth of localism among the interviewees as professional socialisation progresses. Once again the change is common to all the examined young people, independently of the chosen professional sector, whether military or not.

There thus seems to occur, for all the youths of the sample, a loss of trust, confidence and attachment to those ideal aggregates that had appeared to

Table 15. Confidence in Institutions: Trend During Studies.

	Cadets	Students
Church	↗	↙
President	↗	↗
Media	↗	↙
Justice	↙	↙
Parliament	↙	↙
Government	↙	↙
Banks	=	↙
Companies	↙	=
Trade unions	↙	↙
Universities	=	↙
Political parties	↙	↙
The military	↙	↙
The police	↙	↙
Voluntary organisations	↙	↙

be so important at the end of their primary socialisation. Is it professional socialisation and, perhaps, life socialisation that have acted in this direction?

3.2. Attitudes Toward the Military

The trend of the opinions of the two groups regarding the persistence of war diverges sharply. While the number of cadets who strongly believe there will always be war grows significantly, this number falls among the students (see Table 16). The percentage of those who condone war to protect national interests appears to decline in both groups.

The abolition of the armed forces (see Table 17) is opposed most strongly by cadets beyond their second year of study (82% vs. 81%), while among the students there is only a very slight variation in those who support this position (overall they pass from 17.5% to 17.0%). The affirmation that the military is a necessary evil does not see significant differences in agreement according to class year, but only a very slight percentage drop for the whole sample as professional socialisation progresses.

What emerges from these changes in the attitudes of the young people in the sample?

Aside from an expected confirmation of the "militariness" of the cadets compared to their peers, it is interesting to note that they, too, begin to look with less favour on war as a tool for resolving international disputes. This

Table 16. Opinions on War: Trends During Studies.

Agreement	Cadets (%)		Students (%)	
	First and second year	Third and beyond	First and second year	Third and beyond
Human nature being what it is, there will always be war				
1. I agree strongly	39.8	47.9	29.6	24.7
2. I agree somewhat	40.5	32.0	36.6	38.0
Sometimes war is necessary to protect national interests				
1. I agree strongly	35.9	34.8	18.2	15.8
2. I agree somewhat	39.3	36.5	33.2	33.9

Table 17. Opinion on the Military: Trends During Studies.

Agreement	Cadets (%)		Students (%)	
	First and second year	Third and beyond	First and second year	Third and beyond
The military should be abolished				
6. I agree strongly	0.9	2.1	6.2	5.8
7. I agree somewhat	4.1	4.2	11.3	11.2
8. I disagree somewhat	10.0	8.0	23.1	26.3
9. I disagree strongly	81.1	82.1	54.5	52.2
10. No opinion	3.9	3.6	4.9	4.6
The military is a necessary evil				
6. I agree strongly	9.6	6.5	12.3	11.6
7. I agree somewhat	15.0	14.0	23.6	23.1
8. I disagree somewhat	16.3	17.4	21.8	26.4
9. I disagree strongly	54.5	57.9	35.7	34.0
10. No opinion	4.6	4.2	6.6	4.9

Table 18. Interest in Security Issues.

How Interested are you in Defence-related Security Issues?	Cadets %		Students %	
	First and second year	Third and beyond	First and second year	Third and beyond
Very much	58.9	65.6	27.1	26.0
Somewhat	34.8	29.9	43.1	43.5
A little	6.1	3.5	24.4	25.2
Not at all	0.3	1.0	5.4	5.3

does not weaken their belief in the necessity of the existence of the military, however: on the contrary.

For the students the variations are less significant, although they appear to go, moderately, in the direction of greater pacifism.

Interest in military security issues (see Table 18) increases for the cadets as their professional socialisation progresses, while it does not present appreciable variations for their university peers. This datum might be a foreseeable one but it bears pointing out that it leads to a consolidation of the cultural gap between the two groups of future leaders.

This despite the fact that, all things considered, there is a parallel improvement over time in the public image of the armed forces, both in the perception that the cadets have of it and among their university peers, as shown graphically in Fig. 2.

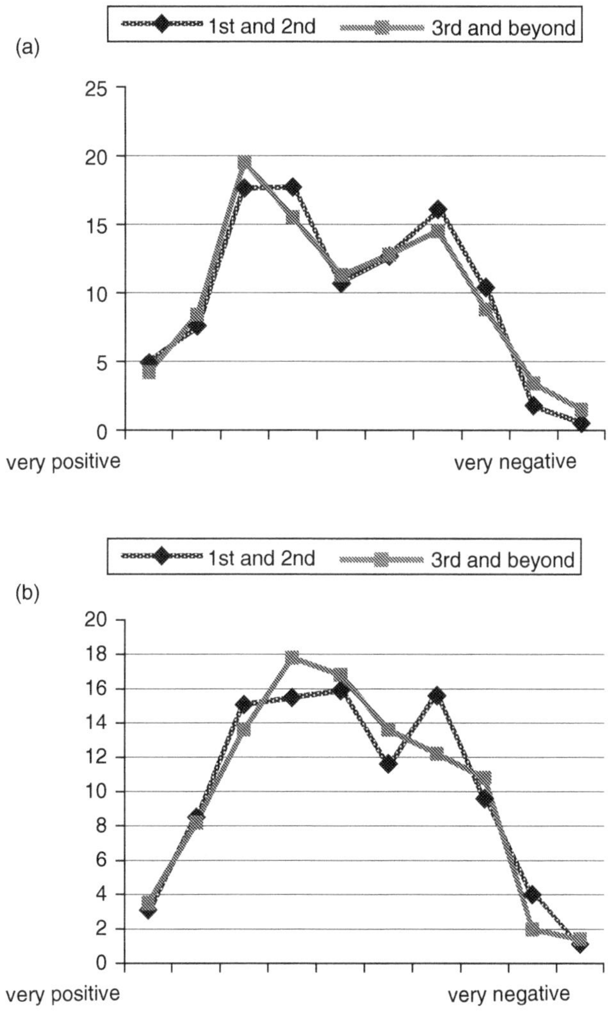

Fig. 2. Public Image of the Armed Forces: Trends During Studies. (a) According to Cadets. (b) According to Students.

The prestige of the military profession, seen also in relation to other professions, does not display any particular variations during the years of study if not that of a rapprochement between the two groups: for cadets in their third year or later it declines slightly with respect to the initial expectations, for their university peers it increases slightly. The substantial difference remains between the perception of the military officer as a profession like any other for the students and the uniqueness and peculiarity attributed to officership by the cadets.

4. SOME CONCLUSIONS

As already mentioned earlier (see Section 2.3), primary (or anticipatory) socialisation plays a very important role for cadets, more important than appears to be the case for the future civilian elites who attend universities. For the future military elites, the professional socialisation that takes place during their years at the academy works in two opposing and contradictory directions.

On the one hand, it increases the particularity and peculiarity of the profession. This occurs for aspects and themes that we can consider characteristic of militariness, such as a stronger belief in the persistence of war, an even stronger belief in the necessity of a national military, increased consideration of the armed forces as a good and a national value and greater interest and involvement in national security issues.

In parallel, the professional socialisation seems to generate in the cadet a greater appreciation for values like patriotism and national tradition, especially military and also of some "operational" qualities for the military officer like determination and team spirit.

On the other hand, the socialisation produced by the training courses tends to attenuate some attitudes of the cadets, bringing them closer to those of their university peers. We thus see some muting of politically conservative positions, a reduction in what I have called here cadets' "institutionalism", and a certain increase both in religiosity and in attachment to one's religious community. In parallel, however, one also notes a decline in confidence in effective democratic governance in one's country: the realisation of fundamental democratic principles, for which there is near-unanimous agreement among the future elites examined here, is seen as the years pass – and perhaps with the accumulation of life experiences – as a task that is still partly to be accomplished. It should be pointed out that this "disillusionment" is more marked for the cadets than for their university peers.

For the university students the trend is less clear-cut, partly due to the greater heterogeneity of the sample, which takes in students belonging to various university faculties. They substantially share with the cadets an increase in religiosity as their studies progress, as well as disenchantment regarding the actual implementation of the fundamental principles of democracy in their country. Although their political leanings stay the same, with the increase in socialisation we see a moderate increase in pacifist tendencies, expressed here in less acceptance for the propositions that war will always exist and that resorting to war is sometimes necessary to protect national interests. Interest – and disinterest – in national security issues remains stable, while the public image of the national armed forces improves slightly.

The cultural differences between the two groups, military elites and civilian elites, can be defined very briefly with a series of "isms" that seem to characterise the future military elites of the examined countries: greater *legalism, nationalism, conservatism, institutionalism* and a more accentuated *militariness* with respect to the average for their university peers.

These differences, which undoubtedly exist and are significant, as seen in the course of this chapter, seem to be prevalently due to the primary socialisation of the two groups. Professional socialisation affects them marginally – and at times in a contradictory fashion. For some values and attitudes the differences attenuate as the training courses progress, for others they increase, but the positions are already substantially determined by the primary socialisation received.

NOTES

1. The original source: Ervin Goffman: The Characteristics of Total Institutions: The Intimate World. In: Donald R. Cressey (ed.): *The Prison, Studies in Institutional Organization and Change*. New York: Holt, Rinehart and Winston, 1961.
2. See, for example, Caforio (1994, 2006) and Janowitz and Wesbrook (1983).
3. See, for example, Caforio (1999) and Dandeker (2000).

REFERENCES

Bachman, J. G., Sigelman, L., & Diamond, G. (1987). Self-selection, socialization, and distinctive military values: Attitudes of high school seniors. *Armed Forces and Society*, *13*(2), 169–187.

Caforio, G. (Ed.) (1994). The military profession in Europe. *Current Sociology*, *42*(3).

Caforio, G. (1999). The italian press and defense problems: An in-depth analysis of a short period. In: Hans Seidel Foundation (Ed.), *The armed forces in a democratic society* (pp. 147–166). Sofia: Hans Seidel Foundation.
Caforio, G. (2006). Trends and evolution in the military profession. In: G. Caforio (Ed.), *Social sciences and the military: An interdisciplinary overview*. London and New York: Routledge.
Caforio, G., & Nuciari, M. (1998). Introduction. In: G. Caforio (Ed.), *The European cadet: Professional socialisation in military academies* (pp. 7–16). Baden Baden: Nomos.
Dandeker, C. (2000). The military in democratic societies. In: J. Kühlmann & J. Callaghan (Eds), *Military and society in 21st Century Europe*. London: Transaction Publisher.
De Fleur, L. B., & Warner, R. L. (1987). Air force academy graduates and nongraduates: Attitudes and self-concepts. *Armed Forces and Society*, *13*(4), 517–533.
Etzioni, A. (Ed.) (1964). *Complex organizations – a sociological reader*. New York: Holt-Rinehart and Winston.
Franke, V. C. (2001). Generation X and the military: A comparison of attitudes and values between west point cadets and college students. *Journal of Political and Military Sociology*, *29*(Summer), 92–119.
Janowitz, M., & Wesbrook, S. D. (Eds). (1983). *The political education of soldiers*. Beverly Hills: Sage.
Jelušič, L. (1997). *Legitimnost sodobnega vojaštva*. Ljubljana: Fakulteta za družbene vede.
McAllister, I. (1995). Schools, enlistment, and military values: The Australian services cadet scheme. *Armed Forces and Society*, *22*(1), 83–102.
McAllister, I., & Smith, H. (1989). Selecting the guardians: Recruitment and military values in the Australian officer corps. *Journal of Political and Military Sociology*, *17*(Spring), 27–42.
Merton, R. K., Reader, G. G., & Kendall, P. L. (Eds). (1957). *The student-physician*. Cambridge: Harvard University Press.
Priest, R., Fullerton, T., & Bridges, C. (1982). Personality and value changes in west point cadets. *Armed Forces and Society*, *8*(4), 629–642.
Priest, R. F., & Beach, R. (1998). Value changes in four cohorts at the U.S. military academy. *Armed Forces and Society*, *25*(1), 125–144.
Ricks, T. E. (1997). The widening gap between the military and society. *The Atlantic Monthly*, *280*, 66–78.

MEDIA AND PUBLIC OPINION

Giuseppe Caforio

ABSTRACT

Data analysis reveals that the sources of information on military security issues that the young elites mainly rely on are first and foremost television news programmes, followed very closely by newspapers and in third place, but lagging considerably behind, is the Internet. So far the information sources appear to be the same ones and to be equally important for the two groups studied, university students and cadets.

However, sizeable gaps have to be registered in the opinions of respondents on the media in general, as, for instance, the assessment of the attitude displayed by the media toward the military, or their interest in defence-related issues, the judgment of the level of information on military issues.

Other cultural differences arise dealing with the public opinion theme, as far as the armed forces' public image is concerned, or on the evaluation of the officers' professional training.

After presenting main data on the theme, this chapter tries to discuss them and to reach some general conclusion.

Cultural Differences between the Military and Parent Society in Democratic Countries
Contributions to Conflict Management, Peace Economics and Development, Volume 4, 107–127

ISSN: 1572-8323/doi:10.1016/S1572-8323(07)04005-2

INTRODUCTION

The issue of public information on military security is a particularly delicate one because it is subject to conflicting pressures and demands.

On the one hand, the general rule of freedom, or rather, the necessity of unfettered information characteristic of advanced democracies, applies here: it is a necessity functional to the very purposes of the military, since in a democratic country every political choice, and therefore also those of military interest, is anchored to the judgement of the "demos" (Dahl, 1989, p. 339), which judges on the basis of what it knows and what is communicated to it. In fact, as Holmes and McConville (2003, p. XI) write:

> ... being a public service, defence and its management is always open to scrutiny from government, international bodies such as United Nations, and from wider population via the mass media. Hence, defence management is carried out under the gaze of the population who can be swift to criticise, even when they do not fully understand what is expected of defence services.

On the other hand, in the area of military affairs, reserve, when not outright secrecy, is often necessary in order to preserve one of the typical parameters of military strategy, surprise. Hence, the familiar and frequent complaints by journalists about "black holes" in the information supplied by military authorities, which according to some[1] threaten the very existence of McLuhan's "global village".

But there is more. Military issues are often alien to the world of knowledge of the average citizen (and at times, even of the average journalist!), so that, here more than elsewhere, information as communication is always an interpretive act as well. What the media find themselves communicating on defence-related issues is often something complex, complicated, comprehensible in different ways and on several levels. And this interpretive necessity has another well-known delicate aspect, namely the possibility that, in some cases, the information/interpretation could become manipulation, an instrument of social control.

It thus seems clear that it is important to understand what the sources of information on military issues are for the young people who are getting ready to become the elites of the examined countries, how they judge these sources and, correlatively, what opinion and appreciation they have formed of the military and of those who are part of it.

These questions are fundamental issues and aspects of analysis of the cultural gap between civil society and the armed forces in the countries examined here.

DATA ANALYSIS

The sources of information on military security issues that the young elites surveyed in our research mainly rely on are first and foremost television news programmes (82.9%), followed very closely by newspapers (79.5%); in third place, but lagging considerably behind, is the Internet (63.9%). So far the information sources appear to be the same ones and to be equally important for the various groups studied, university students and cadets at military academies.

Still on a general level, other sources of information, like radio, weekly and monthly magazines, and political and military newspapers, seem to have less importance. On these, shall we say, minor sources the different surveyed groups begin to differentiate themselves, however. The cadets, obviously, give more importance than their civilian peers to military publications and less to political newspapers, which instead constitute a significant source of information on military issues for political science students (62.5% versus a general mean of 44.1%). This is the first indicator of greater politicisation among the students of this faculty, which would be confirmed by other indicators in the course of the survey.

Again, in a general comparison between military students and university students regarding their reliance on more general information sources common to both groups (television news, newspapers, radio news), for the cadets we see 3 or 4 percentage points less on average than for the university students. The cadets apparently seek information on military problems chiefly from specialised publications in the sector; the percentage gap between the cadets and their university peers is – as expected – considerable here (39 percentage points for special military newspapers and 34 percentage points for professional military publications).

The female component of the surveyed sample follows the average trends of the sample as a whole, with a stronger reliance than the males on television news, and also on radio news. The lower frequency with which military newspapers and professional military journals were read by women was unsurprising.

In any event, considering the percentage overlaps, the sources of information on military security on which young people rely appear to be quite wide-ranging and diverse in the examined countries.

Individual national situations diverge from this general panorama. The print media seem to have less importance in some eastern European countries (Bulgaria and Poland especially) where, besides television news, there seems to be greater reliance on radio news broadcasts and Internet searches.

The future elites of France, Germany and South Africa, and also Poland, give greater than average importance to general news magazines as sources of military information. One can hypothesise that the periodicals of these countries provide quite ample information on the subject; this hypothesis seems to be particularly valid for French youth, who rely much less than the others on television news to bring themselves up to date in this area. This seems to be consistent with the general attitude of the country, where, as last Eurobarometer shows, there is a high trust in the press (see Fig. 1) and a low trust in television news.

It was sought to determine whether a higher distribution of news dailies in the individual country corresponds to greater reliance on them as a source of information on defence issues, but comparison with the UNESCO distribution data (graphed in Fig. 2) belies this hypothesis, which seems to be confirmed only for a few countries, such as Switzerland.

The extensive and differentiated reliance by the young people of our sample on the possible news sources does not mean they find the level of the information contained in them to be satisfactory, however. The general datum shows a prevalence of those who judge the level of information on military issues in their country's media negatively: 48.3%, against the 45.7% who deem the coverage good.[2] Looking at individual groups, it is the political science students who are least satisfied with the level of information (52.4%, 4 percentage points above the average). The cadets, too, show a slightly higher gradient of dissatisfaction compared to the civilian sample as a whole (1.7%).

No substantial differences are recorded in the evaluation according to gender, but there does appear to be strong differentiation here from country to country. As can be seen in Table 1, satisfaction with the level of information is particularly low for a group of countries made up of Turkey, France, Spain and Bulgaria, while it is reasonably close to or above the general mean for all the remaining ones, with high levels for the Netherlands and Switzerland. What appears curious, and definitely deserving of further investigation, is the fact that the four countries with a low level of satisfaction do not seem, at least at first glance, to display common socio-cultural characteristics.

But what is the media's general attitude towards the armed forces? The sample is divided on this point into three equivalent opinion groups: a third of the young interviewees feel that the media's attitude is generally one of support, a third say it is neutral, and a third describes it as hostile.

The least satisfied regarding this attitude are the cadets, while, at the opposite end, a near majority of political science students (44.1%) consider

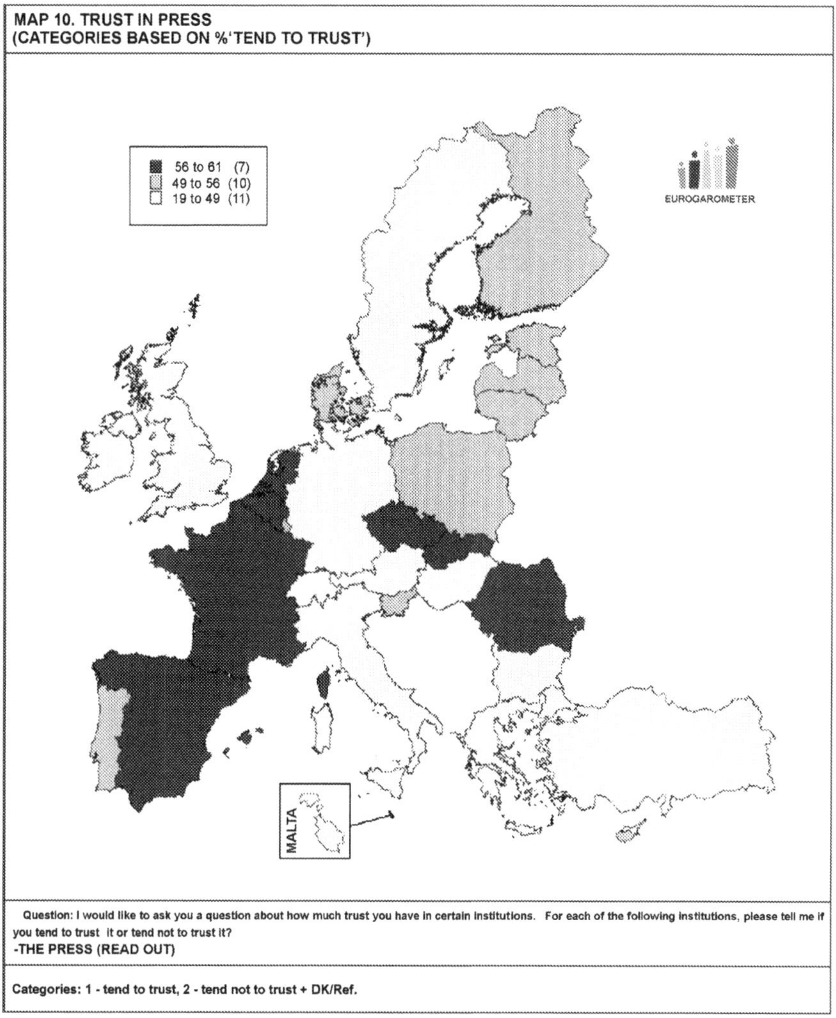

Fig. 1. Trust in the Press of European countries.

the media's attitude to be supportive. Globally comparing the two surveyed groups, civilian and military, 15% more of the cadets judge the media's attitude as hostile than do the civilian students (37% versus 22%).

The assessment of the media's attitude appears to be significantly influenced here by the respondents' declared political positions. As shown in Table 2,

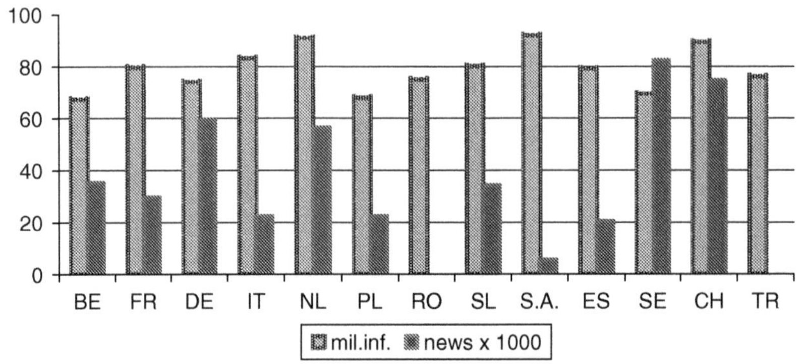

Fig. 2. Newspapers as Source of Military Information by their Distribution. *Source:* Newspaper Distribution × 1000 Inhabitants/5: UNESCO 2000. Data from Romania and Turkey are not Available.

Table 1. Positive Judgement of the Level of Information on Defence Issues by Media.

	Bulgaria	France	Germany	Italy	Nether-lands	Poland	Romania	Slovenia	S. Africa	Spain	Sweden	Switzer-land	Turkey
Very good + somewhat good	**37.2**	**30.1**	47.3	44.1	67.9	48.0	49.4	50.9	45.4	**30.2**	44.4	58.3	**27.1**

Table 2. Media Depiction of the Military by Political Position %.

	Left	Centre	Right
Very supportive + somewhat supportive	42.0	31.6	27.8
Neutral	33.8	35.8	30.0
Somewhat hostile + very hostile	18.1	27.4	38.6
No opinion	6.0	5.1	3.7

those who describe themselves as being on the right appear to be especially critical of the attitude of their country's media towards the military.

Turning to an analysis of the various national situations here as well, we find a group of three countries where a majority of the future elites feel that the mass media give a positive, supportive picture of their armed forces: these are Turkey (59.0%), Romania (55.0%) and Italy (53.6%). Conversely, the young people of another group of five countries give a sharply opposing assessment: Sweden (7.2%), Germany (20.1%), Switzerland (22.6%), Slovenia (25.6%) and the Netherlands (26.5%).

But just how interested are the young people of our sample in defence-related issues? Interest is generally high, 81% for the entire sample, but significantly differentiated according to gender: among the men, 89.3% of the respondents say they are very or somewhat interested, a percentage that falls to 63.4% for the women. An equally marked – and expected – difference is found between cadets and civilian students (94.4% versus 70.1%); among the latter, those who show the most interest in defence-related issues are the political science students (75.3%, a value 5 points above the average for the civilian students as a whole). Interest does not vary significantly with class year[3] in the sample average; it seems to increase slightly during their studies for those who already showed high interest (cadets and political science students), and decrease for those who showed low interest.

Interest also appears to be influenced by political position, proving more widespread among respondents on the political right, and sensitive to position in the Inglehart (1977) index (Table 3)

Breakdown of the data by country does not reveal deep national variations, with the exception of the respondents from Slovenia and Spain, where the percentage of young people interested in defence-related issues is markedly lower than the sample average (respectively 65.2% and 65.8%).

So far we have looked at the sources of information and their attitudes as perceived by the young people of the sample. Having seen the opinion-makers, it is now time to examine the opinions prevalent among the future elites, that is, to investigate the opinions and attitudes these young people have towards national security issues and their own armed forces. For the first aspect the reader is referred to Chapter 4 on Threat Perception in this book; here we shall treat the relationship that the future elites have with the armed forces and the military profession.

It appears central to evaluate first of all what, according to the interviewees, the image of the country's armed forces is in public opinion.

In general, half of the sample feels that this image is not positive, while only 47% consider it good (very good + somewhat good): but this is a

Table 3. Interest in Defence-Related Issues According to Position in the Inglehart Index.

Interested in Defence-Related Issues	Materialistic	Post-Materialistic	Mixed
Very much + somewhat	85.1	72.8	81.0

general datum that needs to be broken down further in order to be meaningful. For the cadets, 51% consider this image to be positive, compared to 44% of the university students as a whole: this sizeable percentage difference could be interpreted as wishful thinking among the cadets. Among the civilian students, those in law and political science give the least positive assessments.

Among the interviewed women, positive judgements on the image of the national armed forces fall three percentage points lower than among the men: 45.1 versus 48.1.

Here, too, the respondents' political positions seem to have some weight. As Table 4 shows, it is again the respondents on the right who are more likely to feel that public opinion in their country has a negative view of the armed forces.

But the most significant and important breakdown is undoubtedly the one by country: more than any general factor, it is local historical and cultural reasons that influence the military's social prestige and public image.

According to this breakdown (Table 5), only five countries show a majority (highlighted in boldface) of respondents who judge the social acceptance and prestige of the armed forces in their countries to be positive. Conversely, the countries where this percentage is particularly low are Bulgaria, Spain, Slovenia, Switzerland and South Africa. A few elements of explanation will be given on some local situations in the part of this chapter devoted to discussing the data; for a more general look at national particularities, see the country papers in the third part of this volume.

Connected to the social prestige of the armed forces is the prestige of the military profession itself, an aspect that we have investigated in greater

Table 4. Perception of Armed Forces' Image by Political Position.

	Left	Centre	Right
Very good + rather good	46.2	48.3	47
Not very good + not good at all	48.6	47.4	52.1
No opinion	5.2	4.3	0.9

Table 5. Positive Image of Armed Forces by Country.

	Bulgaria	France	Germany	Italy	Netherlands	Poland	Romania	Slovenia	S. Africa	Spain	Sweden	Switzerland	Turkey
Very good + rather good	26.5	42.9	40.7	**62.3**	46.7	**50.7**	**64.5**	30.5	35.9	30.3	**62.3**	35.7	**86.1**

depth and the evaluation of which appears particularly interesting since the surveyed sample is made-up of future professionals, some of them future military professionals.

The interviewees' assessment of the military profession was investigated by means of three distinct questions, one more generically directed at evaluating the profession's social image in the country as seen by the respondents, a second aimed at learning the opinion that the interviewees themselves have of officers' professional training, and a third on how they rank the officer's profession as compared to the other, civilian professions. The three questions are strongly correlated with each other in the responses, however, as clearly indicated by the application of Pearson's '*r*'.[4]

On the sample as a whole the public image of the military profession is perceived as prevalently good (44.6%), albeit with a considerable number of respondents who deem it poor (37.5%) and a sizeable share who feel it is considered a profession like any other (14.1%).

The difference in this perception between military students and civilian students does not seem very large: 46.8% of the cadets feel the public image of their future profession is good, compared to 42.9% of the civilian students; a further breakdown by faculty shows the law students to be less inclined than the average in percentage terms to agree with this positive assessment.

But where the difference becomes sizeable is between the male universe and the female universe: in this breakdown, whose results are represented graphically in Fig. 3, the curve that records the histograms relative to women has its frequency maximum in position 5 (intermediate, a profession like another) while the one relative to men reaches its apex between positions 3 and 4, that is, positive.

From the standpoint of political position, we see here, too, a less positive perception among those belonging to the right: only 39.9% judge the military profession's public image positively, compared to 43.7% of those oriented to the left politically and 49.6% of those who place themselves in centrist positions.

A breakdown by country, rendered graphically in Fig. 4, shows a group of four countries – South Africa, Bulgaria, Turkey and Romania – where the profession enjoys the perception of very high prestige among the future elites, while in all the others, with the negative exceptions of Spain and Germany, the percentage of young people who ascribe good social prestige to the military profession ranges between 30% and 40%.

For the sample in its entirety, the evaluation that the respondents give of the professional training provided to officers is more favourable. This is an

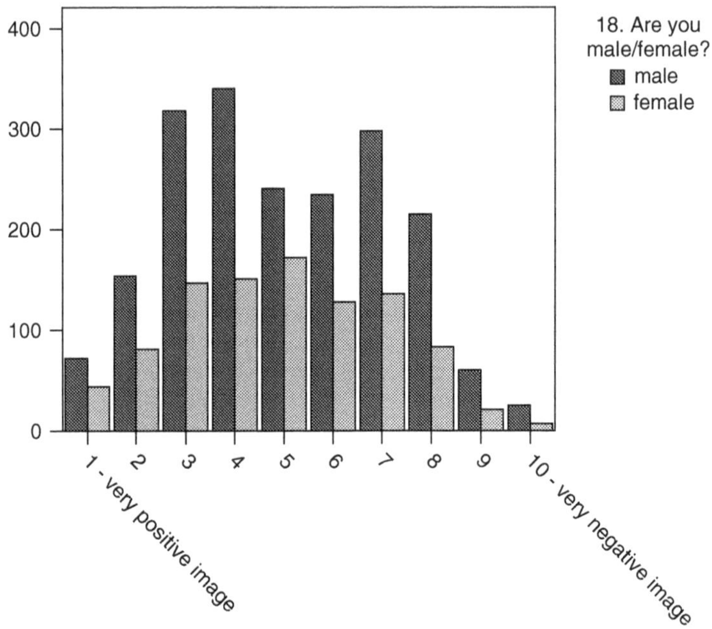

Fig. 3. Public Image of the Military Profession According to Gender.

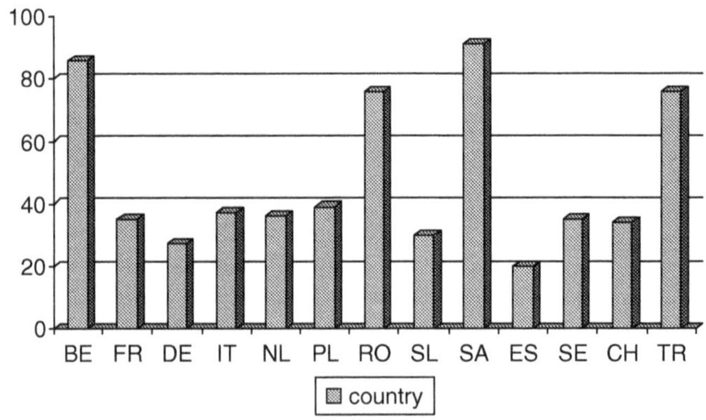

Fig. 4. Perception of the Public Image of the Military Profession by Country.

Table 6. Evaluation of Military Officer Education %.

Evaluation	Military Sample	Civilian Sample
Positive	70.2	44.7
Neutral	15.0	34.0
Negative	14.8	21.3

item of particular interest because the question is aimed at a direct assessment by the interviewee, that is, where the previous one asked interviewees what they thought the image of the officer's profession was among the public, here they are asked what they personally think of the training given to officers.

The difference between the military sample and the civilian one becomes truly marked here, as can be seen from Table 6, where the difference in positive assessments between the two samples reaches almost 26 percentage points, even if one can hypothesise that the high percentage of neutral evaluations of the civilian sample may hide a certain lack of knowledge of the real educational content of officers' professional preparation.

Turning the analysis towards the various faculties represented in the civilian students' sample, we see that it is mainly the political science and law students who display the lowest percentages of appreciation for military education.

Here, too, with the aid of another bar graph, we can see that the males' assessment of the officer's educational process is considerably more positive than that of females. In fact, the curve that records the histograms relative to women has its frequency maximum in position 5, while the one relative to men reaches its apex in position 3, that is, more positive (Fig. 5).

Subdividing according to political leanings, it is the conservative respondents who express the most positive assessments on officer education, with a steady decline as one moves first toward the centre and then toward the left.

The ever-significant breakdown by country presents more balanced data here, as can be seen in Table 7.

Here, too, with the exceptions of Spain and Slovenia, a positive assessment of military education is always given, in every country, by over 40% of the sample, and is very often the majority. It is also worthy of note that the highest percentage of those rating officer education negatively is found among the Slovenian respondents, no less than 37.1%.

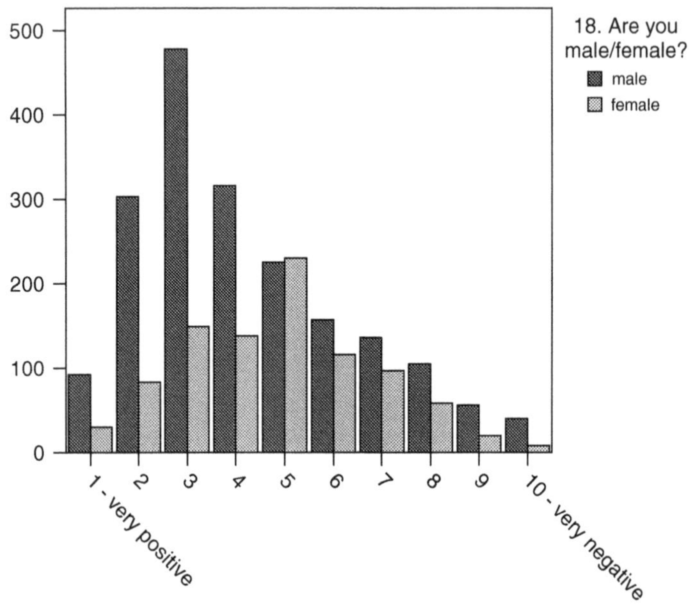

Fig. 5. Evaluation of Officer Professional Training According to Gender.

Table 7. How Do You Rate Military Officer Education?

Rating	Bulgaria	France	Germany	Italy	Netherlands	Poland	Romania	Slovenia	S. Africa	Spain	Sweden	Switzerland	Turkey
Positive	57.0	42.7	69.9	52.1	65.7	51.1	69.3	**31.4**	43.2	**36.4**	69.7	49.0	71.3
Neutral	24.0	38.2	17.1	29.7	18.4	30.5	18.4	**31.4**	27.9	**40.1**	21.5	27.3	18.2
Negative	19.0	19.1	13.0	18.3	15.9	18.4	12.3	**37.1**	29.0	**23.5**	9.0	23.8	10.5

However, when the sample as a whole is asked to rank the most common professions according to social prestige, the officer's profession seems to do quite well, as shown by the resulting scale:

Classification of professions according their to social prestige – sample average:

1. medical doctor
2. diplomat
3. university professor

4. lawyer
5. manager of a company
6. military officer
7. engineer
8. civilian pilot
9. entrepreneur
10. police inspector
11. pharmacist
12. journalist
13. clergyman
14. secondary school teacher
15. civil servant
16. artist

Applying the usual breakdowns, we see that women rank the officer's profession lower than men do, while, unsurprisingly, it is the cadets at the military academies who assign the highest prestige to their profession, and the political science students who rank it lowest (Table 8).

An analysis of change during the education process sees, in the sample average, a drop-off in the prestige of the military profession, falling from the first to fifth year of study.

According to stated political position, the profession's prestige increases gradually as we move from leftist positions to right-wing positions.

But the most significant breakdown is by country, reported in Table 9.

We see from these data how sizeable the national differences are: the ranking of the officer's profession ranges from a large group of countries where it is better than the sample average (seven countries) to others where

Table 8. Classification of the Officer's Profession According to Faculty.

Classification	Military Academy	Economics	Law	Political Science	Others
Military profession	4th	8th	9th	10th	8th

Table 9. Classification of the Officer's Profession by Country.

	Bulgaria	France	Germany	Italy	Nether-lands	Poland	Romania	Slovenia	S. Africa	**Spain**	Sweden	**Switzer-land**	Turkey
Officer	5th	3rd	8th	3rd	3rd	4th	2nd	8th	8th	12th	5th	13th	4th

Table 10. Quality of Recruitment by Country.

I Agree Strongly/Country	Cadets	University Students
Bulgaria	40.0	48.3
France	48.3	34.0
Germany	38.8	31.1
Italy	57.4	36.5
Netherlands	51.6	12.9
Poland	21.6	17.7
Romania	25.8	24.2
Slovenia	31.4	16.7
South Africa	55.8	42.5
Spain	53.8	11.2
Sweden	57.1	26.0
Switzerland	37.4	3.7
Turkey	48.9	25.3

it is considerably worse, particularly Switzerland and Spain. This interesting aspect will constitute a subject for discussion as well.

Examining for the sake of completeness two questions relating to the quality of recruitment of national armed forces, we find a generally positive opinion on this quality but with significant differences between civilian and military respondents, particularly as they break down by country. By way of example, the percentage of strongly positive responses to the statement "I am proud of women and men who serve in the military", shown in Table 10, is significant.

Here we arrive at the extreme case of Switzerland, where less than 4% of the university students interviewed feel they can subscribe to this statement.

DISCUSSION

A discussion on the data analysis just presented allows us to point out, and in some cases clarify, the most interesting aspects regarding the cultural gap between the future civilian and military elites as well as the national characteristics relative to the topic of this chapter, *Media and Public Opinion*.

For what regards the sources of information on defence-related issues for the two elites, the greater reliance of the military elite on their internal sources, clearly shown by the analysed data, was rather expected, even if the percentage gap is perhaps larger than what might have been anticipated. Less expected was that a specific sector of the university students, those enrolled in political science programmes, would express the most dissatisfaction regarding the level of information provided by the media on this subject. However, if we correlate this datum with the greater declared interest in military issues on the part of these students with respect to the other civilian students, we find an element of explanation for this dissatisfaction. Clearly, the political science student, often focused on analysing foreign policy, requires more information than others on the armed branch of this policy, the military one.

Which does not necessarily mean greater favour or propensity toward the military, quite the contrary: it is precisely the political science students who feel that the media's attitude toward the military is too supportive, and who evaluate the armed forces' public image, officers' professional training and the profession's social prestige less positively than the others.

But staying with a more general comparison between the civilian and military groups of students, a truly sizeable gap is seen in the assessment of the attitude displayed by the media toward the military: as shown by the reported data, this gap is 15 percentage points with regard to the assessment of hostility. Basically, the cadets perceive an attitude of marked hostility on the part of the national media, a perception not at all shared by a large majority of civilian students. The military group confirms here a datum frequently found in previous field surveys[5] on officers' mistrust regarding the information sector (and confirmed in the present elites experts survey; see the concluding chapter of this book).

Another expected result is the greater interest shown by the cadets in military security issues than their civilian peers, what may most interest the reader here is a quantification of this gap, which exceeds 24 percentage points. The interest in national defence issues thus seems, in the advanced democracies, to be delegated to a restricted and specialised *couche* of the national elite, the military professionals.

As for the attitude toward the armed forces and the military profession, here, too, we register a gap between the assessment of the armed forces' public image given by the cadets (7 percentage points higher) and the one given by their university peers: it is possible that, as mentioned earlier, wishful thinking is at work here on the part of the group of military students.

But where the disparity takes on the dimensions of a real cultural gap is the direct evaluation given by the respondents of officers' professional training: here the difference in positive assessments reaches 26 percentage points between the military group (70.2%) and the civilian group (44.7%). It is not easy to explain the size of this gap, which cannot depend only on overrating one's own programme of studies with respect to the others.

Examining the set of available data we find that this attitude of the university students is strongly correlated with gender, political position, ranking according to Inglehart's index, and declared interest in defence-related issues. Substantially, and for the civilian group as a whole, there seem to be two elements that impact this gap: gender, owing to the much more critical position of women students on officers' professional preparation (not matched in the positions of the female cadets), and a general cultural attitude that, for the university students, is more left-oriented politically (36% versus 18%), more on post-materialist positions (12% versus 5%), and, as stated earlier, much less interested in national defence issues. Moving to an analysis by country, we find that, although the average appreciation gap is always sizeable in every country (around 20 percentage points),[6] it is the judgements by the university students of a few countries that weigh particularly on the less positive assessment that the civilian group gives of the officers' professional preparation, especially in the case of Switzerland (gap between the two groups 51 percentage points).

This datum is somewhat in conflict with the rather good ranking that the sample as a whole gives to the military profession in the context of the other professions: a 6th place out of 16 that, even in a breakdown by university faculties, never falls below the 10th spot (for political science students). The gap here between the ranking given to the military profession by the military students and the one assigned by the civilian students was clearly expected and does not appear to be particularly significant. Probably what is at work here is an evaluation of de facto social conditions, less influenced by ideological positions and cultural diversities.

The national differences provide the second point of interest of this discussion.

Starting from the examination of the information sources that the young elites rely on for military security issues, an explanation must be found first of all for the low satisfaction that the Bulgarian, French, Spanish and Turkish samples display globally for these sources. The countries of this set are quite different from each other and the possible reasons that we found in the research data (where we found any) are episodic, single and differ from each other.

For Bulgaria and Spain we are assisted by the opinions expressed by current elites in semi-structured interviews, of which we will give an account in the conclusion of this book. Some Bulgarian interviewees assert that their media "mostly refer to scandals or focus on paid PR publications" rather than provide real information. For different reasons, the current Spanish elites also complain of a dearth of information on military issues, claiming that "There are no specialists in the mass media about militarism and defence. That's why they talk poorly about the military affairs and if something is told is just the fact."

For the future Turkish elites the reason seems almost the opposite, the media appear too supportive of the military to give sufficiently objective information to satisfy the university component of these elites in particular. And France? The future French leaders rely in much lower percentages than their European peers on the usual sources to get news and information on military issues: television news, radio news and political newspapers show the lowest frequency of use among the various countries of the sample for what regards these topics. Could there be a correlation between the marked dissatisfaction with the quality of defence-related information and this scarce attention for the traditional media? The question remains open as a study hypothesis.

Looking back through the preceding section I believe no one will have failed to notice that certain characteristics seem to unite groups of countries, where:

1. the future elites display little interest in the subject of military security (Slovenia and Spain);
2. appreciation of the armed forces' public image is particularly low (Bulgaria, Spain, Slovenia, Switzerland and South Africa);
3. the interviewed young people consider the social prestige of the military profession to be modest (Spain, Germany and Slovenia);
4. the sample displays much lower than average appreciation for the officer training process (Slovenia and Spain);
5. the social ranking of the officer's profession is considerably lower than the sample average (Switzerland and Spain).

It is enough to glance over this list to note some recurrences, those shown by the Spanish and Slovenian samples above all, but also the Swiss sample. And since, from a general look at the whole of the results of this survey on future elites (that is, from all the responses to the questionnaire) the same recurrences seem to repeat, in order to get first-hand information that can help us understand certain national situations, it appears opportune to turn here, too, to the results of the expert survey conducted among the present elites in these countries.

For Spain, a substantial historical reason emerges for the opinions and positions expressed, a reason pointed out by an interviewed member of the current Spanish elite who affirms:

> Throughout almost forty years of a totalitarian regime, millions of Spanish men spent a period of their lives as conscripts in military service under the orders of a fascist military and under the influence of an oppressive political power.
>
> Following the consolidation of the democratic process and having been accepted as full members of the European Economic Community in 1986, Spanish democracy faced multiple challenges, one of which, due to the nature of past relations between the AFs and civil society, was that of constructing fruitful and fluid relations between civil society and the military. The social status of Spanish military personnel was not well considered. As a profession, it had lost a great deal of prestige. Anti-military sentiment was increasingly present in the minds of many citizens and made itself felt with greater force and less fear. The very large presence of North American bases and troops on Spanish soil, and the accompanying feeling that national sovereignty had been violated, did nothing to appease that tendency. Civil society identified the army with the Franco era and to move beyond that perception would require a great deal of very patient activity.

For Slovenia, too, specific historical reasons exist that can explain a higher level of anti-militarism or amilitarism than in the other examined countries. According to what Ljubiça Jelusic and Maja Garb, Slovenian researchers who are participating in this research, write (Jelušič & Garb, 2005):

> In 1991, Slovenian public verified its decade long hypothesis that there is no enemy outside the country, but the biggest enemy is its own military. The war in Slovenia, although the decision to form an independent state was encouraged by Serb nationalism and totalitarian perception of Yugoslav federation, was clearly the war between Slovenian people, military and police against Yugoslav Peoples' Army, not against other nations or republics of former Yugoslavia.

The building of a national army later moved along quite untraditional military lines, so that future officers in the Slovenian armed forces arrive at their appointment through a programme at a civilian university, pursued with the status of civilian students who are free to enlist or not at the end of the programme. As these authors again write in the cited essay: "[The] military is becoming like an enterprise, for those who need some adventures or a short-term job, the contract of at least five years is offered. Those who do not accept the military values are not going to be forced into it."

The case of Switzerland appears to be more political than historical and can be traced to the country's geopolitical position in the context of swift and far-reaching international changes. Nothing better than the European

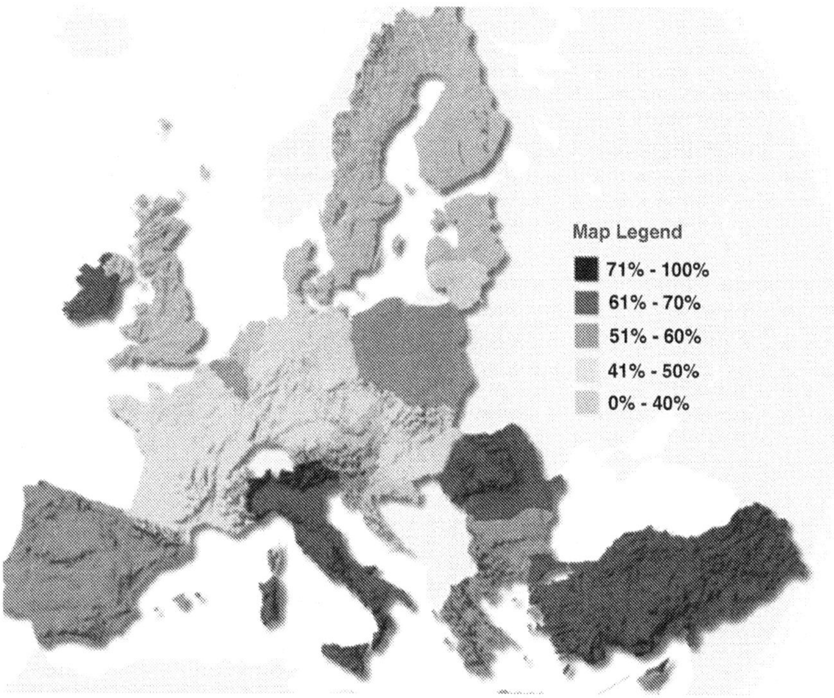

Fig. 6. Switzerland Figure in the European Map. *Source:* Eurobarometer No. 63.

map designed in last Eurobarometer report (No. 63) can give a visual idea of such a situation (see Fig. 6).

Small states that wish to maintain an autonomous, unaligned position are finding it increasingly difficult to do so due to the development of large supranational unions and alliances. This is plainly the case of Switzerland, where the research data point to a clear crisis of national identity that is widely reflected in the surveyed elites' opinions on the tasks, missions and very existence of the national armed forces.

Indeed, a representative of the country's current elite affirms in this regard:

> Switzerland has a very long tradition of neutrality. However, for the last twelve years Switzerland has been in an identity crisis. The main reason is that neutrality has lost its meaning: The cold war is over, Europe is united, there are no real security threats, and the UN charter has outlawed war. Nevertheless, people can't adapt their mindset so fast to

the new situation – they need time to understand and realize that the solutions which worked for the last couple of hundred years will be useless for the future.

It is a crisis situation that is plainly reflected in the credibility and the social acceptance of the military, producing opinion gaps of as much as 51 percentage points between the future military and civilian elites (see "Data analysis" section).

The remaining countries of the sample display less singular and discordant aspects in this survey than those highlighted here, and many similarities in the various attitudes of the individual groups of students examined, at least for what regards the topic dealt with here, *Media and Public Opinion*. A transnational situation emerges that seems to render attitudes more similar, for example, among the political science students of the different countries than between the military students and the civilian students of a single country. It is an aspect of globalisation that appears in any event to be on the increase and not about to go away.

NOTES

1. Furio Colombo, "La fine del villaggio globale", in *La Repubblica*, 19 April 1999, p. 29.
2. The lacking percentage is represented by "don't know/no answer".
3. To get this datum a breakdown by class was used, on the assumption that a contemporaneous survey of students in their first and subsequent years will roughly approximate a longitudinal survey of a single group of students. This assumption is not totally aprioristic: at the Army Academy in Italy, both transversal and longitudinal surveys were conducted and then compared (see Caforio, 1998, p. 44); results were very similar.
4. The correlation coefficient between the three questions is as follows:
Pearson's '*r*'

	Q13	Q38	Q39
Q13	1	.336	.225
Q38	.336	1	.286
Q39	.225	.286	1

5. See Caforio (1994, 1998, 2001).
6. With the exceptions of Germany (just 1 percentage point) and France (9 percentage points).

REFERENCES

Caforio, G. (Ed.) (1994). The military profession in Europe. In: *Current Sociology* (Vol. 42, Issue 3), London: Sage.

Caforio, G. (Ed.) (1998). *The European cadet: Professional socialisation in military academies*. Baden-Baden: Nomos.

Caforio, G. (Ed.) (2001). *The flexible officer*. Gaeta: Artistic & Publishing Company.

Dahl, R. A. (1989). *Democracy and its critics*. New Haven: Yale University Press.

Holmes, R., & McConville, T. (2003). Introduction. In: R. Holmes & T. McConville (Eds), *Defence management in uncertain times*. London: Frank Cass.

Inglehart, R. (1977). *The silent revolution: Changing values and political styles among western publics*. Princeton: Princeton University Press.

Jelušič, L., & Garb, M. (2005). The cultural gap between the military and the parent society in Slovenia. In: G. Caforio & G. Kuemmel (Eds), *Military missions and their implications reconsidered: The aftermath of september 11th*. Elsevier book Series.

THREAT PERCEPTION: NEW RISKS, NEW THREATS AND NEW MISSIONS

Rafael Martínez Martínez and
Antonio M. Díaz Fernández

ABSTRACT

The threats, the potential enemies, the risks and, consequently, the strategies used in each context to face them have all changed. The comparison by countries between futures civil and military elite shows us the palpable differences that exist among both worlds in these questions. Broadly speaking, a very intense inclination among the university students toward the human security could be detected while the cadets are more inclined toward the hard security. Undoubtedly, such a redefinition and adaptation of military missions to the new demands of a globalised world will eventually take precedence.

1. INTRODUCTION

At this stage, it would be stating the obvious to say that drastic changes are afoot on the international stage; but such is the situation. The threats, the potential enemies, the risks and, logically, the strategies used in each context

Cultural Differences between the Military and Parent Society in Democratic Countries
Contributions to Conflict Management, Peace Economics and Development, Volume 4, 129–160

ISSN: 1572-8323/doi:10.1016/S1572-8323(07)04006-4

have all changed. At the beginning of the century, a group of experts appointed by Koffi Annan concluded that in the near future the main threats to world security would come from (i) economic and social disorder – arising especially from poverty, (ii) conflicts between states, (iii) the spread of weapons of mass destruction, (iv) terrorism and (v) transnational organised crime. Likewise, a recent document on EU security strategy entitled 'A secure Europe in a better world'[1] set out the key threats facing Europe: (i) terrorism, (ii) proliferation of weapons of mass destruction, (iii) regional conflicts, (iv) State failure – the collapse of state institutions – and (v) organised crime. The Union proposes three strategic objectives to address these threats:

1. To take steps to tackle the threats and, at the same time, remain aware that, unlike situations in the past, no present-day threat is a purely military one and each one calls for a specific combination of instruments.
2. To build security in our neighbourhood: especially in the Mediterranean area, the southern Caucasus and the Arab world. The quality of international society is dependent on its governments. The best protection for European security is a world in which democratic states practise good governance.
3. Develop an international order based on an effective multilateralism. To achieve as much, the UN system must be strengthened along with regional organisations, with a view to developing a stronger international society, with effective institutions that uphold international law.

In its response to these strategic objectives the EU has to become *more active, more capable, more coherent and more cooperative*. In order to be more active, early, rapid and where necessary robust intervention is essential. A European Defence Agency is needed, as well as armed forces (AFs) that are more rapidly deployable, have greater flexibility and are better equipped and more effective. The EU will require a large volume of civil resources for any post-conflict scenario, will have to widen co-operation and collaboration between its intelligence services in order to produce more accurate assessments to confront the threats and broaden the range of missions in which the EU participates. Greater coherence will ensue wherever conflicts are approached from a regional perspective and justice and home affairs policies are coordinated to persecute actual and potential organised crime. The Common Foreign and Security Policy and the European Security and Defence Policy represent the most coherent ways of fighting against common threats and creating a stronger Europe. However, collaboration must extend across European borders since we face common threats and international cooperation is therefore imperative. Hence, the EU asserts the right to maintain close collaboration with a range of actors[2]: the USA, Russia, the Middle East, Africa, Latin America and Asia. However, as stated in the Barcelona Forum of Culture 2004 by the EU High Representative for the Common Foreign and Security Policy, Javier Solana, European society cannot adopt a hypocritical stance and must be fully aware of the economic effort involved. We will be able to transform a clearly defensive security policy into a security policy that seeks peace; but which is neither a less expensive, nor a softer option.

The future civil and military elites of eight countries of the 'Europe of the 25' (France, Germany, Italy, Netherlands, Poland, Slovenia, Spain and Sweden), four other European countries (Bulgaria, Romania, Switzerland and Turkey) and the Republic of South Africa have made known their overall agreement with the need for this budgetary increase (64% in agreement as against 29% in disagreement). France, Romania, Poland, Germany, South Africa and Italy show the highest degree of agreement with this need (86%, 86%, 82%, 76%, 79% and 74%, respectively), whereas Slovenia and Turkey oppose the idea (by 58% in both cases) and Switzerland and Spain harbour significant reservations over such an increase in the defence budget (41% and 35%, respectively).

On another note, and in total harmony with the European security strategy approved in 2003, future civil and military elites are clear that National Security is increasingly linked to the security of the international system. Thus, over half (54%) are in agreement with the idea that 'We shouldn't think so much in international terms but concentrate more on our own national problems' (in Italy, Holland, Spain, Sweden and Switzerland it amounts to 70%; whereas in Romania, Bulgaria, Poland and South Africa they are more inclined to consider national problems). Likewise, 67% think that 'the national security of my country depends more on international trade and a strong domestic economy than on our military strength' (neither France (68%) nor Italy (56%) support this statement).

Regarding the threats to their security,[3] the future civil and military elites consider the principal ones to be: (i) organised crime, (ii) international drug trafficking, (iii) terrorism in our country and (iv) an armed conflict over the control of vital raw materials (water, oil, etc.). For the future military elites – but not for the future civil elites – mass immigration from foreign countries is also an important threat; something similar occurs but vice-versa with respect to environmental problems such as air and water contamination.

2. THREATS TO NATIONAL SECURITY

When threats to national security are analyzed from a gender perspective, the only noteworthy variation occurs with regard to the fear of an accidental nuclear war, considered as a very significant threat by a quarter of the women interviewed, as well as environmental problems that also greatly concern a third of the women interviewed. When the latter is seen in terms of global warming of the planet, it is perceived as an almost irrelevant threat for the extreme right (very important for 18%) but its importance progressively increases across the political spectrum until it becomes an essential concern for 43% of those interviewed on the extreme left. On the other hand, the importance attributed by more than half of the students on the extreme right to mass immigration from foreign countries is also notable.

The religious factor introduces a further key analytical variable since the number of threats perceived by Orthodox Christians and Muslims is altogether much greater than other religious groupings. Nevertheless, the fact that the Orthodox Christians and Muslims in question are in the main Bulgarians, Romanians or Turks introduces an important geographical factor that might be as if not more explanatory than the religious aspects themselves. As things now stand, the threats considered as very important for Orthodox Christians, much more so than in the eyes of the other religious groups, are ‘organised crime’ (63%), ‘international drug trafficking’ (61%), ‘terrorism in our country’ (58%), ‘a military attack by a foreign country’ (55%), ‘an accidental nuclear war’ (48%), ‘armed conflict over the control of vital raw materials’ (42%), ‘the spread of weapons of mass destruction’ (42%), ‘nuclear war between third-world countries with global consequences’ (40%) and ‘nuclear blackmail by third-world countries’ (26%). The Muslim world, in comparison with the other religions in its ranking of very important concerns, highlights: ‘terrorism’ (62%), ‘an armed conflict over the control of vital raw materials’ (42%), ‘an armed conflict in the Middle East’ (36%) and ‘an accidental nuclear war’ (30%).

In a study of these dimensions, an analytical approach on a country by country basis is indispensable. In the first place, because global averages mask the distinguishing traits of each individual country, as not all realities are necessarily identical; but it is furthermore the case that the number of interviewees per country is neither equal nor is the survey population subject to any logical weighting in relation to the total population of the country,[4] nor are the percentages of future civil and military elites in the study proportional.[5] In short, a country-by-country study of the civil–military gap is not only advisable, but also quite indispensable.

As it is, the country-by-country analysis reveals how organised crime and international drug trafficking are perceived as threats by all university students in all countries with the exception of Spanish and Slovenian students, who do not perceive international drug trafficking as a principal threat (Table 1). In addition to these threats, university students in Bulgaria, France, Italy, Holland, Poland, Sweden and Switzerland also consider environmental problems as a threat, as do Slovenian students without ranking them among their first two. Furthermore, in the case of Bulgaria, France, Italy and Holland, there is also agreement over the perception of terrorism as a threat. The latter is also threatening for German, Romanian, South African, Spanish and Turkish students. The Slovenians and the Swiss join the latter group insofar as they consider an armed conflict over the control of vital raw materials as a relevant threat.

From the military perspective, organised crime and international drug trafficking are considered crucial threats for all countries, with the exception of France in relation to organised crime and Spain in relation to both threats (Table 2). Alongside these threats, terrorism is highly ranked in Bulgaria, Turkey, Romania, South Africa, Sweden and Italy; and in the latter three there are also coincident views as to the perceived threat of mass immigration from other countries. Leaving aside coincident views on a global scale, terrorism and immigration are also threatening for France and Spain, as is immigration for Holland, Slovenia and Switzerland. Finally, for Germans, Poles, Slovenians, Turks, the Spanish and the Swiss, an armed conflict over the control of vital raw materials is thought to be a latent threat.

Civil–military disaccord (Table 3) warns us that there is no country in which similar threats are perceived by the future civil and military elites, although the Germans, the Italians, the South Africans, the Turks and the Swiss only disagree over one point. On the other hand, the biggest rift exists among the French who register three differences. It is also made clear that organised crime is a global threat – except for Spanish and French military cadets – and that unanimity exists over international drug trafficking – except among Spanish cadets and Slovenian and Spanish university students – and that unanimity also exists over terrorism among civil or military elites, or both – except in the case of Poland, Slovenia and Switzerland. Finally, immigration is fundamentally a threat for cadets and environmental problems a threat for civil elites.

Table 1. University Students – Principal Threats to National Security (% of Very Important).

Possible Threats	Bulgaria	France	Germany	Italy	Netherlands	Poland	Romania	Slovenia	S. Africa	Spain	Sweden	Switzerland	Turkey
Mass immigration from foreign countries	17	11	14	**43**	20	17	9	9	**49**	15	9	16	12
Terrorism in our countries	**41**	**42**	**20**	**46**	**23**	6	**68**	15	**33**	**67**	17	2	**74**
International drug trafficking	**68**	**38**	**14**	**33**	**35**	**43**	**61**	10	**50**	20	**22**	**23**	**39**
Organised crime	**66**	**27**	**24**	**43**	**36**	**58**	**66**	**24**	**63**	**24**	**32**	**21**	**52**
Environmental problems such as air pollution and water contamination	**46**	**44**	14	**17**	**26**	**46**	41	**22**	31	20	**26**	**35**	33
Possible indirect involvement in a civil war	25	21	0	6	5	8	26	10	17	18	7	3	27
An armed conflict between African countries with which we maintain co-operative relations	2	19	1	5	1	6	10	2	20	7	3	4	8
An armed conflict in the Middle East	7	25	12	14	17	**20**	20	4	16	19	12	10	31

Attacks on computer networks	19	13	<u>**23**</u>	14	<u>**22**</u>	17	37	16	24	11	<u>**20**</u>	<u>**19**</u>	16
Nuclear blackmail by Third World countries	9	10	2	5	5	7	43	5	13	12	9	5	25
Nuclear war between Third World countries with global consequences	24	11	5	7	9	3	**55**	16	20	24	11	6	32
An armed conflict between Asian countries	9	2	2	10	6	3	11	2	10	7	3	4	16
Proliferation of weapons of mass destruction	33	21	13	13	15	<u>**19**</u>	**54**	13	16	22	<u>**18**</u>	15	37
An accidental nuclear war	<u>**41**</u>	10	3	5	18	12	<u>**60**</u>	<u>**16**</u>	22	<u>**25**</u>	11	7	37
An armed conflict over the control of vital raw materials (water, oil, etc.)	35	21	<u>**25**</u>	10	22	16	**58**	<u>**20**</u>	<u>**33**</u>	<u>**29**</u>	9	<u>**24**</u>	<u>**41**</u>
Military attack by a foreign state	39	<u>**28**</u>	4	6	13	6	<u>**66**</u>	<u>**19**</u>	29	<u>**28**</u>	9	3	<u>**38**</u>

Source: Authors.
Bold & underline type: top five. Only bold type: outside top five – considered by over 50% as 'very important'.

Table 2. Cadets – Principal Threats to National Security (% of Very Important).

Possible Threats	Bulgaria	France	Germany	Italy	Netherlands	Poland	Romania	Slovenia	S. Africa	Spain	Sweden	Switzerland	Turkey
Mass immigration from foreign countries	13	**48**	17	**42**	**22**	18	14	**14**	**73**	**28**	**22**	**48**	15
Terrorism in our countries	**37**	**43**	15	**42**	19	15	**66**	9	**36**	**76**	**21**	1	**63**
International drug trafficking	**57**	**43**	**21**	**28**	**44**	**44**	**69**	**14**	**55**	14	**32**	**41**	**32**
Organised crime	**52**	22	**29**	**50**	**28**	**56**	**73**	**31**	**64**	20	**46**	**31**	**51**
Environmental problems such as air pollution and water contamination	13	33	15	10	19	**29**	**51**	**26**	29	15	18	16	16
Possible indirect involvement in a civil war	14	14	2	2	4	10	35	0	32	9	3	0	17
An armed conflict between African countries with which we maintain co-operative relations	7	**34**	2	1	3	2	6	0	**38**	4	6	4	2

An armed conflict in the Middle East	17	**35**	8	**15**	**22**	21	15	0	20	12	17	11	**45**
Attacks on computer networks	7	22	**23**	3	**24**	**28**	25	6	28	7	**33**	**43**	15
Nuclear blackmail by Third World countries	20	5	7	2	7	10	35	0	27	11	6	1	12
Nuclear war between Third World countries with global consequences	30	6	5	1	13	11	**61**	0	21	14	10	4	17
An armed conflict between Asian countries	10	5	2	6	6	7	9	0	14	4	4	2	13
Proliferation of weapons of mass destruction	**33**	25	**24**	14	12	24	**57**	6	15	**22**	11	13	18
An accidental nuclear war	27	6	4	3	12	18	**57**	3	24	18	9	0	18
An armed conflict over the control of vital raw materials (water, oil, etc.)	10	31	**21**	6	16	**35**	47	**9**	36	**21**	20	**25**	**48**
Military attack by a foreign state	**33**	8	6	5	8	21	**72**	3	26	**29**	9	0	28

Source: Authors.
Bold & underline type: top five. Only bold type: outside top five – considered by over 50% as 'very important'.

Table 3. Coincident and Divergent Views on the Principal Threats to National Security Held by Cadets and Students.

Possible Threats	Bulgaria	France	Germany	Italy	Netherlands	Poland	Romania	Slovenia	S. Africa	Spain	Sweden	Switzerland	Turkey
Mass immigration from foreign countries		C		CS	C			C	CS	C	C	C	
Terrorism in our countries	CS	CS	S	CS	S		CS		CS	CS	C		CS
International drug trafficking	CS	CS	CS	CS	CS	CS	CS	C	CS		CS	CS	CS
Organised crime	CS	S	CS	CS	CS	CS	CS	CS	CS	S	CS	CS	CS
Environmental problems such as air pollution and water contamination	S	S		S	S	CS		CS			S	S	
Possible indirect involvement in a civil war													
An armed conflict between African countries with which we maintain co-operative relations		C							C				

An armed conflict in the Middle East		C		C	CS								C
Attacks on computer networks			CS		C	C					CS	CS	
Nuclear blackmail by Third World countries													
Nuclear war between Third World countries with global consequences							C						
An armed conflict between Asian countries.													
Proliferation of weapons of mass destruction	C		C			S				C	S		
An accidental nuclear war	S						S	S		S			
An armed conflict over the control of vital raw materials (water, oil, etc.)			CS			C		CS	S	CS		CS	CS
Military attack by a foreign state	C	C					CS	S		CS			S

Source: Authors.
"CS": Coincident views held by both Cadets and Students. "S": Students only. "C": Cadets only.

3. NEW MISSIONS FOR THE MILITARY

National security is built around three elements: the threat and the hostile agent that causes it, the assets (material and intangible) that are to be protected and finally, the security strategy to be put in place. In other words, the means and resources that we are prepared to use in order to guarantee our assets. Evidently, the AFs are one of the most appropriate instruments to implement the chosen security strategy. However, when confronted by the new generation of threats, it is worth asking whether the AFs continue to be the most suitable resource. For this reason, it was an opportune moment to question the future civil and military elites over the extent to which, in their opinion, the military was still suited to conventional roles and adaptable to new ones.[6]

Thus, in the global view afforded by Tables 4 and 5, absolutely contiguous views are seen to be held by civil and military elites in relation to the suitability of the military to (i) 'defend your country', (ii) 'provide disaster relief', (iii) 'participate in peace-keeping missions', (iv) 'provide humanitarian aid in foreign countries' and (v) 'fighting terrorism'. However, equal weighting is given to different political or military objectives that should determine the use of military force. Nevertheless, in countries such as Poland (73%), South Africa (64%), Turkey (58%), Sweden (57%), Germany (56%) or France (52%), it is clearly understood that military goals should determine the use of force; whereas in Slovenia (64%), Bulgaria (59%), Switzerland (58%), Italy (52%) and Spain (49%) the idea given most weight is that the use of military force has to be decided on the basis of political goals.

Both the 'defence of the country' and 'the fight against terrorism', the former conventional and the latter of more recent origin, are two missions that unambiguously belong to the combative role of an army. Conversely, the other three missions that were considered by a large majority as appropriate for the army correspond to new roles that are replacing the more conventional defensive ones: 'provision of disaster aid', 'humanitarian aid in foreign countries' and 'participation in peace-keeping missions'. That the cadets support the use of the military apparatus for peace-keeping operations and disaster aid indicates that they have taken on board more willingly than their commanding officers (Martínez, 2000), the redefinition of their roles in response to the challenges presented by the new threats, roles which will continue to be compatible with their more conventional mission.[7] It should not be forgotten that peace-keeping operations: (i) reinforce the supremacy of civil society because the troops are dispatched

Table 4. Views Held by University Students on the Suitability of the Military to Different Types of Mission (% of Approve Very Strongly).

Possible Missions	Bulgaria	France	Germany	Italy	Netherlands	Poland	Romania	Slovenia	S. Africa	Spain	Sweden	Switzerland	Turkey
Defence of your country	**<u>84</u>**	**<u>85</u>**	**<u>87</u>**	**<u>75</u>**	**<u>73</u>**	**<u>93</u>**	**<u>81</u>**	**<u>81</u>**	**<u>91</u>**	**<u>59</u>**	**<u>79</u>**	**<u>59</u>**	**<u>84</u>**
Peace-keeping missions	44	**<u>77</u>**	**<u>57</u>**	41	**<u>51</u>**	38	28	36	**<u>56</u>**	**<u>58</u>**	**<u>70</u>**	**<u>40</u>**	**<u>38</u>**
Peace-enforcement missions	12	28	17	15	20	15	11	6	28	13	26	10	16
Combat missions	15	36	17	7	17	17	10	4	32	10	7	3	19
Disaster relief	**<u>81</u>**	**<u>70</u>**	**<u>79</u>**	**<u>64</u>**	**<u>37</u>**	**<u>74</u>**	**<u>60</u>**	**<u>79</u>**	**<u>72</u>**	**<u>79</u>**	**<u>68</u>**	**<u>81</u>**	21
Humanitarian relief abroad	**63**	**<u>53</u>**	**<u>48</u>**	35	**<u>43</u>**	**<u>65</u>**	46	**<u>66</u>**	49	**<u>72</u>**	**<u>55</u>**	**<u>73</u>**	23
Domestic disorder within our country	**<u>64</u>**	43	26	45	**<u>38</u>**	**53**	33	30	**56**	28	36	21	**<u>28</u>**
Combat drug trafficking	**<u>74</u>**	32	7	**<u>52</u>**	22	**58**	**<u>52</u>**	34	**<u>60</u>**	26	15	16	18
Prevent spread of weapons of mass destruction	**60**	28	19	**<u>53</u>**	28	**<u>66</u>**	**<u>54</u>**	**<u>36</u>**	**56**	43	33	17	**<u>34</u>**
Control mass immigration from abroad	25	19	5	38	13	20	16	12	47	13	7	9	11
Fighting terrorism	**<u>68</u>**	**<u>51</u>**	**<u>28</u>**	**<u>66</u>**	35	**<u>71</u>**	**<u>64</u>**	34	**<u>61</u>**	**<u>53</u>**	**<u>42</u>**	17	**<u>74</u>**
Protect the environment	50	17	9	37	22	44	24	**<u>50</u>**	39	41	20	**<u>41</u>**	18

Source: Authors.
Bold & underline type: top five. Only bold type: outside top five – considered by over 50% as 'very important'.

Table 5. Views Held by Cadets on the Suitability of the Military for Different Types of Missions (% of Approve Very Strongly).

Possible Missions	Bulgaria	France	Germany	Italy	Netherlands	Poland	Romania	Slovenia	S. Africa	Spain	Sweden	Switzerland	Turkey
Defence of your country	**93**	**95**	**90**	**97**	**87**	**99**	**97**	**97**	**97**	**78**	**93**	**98**	**98**
Peace-keeping missions	**53**	**64**	**64**	**75**	**72**	**55**	**53**	**46**	**71**	**70**	**79**	**57**	**56**
Peace-enforcement missions	10	38	28	38	**50**	24	27	17	**66**	33	**56**	12	25
Combat missions	10	**78**	27	38	37	35	19	9	**71**	42	34	13	37
Disaster relief	**90**	**58**	**81**	**85**	**49**	**87**	**67**	**91**	**60**	**73**	**63**	**83**	**42**
Humanitarian relief abroad	40	29	**51**	37	42	**51**	**50**	**54**	**50**	**65**	48	**57**	41
Domestic disorder within our country	**70**	30	17	**55**	31	**66**	39	34	49	44	**59**	**40**	**49**
Combat drug trafficking	**60**	24	9	44	22	**57**	44	21	47	23	27	8	10
Prevent spread of weapons of mass destruction	**70**	47	24	**69**	46	**77**	**66**	43	**60**	45	47	14	20
Control mass immigration from abroad	13	21	7	41	15	26	10	20	**52**	22	18	27	8
Fighting terrorism	**60**	**61**	**32**	**82**	**52**	**80**	**82**	**49**	**66**	**54**	**62**	28	**75**
Protect the environment	**50**	5	16	23	17	42	25	37	42	20	22	17	10

Source: Authors.
Bold & underline type: top five. Only bold type: outside top five – considered by over 50% as 'very important'.

by their respective governments, in some cases even with the approval of their parliaments, (ii) legitimises the military because it brings with it the support of their fellow citizens as is evident from their image in public opinion following their participation in these types of missions[8] and (iii) forces them to work alongside other military personnel and citizens from other countries which creates social interaction, at the same time as it opens new avenues for European collaboration. However, the majority of those interviewed (78%) are quite clear that public opinion in their countries will not tolerate large numbers of casualties in military operations (a particularly acute perception in Bulgaria, Germany, Holland, Slovenia, Switzerland, Spain and Sweden).

Leaving aside the homogeneity of military and civil responses, it is noteworthy, but not surprising, that the responses of the cadets on the question of their adaptability to any role are always given much greater importance. However, there are three exceptions to this rule: providing humanitarian aid in foreign countries, combating drug trafficking and helping protect the environment. It is symptomatic that these three roles are the only ones in which women attach considerably greater importance to their responses on the adaptability of the military to such tasks than men.

Ideologically speaking, the provision of humanitarian aid abroad is a role that finds more support among interviewees on the left (appropriate for 34% on the extreme right as against 68% on the extreme left), and a similar situation occurs with regard to protecting the environment. Conversely, the roles that are increasingly supported on the right as opposed to the left of the political spectrum are the 'defence of your country' (95% as opposed to 60%), 'participation in combat missions' (41% as opposed to 13%), 'preventing the spread of weapons of mass destruction' (57% as opposed to 36%), 'the fight against terrorism' (52% as opposed to 37%) and 'participation in peace-enforcement missions' (31% as opposed to 17%). There are two roles that are only highly rated by the extreme right: 'domestic disorder within our country' (65%) and 'controlling mass immigration from foreign countries' (53%).

Along religious lines, Orthodox Christians lay greater emphasis on 'Preventing the spread of weapons of mass destruction' (59%) and on 'combating drug trafficking' (54%) than any other religious grouping. Alongside the Muslims and displaying equally strong feelings in their perception of the threat, the high ratings given to the adaptability of the military to the fight against terrorism is also noteworthy (70% Orthodox and 74% Muslims). On the other hand, it is notable that the Muslims do not consider the army highly adaptable to the provision of disaster relief (35%) and humanitarian

Table 6. Coincident and Divergent Views on the Adaptability of the Military to Different Types of Missions Held by Cadets and Students.

Possible Missions	Bulgaria	France	Germany	Italy	Netherlands	Poland	Romania	Slovenia	S. Africa	Spain	Sweden	Switzerland	Turkey
Defence of your country	CS	CS	CS	CS	CS	CS	CS	CS	CS	CS	CS	CS	CS
Peace-keeping missions		CS	CS	C	CS		C	C	CS	CS	CS		CS
Peace-enforcement missions					C				C				
Combat missions		C							C				
Disaster relief	CS	CS	CS	CS	CS	CS	CS	CS	S	CS	CS	CS	C
Humanitarian relief abroad		S	CS		S	S		CS		CS	S	CS	
Domestic disorder within our country	CS				S	C					C	C	CS
Combat drug trafficking	S			S			S		S				
Prevent spread of weapons of mass destruction	C			CS		CS	CS	CS					S
Control mass immigration from abroad													
Fighting terrorism	CS	CS	CS	CS	C	CS	CS		CS	CS	CS		CS
Protect the environment								S				S	

Source: Authors.
'CS': Coincident views held by both Cadets and Students. 'S': Students only. 'C': Cadets only.

aid abroad (32%). The radically different stance of protestant countries (Germany, Switzerland and Sweden) rates participation in peace-keeping missions (65%) much more highly than all of the other religious groupings.

An analysis based on the home country of university students (Table 4) shows unanimity over the appropriateness of the military for the defence of their country and only Turkey excludes the capacity to provide disaster relief. Furthermore, France, Germany, Spain and Sweden all display absolute agreement over the five principal roles for which the military are adapted: (i) the 'defence of your country', (ii) 'provision of disaster relief', (iii) 'participation in peace-enforcement missions', (iv) 'provision of humanitarian aid abroad' and (v) 'the fight against terrorism'. Holland, Poland, South Africa and Switzerland agree on four of the five; neither the Dutch nor the Swiss prioritise 'the fight against terrorism', nor the Polish 'peace-keeping missions', nor the South Africans 'the provision of humanitarian aid abroad'. The remaining countries only agree on the adaptability of the army to three of the five missions.

Among the cadets (Table 5), there is overwhelming agreement for 'the defence of your country', 'participation in peace-keeping missions', 'provision of disaster relief' and 'the fight against terrorism' – it is only the Swiss who do not consider that the army is adapted to the latter role. 'The provision of humanitarian aid abroad' is not considered a role to which the army is well adapted by cadets from Bulgaria, France, Italy, Holland, Sweden and Turkey. Bulgarian, Polish and South African cadets, as well as the university students from those same countries, rank the suitability of the army for eight and even nine of the 12 proposed roles at levels of over 50%.

Divergent opinions between civil and military elites on a country-by-country basis (Table 6) show that, as a first relevant point, German and Spanish viewpoints exactly coincide and only Holland and South Africa register two differences. That is to say, there is a high degree of similarity in the responses of cadets and university students on the adaptability of the armies to certain roles. It is, nonetheless, possible to point out that 'participation in peace-keeping missions' finds greater support among cadets and that 'providing humanitarian aid abroad', on the other hand, is supported more by university students.

4. ASSESSMENTS OF FOREIGN POLICY GOALS

Understanding which threats those interviewed considered as the main threats to the security of their respective countries will in turn help us

Table 7. Assessment of Foreign Policy Goals (% of Very Important).

Goals	Cadets	University Students
Improving living standards in less-developed countries	28	39
Worldwide arms control	36	39
Combating world hunger	40	52
Strengthening the United Nations	34	34
Fostering international co-operation to solve common problems, such as food, inflation, and energy	41	52
Preserving world peace	70	71
Preventing the spread of weapons of mass destruction	64	60
Promoting and defending human rights in other countries	45	48
Bringing democratic forms of government to other nations	21	24
Strengthening regional security alliances or agreements (NATO, for example)	32	26
Maintaining the external security of your country	70	56
Fighting terrorism	67	55

Source: Authors.

understand the priorities they assign to foreign policy goals.[9] As is evident from Table 7, prioritisation of foreign policy goals strongly correlates with the main threats to national security. Similarities exist between the ranking of civil and military foreign policy goals.[10] Hence, 'preserving world peace', 'preventing the spread of weapons of mass destruction', 'maintaining the external security of their countries' and 'fighting terrorism' are all important goals in both worlds, although to varying degrees and in different orders. Among cadets, the remaining goals fall below 50% importance and even their fifth priority – 'preventing and defending human rights in other countries' – is attributed less importance by university students who rank it seventh (45% among cadets and 48% among students). For the future civil elites, the principal foreign policy goals are 'combating world hunger', 'fostering international cooperation to solve common problems, such as food shortages, inflation and energy', and 'defending human rights in other countries'. Whereas the cadets have more of a short-term agenda focusing on reactive security issues, university students have a wider one that integrates both reactive security and cooperation and development with other countries, involving preventive and proactive security strategies. This wider range of options has its origin in separate visions influenced by each particular academic background. For instance, 'fighting terrorism' is a priority shared by all cadets, although it is only the third priority for economists; law students relegate it to sixth position and, finally, students of political science place it in seventh position. The second priority for law students is 'fostering international cooperation to solve common problems', which is placed sixth by economists, who rate it below 50%. Similarly, the fifth priority for law students, 'promoting and defending human rights in other countries', is the seventh for economists, and was also rated below 50%. Finally, the interest expressed by law students in 'worldwide arms control' (46%) and the weight given by students of political science to 'strengthening the UN system' (40%) are both worth remarking on.

It is surprising that cadets and university students attach little importance to the 'strengthening of the UN system' in their ranking of foreign policy goals when 76% strongly agree on the need for a stronger United Nations due to the increasing multinational nature of military missions. Something which fits in with the idea supported by 81% that 'it is vital to enlist the cooperation of the U.N. in settling international disputes' (94% for the Swedish). What is more, 58% agree that 'the United Nations should have more control of the AFs of all members' (78% of Slovenians, 72% of the Swiss, 71% of South Africans and 67% of the Spanish); however, this last idea is rejected by 65% of the French, 53% of the Germans, 46% of the Polish and 45% of the Turks. Equally, 57% think that 'the Security Council of the United Nations should be the only power to verify military actions against sovereign status' (only Holland and Turkey oppose this statement; 54% and 52% respectively). A paradigm that is quite logically associated with outright rejection of the idea that the USA (84%); the EU (73%) or NATO (61%) should have freedom to intervene on their own initiative.

Analysis from a gender perspective shows that the values attributed by men shadow the priorities of the cadets and those attributed by women are closer to the priorities of the students, which suggests that there will be a very limited number of women in future military elites (in our data, women represent 12% of cadets and 50% of university students). It may be seen how Third World development and co-operation incites greater interest among women. Thus, women rank 'helping to improve the standard of living in less developed countries' as more important by a margin of 12 points[11]; 'combating world hunger'[12] and 'preventing and defending human rights in other countries'[13] by a margin of nine; 'preserving world peace'[14] by eight and 'fostering international cooperation to solve common problems' by six points. On the contrary, 'strengthening the UN[15] and regional security alliances or agreements' and 'maintaining the external security of your country' are given between four and ten points less by women. When both gender and civil–military variables are considered, differences between men and women are more acute among university students. However, the gender variable only reveals different priorities in the ranking of foreign policy goals among cadets and university students. Although male university students coincide with their female classmates in their ranking of foreign policy goals, only in three cases do they ascribe more than 50% importance to them ('preserving world peace', 'preventing the spread of weapons of mass destruction' and 'maintaining the external security of their countries'), whereas women ascribe an importance of over 50% to seven goals.[16] Another interesting point is that while 'fighting terrorism' was ranked fifth by male university students (below 50%) and third by cadets, women ranked it as their second priority – cadets as well as university students.

From a religious stance, there are no substantial variations in the ranking of foreign policy priorities, but it is a noteworthy fact that 'fighting terrorism' is not in the top five for those who 'do not belong to any confession or who are atheist' and is the top priority for Muslims (75% – very important goal). If we add the civil–military dimension, as much may also be said for students. Thus, atheist university students relegate 'fighting terrorism' to tenth place and Muslim students – knowledgeable of Islam and unsympathetic to Islamic fundamentalism – ascribe greater importance than Muslim cadets to 'fighting terrorism', which is their highest priority. It is also relevant that protestant, Christian orthodox and atheist cadets rank the preservation of world peace above all else, followed by maintaining the external security of their country, and that Catholic cadets (21% Italian, 15% Polish, 14% Spanish, 12% French) and Muslims (96% Turkish) prefer 'fighting terrorism' and maintaining the external security of their respective countries as their principal goals. Undoubtedly, the different kinds of terrorist attacks in the home countries of Catholic and Muslim cadets help explain their priorities.

The ideological variable also sheds further light on the situation. For instance, 'combating world hunger' is a principal goal only for left-wing and extreme left-wing interviewees. On the contrary, 'fighting terrorism' is not a priority for them although it is for the rest. Equally, 'preserving world peace' is the first goal for all but extreme right participants, who place 'fighting terrorism' in first place (78%). In a very general way, it may be observed that, moving from left to right across the ideological continuum, all the proposed options are allocated decreasing levels of importance ('fighting terrorism' and 'maintaining the external security of your country' are exceptions for university students, as are 'strengthening regional security alliances or agreements' for the cadets). The above goals are given greater importance than 'combating world hunger', 'preventing and defending human rights in other countries', 'helping to improve the standard of living in less developed countries' or 'helping to bring democratic forms of government to other nations'. The ranking remains unchanged regardless of whether those interviewed are from a civil or military background, the only difference being that university students ascribe lower levels of importance to them. However, left-wing cadets give great priority to hard security issues ('maintaining the external security of your country' and 'fighting terrorism'), though with percentages that are clearly lower than cadets occupying the middle-ground and the right-wing.

Broadly speaking, an analysis of Tables 8 and 9 gives the impression that university students' ratings are always clearer than those of cadets. Nonetheless, cadets express their preferences more intelligently and convincingly which lead us to the conclusion that they have a clearer picture of what their priorities are and are not. As for the university students, it seems that everything is of outstanding importance for them. In general, the ranking of different goals is not so varied among university students. Cadets, except German ones, attribute 70% importance to their most important goal. With the exception of Bulgarians, Romanians, South Africans, Swedes and the Swiss, the rest of the cadets, as from their fourth priority – as from the third for the Dutch and Turkish – assess importance at levels below 50%. Although, university students from Germany, Italy, Netherlands, Romania, South Africa and Spain all rank their first foreign policy goal as 'very important' at a level below 70%, at the same time, students from Bulgaria, France, Romania, South Africa, Sweden and Switzerland have more than five goals ranked as 'very important' at over 50%.

One conclusion might be that the judgement of the Swedish and Swiss university students is not altogether sound because they consider every item as very important, a similar pattern being repeated in Switzerland, but by its cadets. The antithesis of Sweden is Romania: its cadets perceive all possible goals as very important and its university students exercise greater discernment between the goals they consider significant and the rest.

A detailed country-by-country analysis of the university students' responses (Table 8) shows certain similarities, though the cadets' responses show greater heterogeneity. Thus, 'preserving world peace' is the priority goal for the majority (Bulgaria, Germany, the second priority in South Africa, the third in Poland); 'preventing the spread of weapons of mass destruction' is in the top three in Bulgaria, France, Germany, Netherlands,

Table 8. University Students' Ranking of Foreign Policy Goals (% of Very Important).

Possible Foreign-Policy Goals	Bulgaria	France	Germany	Italy	Netherlands	Poland	Romania	Slovenia	S. Africa	Spain	Sweden	Switzerland	Turkey
Helping to improve less-developed countries	28	30	15	**51**	31	17	45	21	42	43	**51**	**87**	31
Worldwide arms control	44	**51**	**35**	34	10	28	47	28	32	46	28	**78**	29
Combating world hunger	**50**	47	29	**50**	**38**	**48**	47	**43**	**54**	**58**	**58**	**92**	**46**
Strengthening the United Nations	22	35	31	37	23	16	20	25	36	33	**50**	77	10
Fostering inter. co-operation to solve common problems	**58**	**70**	35	41	**43**	43	**56**	**47**	**68**	**49**	47	89	44
Preserving world peace	**76**	**70**	**57**	**60**	**63**	**63**	**69**	**79**	**63**	**68**	**80**	**93**	**74**
Preventing the spread of weapons of mass destruction	**70**	**67**	**62**	**50**	**43**	**65**	**64**	**55**	**50**	46	**65**	**87**	**51**
Promoting and defending human rights in other countries	36	47	34	44	**47**	35	**54**	32	**50**	**53**	**61**	**90**	34
Bringing democratic forms of government to other nations	12	11	8	19	15	15	22	9	32	30	35	**68**	17
Strengthening regional security alliances or agreements	39	21	19	14	26	34	38	12	35	19	17	42	19
Maintaining the external security of your country	**81**	**54**	**49**	**34**	31	**71**	**67**	**46**	**56**	46	**67**	**64**	**62**
Fighting terrorism	**64**	**57**	**40**	58	30	**55**	**57**	30	**52**	**66**	**63**	67	**73**

Source: Authors.
Bold & underline type: top five. Only bold type: outside top five – considered by over 50% as 'very important'.

Table 9. Cadets' Ranking of Foreign Policy Goals (% of Very Important).

Possible Foreign-Policy Goals	Bulgaria	France	Germany	Italy	Netherlands	Poland	Romania	Slovenia	S. Africa	Spain	Sweden	Switzerland	Turkey
Helping to improve less-developed countries	23	13	22	23	26	13	**51**	14	50	19	27	**62**	19
Worldwide arms control	**53**	34	**47**	22	30	30	**57**	43	41	36	20	**69**	26
Combating world hunger	43	23	42	36	36	37	**62**	44	**60**	26	36	**63**	24
Strengthening the United Nations	20	24	42	29	30	23	18	**46**	31	29	42	**67**	22
Fostering inter. Co-operation to solve common problems	37	**41**	33	**47**	26	38	**57**	40	55	29	29	**83**	**39**
Preserving world peace	**93**	**67**	**50**	**62**	**71**	**73**	**91**	**77**	**55**	**67**	**78**	**88**	**59**
Preventing the spread of weapons of mass destruction	**76**	**51**	**65**	**59**	**58**	**61**	**80**	**77**	**56**	**64**	**70**	**82**	**46**
Promoting and defending human rights in other countries	20	37	39	40	**45**	29	**51**	40	43	**40**	**60**	**82**	25
Bringing democratic forms of government to other nations	0	8	15	16	17	19	10	14	40	19	27	**60**	16
Strengthening regional security alliances or agreements	33	24	15	24	30	42	46	35	48	31	24	**58**	38
Maintaining the external security of your country	**93**	**76**	**59**	**53**	**46**	**75**	**83**	**80**	**70**	**76**	**80**	**91**	**80**
Fighting terrorism	**80**	**72**	**46**	**72**	**50**	**60**	**76**	**60**	**53**	**88**	**69**	**89**	**76**

Source: Authors.
Bold & underline type: top five. Only bold type: outside top five – considered by over 50% as "very important".

Poland, Romania and Slovenia, as is 'fighting terrorism' in Italy, Spain and Turkey. A traditional military function such as 'maintaining the external security of your country' appears among the top three in Bulgaria, Germany, Poland, Romania, Sweden and Turkey.

Many countries place international solidarity among their first three preferences. This is the case of France, Slovenia and South Africa, which all support 'fostering international cooperation to solve common problems, such as food, inflation and energy', or Italy that supports 'helping to improve the standard of living in less developed countries', or the Netherlands and Switzerland which favour 'preventing and defending human rights in other countries', or indeed Spain and Switzerland that prefer 'combating world hunger'.

Only in five cases, alongside 'preserving world peace', do we find basic security goals linked to security. These correspond to Bulgaria, Poland, Romania and Sweden which opt for 'maintaining the external security of your country' and 'Preventing the spread of weapons of mass destruction'; the fifth case is Turkey which chose 'worldwide arms control' and 'fighting terrorism'. The location of these countries may help explain the reasons behind these preferences expressed by university students.

Turning to the cadets, we find that they display greater homogeneity in their responses (Table 9). Practically all of them – except those from Germany and South Africa – place the following in the top five: 'preserving world peace', 'maintaining the external security of your country', 'fighting terrorism' and 'preventing the spread of weapons of mass destruction'. For the majority (Bulgaria, France, Poland, Slovenia, South Africa, Sweden, Switzerland and Turkey), the traditional defensive function of their armies is decisive and they opt to 'maintain external security' as their main foreign policy goal. Spanish and Italian cadets give first place to 'fighting terrorism', Romanian and Dutch cadets to 'preserving world peace' and Germans to 'preventing the spread of weapons of mass destruction'; but in the rankings of cadets from Germany, Romania and Spain the external security of their countries occupies second place. Only the Italians and the Dutch relegate their country's external security to fourth place and with lower percentages than the cadets from other countries.

Grouping countries according to their three first preferences results in a majority group with slight variations in its third goal due to a small group (Italy and Netherlands) which does not rank the 'external security of your country' in the top three, and finally South Africa – which in consonance with its geographic location – prioritises topics that are less relevant from a European perspective. Thus, for Bulgaria, France, Spain, Switzerland and

Table 10. Coincident and Divergent Views on Foreign Policy Goals Held by Cadets and Students.

Possible Foreign-Policy Goals	Bulgaria	France	Germany	Italy	Netherlands	Poland	Romania	Slovenia	S. Africa	Spain	Sweden	Switzerland	Turkey
Helping to improve less-developed countries				S									
Worldwide arms control	C		CS										
Combating world hunger				S	S	S	C	S	CS	S		S	S
Strengthening the United Nations								C					
Fostering inter. Co-operation to solve common problems	S	CS		C	S		S	S	CS	S		CS	C
Preserving world peace	CS	CS	CS	CS	CS	CS	CS	CS	CS	CS	CS	CS	CS
Preventing the spread of weapons of mass destruction	CS	CS	CS	CS	CS	CS	CS	CS	CS	C	CS	CS	CS
Promoting and defending human rights in other countries					CS					CS	CS	S	
Bringing democratic forms of government to other nations													
Strengthening regional security alliances or agreements						C							
Maintaining the external security of your country	CS	CS	CS	C	C	CS	CS	CS	CS	C	CS	C	CS
Fighting terrorism	CS	CS	CS		C	CS	CS	C	CS	CS	CS	C	CS

Source: Authors.
'CS': Coincident views held by both Cadets and Students. 'S': Students only. 'C' Cadets only.

Turkey, 'maintaining the external security of your country', 'preserving world peace' and 'fighting terrorism' figure in the top three; for Germany, Poland, Romania, Slovenia and Sweden 'fighting terrorism' and 'preventing the spread of weapons of mass destruction' do not figure among the top three. The latter goal, and 'preserving world peace' and 'fighting terrorism' are the principal foreign policy goals for Italian and Dutch cadets. 'Maintaining external security', 'combating world hunger' and 'preventing the spread of weapons of mass destruction' are the priorities for South African cadets.

Comparing the data on a country-by-country basis and not only from a civil–military perspective can provide insight into the cultural gap between both worlds. By comparing the top five foreign policy goals for cadets and university students, on a country-by-country basis, without considering the exact position of any goal, we can create a typology that will help us envisage future models of civil–military harmony (Table 10). This typology has three different types: total, strong or limited harmony. 'Total harmony' indicates that the civil and military elites have a tendency to consider the same first five foreign policy goals. France, Germany, South Africa and Sweden all fit into this group and we may conclude that the cultural gap in this area and in these countries is inexistent. 'Strong harmony' refers to those countries where there is a coincidence in four of the top five goals: Bulgaria, Romania, Poland and Turkey. Finally, 'limited harmony' is characterised by a more striking civil–military cultural gap in foreign policy goals, which arises in five countries whose goals only coincide in three cases in the top five: Italy, Netherlands, Slovenia, Spain and Switzerland.

5. CONCLUSION

Our analysis of European data leaves us, unequivocally, on the verge of a reform of the role of the AFs. Modernisation will lead not only to defensive armies but also to armies working for peace. Corroboration of the coincident and divergent views expressed by future civil and military elites (university students and cadets) in their prioritisation of the principal threats facing Europe, the foreign policy priorities that should be set by government, and their approval of suitable roles for the army, reveals the existence of quite a closely shared perception of the risks, the definition – in precise terms – of the threat, a degree of approval for the army to be used in international non-combat missions and an important divergence of opinion over the definition of priorities.

In reference to threats to their security, the future civil and military elites consider the principal ones to be: (i) organised crime, (ii) international drug trafficking, (iii) terrorism in our country and (iv) an armed conflict over the control of vital raw materials (water, oil, etc.). For the future military elites – but not for the future civil elites – mass immigration from foreign countries is also an important threat; something similar occurs but vice-versa with respect to environmental problems such as air and water contamination. The Muslim world, in comparison with the other religions in its ranking of very important concerns, highlights: 'terrorism', 'an armed conflict over the control of vital raw materials', 'an armed conflict in the Middle East' and 'an accidental nuclear war'. The country-by-country analysis reveals how organised crime and international drug trafficking are perceived as threats by all university students in all countries with the exception of Spanish and Slovenian students, who do not perceive international drug trafficking as a principal threat. In addition to these threats, university students in Bulgaria, France, Italy, Holland, Poland, Sweden and Switzerland also consider environmental problems as a threat, as do Slovenian students without ranking them among their first two. Furthermore, Bulgaria, France, Italy and Holland, put in the top five as a threat the terrorism. The latter is also threatening for German, Romanian, South African, Spanish and Turkish students.

Inside the military, organised crime and international drug trafficking are considered crucial threats for all countries, with the exception of France in relation to organised crime and Spain in relation to both threats. Terrorism is highly ranked in Bulgaria, Turkey, Romania, South Africa, Sweden, France, Spain and Italy, too. And immigration is a threat for Holland, Slovenia, France, Spain and Switzerland. Finally, for Germans, Poles, Slovenians, Turks, the Spanish and the Swiss, an armed conflict over the control of vital raw materials is thought to be a latent threat. There is no country in which similar threats are perceived by the future civil and military elites, although the Germans, the Italians, the South Africans, the Turks and the Swiss only disagree over one point. On the other hand, the biggest rift exists among the French who register three differences.

Both the 'defence of the country' and 'the fight against terrorism' – the former conventional and the latter of more recent origin – are two missions that unambiguously belong to the combative role of an army. Conversely, the other three missions that were considered by a large majority as appropriate for the army correspond to new roles that are replacing the more conventional defensive ones: 'provision of disaster aid', 'humanitarian aid in foreign countries' and 'participation in peace-keeping missions'. That the cadets support the use of the military apparatus for peace-keeping operations and disaster aid indicates that they have taken on board more willingly than their commanding officers, the redefinition of their roles in response to the challenges presented by the new threats, roles which will continue to be compatible with their more conventional mission. Leaving aside the homogeneity of military and civil responses, it is noteworthy, but not surprising, that the responses of the cadets on the question of their adaptability to any role are always given much greater importance. That is to say, there is a high degree of similarity in the responses of cadets and university students on the adaptability of the armies to certain roles.

Similarities exist between the ranking of civil and military foreign policy goals. Whereas the cadets have more of a short-term agenda focusing on reactive security issues, university students have a wider one that integrates both reactive security and co-operation and development with other countries, involving preventive and proactive security strategies. So, 'preserving world peace', 'preventing the spread of weapons of mass destruction', 'maintaining the external security of their countries' and 'fighting terrorism' are all important goals in both worlds. For the future civil elites, the principal foreign policy goals are 'combating world hunger', 'fostering international cooperation to solve common problems, such as food shortages, inflation and energy' and 'defending human rights in other countries'.

If we confront country by country the top five foreign policies goals, on cadets and university students basis we can do a cultural gap typology.

'Total harmony': France, Germany, South Africa and Sweden. The civil–military cultural gap in this area and in these countries is inexistent. 'Strong harmony': Bulgaria, Romania, Poland and Turkey. There is a little cultural gap in this area in these countries. 'Limited harmony': Italy, Netherlands, Slovenia, Spain and Switzerland. The cultural gap in this area is very strong.

Undoubtedly, such a redefinition and adaptation of military missions to the new demands of a globalised world will eventually take precedence. In the short or medium term, it will mean that the very raison d'être of the army, today orientated around the defence of national territory, will have to adapt to new missions, the outcome of which might very possibly be a much more dramatic re-examination of what armies are and what they should represent. The modernisation of their armies will come about, at which time questions will arise stemming from the globalisation of threats and the required responses: (i) what are they for? (ii) how are they organised? In short, what will armies be like in the 21st century?

NOTES

1. Document adopted by the European Council, 12th of December, 2003 (European Union Institute for Security Studies).

2. This document defends the importance of increasing bilateral relationships with Japan, China, Canada and India.

3. The actual question was: This question asks you to evaluate the likelihood of each of the following threats to the national security of your country. Please use the scale below (Very likely, Rather likely, Not likely, Not at all likely). The list of potential threats was made up of the following: (i) Mass immigration from foreign countries. (ii) Terrorism in your country. (iii) International drug trafficking. (iv) Organised crime. (v) Environmental problems such as air pollution and water contamination. (vi) A possible indirect involvement in a civil war. (vii) An armed conflict between African countries with which we co-operate (viii) An armed conflict in the Middle East. (ix) Attacks on computer networks. (x) Nuclear blackmail by Third World countries. (xi) Nuclear war between Third World countries with global consequences. (x) An armed conflict between Asia countries. (xi) Proliferation of weapons of mass destruction. (xii) An accidental nuclear war. (xiii) An armed conflict over the control of vital raw materials (water, oil, etc.). In the text, we only refer to responses rated as 'very important'.

4. The weighting of interviewees by country was as follows: Bulgaria 4%, France 5%, Germany 12%, Italy 8%, Holland 10%, Poland 7%, Romania 6%, Slovenia 5%, South Africa 6%, Spain 9%, Sweden 10%, Switzerland 10%, Turkey 8%.

5. The proportion of military and civil interviewees by country was as follows: Bulgaria 25% cadets compared to 75% students, France 65%–35%, Germany 37%–63%, Italy 56%–44%, Holland 67%–33%, Poland 40%–60%, Romania 49%–51%, Slovenia 21%–79%, Spain 34%–66%, Sweden 64%–36%, Switzerland 36%–64%, Turkey 39%–61%.

6. The actual question was: The following are some possible uses of the military. Please indicate how much you approve of the *military being used* for the each of the following missions. The list of proposed missions was: (i) to defend our country, (ii) to participate in peace-keeping missions, (iii) to participate in peace-enforcement missions (missions against the will of local parties), (iv) to participate in combat missions, (v) to provide disaster relief, (vi) to provide humanitarian relief abroad, (vii) to deal with domestic disorder within our country, (viii) to combat drug trafficking, (ix) to prevent the proliferation of weapons of mass destruction, (x) to control mass immigration from foreign countries, (xi) to fight to terrorism and (xii) to contribute to the protection of the environment. Reference is only made in the text to 'very appropriate' answers.

7. Hence, in the opinion of the Chief of Army High Command, in 1996: 'foreign operations for humanitarian aid as well as for peace-keeping purposes or those hypothetically to re-establish peace, are not the principal objective of the AFs. The essence of our existence is the military defence of Spain and Spanish interests' (Faura Martín, 1996). Problem such as organised crime, drug trafficking, environmental damage and humanitarian disasters, the transformation of social, political and economic structures are problems which the military contingent will have to confront and for which it has not received sufficient training (Durán & Manuel, 1998).

In order to guarantee that it will be able to fulfill its duties conventional military training has to be interrupted and temporarily replaced by another more specifically orientated towards the roles to be undertaken. The United States army considers that peace missions distract the armed forces from its main aim to such an extent that units assigned to such missions undergo a process of recycling to correct any theoretical and practical deviance they might have experienced (Martínez Isidoro, 1996). It is their understanding that the units participating in peace missions have to receive a specific preparatory training that for the bulk of the army might be considered as 'contaminating'.

8. We believe that there is no room for doubt that the so-called 'new missions' of the armed forces have supposed and do indeed represent the very best opportunity to redefine armies. The successive Directives on national defence issued by Spanish governments since 1992 reiterate, one after another, the need for Spanish society to 'understand, support and feel committed to the objectives pursued' by Defence Policies; for this reason, the government cannot overlook the beneficial effect that peace missions have had on the social acceptance of the armed forces as more than 50% of the population says that participation in these missions has meant that their opinion of the army has improved:

Following the participation of Spain in peace missions, would you say your opinion of the Armed Forces?

Options	1997	1998	1999	2000	Average
Has improved	51	51	52	59	*53*
Has worsened	3	3	2	2	*3*
Has remained more or less the same	39	38	40	32	*37*
Don't know/No Comment	7	8	6	7	*7*
Total	100	100	100	100	100

Source: CIS (*Centro de Investigación Sociológico*) Surveys 2.234, 2.277, 2317 and 2379

9. The actual question was: Here is a list of possible foreign policy goals that your country might have. Please indicate how much importance you think should be attached to each goal. The list of proposed goals was: (i) Helping to improve the standard of living in less-developed countries, (ii) worldwide arms control, (iii) combating world hunger, (iv) strengthening the United Nations, (v) fostering international co-operation to solve common problems, such as food, inflation and energy, (vi) preserve world peace, (vii) preventing the spread of weapons of mass destruction, (viii) promoting and defending human rights in other countries, (ix) helping to bring a democratic form of government to other nations, (x) strengthening regional security alliances or agreements (NATO, for example), (xi) maintaining the external security of your country and (xii) fighting terrorism.

In the text, we only make reference to responses graded as 'very important'.

10. As happened in the USA with the 'Project on the Gap Between Military and Civilian Society' funded by the Triangle Institute for Security Studies (TISS) (Feaver & Kohn, 2001), the answers in both worlds show little similarity, except for the 'maintaining superior military power worldwide' option. A goal that was ranked in

fourth place by the future civil elites, far removed in percentage terms from the aggregate response of both civil and military elites and, of course, from the military response. Both the TISS and ERGOMAS questionnaires are similar, but each one offers a different set of possible answers (eight are similar and four are different) and the different options are those chosen by participants. Nevertheless, considerable similarities exist between European and North American responses. Both place in first place 'Preventing the spread of nuclear weapons or weapons of mass destruction' and 'Fostering international cooperation to solve common problems' – as in Europe, this goal is a more strongly felt one in civil society. It can also be seen how military cadets give more importance to hard security goals, whereas university students tend to support preventive goals such as 'Cooperation with third world countries'. For instance, half of the non-veteran civilian leaders consider that combating world hunger is very important; a view only shared by 15% of military leaders and 20% of active reserve leaders.

11. It should be highlighted that this issue is rated 29% percentage points higher by German women than it is by German men; the same is true for Swedish women (21%) in relation to their men folk, as it is for Swiss women (20%), Spanish women (17%) and French women (16%).

12. By the same token, this issue is rated 25% percentage points higher by German women than it is by German men, as it is by Swedish and French women (23%), Swiss women (18%), Bulgarian women (15%) and Polish women (14%).

13. Once again, higher ratings by a margin of 37% are given by German women to this issue than German men, and the same is true for Romanian women (20%), Spanish women (19%) and French women (18%).

14. Both German and French women (21% and 12% respectively) attach greater importance to this issue than their men folk.

15. On this point, greater importance is attached by Slovenian men (28%) than by Slovenian women, and the same is true for Bulgarian men (18%) and Turkish men (16%).

16. 'Preserving world peace', 76%; 'Fighting terrorism', 63%; 'Preventing the spread of weapons of mass destruction', 63%; 'Maintaining the external security of your country', 60%; 'Combating world hunger' 55%, 'Fostering international cooperation to solve common problems, such as food, inflation, and energy' 54%; 'Promoting and defending human rights in other countries', 53%.

ACKNOWLEDGMENT

We express our thanks to Marian Zulean and Gerhard Kümmel for their help with the analysis of the data presented in this article.

REFERENCE

Durán, R., & Manuel, M. (1998). Nuevos requerimientos de preparación en os los estudios militares ante las nuevas misiones de las fuerzas armadas. *Cuadernos del CESEDEN*, no 24, Madrid, Ministerio de Defensa.

Faura, M. J. (1996). *El ejército español ante los desafíos del siglo XXI*, ABC, 6-VI.

Feaver, P. D., & Kohn, R. H. (Eds). (2001). *Soldiers and civilians. The civil–military gap and American national security triangle institute for security studies*. Cambridge and London: MIT Press.

Martínez Isidoro, R., (1996). La defensa nacional y las operaciones de paz. *Cuadernos de Estrategia*, no. 82. Madrid: Instituto Español de Estudios Estratégicos, Ministerio de defensa.

Martínez M. R. (2000). La proyección social de las nuevas misiones de las FAS. *Cuadernos del Instituto Universitario General Gutiérrez Mellado* (Vol. 1, pp. 106–129).

DEMOCRATIC CONTROL OVER THE ARMED FORCES

Ljubica Jelušič

ABSTRACT

The study on democratic control over the armed forces elaborates on perceptions of the respondents in 13 countries on interaction between democratically elected political power and the military. The views of the civilian and military students are similar on many issues that relate to the role of the military in society. There are also some differences in their opinion. Civilian students are more open towards public statements and the public influence of the military than the military students, who seem to be socialised in subordinate position towards the public, and who understood the military professionalism in terms of professional autonomy. This difference is a result of the professional socialisation and correlates with the professional culture of different occupational and professional groups.

1. THE FRAMEWORK OF THE STUDY

The relation between military organisation and the civilian environment can be shaped in different ways: in some countries, the civilians are executing firm oversight over the armed forces, whereas in some other countries the

Cultural Differences between the Military and Parent Society in Democratic Countries
Contributions to Conflict Management, Peace Economics and Development, Volume 4, 161–176

ISSN: 1572-8323/doi:10.1016/S1572-8323(07)04007-6

military can perform its duties regarding national security in its own, autonomous way, if not even in the way where the military imposes its principles of governance over the citizens. In the contemporary society, the last, i.e. military-dominated political systems are rare. More common are civilian-dominated political systems, in which civilian political leaders control the military in very authoritative way, or where the whole civilian environment through the channels of the democratic control over the military imposes the tasks, the execution of tasks and respect for democracy in the inner-military organisational structures. The redefinition of the roles, organisation and financing are the worldwide adaptation processes that shape the changing relationship between armed forces and the societies in the post-Cold War era (Forster, 2006, p. 1). The issue of the democratic control over the armed forces is sometimes confused with the term civilian control over the armed forces, which can be democratic, but it may happen to be also very authoritative and executed by totalitarian civilian rule (civilian dictatorship). Some authors, like Forster (2006) and Forster, Edmunds, and Cottey (2003), consider the term "democratic civilian control" as interaction between the armed forces and the civilian political authorities. The topic is becoming one of the most likely analysed after the end of the Cold War, mostly due to the expectation that the crisis of military legitimacy that affected mainly the south-western and eastern Europe, would finish in attempts of the military dominance over the civilian political systems. Europe was, as Born, Haltiner, and Malešič (2006) claimed, exposed to the renaissance of an old issue.

In this chapter, we will use the term democratic control over the military, as most common expression of the interaction, in which the armed forces are considered to be controlled by the democratically elected members of the executive, judiciary and representative political power and by the civilian society, to which security interests the armed forces serve. Armed forces can, on the other side, express their views on the defence and security policy of the society in the context and by means, considered to be acceptable in the democratic standard of civil–military relations. Taking into account the methodological limitations of the survey, the chapter will discuss the democratic control as the surveyed population in 13 countries, included into the research, perceives it and not as it objectively is in the respective countries.

Therefore, we are not going to investigate the level of democratic control in the real political systems, because our collected research materials did not allow us to make conclusions about the real status of the democratic control over the military. In order to do so, we would need to analyse the roles and responsibilities of the main branches of the state, concerning the security sector in general, and also the armed forces as part of that security sector. We would have to find out the shared responsibilities of the government and the parliament in keeping a well functioning of the military, division of roles between the executive, legislature and judiciary branches of the state in fulfilling their major roles in national security policy in general. We would have to elaborate on the roles of the parliament, the judiciary and the executive (the head of state, the governmental cabinet, the chief of General Staff) in formulating and implementing the oversight over the armed forces. In addition to the three state braches, civil society makes an important informal contribution to this oversight, while the media contribute by informing the public of the intentions and actions of all state sectors (Born, Fluri, & Johnsson, 2003, p. 20). There are also some other institutions that play the crucial role in overseeing the implementation of the security policy, and among them the Ombudsman as human rights watch and the Auditor General as controller of spending the military budget, should at least be mentioned.

The democratic countries have different structures to execute the controlling roles, because no internationally agreed standards in the field of the democratic oversight exist (Born et al., 2003, p. 22). This behaviour is falling into the domain of the national sovereignty. Having been aware of this fact, the researchers in the project on "Cultural dimensions of civil–military relations in democratic society" decided to survey the public perception of the mutual understanding between high political leaders and the high-ranking military officials, and the perception of sharing common values between high political leaders, high-ranking military officials and the civil society. We posed the questions in this respect to the people who were in education process to become future civilian and military elites (university students and cadets of the military academies/candidates for officer ranks). Our hypothesis was that if the candidates for civilian and military elites have similar perceptions regarding the shared responsibilities between parliament, judiciary, government and civil society in respect to the democratic control over the armed forces, while they are in the process of their professional socialisation, they would develop their student perceptions into firm attitudes while becoming the civilian/military elite members themselves. If the perceptions are close to one another, the civil–military gap is going to diminish in future, if the perceptions are very apart, the civil–military gap will continue to shape the life of the democratic society in future.

The indicators to measure the perception of the democratic control over the military organisation were manifold. We asked the surveyed population about the knowledge that political leaders have about the modern military and about the values that political and military leaders share with country people. Additionally, we tried to find out, what is, according to the surveyed population's opinion, the military's role in the civil society. It was also important to know, how the future elites regard the relation between military profession and the political leadership in terms of military subordination to the political leaders and professional autonomy of the military. The question on social representation or social diversity in the military was also posed. Knowing that we conduct the survey among students who will in the future form the military and civilian elite, we also tried to find out the ratio between the importance of the principles regarding democratic control over the armed forces and the realisation of these same principles in the country of the respondents.

2. KNOWLEDGE ABOUT THE MODERN MILITARY

The clashes between civilian society and the military reasoning sometimes exist because there is a lack of knowledge regarding the main tasks of both parties in the national security complex. The perception of the civilian society on what are the military tasks may be very different from what the military supposes to execute as the national security provider. This misperception may be caused by the tendency of the military to develop professional autonomy within the questions of the national security in general (not only the military security) or by a poor knowledge regarding the modern military structure among members of the civilian society. If the ordinary people have false perceptions, this might lead to the decreasing legitimacy of the military (Jelušič, 1997).

If the political leaders have poor knowledge on the subject, which they are supposed to control and orient its behaviour, the question might arise whether the political leaders are able to execute sufficient control over the armed forces, and if not, what this disadvantage might cause in tendency of the military to get out of the control and execute the military policy in accordance with the military corporate interests. The straight answer cannot be expectation of the military coup d'état or military predominance in political system, because there are other ways of controlling the military behaviour in the contemporary society, for example self-perception of the military to be subordinated to the political system, poor knowledge of the military on inabilities of the political leaders or even international pressure towards the subordinated role of the military in society.

The reasons why the political leaders may have poor knowledge of the military issues may be inherited in the fact that the current elites have no common organised way of getting the knowledge on these issues. The fact of declining the mass armies (Haltiner, 1998), the overwhelming changes of the manning of the military from compulsory military service to the small constabulary all-volunteer forces in many European and North American countries, caused the decrease of commonly shared military knowledge in the society, at least among the male population. The problem is how to fill in the gap that was caused in the civilian knowledge, if the service which helped to understand the basic features of the military, ceased to exist. Is there any other public services or organisations that help political leaders to learn about the military? Usually, the truth is that the political leaders are learning by doing – the politics on national security.

The intention of our survey was to find out if the civilian and military students share the same perception regarding their political elite or not. The respondents gave the evaluation on how knowledgeable are the political leaders about the modern military. The data show that all respondents have some doubts regarding political leaders' knowledge about the modern military. The differences between civilian students and military cadets in their evaluation that political leaders are somewhat ignorant towards the military are not high. The Italian, Swiss and French respondents regarded the knowledge of the politicians on the military in a better way comparing to the respondents from other countries, whereas the Swedish respondents are at the other extreme, claiming the ignorance of the political leaders in the highest percentage (see Table 1)[1].

3. SHARING SAME VALUES

Democratic control over the armed forces may be stronger if the military elites and the political leaders share the same values as the citizens of the country. It means that the gap between military elites and civilians at one side; and the gap between the political elites and the citizens at the other side may show the circumstances in which the democratic control is executed. The data presented in Table 2 show that all respondents recognised the differences in this relation. The military cadets have shown more readiness to claim military leaders having the same values as the country people than the university students.

What is the impression of the political leaders and their values in comparison to the country people? The surveyed population has similar critical opinion on them, as was the case with military leaders. The majority tends to see the gap in sharing same values with citizens. The data show that the

Table 1. Civilian Knowledge About the Modern Military (M).

Sample	Cadets (M)	Students (M)	Total (M)
All countries	2.91	2.81	2.86
Bulgaria	3.13	2.96	3.00
France	2.53	2.77	2.62
Germany	3.12	3.12	3.12
Italy	2.58	2.53	2.56
Netherlands	2.87	2.68	2.81
Poland	3.14	2.99	3.05
Romania	2.72	3.02	2.87
Slovenia	2.86	2.75	2.77
South Africa	2.65	2.66	2.66
Spain	3.07	2.69	2.81
Sweden	3.31	2.93	3.17
Switzerland	2.61	2.60	2.61
Turkey	2.96	2.78	2.85

Q10: How knowledgeable do you think our political leaders are about the modern military? Answers: 1 – very knowledgeable; 2 – somewhat knowledgeable; 3 – somewhat ignorant; 4 – very ignorant.

Table 2. Civil–Military Value Gap.

Sample	Cadets (M)	Students (M)	Total (M)
All countries	1.95	2.19	2.09
Bulgaria	2.17	2.30	2.26
France	1.85	2.29	2.01
Germany	1.78	1.77	1.77
Italy	1.80	2.12	1.94
Netherlands	2.15	2.31	2.20
Poland	2.09	2.34	2.24
Romania	1.97	2.16	2.07
Slovenia	1.74	2.42	2.27
South Africa	1.96	2.11	2.07
Spain	2.10	2.35	2.26
Sweden	2.12	2.23	2.16
Switzerland	1.76	2.30	2.10
Turkey	1.70	2.13	1.96

Q11: Do you think military leaders, in general, share the same values as our country people? Answers: 1 – yes; 2 – no; 3 – not sure; 4 – no opinion.

university students were more inclined to state that the political leaders do not share the same values as the country people and they also have no opinion on this issues more frequently than the military cadets. Bulgarian, Italian, Slovenian, Swedish and Turkish cadets and candidates for military

Table 3. Political Leaders' Values versus Citizens Values.

Sample	Cadets (M)	Students (M)	Total (M)
All countries	2.11	2.18	2.15
Bulgaria	2.43	2.27	2.31
France	1.84	2.30	2.00
Germany	1.90	2.08	2.01
Italy	2.23	2.18	2.21
Netherlands	2.04	2.06	2.05
Poland	2.18	2.28	2.24
Romania	2.18	2.16	2.17
Slovenia	2.29	2.19	2.21
South Africa	2.02	2.06	2.05
Spain	2.14	2.28	2.23
Sweden	2.26	2.23	2.25
Switzerland	1.98	2.07	2.04
Turkey	2.20	2.31	2.27

Q12: Do you think political leaders in general share the same values as our country people?
Answers: 1 – yes; 2 – no; 3 – not sure; 4 – no opinion.

officers were less sure in their evaluation of the political leaders' values. The majority of their answers were between having no opinion and being not sure about the statement (see Table 3).

4. THE ROLE OF THE MILITARY IN SOCIETY

The principles of democratic control of the military claim the subordination of the military to the political authorities. This subordination may be understood in very different ways, although there are some general commonly expected ways of military behaviour, which should be implemented in every country, where the democratic control is introduced. One of these commonly agreed (not formally proclaimed, but introduced on the basis of good practices) principles is the public appearances of the military leaders, who are not allowed, or allowed to the certain extend, to make public statements on the behaviour of the members of the government. In some countries, the public also expects the military to restrain from public criticism about the parent society.

The German, Slovenian, Swedish and Swiss respondents disagreed to a certain extend, above average of the total of respondents, with the statement that the military should not publicly criticise the members of the government. It means that they are more ready to accept the military's public

Table 4. Military should/not Criticise the Government.

Sample	Cadets (M)	Students (M)	Total (M)
All countries	2.09	2.42	2.27
Bulgaria	2.04	2.45	2.35
France	1.48	2.04	1.68
Germany	2.52	2.77	2.68
Italy	1.80	2.11	1.93
Netherlands	2.23	2.28	2.25
Poland	2.16	2.34	2.27
Romania	2.03	2.44	2.24
Slovenia	1.91	2.74	2.56
South Africa	1.70	2.16	2.02
Spain	1.70	2.17	2.00
Sweden	2.30	2.67	2.43
Switzerland	2.45	2.64	2.57
Turkey	1.97	2.11	2.05

Q17: What is your opinion on the following statements concerning the military's role in civil society?
A: Members of the military should not publicly criticise members of the government.
Answers: 1 – agree strongly; 2 – agree somewhat; 3 – disagree somewhat; 4 – disagree strongly; 5 – no opinion.

statements on the government. French and Italian respondents are less ready to accept the possibility of having democracy also in the case of the military's public appearances. They agreed to the highest level and far below average of the respondents with the statement, that the military should not publicly criticise members of the government (see Table 4).

This statement caused higher disagreement between university students and cadets. In all countries, the university students disagreed to the higher level with abandonment of the right of the military to criticise the government. It seems that military cadets are exposed to the specific socialisation in which they are trained to keep away from public criticism. The self-imposed limitations in criticism regarding the government or parent society were confirmed in military agreement with statement on political rights of the military's members. Military cadets did not agree with permission given to the members of the military to publicly express their political views just like any other citizen (see Table 6). In this case, the university students proved to be more democratic in recognising same human rights to the military people as to the civilians.

Similar findings were result of the question in which the respondents expressed their agreement with the statement that the military should not

Table 5. The Military should/not Criticise the Parent Society.

Sample	Cadets (M)	Students (M)	Total (M)
All countries	2.23	2.39	2.32
Bulgaria	2.04	2.12	2.10
France	2.01	2.08	2.04
Germany	2.93	2.97	2.96
Italy	2.11	2.15	2.12
Netherlands	2.27	2.27	2.27
Poland	1.99	1.92	1.95
Romania	2.10	2.33	2.22
Slovenia	2.26	2.77	2.66
South Africa	1.71	2.17	2.03
Spain	1.60	1.90	1.80
Sweden	2.38	2.77	2.52
Switzerland	2.73	2.75	2.74
Turkey	1.99	2.16	2.09

Q17: What is your opinion on the following statements concerning the military's role in civil society?
B: Members of the military should not publicly criticise their parent civil society.
Answers: 1 – agree strongly; 2 – agree somewhat; 3 – disagree somewhat; 4 – disagree strongly; 5 – no opinion.

publicly criticise their parent society (see Table 5). German, Slovenian, Swedish and Swiss respondents are more open towards the military and would, above average, agree with the military criticism of the parent society. The opinions of the students and of the military cadets were very similar.

The agreement of having "citizens in uniform" was checked with the statement that the military should be allowed to publicly express their political views. Tables 6–8 show that military cadets agreed with such option, above average, in Germany and Switzerland.

There were no doubts regarding the open political influence of the military. The majority of the respondents disagreed with the statement that the military should have political influence in the society (see Table 9).

5. DEMOCRATIC PRINCIPLES: IMPORTANCE AND REALISATION

The survey aimed at the comparison of the importance of the democratic principles for the respondents personally and of the principles' realisation in the country of the surveyed respondents. The results of the comparison

Table 6. Citizens in Uniform Express their Political Views.

Sample	Cadets (M)	Students (M)	Total (M)
All countries	2.37	2.00	2.16
Bulgaria	2.61	2.25	2.33
France	2.94	2.23	2.70
Germany	1.97	1.74	1.83
Italy	2.82	1.95	2.45
Netherlands	2.36	2.35	2.36
Poland	2.15	1.98	2.05
Romania	2.01	1.80	1.90
Slovenia	2.80	2.08	2.24
South Africa	2.70	1.96	2.19
Spain	2.60	2.03	2.23
Sweden	2.02	1.74	1.92
Switzerland	1.78	1.67	1.71
Turkey	3.05	2.66	2.82

Q17: What is your opinion on the following statements concerning the military's role in civil society?
C: Members of the military should be allowed to publicly express their political views just like any other citizen.
Answers: 1 – agree strongly; 2 – agree somewhat; 3 – disagree somewhat; 4 – disagree strongly; 5 – no opinion.

Table 7. Military should Defend the Government's Views.

Sample	Cadets (M)	Students (M)	Total (M)
All countries	2.62	2.52	2.57
Bulgaria	3.16	2.25	2.45
France	3.07	2.76	2.96
Germany	2.50	2.54	2.52
Italy	2.98	2.52	2.79
Netherlands	2.29	2.42	2.33
Poland	2.98	2.75	2.85
Romania	2.93	2.65	2.79
Slovenia	2.88	2.89	2.89
South Africa	2.12	2.14	2.13
Spain	3.16	2.65	2.83
Sweden	2.12	1.98	2.07
Switzerland	2.05	2.44	2.30
Turkey	3.05	2.76	2.87

Q17: What is your opinion on the following statements concerning the military's role in civil society?
D: It is proper for the military to explain and defend in public the policies of the government.
Answers: 1 – agree strongly; 2 – agree somewhat; 3 – disagree somewhat; 4 – disagree strongly; 5 – no opinion.

Table 8. Military Advocacy of Defence Interests.

Sample	Cadets (M)	Students (M)	Total (M)
All countries	2.05	1.93	1.98
Bulgaria	2.15	1.54	1.68
France	2.56	2.04	2.39
Germany	1.93	1.87	1.89
Italy	2.15	1.84	2.02
Netherlands	2.07	2.16	2.10
Poland	1.86	1.85	1.85
Romania	1.94	1.67	1.81
Slovenia	2.67	2.09	2.22
South Africa	1.83	1.77	1.79
Spain	2.24	1.92	2.03
Sweden	1.87	1.74	1.83
Switzerland	1.71	2.16	1.98
Turkey	2.22	2.20	2.21

Q17: What is your opinion on the following statements concerning the military's role in civil society?
E: It is proper for the military to advocate publicly the military policies it believes are in the best interests of the country.
Answers: 1 – agree strongly; 2 – agree somewhat; 3 – disagree somewhat; 4 – disagree strongly; 5 – no opinion.

Table 9. Military should have Political Influence.

Sample	Cadets (M)	Students (M)	Total (M)
All countries	2.87	3.20	3.05
Bulgaria	2.63	3.13	3.01
France	3.05	3.17	3.09
Germany	3.09	3.28	3.21
Italy	2.93	2.82	2.88
Netherlands	2.95	3.24	3.05
Poland	2.87	3.08	3.00
Romania	2.40	2.90	2.65
Slovenia	3.48	3.34	3.37
South Africa	2.89	2.81	2.83
Spain	2.99	3.39	3.26
Sweden	2.33	2.80	2.50
Switzerland	2.98	3.65	3.40
Turkey	3.25	3.32	3.29

Q17: What is your opinion on the following statements concerning the military's role in civil society?
F: It is proper for the military to have direct political influence in the society.
Answers: 1 – agree strongly; 2 – agree somewhat; 3 – disagree somewhat; 4 – disagree strongly; 5 – no opinion.

would show if respondents are aware of the necessity of democratic control over the armed forces. The principles of democracy have been surveyed on the level of the individual like: equality of people, regardless of gender, race, religion; respect for the individuals and their basic freedoms like: freedom of assembly, ideas, speech, press, safeguard of the individual opportunities and responsibilities; on the level of the respect for the way of life within the country, subordination of the military to the political leadership and the integration of the military in the parent society; and finally on the level of peaceful relations with other societies in the world.

Majority of respondents answered that the mentioned principles are very or rather important for them, and at the same time, the majority said that these principles are rather unrealised or unrealised at all within their respective countries. The respondents were expressing the agreement with the principles that affects their personal or group standard of democracy, and they were also very much in favour of the integration of the military to the parent society. The importance of the military subordination to the civilian political leaders was slightly lower than other principles. Regardless of the importance of this principle, the majority realised its high realisation in their countries. So, we may conclude that higher level of realisation of the principle of subordination of the military to the political leaders diminished the importance of this principle for the respondents. All other principles are according to the respondents' opinion less realised within the countries. That explains their higher awareness of the importance of the (less realised) principles, like integration of the military in the parent society, safeguard of the individual opportunities and responsibilities, respect for individuals, or equality of people (Table 10).

6. INTERACTION BETWEEN THE MILITARY ELITE AND POLITICAL LEADERS

The interaction between the military and political elite has been surveyed through different indicators, among them we asked the respondents to express the agreement with the statements in which the subordination of the military professionals to the political leadership was indicated. On the other hand, we also tried to find out, how much our respondents agree with the process of recognising the professional autonomy of the military. The respondents were very unique in expecting the subordination of the military profession to the political leadership. On the contrary, the two samples have had different opinions on the statement that the politicians should give

Table 10. Importance and Realisation of the Democratic Principles.

Sample from all countries	Cadets (M)		Students (M)		Total (M)	
Importance (I) versus realisation (R)	I	R	I	R	I	R
Equality of people	1.53	2.13	1.33	2.36	1.42	2.26
Respect for individuals	1.38	2.30	1.27	2.45	1.32	2.38
Basic freedoms of the individuals	1.46	1.80	1.32	2.03	1.38	1.93
Respect for the national basic law	1.44	2.20	1.58	2.28	1.52	2.25
Safeguard of the individual opportunities and responsibilities	1.63	2.30	1.57	2.48	1.60	2.40
Defence of the societal system and the way of life of the country	1.68	2.20	1.83	2.28	1.76	2.25
Peaceful relationship with the other societies in the world	1.64	1.82	1.59	1.90	1.61	1.87
Subordination of the military to the political leadership	2.11	1.80	2.17	2.00	2.15	1.91
Integration of the military in the parent society	1.76	2.48	2.29	2.57	2.05	2.53

Q35: How important are the following principles for you?
Answers for importance: 1 – very important; 2 – rather important; 3 – rather unimportant; 4 – very unimportant; 5 – no opinion.
Q36: How well do you consider that each of the principles is realised in our country?
Answers for realisation: 1 – completely realised; 2 – rather realised; 3 – rather unrealised; 4 – unrealised at all; 5 – no opinion.

Table 11. Agreement with the Statements on Military and Society.

Sample	Cadets (M)	Students (M)	Total (M)
The military profession is subordinate to the political leadership	1.84	1.95	1.90
Politicians must give professional autonomy to the military	1.92	2.36	2.16
The military should represent the parent civil society with regard to the social and ethnic groups and classes	2.41	2.47	2.44

Q37: How far do you agree with the following statements?
Answers: 1 – agree strongly; 2 – agree somewhat; 3 – disagree somewhat; 4 – disagree strongly; 5 – no opinion.

professional autonomy to the military. The majority of the military cadets agreed somewhat and strongly with this statement. University students had different opinion – they disagreed with the transfer of the professional autonomy to the military (see Table 11).

On the basis of the respondents' view, we may conclude that the ideal of social and ethnic representation of the society in the military is the outdated model of the military. Cadets and students shared similar opinion in disagreement with the statement that the military should represent the parent civil society with regard to the social and ethnic groups and classes. It might be that all respondents are more and more aware of the obstacles posed to the proportional social representation which has never fully occurred in past.

7. CONCLUSION

The democratic control over the armed forces is one of those issues that show some differences between university students and military cadets in all surveyed countries, but we cannot say that these differences may be observed in the same countries as consistent pattern. In most cases, the future elites represented the prevailing policy in their respective countries. For example, Germany has introduced the concept of the citizens in uniform as a pattern of diminishing gap between the military professionals and civilians. German students and cadets consequently agreed with all statements in which we stated the autonomous and socially engaged military, like military should criticise members of the government and civil society, should express publicly their political views and should defend publicly the military policies. But when it comes to the direct political influence of the military, also German students and cadets would highly disapprove such actions.

The respondents were asked about their perception of the interaction between the military elite and political leaders. All respondents have shown some doubts in the politicians' knowledge of the modern military. As the values of the military elite are concerned, the military cadets are more inclined to diminish the perceived gap in sharing the same values with the parent society, while students, on the other hand, less likely believe in the coherence of the military–civilian values. The students also perceive the gap between the civilian political elite values and the parent society values more likely than the military cadets.

The opinion of the respondents regarding the military criticism of the government and of the parent society was dispersed. The military cadets were less prepared to agree with public critical statements of the military than civilian students. Military cadets in comparison to the students expressed lower agreement with the right of the military to publicly express their political views like any other citizens. Students and cadets have had similar opinion, when they did not agreed with the statement that military should defend the policies of the government. University students again agreed to the higher extend with the military advocacy of the policies it believes are in the best interests of the country. This result confirm previously mentioned more moderate attitude of the students towards the democratic and human rights of the military. The cadets, on the contrary, more firmly agreed with the prohibition of all military attempts to have public appearances. All respondents disagreed with possibility that the military has direct political influence in the society. All respondents are aware and evaluated as important for them the principles of democracy in society, but they also stated that the majority of these principles are rather unrealised in their countries.

The interesting finding concerns the realisation of the military subordination to the civilian political power, which is, according to the respondents' views higher than in cases of other democratic principles. The professional autonomy of the military was more relevant to the military cadets as to the university students. The general conclusion leads us to the finding that all respondents are aware and agree with the importance of the democratic control over the military. The only cases where there are different opinions between the military cadets and university students are regarding the right of the military to publicly make statements and the transfer of the professional autonomy to the military. Students are more democratic than cadets in leaving the military its right to have public influence, and cadets are more likely to expect the professional autonomy of the military than the civilian students.

NOTE

1. The data in all tables are presented by Mean values.

REFERENCES

Born, H., Fluri, P., & Johnsson, A. B. (2003). *Parliamentary oversight over the security sector: Principles, mechanisms and practices*. Geneva: Geneva Centre for the Democratic Control Over the Armed Forces, Interparliamentary Union.

Born, H., Haltiner, K. W., & Malešič, M. (2006). *Renaissance of democratic control of armed forces in contemporary societies*. Baden-Baden: Nomos Verlag.

Forster, A. (2006). *Armed forces and society in Europe*. Hampshire, New York: Palgrave MacMillan.

Forster, A., Edmunds, T., & Cottey, A. (2003). *Soldiers and societies in postcommunist Europe. Legitimacy and change*. Hampshire, New York: Palgrave MacMillan.

Haltiner, K. W. (1998). The definite end of the mass army in western Europe? *Armed Forces & Society*, 25(1), 7–36.

Jelušič, L. (1997). *Legitimnost sodobnega vojaštva (Legitimacy of the military)*. Ljubljana: Fakulteta za družbene vede.

NEW MISSIONS AND THE CHANGING CHARACTER OF MILITARY ORGANISATIONS

Lindy Heinecken

ABSTRACT

In the post Cold War era, military organisations have grappled with the challenge of how to bridge the gap between their mandate, the demands placed upon them by the new security environment and other pressing political concerns. To reflect on this, this chapter examines the responses of officers and civilian students from 13 countries on a range of issues, namely how they perceive the use of armed forces in various missions, the priority assigned to these missions; the importance and mandate of international security organisations; the status of the military within society as their role becomes more international; and the willingness of citizens to serve in the armed forces, given that these missions are often abroad. Judging from the findings, it appears as if there are a number of critical concerns regarding the future role, functioning and character of military organisations, which may be attributed to the emergence of a civil–military gap in many societies.

Cultural Differences between the Military and Parent Society in Democratic Countries
Contributions to Conflict Management, Peace Economics and Development, Volume 4, 177–199

ISSN: 1572-8323/doi:10.1016/S1572-8323(07)04008-8

INTRODUCTION

Contrary to what was expected the end of the Cold War has not seen the decline in the relevance of armed forces. In fact, armed forces across the world are busier than ever before, but not for what they are trained for – to fight wars. Today armed forces are deployed in an array of tasks to combat threats of a non-military trans-national nature most of which are rooted in political, economic, societal, environmental and to a lesser extent military considerations (Smith, 2000, pp. 77–91). Typical examples include the threat posed by organised crime, terrorism, arms trafficking, illegal international immigration, global environmental degradation and disease.

To combat these threats, armed forces are increasingly deployed together with alliance partners in missions commonly referred to as military operations other than war (MOOTW). Depending on the task in hand, these have ranged from classic peacekeeping and humanitarian missions to more muscular peace-enforcement operations abroad, to rendering assistance to police in controlling mass immigration, ethnic conflicts, urban terror and criminal activities within their own territories. What makes these new threats so different is that even where they pose no direct threat to national security or even a state's interests, the international community has been unable to ignore them either for moral, humanitarian, political or economic reasons.

This has sparked huge debates both within the armed forces and broader society about the use of the armed forces in such roles, the priority assigned to them and the role international security organisations should play in co-ordinating, facilitating and controlling the use of armed forces in combating threats to global peace and stability. However, the extensive deployment in these missions has placed enormous strain on national armed forces at a time when public support has given way to other more pressing social concerns. Most armed forces were (and some still are) trained, structured and funded for their core function – warfighting. What these missions required was more adaptive, flexible and mobile armed forces to deal with a broad range of tasks. This posed considerable organisational challenges to armed forces, as a growing mismatch between military missions and the capabilities needed by the armed forces to meet these obligations emerged in terms of personnel, equipment and overall capacity (Feaver & Kohn, 2001, p. 467).

As regards personnel, the increasing realisation that one would be deployed in (dangerous) missions far away from home, often under arduous conditions in some foreign country has resulted in increasing problems of recruitment and retention. In an attempt to meet recruitment deficits many armed forces have been obliged to lower recruitment standards and enrol groups previously considered unsuited for military service (Morgan, 2001, pp. 104–105). Any return to conscription to solve recruitment deficits or obtain the necessary skills is considered neither economically viable, nor socially acceptable. Some ascribe this recruitment dilemma as "indicative of a weakened link between the armed forces and society" – a consequence of the decline in the status and growing distance between civil society and the military (Morgan, 2001, p. 105).

With this brief background, the aim of this chapter is to analyse the responses of officers and civilian students towards a range of issues concerning the deployment of armed forces in these new missions, the priority assigned to them, the importance of international security organs, the status of the military in society and willingness of citizens to serve in the armed forces. An evaluation of the empirical results justifies the concern that a civil–military gap does exist and evokes a number of critical concerns regarding the future role, functioning and nature of military organisations.

DATA ANALYSIS

Use of Military in Various Missions

The increasing deployment of the armed forces in MOOTW raises the question of whether the armed forces should be used in these tasks where they are required not to fight, but to protect, help and save mostly civilians in countries to which they often feel no allegiance. Accordingly, respondents were asked to comment on whether they approved or disapproved of the use of the armed forces in a wide spectrum of tasks (see Table 1). If one analyses the combined positive responses[1] of the various uses of the military very clear trends emerge.

Firstly, there is widespread support for the military to be used in a wide range of missions, with the highest support for roles that involve defence of the homeland/country (96%), disaster relief (92%), peacekeeping operations (91%), rendering humanitarian relief (86%), fighting terrorism (82%) and combating the spread of weapons of mass destruction (77%). As regards law-enforcement tasks, the military's involvement in curtailing domestic disorder (69%), drug-trafficking (58%) and controlling mass immigration (46%) is slightly less supported. Of interest is that those missions that

Table 1. Support for Military Missions by Country (in Percentage).

Variable	Frequency	Country												
		Bulgaria	France	Germany	Italy	Netherlands	Poland	Romania	Slovenia	South Africa	Spain	Sweden	Switzerland	Turkey
Defend country	96	96	95	98	96	97	99	99	97	97	89	99	89	98
Peacekeeping	91	84	96	94	91	97	92	80	81	90	90	98	87	86
Peace-enforcement	59	65	70	57	68	77	57	55	30	73	46	86	40	61
Combat missions	53	34	86	53	51	74	59	46	20	78	37	66	22	59
Disaster relief	92	97	93	98	93	86	97	87	99	95	93	95	94	69
Humanitarian relief	86	87	74	91	79	88	82	83	93	80	81	88	93	74
Weapons mass destruction	77	86	80	66	89	80	93	92	78	86	71	44	55	71
Fight terrorism	82	89	87	76	90	83	95	95	75	89	76	85	58	90
Domestic disorder	69	91	63	52	87	74	76	68	56	82	62	82	63	61
Drug trafficking	58	84	53	25	77	61	78	80	60	79	60	50	40	51
Control mass immigration	46	55	41	18	74	41	66	44	42	79	47	39	50	37
Protect environment	58	78	45	38	66	54	69	57	81	78	58	53	69	39

evoked the most likely use of the legitimate use of force or violence, namely peace-enforcement (59%) and combat missions (53%), received the least support (Table 1).

In terms of country comparisons, there was consensus that the military should be used to protect the country (>95%), although the degree of support by country varied, particularly with respect to Spain and Switzerland (<90%). Support for participation in peacekeeping missions was also a high priority, with below average support by only those countries "new" to peacekeeping – Bulgaria, Romania, Slovenia – but even here support was >80%.

Far more marked differences were observed between countries on the deployment of the armed forces in peace-enforcement missions and support for combat missions. Respondents from Sweden, Netherlands, South Africa and France were far more supportive of the use of the military in both peace enforcement (>70%) and combat roles (>65%), than the other nations. Countries that displayed the lowest level of support for these missions include Bulgaria, Romania, Slovenia, Spain and Switzerland, with Poland and Germany being somewhat more divided.

As regards those tasks that involve the rendering of humanitarian aid, disaster relief and matters affecting global security such as the proliferation of weapons of mass destruction or terrorism, a number of noteworthy findings emerged. Most approved of the military being used in disaster relief operations (86%–99%) with the exception of Turkey where only 69% supported the use of the military in this role. A similar high level of approval was afforded to the use of the armed forces for humanitarian aid missions abroad – Switzerland, Germany and Slovenia being the most supportive (>90%), the remaining countries over 80% and the lowest France and Turkey (74%).

Most of the respondents also supported the use of the military to combat threats to global security. Over 80% supported the use of the military to prevent the proliferation of weapons of mass destruction, with the exception of Swedish, Swiss and German respondents. Similar sentiments were observed regarding the use of the military to fight terrorism, with the exception that only 58% of Swiss respondents considered the military appropriate for these missions.

Concerning those missions typical of policing functions, a different picture emerged. On average there was considerably less support for the use of the military to curtail domestic disorder, with the exception of Bulgaria, Italy, South Africa and Sweden (>82% support). On the matter of drug-trafficking countries were very divided with Bulgaria, Italy, Poland,

Romania and South Africa supporting such involvement (>77%), while others such as Switzerland (40%) and Germany (25%) opposed this. On the use of the military to control mass immigration, once more South Africa, Italy, Poland and Bulgaria were on average more supportive of the military in these than other nations, most notably Germany. On the matter of military's role in environmental protection, countries were polarised – some supporting involvement (Slovenia, South Africa and Bulgaria), others being more opposed, most notably Germany and Turkey.

Influencing the outcome of these results were the difference in the opinions of the cadets and students. Cadets were far more supportive of the military being used in missions that could entail the use of force such as combat missions (70% versus 39%) and peace enforcement (77% versus 50%). Cadets were also more inclined to support the use of the military in peacekeeping missions (96% versus 87%) and to prevent the proliferation of weapons of mass destruction (80% versus 75%). Much lower down the scale was soliciting the military to control mass immigration from foreign countries, but even here cadets (51%) were more in favour of using the military in this role than students (42%) (Table 2).

Another marked difference in opinion is that students were far more supportive of the military being involved in humanitarian aid missions, to combat drug-trafficking and to contribute to the protection of the environment, than cadets. This confirms the sentiment that civilians are less likely to endorse those roles that involve the use of force and appear more willing to support the use of the military in non-warfighting roles.

Table 2. Support for Military Missions by Cadets/Students (in Percentage).

Variable	Frequency	Cadets	Students
Defend country	96	98	94
Peacekeeping	91	96	87
Peace-enforcement	59	77	50
Combat missions	53	70	39
Disaster relief	92	94	91
Humanitarian relief	86	85	87
Weapons mass destruction	77	80	75
Fight terrorism	82	83	80
Domestic disorder	69	73	66
Drug trafficking	58	56	59
Control mass immigration	46	51	42
Protect environment	58	54	62

Priority Assigned to Military Missions

These responses concurred with another set of questions relating to issues of war and peace and the growing importance of international organisations in regulating global security. In line with the above-mentioned findings most respondents agreed that "today peacekeeping and other non-combat activities should be central to the military function" (74%) and that the "military should be prepared to cover the whole spectrum of possible missions (from war, to aid the civil power) (79%)". Less than half of respondents still felt that "the most important role of the military is preparation for the conduct of war (48%), although there was the realisation that "war is sometimes necessary to protect the national interest" (60%) and that "human nature being what it is, there will always be war" (71%). However, only 52% felt that "strong armed forces improved their image through the world".

Once more marked differences were observed among the respondents of the various countries on what should be the core function of the armed forces. Most agreed (>66%) that peacekeeping and other non-combat activities should be central to the military – some nations granting them high priority, namely Romania, Poland and Sweden (<81%), others affording them average support, such as Germany, the Netherlands and South Africa (<77%), with Switzerland and Turkey the least support. Similar trends were observed on this issue of whether the military should be prepared to cover a whole spectrum of possible missions – Romania, Sweden and Poland largely agreeing (>85%), Switzerland and Turkey being less supportive (<69%).

As before, while most countries supported the involvement of the military in peacekeeping operations, vast differences existed when it came to use of the military for the conduct of war. The nations in agreement that the most important role of the military is preparation for and the conduct of war include France, Turkey, Bulgaria, Netherlands and South Africa (>70%) while those least supportive included Germany, Slovenia, Spain and Switzerland. Incidentally, these four countries were less inclined to support war "if necessary to protect national interest" (<50%), with once more France, South Africa, Netherlands and Turkey, being the more "warriorlike" nations (>73%) (Table 3).

On the issue of whether "human nature being what it is, there will always be war" some nations such as France, Poland, Slovenia, South Africa, Germany felt more so (<77%) than Spain, Turkey, Bulgaria and Italy (<67%). The only nations which considered strong armed forces improved

Table 3. Priority Assigned to Missions by Country (in Percentage).

Variable	Frequency	Country												
		Bulgaria	France	Germany	Italy	Netherlands	Poland	Romania	Slovenia	South Africa	Spain	Sweden	Switzerland	Turkey
Today peacekeeping and other non-combat activities should be central to the military	74	73	71	77	70	77	81	93	85	77	74	79	69	66
The military should be prepared to cover a whole spectrum of possible missions	79	82	83	83	80	81	85	94	83	84	80	89	69	69
The most important role of the military is preparation for and conduct of war	48	72	91	20	50	50	50	66	22	70	38	41	32	74
Sometimes war is necessary to protect national interest	60	65	86	48	66	74	54	66	49	79	41	64	47	73
Human nature being what it is, there will always be war	71	65	84	77	67	71	82	69	84	78	57	68	71	64
Strong armed forces improve our image through the world	52	67	84	42	58	47	76	74	28	67	42	44	23	62

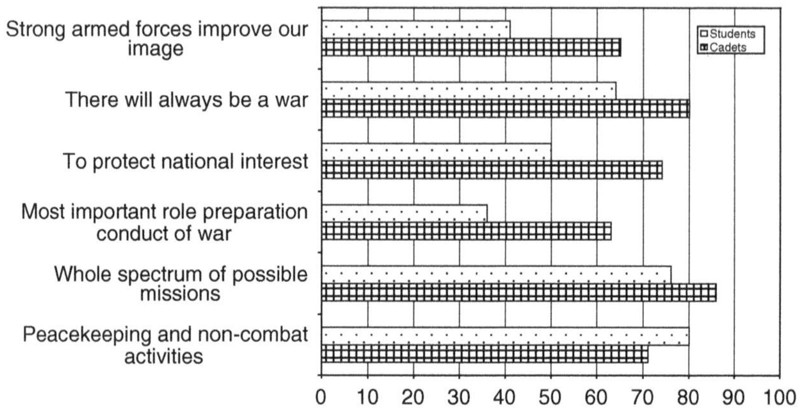

Fig. 1. Priority of Military Missions by Cadets/Students (in Percentage).

the image of their nation throughout the world, were France, Poland, Romania and to some extent Bulgaria and South Africa.

As with the previous responses to the questions on support for various missions, students felt that the military should assign greater importance to non-combat activities and were less inclined to support the "combat role of the military" (36% versus 63% cadets) (Fig. 1). They were also less accommodating towards the notion that war is sometimes necessary to protect national interest and that given human nature that there will always be war. Nor did they support the contention that strong armed forces improve the nation's image throughout the world. This once more confirms the hypothesis that civilians afford less importance to the legitimate role and purpose of the armed forces – namely warfighting (Fig. 1).

This does not imply that the value of armed forces in countering "new threats" is not valued. What has been called into question is the traditional missions and the resources allocated to national armed forces (Raitasolo & Siplila, 2004, p. 248). In fact, by far the majority thought that the defence budget should be raised considerably (35%) or somewhat (29%). The only countries that were not in favour of the defence budget being raised were Turkey, Switzerland, Spain and Slovenia. Although cadets were considerably more in favour of increasing the defence budget, only 13% of students thought it should be lowered and 28% that it should remain as it is.

Role of International Organisations

In terms of the international context, the fact that armed forces are now operating in a global environment implies that they have to link their security strategy and policies to those of coalition partners. The implication is that more and more decisions of common security concern are decided upon at international or regional forums. Being part of such forums ensures some control over transnational processes that impact on nation-states. This affects a whole range of issues, from the ability of states to use force unilaterally in pursuit of their own security policy, to human resource policies that have a direct impact on national policies affecting the armed forces (Dandeker & Weibull, 1999, p. 88). However in recent years, the lack of UN Security Council mandate and related diplomatic disputes within the international society has become a matter of growing concern (Raitasolo & Siplila, 2004, p. 252).

Consequently, respondents were asked to comment on the mandates of various international security organizations. Here most agreed that the increasing multinational character of military missions shows the need for a stronger United Nations (77%), but that this mandate did not extend to the control of the UN of the armed forces of member states (58%), nor for the UN Security council to act as the only power to verify military actions against sovereign states (56%). There was even less support for NATO (34%), the USA (13%) and for the EU (23%) to intervene on their own initiative. On all accounts, there were significant differences in the views of respondents of the various countries (0<001).

Countries with above average support for the need for a stronger UN were South Africa, Germany and Sweden (>83%) with Turkish respondents less inclined to agree that UN needs to be strengthened (65%). However, only Slovenia, South Africa, Switzerland (>72%) strongly supported the need for more control of the armed forces of member states by the UN, with support by France, Germany, Poland and Turkey being <50%. Similarly, Slovenia, South Africa, Switzerland and in this case also Germany (>64%) were more inclined to support the right of the Security Council to act as the only power to verify military actions, with Turkey once displaying the lowest level of support (38%) (Table 4).

As regards the right of NATO, the USA and the EU to intervene on own initiative, not many nations supported this. Only the Netherlands, South Africa and Germany showed some support (>44%) for NATO to intervene on its own initiative. Countries most opposed to the USA having such a mandate include Germany, Slovenia and most notably

Table 4. Support for the Role of International Organisations by Country (in Percentage).

Country	Frequency	Bulgaria	France	Germany	Italy	Netherlands	Poland	Romania	Slovenia	South Africa	Spain	Sweden	Switzerland	Turkey
The increasing multinational character of military missions shows the need for stronger UN	77	75	72	84	79	74	77	77	71	87	70	83	78	65
UN should have more control of the armed forces of all members	58	53	33	44	59	60	46	62	80	72	67	60	72	50
The Security Council of the UN should be the only power to verify military actions	56	47	58	66	56	43	46	57	72	65	56	49	64	38
NATO should have freedom to intervene on its own initiative	34	26	34	44	33	50	38	38	16	48	28	30	14	36
USA should have freedom to intervene on its own initiative	13	11	13	7	13	23	22	15	7	27	10	9	3	14
The EU should have freedom to intervene on its own initiative	23	27	29	26	24	31	30	33	13	30	18	21	6	17

Table 5. Support for the Role of International Organisations by Cadets/Students (in Percentage).

Variable	Frequency	Cadets	Students
The increasing multinational character of military missions shows the need for stronger UN	77	81	74
UN should have more control of the armed forces of all members	58	55	61
The Security Council of the UN should be the only power to verify military actions	56	57	56
NATO should have freedom to intervene on its own initiative	34	38	30
USA should have freedom to intervene on its own initiative	13	13	12
The EU should have freedom to intervene on its own initiative	23	25	21

Switzerland (<10%) and for the EU to have this right – Switzerland, Slovenia and Turkey (<20%).

Although the responses observed for cadets/students were statistically significant on a five-point scale, it is of interest to note that there was considerable agreement that neither NATO, the USA nor the EU have the right to intervene on their own initiative.

On matters that have a more direct impact on military affairs, the level of agreement differed somewhat. Cadets felt considerably stronger than students (81% versus 74%) that the increasing multinational character of military missions shows the need for a stronger UN. However, cadets (55%) were less supportive of the idea that the UN should have more control of the armed forces of all member states (61%) (Table 5).

IMPORTANCE OF THE MILITARY TO SOCIETY

The next set of questions related to the relative importance or status assigned to the military by society. As with the previous question on the use of the military to defend the country, the response to the question of whether the military exists for defence of the country and its interests is confirmed (>91% agreed). Although respondents were a little more divided, the majority also thought that the military job guarantees peaceful and free trade in the international arena (62%).

However, on the importance of the military in society, only 12% agreed that the military should be abolished although a third thought of the military was a "necessary evil". Concerning the importance of the military as an institution within society, only 24% rated the military as "the most

Table 6. Status of the Military in Society (in Percentage).

Variable	Agree Strongly	Agree Somewhat	Disagree Somewhat	Disagree Strongly	No Opinion
Exists for defence of country and interests	59	32	7	2	1
Guarantees peaceful and free trade in international arena	23	39	28	7	3
Should be abolished	4	8	18	65	4
Is a necessary evil	11	20	21	44	5
Is the most important part of public life	6	18	37	33	4
Should be representative of broader society – social and ethnic groups and classes	15	36	27	14	8

important part of pubic life" with 70% holding the opposite view. In terms of the need of the armed forces to be representative of broader society, the responses were almost equally divided (Table 6).

These responses were influenced, as before, by the perception of the various participating countries of their armed forces. For example, Spain (77%) and Switzerland (71%) were less in agreement that military exists for the defence of the country and its interest. In terms of the whether the military job implies the guarantee of peaceful and free trade in the international agreement, some mostly agreed – Italy, Netherlands, South Africa, Romania and Sweden, while other such as Switzerland, Slovenia and Poland felt less so (<41%) (Table 7).

Few countries thought that their armed forces should abolished, although a notable 29% of Swiss and 20% of Spanish respondents considered this. Respectively, quite a few countries thought of their armed forces as a necessary evil – Bulgaria, Slovenia and Switzerland (>40%). Given this, it is not surprising that once more the Swiss and Spanish felt less inclined to support the view that the military is the most important part of public life. Countries that held their armed forces in some esteem were South Africa (42%), Turkey (41%), Italy (39%), Sweden (37%) and Bulgaria (36%).

On the need for the armed forces to be representative of broader society, South Africa rated this as high prerogative (69%) and so did Swedish respondents (63%). On an average the other countries were ambivalent, with the exception of those from Slovenia (32%) who did not ascribe a great deal of importance to representivity (Table 6).

Table 7. Level of Agreement on Status on Military in Society by Country (in Percentage).

Variable	Frequency	Country												
		Bulgaria	France	Germany	Italy	Netherlands	Poland	Romania	Slovenia	South Africa	Spain	Sweden	Switzerland	Turkey
Exists for defence of country and interests	90	98	95	93	92	91	98	96	94	95	77	94	71	94
Guarantees peaceful and free trade in international arena	68	52	68	57	84	79	41	74	41	77	61	74	31	68
Should be abolished	12	4	2	6	11	16	10	6	12	12	20	7	29	12
Is a necessary evil	30	43	36	25	25	21	13	33	41	27	32	37	40	29
Is the most important part of public life	24	36	22	12	39	18	19	32	8	42	10	37	10	41
Should be representative of broader society – social and ethnic groups and classes	50	44	47	54	43	58	41	41	32	69	45	63	55	48

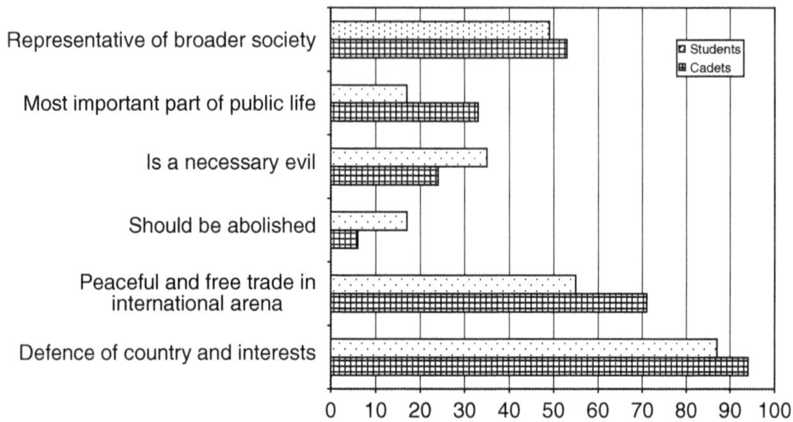

Fig. 2. Level of Agreement on Status on Military in Society by Cadets/Students (in Percentage).

As with the previous questions, the responses of cadets and students differed significantly on each of the variables analysed. From the results it is patently obvious that cadets assigned a greater value to the importance of the military for society than their civilian counterparts (Fig. 2).

Conscript Versus All-Volunteer Forces

One of the arguments in favour of maintaining conscription is that it ensures that the military remains representative of broader society and abides to the democratic ideals of society. However, conscription has hidden costs and for most countries an AVF is the most viable economic and social alternative, although as previously mentioned, it does pose problems in terms of the ability of the armed forces to recruit and retain adequate numbers of "suitable" personnel.

In this regard, it is clear that most respondents did not support the concept of universal conscription. Only 43% of all respondents felt there is a natural link between democracies and conscription, although a substantial number (58%) supported the view that it does ensure a steady exchange of values between society and the military. On the matter of gender equality, only 37% thought that the draft should include women. Most felt that the AVF is better suited to MOOTW (70%), although respondents were divided over whether conscription is more or less costly to the national economy. Regarding those who serve in the military, most (70%) were proud of those who serve in the military, even though they did not think the armed forces were attracting high-quality motivated recruits (45%) (Table 8).

Countries that felt most strongly that there is a natural link between democracies and conscription were Sweden, Germany (which still have conscription), France and the Netherlands (>52%). Those who held the opposite view were Slovenia, Spain, Bulgaria and Italy. Virtually the same response was obtained to the question of whether the draft guaranteed a steady exchange of values between society and the military. In terms of gender equality, the Netherlands and South Africa were far more in favour of extending the draft to include women (>67%) – most opposed was Romania, Poland, Bulgaria and Slovenia (<20% support).

Most countries also thought that the shift to an AVF was better suited to new missions (>70%), with the exception of Switzerland (48%) and to a lesser extent Sweden and Germany (61%) – all of which still have conscription. The cost of conscription to the national economy appeared to be a contentious issue, with some countries feeling strongly that conscription costs too much – Romania (77%), Bulgaria and South Africa (69%) with France, Germany and Sweden (<34%) holding largely the opposite view.

On the aspect of those serving in the military nations most proud of those in uniform include Bulgaria, France, Germany (>81%), those less so – Poland, Spain and Switzerland (<60%). However, only the Netherlands (73%) and Turkey (61%) thought that their armed forces attracted "high quality motivated recruits", the remaining countries were divided, with France, Germany, Slovenia and Spain holding the opposite view (<32%). Although most countries were largely in agreement that all citizens should be willing to fight for their country, only half of Swiss and 26% of Spanish respondents supported this view. Nor did Spanish or Swiss respondents think that good citizenship is related to service in the military in defence of the country (Table 8).

On some of these questions cadets and students had consensus – especially where this pertained to the inclusion of women in the draft and support for the shift to an AVF. On the importance of conscription in ensuring that the military does not become too removed from society in terms of democratic practices, cadets felt far stronger than students that this was so. Cadets were also more proud of their compatriots in uniform and did not agree to the same extent as students (38% versus 53% cadets) that the military does not attract high-quality recruits. Yet, only 46% of students thought that all

Table 8. Military Organisation: Conscription versus AVF by Country (in Percentage).

Variable	Frequency	Country												
		Bulgaria	France	Germany	Italy	Netherlands	Poland	Romania	Slovenia	South Africa	Spain	Sweden	Switzerland	Turkey
There is a natural link between democracies and conscription	43	25	54	57	34	52	37	42	15	47	20	59	48	48
The general military draft should include women too	37	18	31	36	35	74	14	11	19	67	53	51	27	25
The draft guarantees a steady exchange of values etc between society and military	58	45	77	74	47	70	33	47	41	80	41	68	57	60
An AVF fits better than conscription regarding requirements for new missions	70	87	84	61	82	63	67	90	88	71	71	59	48	72
Looking at the whole national economy, conscription causes more costs	51	69	30	31	52	50	62	77	61	69	47	34	50	60
I am proud of woman and men who serve in the military	70	82	84	70	81	78	60	74	70	79	59	79	46	65
The armed forces are attracting high-quality, motivated recruits	45	47	28	32	56	73	36	48	26	48	23	56	–	61
All citizens should be willing to fight for their country	61	68	75	62	70	53	83	66	58	66	26	62	50	73
Strongest indicator of good citizenship is performance of military in defence of country	36	48	28	36	40	33	50	44	28	52	19	44	20	43

Table 9. Support for Conscription by Cadets/Students (in Percentage).

Variable	Frequency	Cadets	Students
There is a natural link between democracies and conscription	43	56	33
The general military draft should include women too	37	39	36
The draft guarantees a steady exchange of values etc between society and military	58	72	47
An AVF fits better than conscription regarding requirements for new missions	70	69	70
Looking at the whole national economy, conscription causes more costs	51	45	55
I am proud of the woman and men who serve in the military	70	85	58
The armed forces are attracting high-quality and motivated recruits	45	53	38
All citizens should be willing to fight for their country	61	80	46
Strongest indicator of good citizenship is performance of military in defence of country	36	51	25

citizens should be willing to fight for their country, compared to 80% of cadets and few considered (25%) that good citizenship relates to performance of military service in defence of one's country (Table 9).

DISCUSSION

Although the issues associated with the civil–military gap debate have remained much of the same over the years, tension in civil–military relations has heightened in the post-Cold War era due to a number of new systemic forces (Cohn, 1999, pp. 2–4). In an international security environment where armed forces are expected to be more than national warfighting institutions, commanders have grappled with ways to bridge the gap between their mandate (to prepare for war), the demands placed upon them in terms of the new security environment (maintaining peace and global security) and the need to accommodate other political imperatives imposed upon them by broader society.

This has given rise to much debate on the future tasks of armed forces. With no visible threat to the nation and the rejection by society of the military to conduct war, most countries have approved of their armed forces serving in a wide range of missions. The irony is that while civil society acknowledges that armed forces exist primarily to defend the state's territory, they rebuke the use of the armed forces in missions that involve the legitimate use of force. This appears to be a universal trend at least among countries participating in this study.

In terms of country comparisons, although *all* support the use of the military to defend the country and for peacekeeping operations, marked national differences emerged on whether the military should be deployed in peace-enforcement and combat operations. Here countries can be placed in two distinct groups – France, Sweden, the Netherlands and South Africa being the most supportive of the use of the military in missions that sanction the legitimate use of force, with Slovenia, Spain and Switzerland being most opposed. For Switzerland, its (past) strong commitment to neutrality could be an influencing factor – for Spain and Slovenia, the explanation is less apparent. Another key finding is that civilian students were significantly more opposed to the use of the military in roles that may involve collective violence.

With respect to the use of the military in rendering assistance to civil society (national or international) to relieve human suffering, there was general consensus among nations that the military should assist in disaster and humanitarian aid missions. These findings concur with those of (Kuhlmann, 1994, p. 96) that "the average European military officer broadly accepts the idea of being deployed to give assistance in civil disasters and those concerning foreign humanitarian and development aid". In fact cadets were even more supportive of their deployment in disaster relief missions than students, although the latter was more inclined to support the use of the military in humanitarian relief missions. The divergence in opinion is easy to explain, as the rendering of assistance in the wake of natural disasters has always been an accepted role for the military, while humanitarian relief aid is generally considered the function of relief organisations or NGOs.

On the use of the military to curtail the spread of weapons of mass destruction most countries supported this, with the notable exception of Sweden and Switzerland. Swiss respondents were also the least supportive of the military being used to fight terrorism. Although on average students supported the use of the military in both these roles, cadets were more supportive of such involvement on both accounts. Rather more distinct divisions emerged between countries and cadets/students on the involvement of the military in more policing type functions, most of which can be related to the political, socio-cultural and geopolitical factors impacting upon their threat perception.

In general it appears that in countries where the armed forces have the legal sanction and are routinely used to maintain domestic order functions, such activities are more readily supported even though they are more "policing type activities". Also, where the country directly faces a particular threat such support is even greater. For example, although most countries face a drug-trafficking problem, those countries that serve as major tran-shipment points such as Bulgaria, Poland, Italy, Romania and South Africa were more supportive of their armed forces assisting in combating this crime, than countries with a lesser drug problem.[2] Of note, is that both Germany and Swiss respondents expressed their reservation about the military's involvement in combating drug-trafficking. Once more, these results concur with those of previous studies (Kuhlmann, 1994, p. 98) and in the case of Germany, is clearly linked to the fact that the maintenance of internal security is for the most part the responsibility of the police forces of the different Lander.

Although there was less support for the use of the military to control mass immigration from foreign countries, this too depended on how this threat was perceived. South Africa faces a massive influx of displaced persons from Zimbabwe and elsewhere in Africa into the country and Italy, illegal immigrants from South Europe and North Africa. Consequently, both these countries were significantly more in favour of their armed forces being used in this capacity. The use of the military to protect the environment only appears to have support in Slovenia, South Africa and Bulgaria. Of all the countries, Turkish respondents were most strongly opposed the use of their armed forces in any of these internal domestic roles.

Similar responses were obtained to questions relating to the priority assigned to the various missions. The sentiment is that the military should move away from being a warfighting institution, to one where their skills can be used more constructively. Of interest, is that of all the countries, Switzerland and Turkey were the most opposed to the armed forces being used in a broad range of missions – but for different reasons. Switzerland is clearly the most anti-militarist, affords the lowest percentage of its GDP (1%) to defence and thought significantly less of its armed forces in terms of their importance to society. Turkey, France and South Africa appear consistently more "warriorlike" and also afforded their armed forces greater social standing than other countries. Once more, students were less supportive of the need for the military to prepare and conduct war and assigned a lesser value to the military's relevance in terms of enhancing the country's image throughout the world.

With most of these missions taking place in international theatre, there was overall agreement that such missions should take place under the UN Flag. However, countries were divided over the extent of control the UN should exercise over national armed forces, as well as the power of the

Security Council. Although there was more support for NATO's right to intervene on its own accord than for the USA or EU, most countries did not sanction unilateral action by any of these bodies. Here there was more or less agreement among respondents, except that cadets afforded both the UN and NATO greater support to intervene on own initiative. However, students were more inclined to support the idea that the UN should exercise greater control over the armed forces. From this one may conclude that there is support for global organizations only if subject to broad consensus among member states.

Moving on to the relevance and status afforded to the military by society, the same pattern of responses emerged on the importance of the military to society. When the mean averages are examined, it is clear that some nations value the military significantly more than others. Comparatively Spain and Switzerland were more aloof about the military, did not consider that the armed forces exist for the defence of the country and their interests, and regarded the military as "a necessary evil". On all accounts students were considerably less appreciative of the value of the military to society. In this regard Weibull (1994, p. 70) points out in earlier research that the lack of appreciation for the officer's job and how politicians value military expertise, is most dissatisfying. It is dissatisfying, because it not only affects morale, but the ability of the military to attract and retain people of the right quality, which ultimately impacts on military effectiveness.

One of the challenges AVF face is the ability to recruit suitable candidates. Most consider professional armed forces more suited to these new missions. The arguments that conscription keeps the military in touch with society is not widely supported and many consider conscription too costly for the economy. As to be expected students were more opposed to conscription, but at the same time did not think the military was attracting good quality recruits. They were also less willing to serve in the military, whether to defend the country or as a token of good citizenship. This finding reinforces the problematic sketched earlier of the challenge facing armed forces of not only ensuring that they remain representative of broader society, but of attracting the kind of personnel required to serve in missions to maintain peace and security around the world.

CONCLUSIONS

While it is difficult to make broad generalisations based on obvious national differences and nature of the sample, there are a number of observations one can make concerning the civil–military gap issue. Firstly, there is definite move away from the military organisation being used as a warfighting force to their use in more constructive roles that enhance world peace, stability and the personal safety of citizens. While these roles afford armed forces a certain "new found" legitimacy, the question can be asked to what extent have armed forces made the conceptual, organisational and material shift to adjust to what society expects – or is it the other way round? Does military leadership need to convince society that the emphasis placed on these roles wears away the warrior culture that underpins military effectiveness and that they still need to train for war to enable them to do the other tasks. Here there appears to be a mismatch vis-à-vis what the military is trained for, what civil society wants from the military and what the politicians regard as national and foreign-policy priorities.

A second concern is the impact the internationalisation or globalisation of security has on the relevance and status of national armed forces. In all the countries examined, a high level of support is given to missions that take place under the banner of international security organisations such as the UN and NATO. However, the consequence of so-called collective defence is that armed forces not only become more removed from society, but society comes to see their protection in internationalist terms, implying that it is no longer as important to have strong national armed forces when one is in an alliance. Haltiner (2003, p. 363) raises similar concerns stating that trust in collective security can lead to nations minimising their defence efforts. The impact this has on civil–military relations (as confirmed by this study) is that where the military as a political tool becomes less significant and fades from public view, it starts to pose other problems for armed forces in terms of funding, recruitment and retention.

This raises a third issue linked to conscription and the inability of AVF to attract suitable personnel. One of the greatest concerns with the end of conscription is that society will become disconnected from their armed forces, exacerbating problems of recruitment and retention. Recent misdemeanors by soldiers in Iraq emphasize the importance of deploying suitable and adequately trained soldiers on international missions. However, as this study confirms most do not consider that the armed forces are recruiting high-quality recruits, nor do they consider serving in the armed forces a citizenship obligation or even (with the exception of South Africa) that being representative of broader society is a social imperative. A disturbing thought with the growing disconnect between the military and society, which can be described more as apathy than hostility, is who will serve as the future defenders of national and international peace and security?

This justifies that there are reasons to be concerned about the widening civil–military gap in many societies.

NOTES

1. As most responses were in the affirmative, the responses approve very strongly and rather approve were combined and discussed accordingly. Thus, in terms of the statistical analysis it may appear as if there is little difference in the percentages given, while in fact the difference was most likely within the five categories when compared by country. However, as the aim is to determine the level of overall support for the various missions, combining the positive responses for the purpose of discussion is justified.

2. Bulgaria serves as a transhipment point for cocaine to Europe, Italy as a gateway of Latin American cocaine and Southwest Asian heroin to Europe, Poland a major producer of synthetic drugs for the international market, Romania major transit country for heroin to the Balkans and South Africa, which is the world's largest market for illicit methaqualone, marijuana and a range of other drugs, http://www.cia.gov/cia/publications/factfook/docs/profileguide.html

REFERENCES

Cohn, L. (1999). The evolution of the civil–military "Gap" debate. Paper prepared for the TISS project on the gap between the military and civilian society, http://www.poli_duke.edu/civlmil/cohn_literature_review.pdf

Dandeker, C., & Weibull, E. (1999). *Facing uncertainty: Flexible forces for the twenty-first century*. Karlstad: Klaria Tryckeri.

Feaver, P. D., & Kohn, R. H. (2001). Conclusion: The gap and what it means for American national security. In: P. D. Feaver & R. H. Kohn (Eds), *Soldiers and civilians: The civil–military gap and American national security* (pp. 459–473). Cambridge, MA: MIT Press.

Haltiner, K. (2003). The decline of the European mass armies. In: G. Caforio (Ed.), *Handbook of the sociology of the military* (pp. 361–384). New York: Kluwer Academic/Plenum Publishers.

Kuhlmann, J. (1994). What do European officers think about future threats, security and missions of the armed forces? *Current Sociology, 42*(3), 87–101.

Morgan, M. J. (2001). Army recruiting and the civil–military gap. *Parameters, 31*(2), 101–115.

Raitasolo, J., & Siplila, J. (2004). Reconstructing war after the cold war. *Comparative Strategy, 23*(3), 239–261.

Smith, P. (2000). Transnational security threats and state survival: A role for the military. *Parameters, 30*(3), 77–91.

Weibull, E. (1994). European officers' job satisfaction and job commitment. *Current Sociology, 42*(3), 57–70.

INTEGRATION OF WOMEN INTO THE ARMED FORCES: IS THERE A GAP BETWEEN THE ATTITUDES OF CIVILIAN ELITES AND MILITARY ELITES?

Tibor Szvircsev Tresch and Demet Varoğlu

ABSTRACT

Since the end of the Cold War, women's integration in the armed forces has been an issue of increasing interest in Europe. The full integration of women into the armed forces is decided on at the divide between voluntary and compulsive service. There is no big civil–military gap in the approval given that military services were mandatory for women. If service is optional, however, there is a clear civil–military gap to be seen in most countries. The differences between the countries, however, must be taken into account as well. There is no standard European attitude concerning the integration of women into the armed forces.

Cultural Differences between the Military and Parent Society in Democratic Countries
Contributions to Conflict Management, Peace Economics and Development, Volume 4, 201–224

ISSN: 1572-8323/doi:10.1016/S1572-8323(07)04009-X

1. INTRODUCTION AND RESEARCH HYPOTHESES

Since the end of the Cold War, women's integration into the armed forces has been an issue of increasing interest in Europe. As a result of the shift from mass-based to volunteer forces, the recruiting process is being reshaped. The armed forces increasingly have to compete with other companies for well-qualified personnel on the labor market. In the process, women become the focus of attention. At the same time, a demographic development reshaping the workforce structure can be observed on all social levels as a result of which the percentage of women in the total workforce is rising. Sociocultural changes in family structures as well as changed gender role conceptions act in favor of women's integration into a wide variety of working processes (Kümmel, Klein, & Lohmann, 2000).

As a consequence of changed social, cultural, international and military-strategic factors, an increasing integration of women into the armed forces is to be perceived.[1] In this context, the question arises, how the public perceives this integration of women into the armed forces and how well it is accepted. This can be discussed by means of three dimensions. The first is based on the main topic of gender studies, i.e. on a possibly differing perception of the acceptance of female personnel in the armed forces by men and women, respectively. A second dimension can be discussed along the axis of civil persons vs. military persons. Do these two groups view women's integration into the armed forces differently? Is there a civil–military gap? Technically, these two dimensions are segmented into four categories: In our study, we discuss male cadets, male students, female cadets and female students with specific emphasis on the topic. The third dimension of our civil–military gap study concerns the specific nations: Is the integration of women into the armed forces judged differently in specific nations and if so, are there specific structures to be discerned? In the first part, current trends in research and their inherent theoretical approaches on the integration of women into the armed forces will be presented. In the following empirical part, the equality of people, regardless of gender, race and religion will be discussed on a general level. Subsequently, the general acceptance of service for the public will be discussed without going into gender issues. In the third part, we will specifically deal with the issue of conscription for women. In the last and longest section of the empirical chapter we will examine the acceptance of women in the armed forces and analyze in detail five arguments in favor of excluding women from military professions and functions. The findings in the last chapter conclude this contribution.

2. CURRENT RESEARCH

In the modern period, which is between 1900 and 1945, women in the military formed a separate corps or were totally excluded. For example, in Russia, during the World War I, the "Battalion of Death" was composed of all-female soldiers. However, this battalion could never serve as an all-female unit in the war. They fought together with hundreds of male soldiers at the front (Carreiras, 2004, p. 15; Kümmel, 2002, p. 627; Goldstein, 2001, pp. 72–73, 76). In the late modern period, which is between 1945 and 1990, women were partially involved in the military, and when we come to the postmodern period, which begins in 1990s, there is full integration of women into the military (Kümmel, 2002, p. 627). Even though Kümmel's (2002) statement on full integration is an overgeneralization for many countries,[2] it seems difficult to erase the women's presence and their walk towards a more powerful stance in military.

In the two world wars, and shortly thereafter, women were employed mainly in the nursing sector, i.e. as nurses (Carreiras, 2004; Nuciari, 2002, p. 2; Creveld, 2001, p. 206; Williams, 1989, p. 14). If women were to be employed in combatant functions at all, it was done secretly, as the example of the Briton Olivia Aykin, who was trained to use a weapon in World War II, illustrates:

> Aykin was told that if Hitler learned that British women were being trained to use weapons, and especially if any pictures were taken of them doing so, he could use it as propaganda to show that Britain was so short of men that is was necessary to train women. By implication, therefore, the only reason a country might allow its women to be trained killers was if men were scarce and the country was weak (Peniston-Bird, 2000, p. 175).

Possible functions for women have become more numerous and their chances to be admitted into the armed forces have increased, especially since the end of the Cold War (Hurri, Meyer Schweizer, Flückiger, & Stüssi-Lauterbach, 1992, p. 11). However, the handling of women's integration into the armed forces varies from state to state.[3] According to Kümmel et al. (2000) there are three ways in which women can serve in the military: (1) in all non-combatant functions; (2) in troops with combatant functions,[4] but not in special functions; (3) without exception in all functions. British woman soldiers, for example, are employed in all combatant functions alongside their male colleagues. This, however, does not apply to units whose assignment is to kill the enemy in close combat. The reason for this is that the female presence is assumed to interfere with the effective fitness for combat (Nielsen, 2001, p. 32). However, and increasingly so, the successful handling of an assignment depends not so much on physical power and manual dexterity alone, but rather on a synthesis of human qualities such as commitment, combat morale, group cohesion and technical knowledge. Because of this shift regarding military abilities, arguments seeking to restrict women's integration because of their physical restrictions are now obsolete (Micewski, 1997, p. 16).

The rising quota of women in Europe's armed forces can be understood as a side effect of at least three factors (Szvircsev Tresch, 2005, p. 141).

1. With social change, role models and attitudes of the sexes change. The change manifests itself among other things in the professions people choose. Professions that were formerly exercised exclusively by men (e.g. jet pilot) or women (e.g. kindergarten teacher) are opened to the other sex. Professional fields that are strongly dominated by men cannot remain unaffected by this change; the change may merely be delayed.
2. In modern times, work in the armed forces is not anymore based on physical strength alone. The technological progress (computers, digitalization, etc.) has created more and more areas of work in the armed forces that are not gender-specific. In logistics, command and support especially, gender issues are becoming increasingly irrelevant. Women are thus given better *chances* to access military professions.
3. With the abolition of conscription and the professionalizing of the armed forces the automatic influx of young men (conscripts) ceases. The professionalized forces do not succeed in recruiting male personnel in sufficient numbers on the labor market. Thus, the employment of women becomes indispensable. In this case, women seem to gain access to the armed forces through a negative trend (pressure of the labor market, not enough men willing to serve).[5]

According to Harris (1997, p. 25), the nature of today's conflicts requires military personnel with qualifications that are usually rather perceived as typical of women professions.[6] This applies even more to peacekeeping operations. In societies in which equality of women and men is more developed, the integration of women into the armed forces is met with less opposition (MFD-Zeitung, 1995). Typically, women are still predominantly found in staffs and in subsidiary functions (Nuciari, 2002, p. 10).

The integration of women into the armed forces has long been impeded by restrictions of combat functions. Besides the argument according to which women do not meet the physical prerequisites for combat,[7] there has also been the moral notion of women's traditional need for protection (for a critical discussion of this issue, see Armor, 1996, p. 23; Kümmel et al., 2000, p. 53). Additionally, conservative analysts fear that group cohesion would suffer if women served in military units. Moreover, if women were included in the military, they could possibly become the victims of sexual assaults by either their own male colleagues or, when captured, by the enemy (Winslow & Dunn, 2002, p. 652; Creveld, 2001).[8] Creveld sees the influx of women into the military as one of the reasons for the decline and fears that the armed forces would not be able to fight in combat any more (2001, p. 15f). There is also the possibility that male soldiers put themselves, their unit and mission at risk in order to protect their female comrades (Winslow & Dunn, 2002, p. 652; Micewski, 1997). Therefore, Micewski (1997, p. 21) demands that there should be a distinction between combat functions and combat action of women. He suggests that female soldiers be trained for certain combat functions but not automatically sent into combat in those functions.

There are many empirical studies on the integration of women into the armed forces. However, in most cases, only military personnel were questioned on their attitudes, rarely civilians. In a survey among members of the German Bundeswehr, 51% of German male soldiers, but 84% of female soldiers, spoke out in favor of a full opening of the military to women (Kümmel & Werkner, 2003). Generally, Kümmel and Werkner found that male soldiers are overall more skeptical of a full integration of women into the armed forces than female soldiers. In a large-scale re-analysis on group cohesion in the U.S., Rosen et al. (1999, p. 377) found out that according to male soldiers, group cohesion in particular would suffer with a high female quota.

In the following empirical section we shall examine if there is a civil–military gap regarding the issue of women's integration into the armed forces. Recent U.S. studies suggest that this is the case. Miller and Williams (2001, p. 368) asked civilian and military elites if they think women should be allowed to serve in all combat functions. In comparison to 57.5% of the civilian elite only 37.6% of the military elite agreed with this statement. The authors note, "our data confirmed the claim that there is a gap between civilians and military elites on issues of gender and sexual orientation" (p. 386).

3. EQUALITY OF PEOPLE, REGARDLESS OF GENDER, RACE, RELIGION

In our study, which was carried out in 13 countries, 93% of those questioned said they deem the equality of people, regardless of gender, race and religion as rather or very important. There is thus a consensus on fundamental principles in society. There are, however, two significant differences: In general, equality is more important to women than it is to men, and cadets regard this issue as less important than students. The cadets' view seems to be reflecting their internalization/normalization of the highly stratified institution they belong to, and the male-dominance of the military occupation.

The perception of the realization of this equality principle shows a discrepancy. Only 61% of those questioned think that equality is rather or completely realized in their countries (men: 68%, women: 48%). The results show that especially female students have a critical attitude. The older the people questioned, the more they tend to think that those principles have been realized in the specific countries (CC = 0.16).

The realization of equality is perceived very differently in the specific countries (Fig. 1). Mainly in eastern European countries and Turkey, but also in Spain, only a minority thinks that this principle has been realized. The highest approval rate is seen with consolidated democracies like

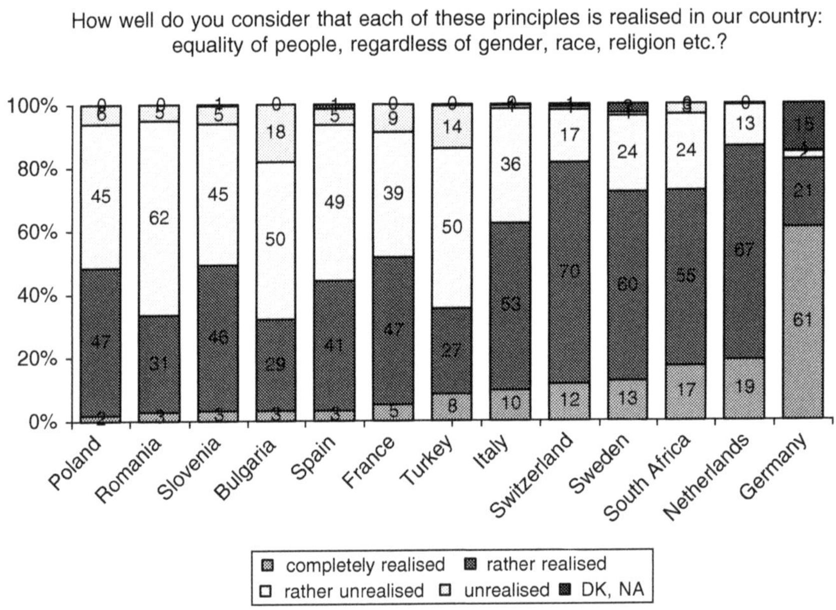

Fig. 1. Realization of Equality of People, Regardless of Gender, Race and Religion (by Country in Percent).

The Netherlands (completely or rather realized: 85%), Switzerland (82%), Germany (82%) and Sweden (73%). The Germans questioned show a particularly marked digression from these patterns. On the one hand, a majority believes that equality is completely realized; on the other hand, the number of people not responding is extremely high.

4. ACCEPTANCE OF A GENERAL AND MILITARY SERVICE FOR THE PUBLIC

In this section, the general acceptance of those questioned towards some form of service for the public will be determined. First, we will discuss the acceptance of a general service for all male citizens, then for women. Lastly, the views of the respondents on including women in the general military draft are discussed.

4.1. General Service for Men

Out of those questioned, only 59% approve of some form of compulsory service for society for all men: 74% of cadets share this opinion compared to only 48% of students (CC = 0.29). There is also a difference between sexes (CC = 0.23): 67% of men, but only 44% of women approve of compulsory service for men with female students displaying a particularly low approval rate of 41%. Equally, people with post-materialistic (45%, CC = 0.17) or left-wing views (46%, CC = 0.21) show a below average approval rate. Strongly supportive of a general service for men are people from countries that continue to have conscription (Bulgaria and Germany: each 77%, Switzerland: 71%, Turkey: 69%. See Fig. 2). Countries that have switched to all-volunteer forces tend to be opposed to a compulsory service for men (Spain, Slovenia, South Africa and Italy, as an exception to the rule: Poland).

4.2. General Service for Women

The respondents view a general compulsory service for women more skeptically. Only 37% of them can imagine such conscription put into force. People with right-wing political attitudes are supportive of the idea above average at 44% approval (left-wing: 32%, CC = 0.15). Again, it is the older

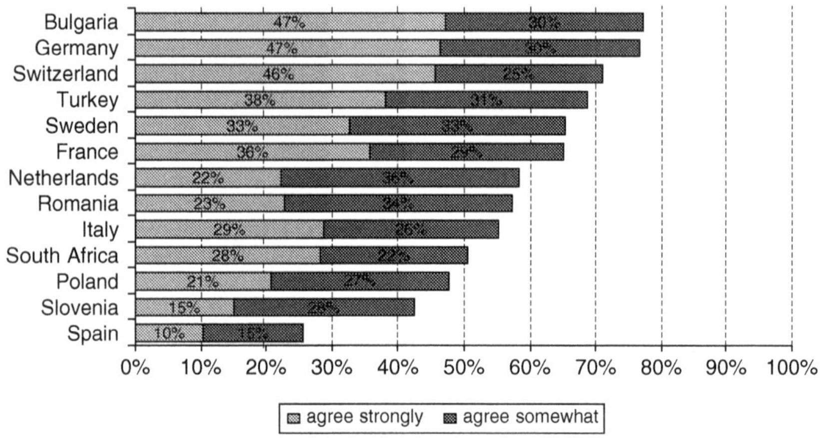

Fig. 2. Approval of National Service for all Male Citizens (in Percent).

people in the survey, from 25 years and above, who tend to support a compulsory national service for women.

On the country level, the approval rates differ strongly (Fig. 3). Only in Germany does a majority of people approve of a compulsory national service for women. A possible explanation for this could be that Germany already has compulsory service for men and that the integration of women would therefore be a smaller step.

People from states in which the welfare of the public is traditionally held in high esteem and in which service for the res publica enjoys high social acceptance are more open towards a compulsory national service for women (The Netherlands: 47%, Sweden: 46%, Switzerland: 46%). Minimal approval rates are seen in eastern European countries (Slovenia: 26%, Poland: 16%, Romania: 14%), as well as in Spain (21%). Spain has always been seen to be skeptical towards compulsory services. Bad experiences from the past military dictatorship seem to be a factor in this (Ajangiz, 2002). Also, the aforementioned nations are deeply rooted in Catholicism and have a more traditional concept of women's role in society than other European countries.

In some instances, there are great differences between cadets and students on a national level (Table 1). In all countries with the exception of Italy, a universal service for women gets more approval from cadets than from students. Significant differences concerning the answers given can be seen in

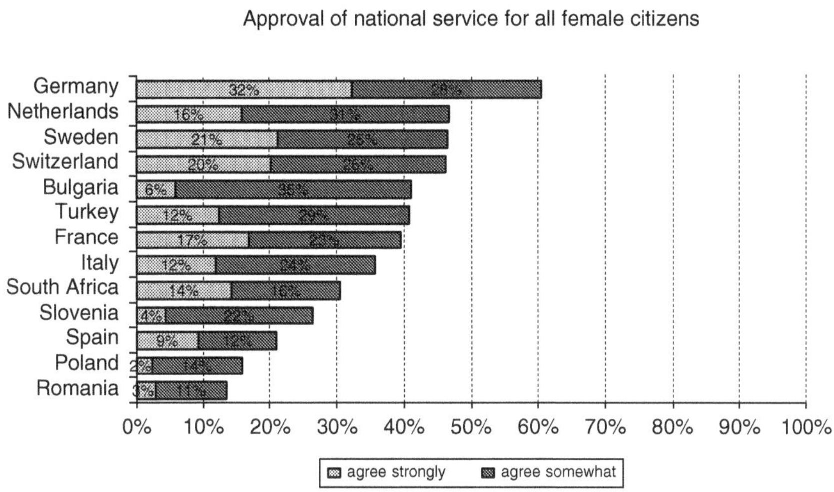

Fig. 3. Approval of National Service for all Female Citizens.

Table 1. Approval of National Service for All Female Citizens (Students and Cadets, Agree Strongly and Agree Somewhat, in Percent).

Country	Students	Cadets
Germany	60	62
Switzerland	40*	56*
Bulgaria	42	44
Turkey	37	47
Italy	37	35
Netherlands	33*	53*
Sweden	32*	55*
France	32	43
South Africa	28	34
Slovenia	26	29
Poland	16	17
Spain	8*	45*
Romania	5**	21**

Note: $*p<0.01$; $**p<0.05$.

The Netherlands, Romania, Spain, Sweden and Switzerland. In Spain, there are very marked differences between cadets and students. Of the students, only 8% to that of 45% of the cadets approve of a universal service for women. In Germany, Switzerland, The Netherlands and Sweden, there is a majority of cadets who approve of universal service for women. In no country, except Germany, does a majority of students support the idea. On a European level, female students with 26% are least supportive of universal service for women, followed by male students (39%). With military personnel, there is no difference between sexes (male cadets: 45%, female cadets: 44%).

4.3. Universal Service for Women

Of all people questioned, 36% agree somewhat and strongly that the general military draft should include women too. This rate of approval is comparably high as with the issue of universal service for women. It can be said that people who approve of a universal service for women would also support a military draft for women (CC = 0.52).

Students and cadets differ only minimally in their approval of a mandatory military draft for women. The picture becomes, however, more interesting if we differentiate according to study subjects and sex (Table 2).

Female cadets are most in favor of a military draft for women: 50% of them are for the draft. At 42%, male students are also particularly supportive of the draft. Conversely, it is above all the female students who do not like the idea at all: 65% of them disagree. Male cadets at 60% reject the idea of a compulsory military service for women. A statistically significant civil–military gap between students and cadets can only be seen in Italy, Romania, Sweden, Switzerland, Spain and Turkey (Table 3).

Table 2. Agreement with Statements about the Military: The General Military Draft should Include Women too.

	Male Cadets	Female Cadets	Male Civilian Students	Female Civilian Students
Agree strongly	15%	21%	15%	8%
Agree somewhat	23%	29%	27%	22%
Disagree somewhat	29%	25%	27%	30%
Disagree strongly	31%	24%	28%	35%
No opinion	2%	1%	3%	5%
N	1140	148	817	797

Note: CC = 0.151, $p > 0.001$.

Table 3. Approval of Conscription for all Female Citizens (Students and Cadets, in Percent).

Country	Students	Cadets
Netherlands	83	69
South Africa	68	64
Spain	46*	67*
Sweden	38**	57**
Germany	39	32
Italy	37*	33*
France	31	30
Switzerland	26*	29*
Turkey	29*	19*
Slovenia	20	17
Bulgaria	19	13
Poland	17	11
Romania	14**	8**

Note: $*p<0.01$; $**p<0.05$

It is rather the cultural differences that are to be noted. There are three distinct groups of countries. The first group is composed of the former communist states such as Romania, Bulgaria, Slovenia and Poland. These countries are against the military draft being expanded to include women. Respondents from The Netherlands, South Africa, Sweden and Spain are of an entirely different opinion. Absolute majorities speak out in favor of a military draft for women. Germany, Italy, France, Switzerland and Turkey make up an intermediate group. A common feature of these countries is their large mass armies, which have known a long tradition of conscription. Still, they overall reject the military draft for women.

5. INTEGRATION OF WOMEN INTO THE ARMED FORCES

Besides the general issue concerning the military draft for women, the question of full integration of women into the armed forces was also asked. Full integration is regarded as achieved if women are employed in combatant functions as well. The question on integration was asked for two different situations. What was of interest were the opinions of the respondents in the hypothetical case of a compulsory draft for women, first, and in the case of a volunteer service for women, second (Table 4).

Table 4. Do you Support the Full Integration of Women into the Armed Forces? (in Percent of Valid Answers).

	On a Compulsory Basis			On an Optional Basis		
	All	Students	Cadets	All	Students	Cadets
Yes in all (also combat) roles	21	19	23	55	61	47
Yes, but not in combat roles	22	19	27	31	26	37
No	50	53	46	11	9	15
No opinion	7	9	4	3	4	1
N	2799	1554	1235	2937	1631	1296
	CC = 0.123, $p<0.001$			CC = 0.174, $p<0.001$		

In the case of a mandatory draft for women, neither students nor cadets approve of a full integration of women into the armed forces. However, the answers differ significantly on the civil–military axis. The cadets are somewhat more supportive of integration than the students, but only under the condition that women are not used in combat (cadets: 27%, students: 19%). Just the opposite is seen, given the case that women are admitted into the armed forces on a voluntary basis. In this case, civilian students are much more supportive of women's integration into the military and, most importantly, of their full integration, i.e. with combatant functions (61%; cadets: 47%). Only very few students would exclude women from the military if their service was voluntary (9%). This is in stark contrast to the case of a compulsory draft, where a majority of students is disapproving (53%).

In the case of a voluntary service for women, the overall sample additionally reveals differences in the approval of full integration between postmaterialists (69%) and materialists (45%), leftists (65%) and rightists (49%), as well as between respondents who are not religious (62%) and strongly religious people (52%; CC = 0.16).

Again, the difference between states is bigger than between cadets and students (Table 5). A full integration of women including combatant functions on a compulsory basis is supported in no country. Only Spain and Sweden nearly approach the 50% margin. Here, the answers of students and cadets differ significantly; this is also true in France, where almost no cadet agrees to a full integration of women under a compulsory draft. Respondents from France (68%), Germany (61%), Italy (58%), Poland (70%), Slovenia (71%) and Switzerland (67%) are especially strongly opposed to a compulsory service for women.

Table 5. Agreement to Full Integration of Women with Combat Roles on Optional Basis or Compulsory Basis (in Percent).

	On Compulsory Basis: Full Integration of Women with Combat Roles: Agreement		On Voluntary Basis: Full Integration of Women with Combat Roles: Agreement	
	Civil	Military	Civil	Military
Spain	42*	50*	88*	79*
Sweden	35**	49**	81	79
France	15**	1**	74**	21**
Switzerland	16	17	72**	44**
Slovenia	5	9	72*	43*
Bulgaria	14	11	63*	38*
South Africa	24	22	60*	37*
Netherlands	36	34	57	55
Romania	17	15	57	49
Italy	16	10	51**	33**
Germany	14	18	49	49
Poland	12	3	45**	23**
Turkey	7	6	33**	10**

Note: $*p < 0.05$, $**p < 0.01$ significant between civilian students and cadets.

Whereas in case of service on a compulsory basis, a civil–military gap cannot be seen in most states, this differs in case of a voluntary service for women. In 9 out of 13 states (Spain, France, Switzerland, Slovenia, Bulgaria, South Africa, Italy, Poland and Germany), civilian students are significantly more supportive of women's full integration including combatant functions if they serve on a voluntary basis (Table 5). Critical of integration are in particular respondents from Turkey and Poland. Likewise, below average approval is seen in Germany and Italy. It is also striking to see a discrepancy in the answers of French respondents. While a 75% majority of students supports a full integration if service is voluntary, only a fifth of cadets agree.

The approval of women's full integration into the armed forces differs not only along a civil–military gap, but differences between states are also significant, if not even more pronounced. It becomes clear that not the adherence to the military or the civil elite is decisive, but rather the political culture and the value system of the specific country a respondent has been brought up in.

5.1. Arguments for the Exclusion of Women from Military Professions and Functions

When the question is asked if one agrees that women take up military professions and functions, there are five patterns of arguments of exclusion also to be found in theory and literature, which can be noticed: (1) arguments saying that women are exposed to danger in military operations; (2) arguments concerning jobs: women are seen to compete with men in military professions; (3) arguments of efficiency: combat units with men and women are allegedly less efficient than single-sexed units; (4) arguments of morale: because of religious and ethical reasons, women should not be allowed to fight in combat missions; (5) arguments of disturbance: women disturb cohesion in male combat units.

Overall, 38% of all respondents are against women in military professions and functions (1,156 out of 3,015 respondents). Male military students are particularly critical with 48% disapproving of women in military professions or functions (Table 6). Male civilian students disapprove at 37%. Female respondents are much less inclined towards the exclusion of women. 27% of female cadets and 29% of female students have difficulty granting women full access to all functions and professions within the military.

Materialistic and post-materialistic attitudes according to Inglehart (1977) also influence attitudes towards women and their full access to all military professions. Materialists show an above average tendency to keep women away from military professions and functions (44%), post-materialists, on the other hand, are more open towards women's rights (disapproval: 28%). The older the respondent, the less will he or she be opposed to the full integration of women into the armed forces. Most reservations are found with young adults who are up to 20 years of age (44%). Political attitudes, as well, influence the acceptance of women in the armed forces (leftists: 32% against women in military professions and functions, rightists: 44%). Religious attitudes too are also quite influential regarding the attitudes towards women's integration into the armed forces. The more religious a person, the more reservations he or she will have concerning the accessibility of military professions and functions to women.

The most significant differences are again to be found between two groups of countries: while respondents from Spain, Sweden and Switzerland have only little to object concerning the involvement of women in the armed forces, there are absolute majorities of respondents found in Turkey, Bulgaria, The Netherlands and in particular in Romania who are against women having jobs and assuming functions within the military (Table 7).

Table 6. Against Women in Military Jobs and Functions According to Socio-Demographic Factors (in Cases and Percent).

	Item	Against Women in Military Jobs and Functions (Cases)	All Answers for the Item (Cases)	Percent Against Women in Military Jobs and Functions (%)
Civil–military	Male cadets	553	1165	48
	Female cadets	41	153	26
	Male students	311	838	37
	Female students	241	827	29
Inglehart scale	Materialist	315	718	44
	Post-materialist	109	386	28
	Mixed type	688	1776	39
Age	Less than 20	243	544	44
	20 to 24	673	1748	39
	25 to 29	189	533	35
	30 and up	37	118	31
Political identification	Left	264	814	32
	Middle	415	1066	39
	Right	433	976	44
Religiousness	Strongly religious	277	650	43
	Moderately religious	374	905	41
	Not clear	138	374	37
	Not religious	279	866	32
Total		1156	3015	38

In the eyes of those opposing women's integration, what are the reasons against the involvement of women in military professions and functions (Fig. 4)?[9]

The greatest difficulty in the integration of women into military professions and functions is perceived to be the full deployability of women in combat. Here, the argument of pregnancy is given the most weight: 57% of deniers view this as an important, or very important, reason. Similarly, the fear that women could be abused during captivity is cited by a majority of respondents (55%) opposing the full integration of women. Arguments according to which men cannot fight effectively in units also comprising women and according to which the death of women has a demoralizing effect on the fighting men, as well as the assumed disturbing influence women would exert on group cohesion, are approved by a narrow margin.

Table 7. Against Women in Military Jobs and Functions by Countries (in Cases and Percent).

Country	Against Women in Military Jobs and Functions	All Answers of the Country	Percent Against Women in Military Jobs and Functions (%)
Spain	40	270	15
Sweden	56	295	19
Switzerland	62	300	21
Slovenia	54	164	33
France	49	137	36
Poland	83	224	37
South Africa	74	190	39
Germany	147	368	40
Italy	99	226	44
Turkey	136	253	54
Bulgaria	68	121	56
Netherlands	160	287	56
Romania	128	180	71
All Countries	1156	3015	38

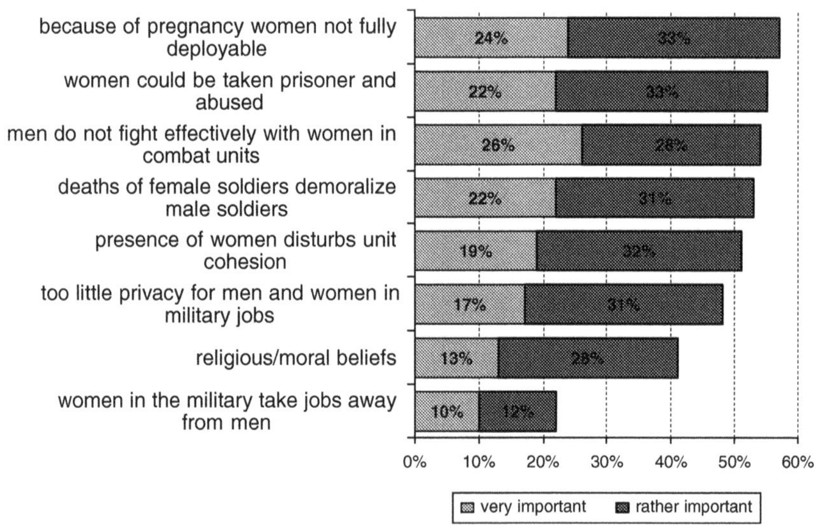

Fig. 4. Arguments against Integration of Women in Military Jobs and Functions (in Percent) ($n = 1136$–1159 Respondents).

Of less importance seems to be, above all, the argument that women might take jobs away from men (22%) or that religious or moral reasons forbid the admission of women into the armed forces (41%). But how are these specific arguments for exclusion assessed by cadets and students? Are there significant differences to be found?

5.1.1. Argument of Endangerment

Mainly students believe at an above average proportion that women could be taken prisoner and be abused (female students: 66%; male students: 58%). This is contrary to the view of female cadets, only a third of whom share that fear. With male cadets too, only a minority is of that opinion (48%). The correlation is highly significant ($CC = 0.17$, $p < 0.001$). Mainly men view the argument that the death of female soldiers will demoralize male soldiers and the public as important. Therefore, they give the endangerment of women by death much weight.

5.1.2. Job Argument

The argument that women in the military take jobs away from men is generally doubted (Fig. 4). In the assessment of this issue, there is no civil–military gap. A gap between the sexes too, is only minimal. The statement is not at all supported by female cadets:7% (male cadets: 23%, male students: 21%, female students: 22%). This is not surprising, as female cadets are already in a military profession and do not want to see themselves as competing with men.

5.1.3. Efficiency Argument

As far as the full availability of women in the armed forces is concerned, pregnancy is perceived to be the biggest problem. Of the 1,156 respondents who are against full integration of women into military jobs and functions, 57% consider this argument as very or rather important. Approval of this notion is above average with male cadets and female students (each 60%), lower with male students (52%). Strongly differing are the answers given by female cadets (39%). It is also them who regard the argument "men will not fight as effectively with women present in combat units" as of only minimal importance (24%). Contrary to this, male cadets opposing the integration of women at 60% give much weight to the efficiency argument. It also becomes clear, however, that concerning the efficiency argument, there is not so much of a civil–military, but a clear gender gap.

5.1.4. Argument of Morale

Religious and ethical criteria of exclusion are generally not regarded as particularly important (Fig. 4). Only some 41% of the respondents opposed to women's integration consider them to be important. There is a marked civil–military gap to be noted in this issue ($CC = 0.15, p < 0.01$). Cadets only to a minimal extent see religious/moral reasons for exclusion (male cadets: 35%, female cadets: 36%). Conversely, male students (46%) and female students (51%) give more weight to these issues.

5.1.5. Argument of Disturbance

"The presence of women could disrupt small unit cohesion" is judged differently by women and men. Among those opposing integration of women, 61% of male cadets and 48% of male students attribute very great or rather great influence to the argument of disturbance. Women see this issue as less problematic. Only one-third (civil and military) agrees with the notion. That women and men in military jobs have too little privacy is judged similarly by male cadets, male students and female students (between 46% and 53%). Here, it is again female cadets who are out of line. Only 20% agree that this would be a very or rather important issue in the integration of women into the armed forces.

5.2. Typological Classification According to Arguments for Exclusion

In order to establish a basis for the analytical interpretation of the arguments for exclusion, we looked out for clusters out of the 1,156 respondents who were against women being admitted into military jobs and professions. A satisfactory way to explain the variance is the use of a five-cluster model. In the latter, out of the 1,156 respondents, 1,018 can be unambiguously allocated. The five types are characterized as follows:

Slightly disapproving respondents (175 respondents, 17% of all valid cases) are opposed to a full integration of women into military jobs and functions without prioritizing a specific argument for exclusion (Fig. 5). It appears that the integration of women into the armed forces seems inappropriate to them out of a rather diffuse attitude. A particularly large portion of this type of attitude is shown by post-materialists and religious persons.

Argument of morale: In 22% of all valid cases (226 respondents) the religious–moral argument stands out. With this goes the notion that women are not fully deployable due to pregnancy and could be abused in captivity.

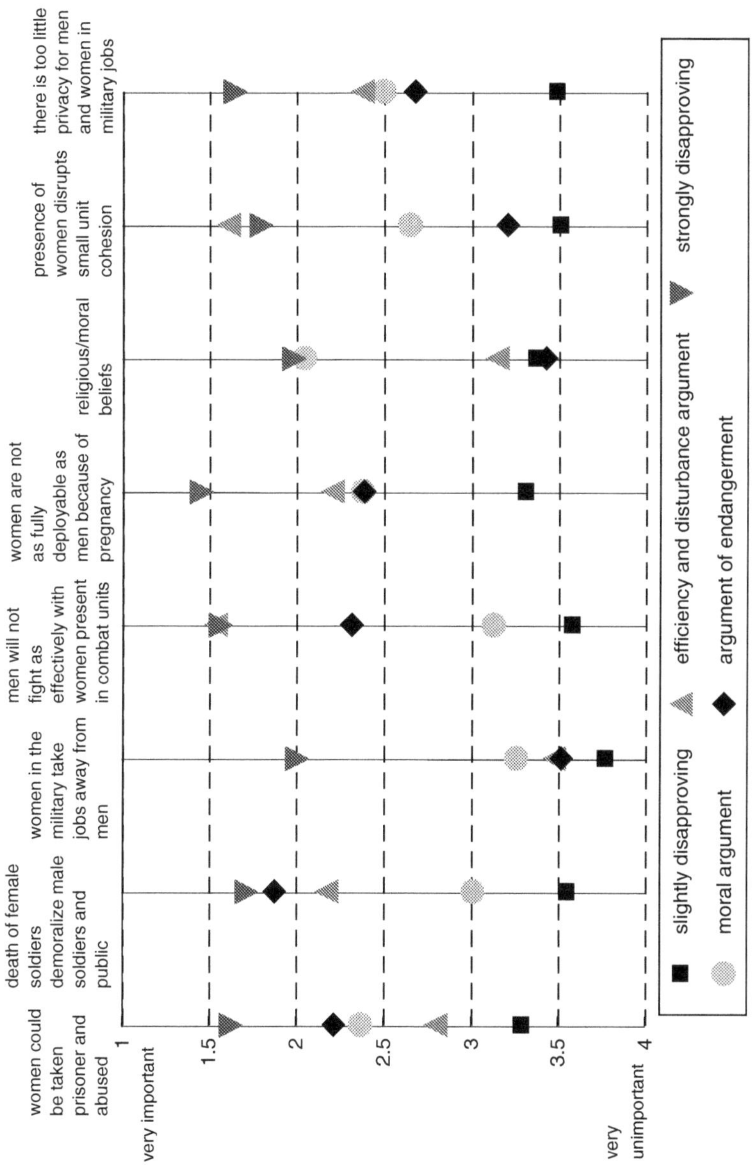

Fig. 5. Typological Classification of Arguments for Exclusion of Women in Military Jobs and Functions.

The dignity and vulnerability of women seem to be at the center of these notions. Therefore, it is not surprising that especially very religious people belong to this type. The percentage of people aged up to 20, as well as of post-materialists, is also high.

Efficiency and disturbance argument: In the opinion of 21% of the respondents who gave valid answers (214 persons) women are, above all, a disrupting factor and their presence diminishes cohesion in small groups. This is linked to reduced combat fitness and efficiency: men allegedly can't fight properly if women are present. In this type, we find in particular people over 25 years of age, people with right-wing political attitudes, as well as materialists.

Argument of endangerment: This type focuses on the danger that women could be abused in captivity. Even more weight is given to the demoralizing effect of women dying in combat; these respondents think that men and the public back home cannot accept dead women. 20% of all valid cases (199 persons) share this view. Above average is the share of non-religious persons in this group.

Strongly disapproving: 20% of the respondents who gave valid answers (204 persons), consider all of the eight proposed arguments against the full integration of women into military jobs and functions to be very important. They fear that women would exert negative influence on all levels. Their opposition against the involvement of women in the military seems to stem from principal attitudes. Even the argument least approved of in the survey, according to which women take away jobs from men, is considered rather important in this group. It is striking that very religious people are often found in this group.

Cadets and students are distributed in different ways in these five types. An above average portion of male cadets thinks that women in the military are a disturbing factor (28%, see Fig. 6). Conversely, female cadets' attitudes are rather diffuse, with 47% of them finding none of the cited arguments important. Most likely to be cited as important by female cadets are religious-moral arguments. Male students do not cite any group at an above average level. Most likely to turn up is the argument of endangerment. Female students emphasize religious–moral arguments (29%). Also, they are the ones who are most supportive of the strongly dissenting type.

The difference in the assessment of the exclusion arguments is highly significant with respect to gender and civil–military (CC = 0.28). It can be seen that, above all, male cadets are skeptical towards a full integration of women into military jobs and functions.

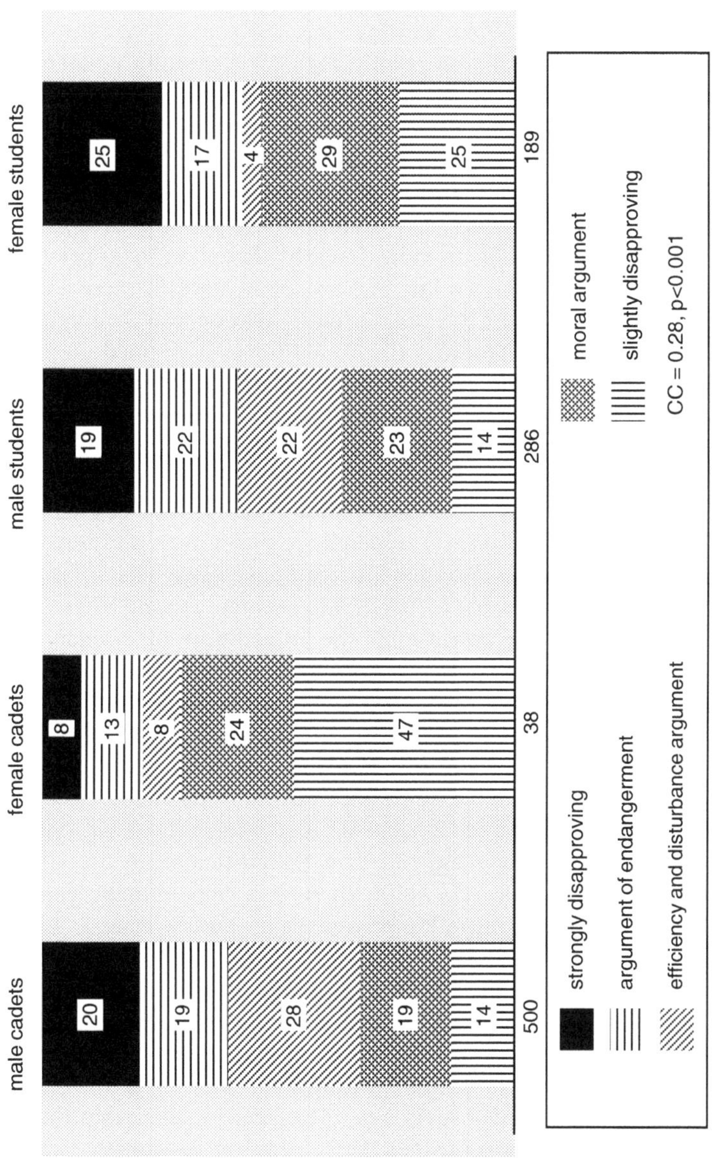

Fig. 6. Clustering of Arguments for Exclusion by Male and Female Cadets, and Male and Female Students (in Percent).

6. CONCLUSIONS

Respondents in consolidated democracies view the equality of people regardless of gender, race and religion as most realized. Generally, equal rights are more important to women than to men. Mainly people from post-communist countries consider equality as not yet achieved.

A service to the public (military or civil service) for women is supported by 37% of respondents while 59% of respondents approve of a compulsory service for men. In countries where the welfare of the public is held in high esteem and a service to the public is valued highly, there is more approval of a compulsory service for women. Only in 5 out of 13 states is there a civil–military gap (The Netherlands, Romania, Spain, Sweden and Switzerland).

The full integration of women into the armed forces is decided on at the divide between voluntary and compulsive service. There is no big civil–military gap in the approval given that military services were mandatory for women. Here, cadets as well as students express their reservations. Of all respondents, only 37% approve a military draft for women. If service is optional, however, there is a clear civil–military gap to be seen in most countries. If the service is voluntary, students are much more supportive of full integration of women into the armed forces than cadets. The differences between countries, however, must be taken into account as well. There is no standard European attitude concerning the integration of women into the armed forces. It appears rather that respondents especially in western European countries are more open-minded towards full integration of women. People who are against women taking on military jobs and functions will most likely cite efficiency arguments like the limited deployability during pregnancy, as well as reduced combat fitness of men in the presence of women. The endangerment argument is considered an important reason for the exclusion of women, too. It is feared that women could be captured and abused. On the one hand, there is a civil–military gap, on the other; the difference in attitudes between men and women is highly significant (gender gap).

Regarding voluntary service of women, people with left-wing views and non-religious respondents are much more in favor of integration than people with right-wing views and strongly religious respondents. Women are also clearly more supportive of full integration than men. Here, the biggest gap is between female and male cadets. We, therefore, conclude that there is not only a civil–military gap regarding the integration of women into the armed forces, but also a gender gap and a gap between specific countries.

NOTES

1. Nielsen (2001) shows that in the last four decades (from 1961 to 2001), the number of women within NATO forces has gone from 30,000 to 288,000. Mainly the Scandinavian countries, but also France, The Netherlands and Great Britain have long been admitting women to the armed forces and also to combat functions. The Mediterranean countries opened their armed forces to women especially in the 1980s and 1990s, but with limitations. Preparations to enter the EU have accelerated the implementation of equal rights for men and women in Czechia, Hungary and Poland significantly (Nielsen, 2001, p. 32).

2. Women, still have a token (minority) (Kanter, 1977) status in the military. The percentage of women in the armed forces of NATO countries by the year 2004 range between 0.47 (Poland) and 19.2 (Slovenia) and the average percentage for all 23 NATO countries are 8.09 (www.nato.int/ims/2004/win/stregnth.pdf).

3. Accordingly, in Germany, women's right to be admitted to armed functions was eked out legally, as is illustrated by the case of Tanja Kreil. See Kümmel et al. (2000, p. 15)

4. According to Micewski (1997, p. 15), combatant functions are generally understood as functions whose main objective is to fight under fire and through this immediate use of physical violence incapacitate the enemy.

5. See also Kümmel et al. (2000, p. 31), Harris (1997, p. 25), Titunik (2000, p. 243), Nuciari (2002).

6. The same line of argument is also made for women in management (Helgesen, 1995). However, even though contemporary leadership requires more femininities it still has not shattered down the glass ceiling and women are still a minority in higher managerial positions.

7. The U.S. army has six categories of jobs in which women can serve with some limitations: infantry, armor, short-range air defense, cannon artillery, combat engineers and special forces. The highly severe physical strain as well as the interference of group cohesion are given as reasons (Wojack, 2002).

8. Sexual harassment in the armed forces is one of the biggest taboos. In the U.S. army, the likelihood of being molested is between three and four times bigger than in civil life according to various estimates (Kümmel et al., 2000).

9. In the following calculations, only those respondents were included who were against the involvement of women in military functions.

REFERENCES

Ajangiz, R. (2002). The European farewell to conscription? In: L. Mjøset, S. van Holde (Eds), *The comparative study of conscription in the armed forces* (Vol. 20, pp. 307–333). Amsterdam: Elsevier Science.

Armor, D. J. (1996). Race and gender in the U.S. military. *Armed Forces & Society*, *23*(1), 7–27.

Carreiras, H. (2004). *Gender and the military: A comparative study on the participation of women in the armed forces of western democracies*. Ph.D. dissertation. European Research Institute, Florence.

Creveld, M. van (2001). *Frauen und Krieg*. München: Gerling Akademie Verlag.

Goldstein, J. S. (2001). *War and gender*. Cambridge: Cambridge University Press.

Harris, M. (1997). Die Anerkennung der Rolle der Frau in den Streitkräften der NATO. *NATO Brief*, *3*(45), 25–26.

Helgesen, S. (1995). *The female advantage*. New York: Doubleday.

Hurri, J., Meyer Schweizer, R., Flückiger, P. J., & Stüssi-Lauterbach, J. (1992). *Frauen in den Streitkräften*. Brugg: Verlag Effingerhof AG.

Inglehart, R. (1977). *The silent revolution: Changing values and political styles among western publics*. Princeton: Princeton University Press.

Kanter, R. M. (1977). Some effects of proportions on group life: Skewed sex ratios and responses to token women. *American Journal of Sociology*, *82*, 965–990.

Kümmel, G. (2002). When boy meets girl: The feminization of the military. *Current Sociology*, *50*(5), 615–639.

Kümmel, G., Klein, P., & Lohmann, K. (2000). *Zwischen Differenz und Gleichheit: Die Öffnung der Bundeswehr für Frauen*. Strausberg: Sozialwissenschaftliches Institut der Bundeswehr.

Kümmel, G., & Werkner, I.-J. (Hrsg.) (2003). *Soldat, weiblich, Jahrgang 2001*. Sozialwissenschaftliche Begleituntersuchungen zur Integration von Frauen in die Bundeswehr- Erste Befunde. Berichte/Reports/Rapports 76. Strausberg: Sozialwissenschaftliches Institut der Bundeswehr.

MFD-Zeitung. (1995). Offizielles Organ der Schweizerischen Verbandes der Angehörigen des MFD. 55 Jahrgang, April, 41–43.

Micewski, E. R. (1997). *Frauen und Streitkräfte. Aspekte des Zuganges von Frauen als Soldatinnen zum Österreichischen Bundesheer*. Studien und Berichte 5/97. Schriftenreihe der Landesverteidigungsakademie. Wien: Institut für strategische Forschung.

Miller, L. L., & Williams, J. A. (2001). Do military policies on gender and sexuality undermine combat effectiveness? In: P. D. Feaver, & R. H. Kohn (Eds), *Soldiers and civilians. The civil–military gap and American national security* (pp. 361–402). Cambridge: MIT Press.

Nielsen, V. (2001). Frauen in uniform. *NATO Brief*, *2*(49), 30–34.

Nuciari, M. (2002). *Women in the military: Contributions and problems*. Conference paper. Geneva: Geneva Centre for the Democratic Control of Armed Forces (DCAF).

Peniston-Bird, C. (2000). Ambiguity, contradiction and possibility. In: G. J. DeGroot, & C. Peniston-Bird, (Eds), *A soldier and woman. Sexual integration in the military* (pp. 175–184). Essex: Pearson Education.

Rosen, L. N., et al. (1999). Gender composition and group cohesion in U.S. army units: A comparison across five studies. *Armed Forces & Society*, *25*(3), 365–386.

Szvircsev Tresch, T. (2005). Europas Streitkräfte im Wandel: Von der Wehrpflichtarmee zur Freiwilligenstreitkraft. Eine empirische Untersuchung europäischer Streitkräfte 1975 bis 2003. Dissertation, Zürich: Universität Zürich.

Titunik, R. F. (2000). The first wave: Gender integration and military culture. *Armed Forces & Society*, *26*(2), 229–257.

Williams, S. (1989). *Women and war*. England: Wayland Limited.

Winslow, D., & Dunn, J. (2002). Women in the Canadian forces: Between legal and social integration. *Current Sociology*, *50*(5), 641–667.

Wojack, A. N. (2002). Integrating women into the infantry. *Military Review*, *6*(82), 67–74.

NATIONAL DIFFERENCES IN MILITARY VALUES AND CIVILIAN VALUES: IS THE GAP CULTURE-FREE OR CULTURE-BOUND?

Marina Nuciari

ABSTRACT

In this research the starting point was that a certain gap between military and civilian culture could exist, because of the inevitable difference between typical military values and new values arisen in contemporary societies, with special reference to Western affluent societies. It seems that this hypothesis belong to the culture-free side, since it rests on the concept of a military culture made of specific values, which are the same in every society. There is anyway a different viewpoint, following the trends of studies developed in the intercultural relations domain, mainly dealing with business internationalisation and cross-cultural management topics, generally known as the culture-bound thesis. In the culture-free assumption the consequence should be a pressure of social change on a supposed unique military; in the culture-bound conception a mutual and systemic adaptation of different institutions within each inclusive society driven by one's own culture could be expected. Findings in this research show that if

Cultural Differences between the Military and Parent Society in Democratic Countries
Contributions to Conflict Management, Peace Economics and Development, Volume 4, 225–237

ISSN: 1572-8323/doi:10.1016/S1572-8323(07)04010-6

a relative gap can be observed between military and civilian students, this varies greatly according to different groups of countries. Distances seem to be larger in countries belonging to the post-modern cluster (Sweden, Switzerland, Spain, France, Italy, the Netherlands), and lowering down in modern countries such as Slovenia, Bulgaria and Poland, and even less appreciable in Romania, South Africa and Turkey. This could give some support to the culture-free thesis, according to which military culture is specific and find more convergences with so-called traditional societies than with modern or post-modern cultures. But results are not as sharp as needed, and the culture-bound thesis cannot anyway be rejected.

1. PREMISE. CULTURE-FREE OR CULTURE-BOUND ARGUMENTS

After having read the results from the analyses of the cross-cultural comparisons, a question arises whether the gap between military and civilian culture has the same features in every country or it shows any differences. In other words, is the gap culture-free or not? Is there anything in each civilian culture so that military and civilian values do differ or not?

The question can be also addressed from a slightly different point of view:

1. contemporary civil society stands on values different from military culture's values;
2. this statement stands on two assumptions:
   a. military culture is given, every time and everywhere
   b. civilian culture, on the contrary, can change;
3. there was a type of society where military and civilian cultures were coincident or, at least, rather convergent;
4. there is now a type of society where military and civilian cultures are divergent;
5. is this relationship between military and society giving rise to a sort of linear continuum from convergence to divergence, or is it a non-linear relationship?
6. if it gives rise to a linear continuum, and if military culture remains the same, then the gap is inevitably growing, and divergence is the result;
7. but if we assume that military culture can also change, then the supposed gap can differ from persisting convergence (cultural change occurs and impacts the society and the military at the same time), to various combinations of partial convergences (or partial divergences).

Table 1. Military Culture in the Two Theses.

Culture-Free Thesis	Culture-Bound Thesis
1. Military culture is the same everywhere	1. Military culture is part of any given culture
2. Military culture stands on traditional values	2. Military culture can adapt to modern values
3. Military culture tends to remain the same	3. Military culture changes with cultural change
4. Military culture becomes necessarily divergent when civilian society shifts from tradition to modernity and further	4. Military culture is influenced by broader culture, so that it tends inevitably to converge with civilian society

A tentative table can be of some help in considering this complex topic (Table 1).

In this research the starting point was that a certain gap between military and civilian culture could exist, because of the inevitable difference between typical military values and new values arisen in contemporary societies, with special reference to Western affluent societies. It seems that this hypothesis belongs to the culture-free side, since it rests on the concept of a military culture made of specific values, which are the same in every society. Many pieces of comparative researches concerning military culture under various points of view have reached similar conclusions: military culture is more similar among different national militaries than the culture of one's own society. When the subject of the comparative cross-national researches are professional officers, the relative similarity among officers of different countries is explained by means of a set of traits typical of a professional group, where the single professional is inculturated in a peculiar and given domain, characterised by a defined function, a related knowledge, value set, corporatism, that is, all the dimensions defining the nature of a professional group. A similar point of view is found also in organisational comparative research dealing with managerial behaviour, where the convergence theory (Kerr, Dunlop, Harbison, & Myers, 1960) states that similar contextual factors push toward similar organisational assets and managerial behaviours, and the contingency theory (Lawrence & Lorsch, 1967; Thompson, 1967) states the necessary similarity of rational organisational behaviours in similar environments independently from national cultures.

1.1. Culture-Free Conceptions of Military Culture

For those who rely on a culture-free thesis, military culture is then definable by a rather specific set of elements, conceived to be the same in any national society. References in the literature are many and well-known. The famous I/O model proposed by Charles Moskos in 1977 and subsequent revisions (Moskos, 1977, 1986) defines the Institutional orientation of soldiers (no matter what role and rank they can have), as a peculiar set of values, norms and rules of behaviours where community prevails over the individual, obedience is a virtue, commitment is based on a moral compliance and reference groups for career evaluation and professional goals are internal and coincident with the military institution. Charles Cotton (1988) in his typology of various military organisations distinguishes between a convergent and a divergent military, where the divergent military is thought as a rather closed and communitarian institution, rather removed from the parent society and because of this functional and convergent with traditional, pre-modern societies and destined to become more and more divergent from modern, industrial and affluent current societies. To a certain extent, it could be said that there is a definition of military culture which can sustain the culture-free thesis in the sense that the military must remain free from the eventually changing culture of civilian society, because its values and behavioural norms are functionally adequate for its peculiar goals, and since these goals remain the same, then military institution cannot adapt to and follow society's cultural change without losing effectiveness becoming unable to offer adequate performances. This thesis is also sustained by those scholars, like Geser (1995), who recognise the evident hisomorphism of military organisations, notwithstanding different types and levels of development of societies all around the world and along history.

At a general level, the majority of scholars dealing with the study of military institutions and armed forces and society relationships belongs to this group, considering the unavoidable peculiarity of the military, in any society at any time.[1]

1.2. Culture-Bound Conceptions of Military Culture

There is anyway a different viewpoint, following the trends of studies developed in the intercultural relations domain, mainly dealing with business internationalisation and cross-cultural management topics. The acceptance of cultural diversity within a globalised business world has sustained a research domain where the diversity of societies is considered as an inevitable character, linked to cultural variety and making reference to cultural relativism. The well-known debate between unilinear and multilinear path of development within social change scholars in the Fifties, and the highly important studies by Shmuel Eisenstadt (1984, 1992) on different traditions and modernities can be recalled here just to show how the topic reaches a wide scope and it deals with a central sociological issue, namely culture variety, socio-cultural change and its expected and unexpected consequences.

Within sociological studies on the armed forces, the cross-cultural viewpoint has been developing in the last decades giving rise to many comparative researches where the underlining assumption – notwithstanding the specific topic considered in each research project – is the inevitable stress to which military culture has been subjected because of the many changes of contemporary society, changes that have been differently shaped and managed by the various national societies so that diversities in institutional assets are normal and impact differently on national armed forces. The consequence should be then a variety of cultural adjustments, caused by national civilian cultures' pressure on a supposed unique military (in the culture-free assumption), or by a mutual and systemic adaptation of different institutions, and armed forces are part of this change within each inclusive society driven by one's own culture (in the culture-bound conception).

2. THE GAP BETWEEN MILITARY CULTURE AND CIVILIAN CULTURE

It is rather evident that the question of a gap between civilian and military culture is intrinsic to the culture-free thesis: as long as military culture can remain untouched, and the society changes, the divergence between them inevitably grows; the point is if this divergence is necessary and it envisages anyway an advantage for society, or if, on the contrary, divergence is felt as a loss of control on armed forces by civil society, thus giving rise to efforts bound to bridge the gap, which usually put military culture under pressure to change and to assimilate as far as possible to civilian culture. This second output enhances the culture-bound thesis: armed forces and their personnel in different countries, notwithstanding the bulk of peculiarity of the specific role that is common to every professional group within modern society, are inevitably affected by values, norms and structural organisation of the parent society, that is, by civilian society culture, they think, feel and act accordingly, and they change along the same lines. Under this viewpoint the cultural gap can exist along the path from pre-modern to modern to post-modern society, but it is lower and rapidly abridged by means of processes of systemic adjustment.

It would be simplicistic and even unwise to choose the one or the other thesis: much more promising is to look for a synthesis, observing that:

- A certain definition of the contents of *military culture* does exist and it is widely accepted. In the last years it has become usual to speak of a *traditional* (or even *conventional*) military culture, thus assuming that something is changing or it has changed.
- When speaking of a traditional military culture, reference is done to a given set of values, to some peculiar priorities in social life, to the preference for certain basic moral criteria, that are usually considered as typical of so-called traditional pre-modern societies: prevalence of ascribed in-group norms, large social hierarchies acceptance, absolute authority legitimacy often religiously founded, obedience and personal loyalty to one's in-group and master.
- The occurrence of a gap between military and civilian culture can thus be seen as the consequence of the passing of traditional society toward modernity, and even more from modernity to a post-modern assessment of social institutions, causing and widening the cultural diversity between typical military values and new post-modern values within civil society at large.[2]
- The awareness of cultural diversity among different societies also plays a role in the consideration that the military–civilian gap can differ according to different societies: according to Hofstede's school of cultural dimensions affecting national cultures' differences, military culture could be defined as intrinsically collectivist, highly hierarchical, strongly adverse to uncertainty and even more feminine than masculine in that it stresses conservation more than innovation.[3] The dimensions taken from cross-cultural research to explain cultural differences and applied to single organisations can show that each organisation adjusts to change according to its national culture characters: this can be done also by military organisations, thus giving rise to different type of military–civilian gap as well.

3. SOME COMMENTS ON FINDINGS FROM THE CROSS-NATIONAL RESEARCH ON CIVILIAN–MILITARY GAP

Findings collected by this research cover a rather large set of topics, and they are presented in the chapters devoted to each relevant topic where a supposed distance between military and civilian actors can be found. The peculiarity of our data is that they have been collected from two distinct groups of respondents, young cadets from military academies and their "civilian counterpart", university students of various faculties. This fact is important since we deal here with opinions, preferences, value-based judgements and evaluations expressed by groups which can be considered as future elites in their societies, military elites and civilian elites. These are in fact the definitions used by authors to address respondents. Our task is to try to make some general comparison, looking for some macro-variables useful to compare not single aspects or countries but general trends or groups of nations.

3.1. Countries, Nations, Cultures

Findings come from 13 countries, the majority of them belonging to Western Europe (France, Germany, Italy, Netherlands, Spain, Sweden, Switzerland), some of them with a past in the so-called Eastern Europe (Bulgaria, Poland, Romania and Slovenia), and two countries not belonging to the West stricto sensu (Turkey and South Africa), characterised by diverse cultural traditions but anyway highly affected by a westernised culture. A variety as such induces to see whether it is possible to use cross-cultural dimensions to form cultural areas, and to consider not simply nations but clusters of nations as different cultures.

It is redundant here to recall arguments and critics about the *habitus* of cross-cultural studies to use *culture* and *nation* as more or less synonymous, and to make generalisations such as the concept of *national culture* taken as a variable valid to distinguish and give sense to groups of individual sharing or not the one or the other behaviour or value. There are anyway reasons to think that belonging to a certain administrative and political unit called "nation" makes sense in that it gives people a shared identity and it refers to a number of shared values and norms. National cultures differ from one another, but cross-cultural comparison has recognised the weight of some more general dimensions, according to which single national cultures can be grouped into macro-areas where similarities are more evident than diversities.

It has appeared worthy here to make use of the most common set of comparative concepts, used by Inglehart et al. in the WVS programs (Inglehart, Basanez, Dìez-Medrano, Halman, & Luijkx, 2004). Theories derived by world values surveys state that the large majority of national cultures can be grouped in clusters according to the cross-tabulation of two basic dimensions, whose definition is clearly stated by Inglehart as it follows: Traditional authority vs. Secular-Rational authority on the one hand, Survival values vs. Self-Expression values on the other.[4] The cross-tabulation of these two basic dimensions permits to have four theoretical types of culture, three of which more plausible and made of specific value sets where the well-known distinction among traditional–modern–post-modern society can be recognised.

> The Traditional/Secular-rational values dimension reflects the contrast between societies in which religion is very important and those in which it is not – but deference to the authority of God, Fatherland and Family are all closely linked. In traditional societies, a main goal in most people's lives is to make their parents proud; they idealized large families, and have large numbers of children. They also have high levels of national pride, favour more respect for authority and reject divorce, abortion, euthanasia and suicide. Societies with secular-rational values have the opposite preferences on all these topics. The Survival/Self-expression dimension taps a syndrome of tolerance, trust, subjective well-being, political activism and self-expression that emerges in post-industrial societies with high levels of existential security. People in societies shaped by insecurity tend to emphasize economic and physical security above all, and feel threatened by foreigners, by ethnic diversity and by cultural change (…) They emphasize economic and physical security more than autonomy and self-expression, have relatively high levels of faith in science and technology, are relatively low on environmental activism and relatively favourable to authoritarian government. Societies high on Self-expression values tend to have opposite preferences on all these topics (Inglehart et al., 2004, pp. 12–13).

The combination of Traditional values and Survival values defines the traditional culture, the opposite combination of Secular-rational values and Self-expression values defines the post-modern culture, and modern culture is placed at an intermediate stage made of Secular-rational values combined with an advanced level of survival values, when industrialisation permits and gives prominence to economic growth and security needs assurance by means of an increasing diffusion of welfare and social guarantees.

The argument here is that there is some consistency with the position of a country in the cultural map, that is with its position along the tradition–modern–post-modern path, and the quality of the gap between military and civilian culture in each country.

According to the culture-free conception of military culture, the gap should emerge in modern societies and be rather prominent only in post-modern societies; but the culture-bound thesis could explain why modern and post-modern societies can have different types and degrees of military–civilian cultural gap (and even no gap at all), by adopting the dimensional analysis proposed and developed by means of the Hofstede (1991) research findings. Military culture could differ or not from its own national culture depending on its relative rank on dimensions such as Collectivism/Individualism, Power Distance, Uncertainty Avoidance or Masculinity. In this chapter, however, comments will be dealing only with the first part of the argument, since an application of Hofstede measure tools has not been considered reliable for our data.

3.2. Clusters of Countries

According to WVS last version of the Cultural Map, the 13 countries of this database belong to three different quadrants, and their relative position differs greatly according to the two above-mentioned dimensions. If considered according to their relative axial proximity, four clusters can be formed, namely: a Post-modern Protestant group (Switzerland, Netherlands, Sweden, to which Germany could be added), a Post-modern Catholic group (France, Italy, Spain), a third Modern East-European group (Bulgaria, Poland, Romania and Slovenia) and a fourth group where the similarity trait is given by country position within the Traditional quadrant (Turkey and South Africa). A distinction as such does not mean that countries within the same cluster are absolutely similar: distances from one another are great, testifying the high level of socio-cultural diversity within Europe and among the 13 countries in themselves. Taking into account the meaning of the two dimensions, Bulgaria, Romania, Poland, Turkey and South Africa belong to the left half of the map, where the Survival values pole predominates; but Bulgaria is high on Secular–Rational Values and belong to the upper left half of the Map where modernity values are typical, while Romania is much lower and nearer Traditional society, like Poland; Turkey and South Africa occupy a position strongly inclined to traditional culture for certain traits, but they are more advanced toward Self-expression values. In the right-side half of the map we find all the remaining countries in the upper right quadrant: Sweden, Netherlands and Switzerland score high on both Self-Expression Values and Secular–Rational Values, a combination that Inglehart defines as already post-modern; Germany is high on Rational Values but less inclined to Self-expression values than the three previous countries. Post-modern but comparatively less secularised are countries such as France, Italy and Spain. According to their relative degree of similarity and diversity, the 13 countries display different positions along the move from traditional to modern to post-modern cultures, and these different cultures could imply different types of civil–military relationships.

Comparison among the 13 countries will be done considering only a selection among the huge amount of findings collected by the structured questionnaire, namely values and norms where a clearer cultural influence can be ascribed. The choice to consider values, in the distinction made here by Haltiner & Weibull in "basic value orientations" and "global-cosmopolitan orientation",[5] has seemed more adequate since values and beliefs are more permanent than opinions and preferences (which are influenced, on the contrary, by events and many other contingencies). Definitions here used, moreover, such as "traditional", "modern" and "post-modern" culture, are based on value dimensions.

A general outlook at findings induce to think that the culture-bound thesis has more good reasons to be adopted, since differences between students and cadets are lower than expected under many respects, and in many countries.

As far as religiosity is concerned, regular church attendance and general conformity to religious rites has been considered to be part of a traditional orientation: as it has been proved by Haltiner & Weibull's analysis, this trait is not particularly widespread in the military segment per se; cadets and students show high religiosity in countries like South Africa, Poland and Italy, and the first two countries are part of the traditional quadrant, while Italy is one of those post-modern countries nearest traditional values; on the contrary, a generalised minor religiosity is declared by respondents of the two groups in countries belonging to the upper side of the cultural map, where secular and rational values are predominant, that is in Germany, Bulgaria, the Netherlands, Sweden and Switzerland. Turkish cadets are far less church attendants as well, and this also can be explained by means of the peculiar socio-political history of the country. In other countries such as France, Spain and Switzerland (where secularisation is winning less than in the other post-modern countries) young officers "show a slightly higher degree of church attendance and thus a more traditional behaviour than their civilian counterparts".[6]

Another value domain affected by the passing of traditional society toward modernity and post-modernity is the local–cosmopolitan orientation. Two groups have been selected according to respondents' high rate of sense of belonging assigned to cosmopolitan or to local reference groups; in our findings, there is a certain gap between students and cadets in those countries where a transition is occurring from a certain type of modernity to the mainly post-modern culture of Western Europe: in Bulgaria, Poland, Romania and Slovenia the cosmopolitan oriented group is mainly formed by civilian students than by their military counterparts, the same happens for Spain; also in transitional countries such as Turkey and South Africa, more students are cosmopolitan than cadets are; in countries rated as post-modern in the Inglehart's Cultural Map, both students and cadets show cosmopolitan orientations in similar percentages. Again, according to the culture-bound thesis, a certain gap between civilian and military culture can occur in the transition from a traditional to a modern society, and from a modern to a post-modern society, but it is destined to be overcome by the adjustment of the military to the inclusive societal cultural models.

A rather traditional scheme to compare value sets is the Materialist–Postmaterialist scale. Leaving aside the critics addressed to this Inglehart artefact, in the questionnaire items have been asked in order to distinguish a possible gap between the two groups of respondents. Three results are noteworthy: the first is that post-materialism is rather low: the majority of respondents shows a prevailing materialist outlook, somehow corrected by a minor number of post-materialists; the second result is that there is no gap, or a very small one, since in all countries students and cadets give more or less the same answers; the third is that, when a certain difference does exists, more cadets tend to give more materialist answers than students. According to countries, post-materialists respondents are higher in numbers in countries belonging to the post-modern quadrant of the map (Sweden, Spain, France, Netherlands, Switzerland); on the contrary, countries whose position is located in the quadrant where survival values prevail show higher level of materialism (Bulgaria, Poland, Slovenia, Romania, South Africa and Turkey). Germany and Italy are the most materialist, relatively speaking, among upper-right quadrant countries. Generally speaking, it seems that cadets and students follow the same trend according to the one prevailing in one's own country, thus giving reason to the culture-bound approach.

A confirmation of this can be found in the acute and deep analysis made in this volume by Haltiner & Weibull in the sphere of dailylife values considered more or less important by cadets and civilian students with reference to two distinct domains, private life (children education) and the military as an institution: the authors' conclusion is that both cadets and students do not differ so much in the structure of their value set, and when they differ it is more with reference to the specific of their professional role for cadets, than because of a radical divergence as toward civil life value orientation between the two groups. This is also my opinion, with a final comment: if a relative gap can be observed between military and civilian students, this varies greatly according to the various countries, better, according to groups of countries. Distances seem to be larger in countries belonging to the post-modern cluster (Sweden, Switzerland, Spain, France, Italy, the Netherlands), and lowering down in modern countries such as Slovenia, Bulgaria and Poland, and even less appreciable in Romania, South Africa and Turkey. Notwithstanding the fact that these differences are not radical and should be taken with caution because of the relative small size of national samples, this could give some support to the culture-free thesis, according to which military culture is specific and find more convergences with so-called traditional societies than with modern or post-modern cultures. But this result could also be considered as another mark of the well-known distinction between traditional, less differentiated society and current modern or post-modern highly differentiated and specialised societies, where the military plays its own specific and peculiar role as any other professional or subcultural group.

NOTES

1. See for instance Boene (1990), How unique should the military be? already cited.
2. See for these definitions the several works by R. Inglehart and his World Values Surveys Group.
3. Hofstede (1991 and further editions), *Cultures and Organizations. Software of the Mind*, London, McGraw-Hill
4. Last reference of these definitions is in Inglehart et al. (2004), *Human Values and Beliefs*, already cited.
5. Haltiner and Weibull (2007) *Value orientations and Political Attitudes among Future Military and Civilian Elites*, in this volume.
6. Haltiner & Weibull, *cited*, in this volume.

REFERENCES

Boene, B. (1990). How unique should the military be? *European Journal of Sociology*, *31*, 3–59.
Cotton, Ch. (1988). The institutional organizational model and the military. In: C. C. Moskos Jr. & F. R. Wood (Eds), *The military: More than just A job?* (pp. 39–55). London/New York: Pergamon/Brassey's.
Eisenstadt, S. N. (Ed.) (1984). *Patterns of modernity*. New York: New York University Press.
Eisenstadt, S. N. (1992). A reappraisal of theories of social change and modernization. In: H. Haferkamp & N. J. Smelser (Eds), *Social change and modernity*. Berkeley: University of California Press.
Geser, H. (1995). La nuova sfida dell'ordine mondiale: una prospettiva organizzativa. In: A. Gobbicchi (Ed.), *La professione militare oggi*. Milano: Angeli.
Hofstede, G. (1991). *Cultures and organizations: Software of the mind*. London: McGraw-Hill.

Inglehart, R., Basanez, M., Dìez-Medrano, J., Halman, L., & Luijkx, R. (2004). *Human values and beliefs. A cross-cultural sourcebook based on the 1999–2002 values surveys*. Mexico: Siglo XXI Editores.

Kerr, C., Dunlop, J., Harbison, F., & Myers, G. (1960). *Industrialism and industrial man*. Boston, NY: Harvard University Press.

Lawrence, P. R., & Lorsch, J. W. (1967). *Organizations and Environment*. Cambridge, MA: Harvard University Press.

Moskos, C. C., Jr. (1977). From institution to occupation: Trends in military organisation. *Armed Forces & Society*, *4*(4), 41–50.

Moskos, C. C., Jr. (1986). Institutional and occupational trends in armed forces: An update. *Armed Forces & Society*, *12*(3), 377–382.

Thompson, J. D. (1967). *Organization in action*. New York: McGraw-Hill.

PART III:
COUNTRY PAPERS

CIVIL–MILITARY RELATIONS IN BULGARIA

Yantsislav Yanakiev

1. MAIN DEVELOPMENTS AND ACHIEVEMENTS

There is no doubt that democracy explicitly supposes unlimited civilian supremacy over the military. Therefore, the process of building democratic civil–military relations (CMR) and establishment of democratic control over the military is the key element of the social transition in Bulgaria and the transformation of the Bulgarian Armed Forces (BAF) from "guards of the power" into an "instrument of foreign policy". The essence of this process is in establishing democratic control over the military plus building up a mutual understanding and confidence as well as redefining the military professionalism.

The military institution in Bulgaria traditionally attracts high public support both before and after 1989 (Yanakiev & Domozetov, 2000). Public opinion polls found confidence in the Army as an institution to have varied between 63% and 70% for the initial years after the democratic changes in Bulgaria, and lack of confidence, between 10% and 12% (Yanakiev, 1999). This high level of confidence has been sustained until recently.

The high rating of the BAF compared with the other state institutions is probably due to several factors. First, in the period of social transformation in Bulgaria, the BAF has come to be seen by the public as truly national institution and a guarantee for the ongoing process of democratization of

Cultural Differences between the Military and Parent Society in Democratic Countries
Contributions to Conflict Management, Peace Economics and Development, Volume 4, 241–246

ISSN: 1572-8323/doi:10.1016/S1572-8323(07)04011-8

the country because it has remained aloof from politics. At the same time, it is unanimously acknowledged to have functions vital to the nation. Second, the ongoing process of differentiation of political and professional ranks in the top echelon of military administration and the establishment of a system of civilian control over the military has raised the prestige of the armed forces as a democratic institution. Third, the BAF accomplishes new tasks such as participation in international peacekeeping and humanitarian missions under the United Nations aegis, joint exercises within North Atlantic Treaty Organization (NATO) and the European Union (EU). The armed forces are thus perceived as an institution helping in the acceleration of Bulgarian integration in Euro-Atlantic defense and security structures and promoting international prestige of Bulgaria.

It is important to underline that the comparison between the public confidence in the military, as an institution, and the prestige of military profession show that they do not match. This situation has been changing slowly during the last decade but divergence still exists. The analysis of data from recent opinion poll (Yanakiev, 2003) shows that the public rates the military in the "golden middle" or at 10th place out of 20 most common professions and occupations. The Bulgarians perceive the military profession as one devoted to the "common good", which is of value to the others and important for the society. At the same time, compared with other professions it is not rated among the most prestigious. The main reason for this rating, in contemporary Bulgarian society, is materialistic rather than post-materialistic ones.

The divergence between the public image of the military institution and the military profession is a very important question because in the situation when there is a widespread perception of low war probability it could result in role crisis among the military professionals. The surveys clearly indicate some changes in public opinion about the military because of their participation "in real action" (international peacekeeping missions, international military cooperation, etc.). In this regard, broadening of missions and tasks of the BAF towards support to civil society and participation in missions abroad will help promoting positive image of military profession.

One of the most important achievements of the CMR is the successful process of national consensus building on the strategic priorities of Bulgarian foreign and security policy – accession into Euro-Atlantic defense and security structures among the political parties, the President, the National Assembly and the government. This consensus is expressed in decisions made on the Defense and Security sector Reform (D&SSR); Bulgaria's accession to NATO and EU; contribution to fighting international terrorism; enlargement of the participation in NATO and EU-led Peace Support Operations (PSOs).

In addition, the consensus is expressed in maintaining a comparatively high level of defense spending during the transition period. Despite financial constrains there exists political will and declared commitment of the government to keep the annual defense budget within 2.6% of the GDP for the period 2005–2007 and the forecasted relative share of annual defense expenditures within the same framework for the period 2007–2015 (Long-Term Vision for Development of the Armed Forces – 2015, 2004).

Another important achievement of the CMR during the process of democratization in Bulgaria is the development of the legal and doctrinal basis of the D&SSR and regular update of the basic defense policy instruments. Among these basic documents are the Armed Forces Act (1995); the National Security Concept (1998); the Bulgarian Military Doctrine (1999); the White paper of the Armed Forces and Defense (2001); Military strategy of the Republic of Bulgaria (2002); Agenda 2004 on the reform of the Armed Forces; the Strategic Defense Review (2004); the Long-Term Vision for Development of the Armed Forces – 2015 (2004); the Plan for the buildup and modernization of the armed forces by 2015.

The existing political consensus as well as the developed legal and doctrinal basis of the reform made possible substantial progress in the reorganization and restructuring of the BAF. The typical totalitarian status of "a state within the state" has changed.

The reform of the armed forces began in 1997. Based on the Force Structure Review in 2002, the government approved an updated Plan for the buildup and organization of the armed forces of the Republic of Bulgaria by 2004. This Plan is based on the optimization of the personnel and organizational structure of the Bulgarian army. We are applying a model as a result of which the peacetime personnel of the Bulgarian army is 45,000 while the wartime strength amounts to 100,000.

A significant step towards establishing All Volunteer Force (AVF) was made in the context of implementing D&SSR. The process of forming a 100% armed forces manned on a volunteer basis will be completed by 2008. Until the end of 2006, the Air forces and the Navy were be fully equipped with volunteer soldiers (Long-Term Vision for Development of the Armed Forces – 2015, 2004).

Despite the important developments in the CMR in Bulgaria during the past 15 years of democratic changes, there exist some points of tension that deserve attention. They can be summarized in three main groups.

2. POINTS OF TENSIONS

The first group of tensions concerns social aspect of CMR and is related to the significant and, for the first time in the New Bulgarian history, personnel reduction under the Plan 2004 for restructuring and reorganization of the BAF. The problem is that the reduction was carried out with insufficient care to preserve young officers. In addition, the resettlement and social adaptation programs for redundant military officers have been not successful. All these failures caused difficulties in social reintegration of dismissed military personnel, tensions on the labor market and in the society as a whole.

The second group of tensions concerns the defense planning and implementation of D&SSR. There still exist divergence between the vision and understanding of the politicians and the military. The military leaders insist on preparation of the armed forces to tackle the worst scenario (war and territorial defense), which is the main function of the BAF according to the Constitution, but at the same time it is the last probable scenario. The politicians would like to have armed forces prepared for the broad spectrum of new missions that is the most probable scenario of employment of the BAF according to the 2004 Strategic Defense Review.

In addition, there were tensions in the process of learning the meaning of democratic control of the armed forces by civilians as well as in the process of adoption of new laws and other legal acts on the armed forces. Clear example in this regard is the existing, at least in the beginning of democratic changes in Bulgaria, misunderstanding of the role of the civilians and the military in defense system management. There were attempts of some civilians to take operational control over the military, to replace the military in command and control of the troops and, on the other side willingness of some of the high ranking military to act as politicians.

Particular attention deserves the third group of tensions, which is related to decision-making process when Bulgarian troops are sent to participate in international missions. There were tensions with respect to the first Bulgarian peacekeeping mission (Cambodia, 1992–1993) because of the poor selection, training and equipment of the troops as well as negative public opinion for sending Bulgarian soldiers abroad. The new situation when the Bulgarian participation in coalitions of willing is broaden, there is still lack of joint civil–military decision-making based on joint civilian and military expertise.

What are the causes of the existing tensions in CMR?

One of the most important is the not efficient legislative basis for regulation of civil–military relations and democratic control over the military, which sometimes block effective decision-making process. For example, the role, the functions and the responsibilities of the President of the State as the Supreme Commander-in-chief of the BAF are not properly defined in the legislation as well as the interrelations with the Council of Ministers in the security sector management process.

Another factor is the primitive understanding of the way civilian and military experts have to work together. The "division of labor" is the currently accepted model, which results in lack of joint efforts in decision-making. The Ministry of Defense (MoD) and the General Staff (GS) still function as two separate structures. The Chief of the GS is formally subordinated to the MoD as well as the President. According to the armed forces law, the Chief of the GS has the authority to re-sign the ministerial orders regarding the armed forces.

Last but not the least, there still exists lack of political education among the military and strategic education and knowledge among the civilians in the MoD and security sector structures.

To summarize, there is an important change in the substance of the tensions in CMR in Bulgaria. In the initial years after the democratic changes in 1989, the main issue was about the limits of civilian control, the borders of pure military expertise, etc. Now, the main issue is how to manage the new situation caused by the dynamics of the complex D&SSR, the new tasks of the BAF, the participation in international coalitions and the need to participate in multinational decision-making process. All these challenges demand joint political–military effort.

3. ROOM FOR IMPROVEMENT

Theoretically and practically, the Parliament and the Government have enough instruments for democratic control over the military. The problem is that these instruments are not used effectively. Political (Parliamentary) control is not effective enough because it is too general. The parliamentary committees are frequently "crisis management bodies" instead of places where consensus on the future of the BAF has to be built. Political control has to be expanded in addition to MoD and GS towards the staffs of the services and large units commanders in order to have broad information of the performance of the BAF. In addition, there is a lack of specialization among policymakers on broad spectrum of security and defense issues. Moreover, there exists unrealistic belief in many of the Bulgarian political and military leaders that once the formal requirements of the civilian democratic control are met the control itself will be guaranteed.

Last but not the least, civil society control over the security policy formulation and implementation is undeveloped. The inertia of old thinking still remains "military issues are domains of military experts", ergo – the public is not prepared to understand these issues. As a result, there exists lack of interest among the general public in defense and security issues as well as little influence on decision-making in security and defense policy formulation.The most important issue that both the military leadership and politicians has to face is how to manage the new situation caused by the dynamics of the complex defense transformation, the new tasks and missions of the BAF, involvement in international coalitions and the need to participate in multinational decision-making process, i.e. to make the important step from managing defense reform towards planning and managing of the transformation of defense and the armed forces.

There is clear need to update legislative and doctrinal basis for national security after Bulgarian accession in NATO and to define the role of the BAF in the new missions, in the collective defense in multinational environment, joint education and training with the Ministry of Interior, Civil Protection Agency, etc. The new/updated legislation has to change the focus from defense towards security sector oriented developments.

REFERENCES

Long-Term Vision For Development of The Armed Forces – 2015. (2004). www.md.government.bg \Long-term vision for development of the Armed forces – 2015.htm

Strategic Defense Review Policy Framework. www.md.government.bg\Strategic defense review_Policy framework.htm

Yanakiev, Y. (1999). The military. In: N. Genov & A. Krasteva (Eds), *Bulgaria 1960–1995 trends of social development* (pp. 292–300). Sofia: National and Global Development.

Yanakiev, Y. (2003). Views of the Bulgarian public on security, defense and the military. In: M. Vlachova (Ed.), *The public image of defense and the military in central and eastern Europe* (pp. 251–268). Belgrade: Geneva Center for Democratic Control of Armed Forces and Center for Civil-Military Relations available in Internet: http://www.dcaf.ch/publications/e-publications/Pub_Image_Defence/Yanakiev.pdf

Yanakiev, Y., & Domozetov, C. (2000). *Public Perceptions of Euro-Atlantic Partnership: Security and Defense Issues (The Case of Bulgaria)*. NATO Office of Information and Press, Final Report NATO-EAPC Institutional Fellowship, http://www.nato.int/acad/fellow/98-00/yanakiev.pdf

CIVIL CULTURAL AND MILITARY MODELS IN FRANCE: COMMON MODELS?

Claude Weber and Axel Augé

INTRODUCTION

Good working relationship between civilians and military has been one of the key priorities of French Politicians in the last decade. President Jacques Chirac has himself in a political speech in 1996 mentioned a professionalisation of the military corpus which has raised concerns of the future of French armed forces and led to the transformation of the relationship between the military and non-military sector. A good example of this cultural transformation could be noted in the creation of the so-called JAPD (Journée d'Appel à la Préparation de Défense) which is a one day event during which the French young population is given the opportunity to have an insight into the military environment.

We defend the idea here that being given the chance to become a professional of the French armies is synonym of a real cultural opening of the military to the civil society. It is also seen as a practice which could easily be compared to non-military practices as opposed to military models. Our hypothesis is that there are more and more bridges between military and civilian cultures and that the key specificities of the military system stay in some of their duties and key operational functions.

Cultural Differences between the Military and Parent Society in Democratic Countries
Contributions to Conflict Management, Peace Economics and Development, Volume 4, 247–253

ISSN: 1572-8323/doi:10.1016/S1572-8323(07)04012-X

METHODOLOGY

As regards the methodology used in this study, quantitative approach through questionnaires and qualitative technique through interviews were chosen. One of the biggest difficulty was to translate the questions from French into English and respect authors's first intentions.

Corpus of analysis: A total of 149 people made up of 90 military students, 47 non-military students and 12 informers.

Two populations were polled: a military one made of students from the French military Academy of St-Cyr and one of civilians composed from several universities. Our civil population came from Law students in public and private institutes and from students in Politics mainly from one of the top Institutes of Political Studies school in Paris called IEP (Institut d'Etudes Politiques).

Interviews: We met 12 people: four journalists from different background, three members of the university community, four military officers and one politician.

Let's say a few words about the military population. In St-Cyr there are actually three schools all with different recruitment procedures: ESM, Ecole Spéciale Militaire (The Military Special School) – EMIA: Ecole Militaire Interarmées (The Inter-Armed Military School) and EMCTA: l'Ecole Militaire du Corps Technique et Administratif (The Technical and Administrative Officers Military School) (Table 1).

About 100 questionnaires have been dispatched in the military population by students of the ESM (considered as one of the most prestigious formation, students are recruited following excellent results in some of the national competitions) and students of the EMIA (people who were already NCO before). These two populations do not have the same profile in terms of age, origin, military experience, etc., as these factors could have influenced the results of our analysis.

Table 1. Military Corpus: Distribution $N = 90$.

Level of Officers Formation	Effective (ni)	Frequency (%)
ESM – 1st year	29	32.2
ESM – last year	12	13.3
EMIA – last year	29	32.2
EMIA 2 – 1st year	20	22.2
Total	90	100

We noted that the answers given by the ESM students were extremely logical and full of prejudgement while the answers of their counterpart military students of EMIA were more open, because they have a better experience of the military profession. Almost all of them had a military work experience before joining Coëtquidan military school.

RESULTS IN NATIONALS SPECIFICITIES

There is a real proximity between the answers given by the military students and those given by the others. Nowadays the links between the civilian and military have strengthened: communication has improved, initiatives such as the JAPD have facilitated these links, etc. The end of conscription increases the proximity between the army and the population.

One point of analysis clearly shows that the military culture and its specificity is due to its professional specificity, i.e., preparing soldiers to die and to kill. In this specificity, we can analyse the military functional principle which resists cultural connection with civil society. Thus, as all jobs, military jobs require special professional culture. Two factors underline those professional dimensions: firstly, religion and professional values such as affection to the Nation, discipline, respect of traditions, loyalty and secondly, the integration of women in the army. These two aspects have been the most underlined in our research.

Importance of Values for Military Officers

In spite of a more open culture from the military towards civil society, a phenomenon which author Morris Janowitz calls in French the "civilianisation"[1] of army, in which he reflects that some aspects of military jobs are more concerned with a cultural connection of civilians and their model. But religion and professional values are not affected by those transformations and cultural changes. In this point of view, the political control remains stable. *"The politicians decide and the militaries executes. Each actor stays in his area" (General Officer met)*. "The political control is exercised in accordance with legal framework in democratic country. There is stability between politicians and military leaders on democratic control. Political control of armed forces is made by the government" (*Journalist*).

In France, it is not usual to see a military making comments on political mechanisms. Even in the Department of Defense where the high officer works with politicians, a good relationship must prevail: the officer has to come under any political power.

Religious Values

Religion is the first specific aspect which is attached to professional military culture, that is to say one can see cultural differences between military and civil students. The factors "beliefs and religion" show different attitudes in both populations. The attachment to religion is strong and can be explained by the fundamental specificity of the job: preparing soldiers to die and to kill (Table 2).

According to a survey carried on military students, 71 percent admitted that they are practicing catholic religion against only 57 percent among civil students. There is an important percentage of atheists in civil students (23 percent against 15 percent in military population). The above statistics table indicates that a large majority of military student is from a catholic faith; about 7 military students out of 10 on average. The number of no answers is really small: only 7.8 percent. This indicates again how important it is to show the impact of religion in our sample.

Specific Professional Values

The military duties and functions determined by the specific values attached to the profession make it difficult to convert them into civil roles.

Solidarity and Belonging to One Body. This is a key element to military students. That notion has a stronger meaning in the army than in a non-military society. It implies a great sense of hierarchy and discipline. A duty to obey and representation a strong sense of mutual aid between "brothers

Table 2. Military Students: Membership Confessionnal Shown, Occasional Religious Practical.

Religious Membership	Effective	Frequency (%)
Catholicism	64	71.1
Protestantism	3	3.3
Orthodox	1	1.1
Muslim	1	1.1
None: atheism	14	15.6
No answers	7	7.8
Total	90	100

in arms". The importance of solidarity is very strong, in fact, it represents 100 percent of the military population.

Attachment to the Nation, Abnegation and Spirit of Sacrifice. All students we have met, have recognised the great importance of these values. In relation with their professional socialisation, 95 percent of the military students said having a great attachment to the nation, a value of their devise: Honnor and Homeland. Whereas civil students are more naturally enclined to their own satisfaction and private lives.

Respect of Traditions. Military stay strongly attached to traditions and to their transmission necessary to the professional value based on respect of older military. They are 76 percent to consider this value important against only 54 percent in civil student population. In spite of individualisms growing up which transform social link in civil society and which transform social institutions like Family, State, Institutional Church (catholicism for example), army product-specific social link named "esprit de corps" and solidarity was founded on principle of "*federative adversity*"[2] and traditions.

Army and Gender: The Role Played by Women in the Army

The question about what role a woman can play in a fight or during the war is very controversial and remains for military and civil students an issue which is worth raising. If 88 percent among the military students are favourable to women integration as volunteers only 20 percent accept the idea that women soldiers could go to battle as their counterpart men. Amongst the military students, 65 percent disagree with the participation of women in fighting. The same trend can be noticed among civil students. Asked about a possible participation in fighting as volunteers, 72 percent among civil students is in favour. Concerning a compulsory participation of women in the army, 61 percent is against.

Thus, for the military students, women have the full right to go to battlefields and can aspire to have any post except from the key strategic ones. For civil students, the women can take part in any actions involving fighting but only as volunteers. These scenarios are really different depending on the type of the populations we have met: some clearly show that the role played by women in the military must be limited to some minor responsibilities such as military secretary, administration, military health which are considered as female jobs.

Several reasons have been given to explain these positions. For military students, 80 percent think that women in the battlefield can be a big trouble element for the group: demoralisation, possibility to be captured or kidnapped by enemies, element of violence, i.e., more likely to be raped. For civil students, who are opposed to women integration in fighting, the same reasons are mentioned. This strong opposition among civil and military students about women integration shows a general image of domination of males in the army and particularly in the battlefield a "macho culture" is predominant. In fact, for many males military, army and military jobs still appear traditionnally like a man job more particularly when it concerns fighting. In this conception, women cannot have same responsibilities in fighting. If feminisation[3] is a process which cannot be avoided in the army, several men in the army still believe that the women's role must be attached to actions and positions considered as reserved to females. Mentally speaking, it will be difficult to change this specific point.

CONCLUSION

French citizens have a history for their striking lack of interest in defence matters, except in times of crisis. In this perspective, professionalisation does not seem to have made things worst. On the contrary, the debate generated by this unprecedented revolution in the armed forces and the light shed on it have contributed to the positive evolution of opinions and representations of this institution. Civilian and military relationship and communication have improved. There is still a need of establishing a close link between University and Research and a more transparent military professionalism which would definitely lead to the recruitment of more diverse workforce in which women and the so-called "visible" minorities would play a more strategic role. It is important that military training continues to strengthen the exchanges between military and civilian society since the former has been professionalised.

The military body is essentially functional and is mainly limited to the execution of missions. This functional role has been intensified since the process of professionalisation started and without that, it is not possible to understand the proximity between the military culture and the civil one. Moreover professionalisation in the French army does not mean total changes about the whole military institution but simply adaptation. The cultural models which establish connection or link between military and civil students are more important than those which tend to separate them.

NOTES

1. For more details, to consult : Feaver Peter D., "The civil-military problematique: Huntington, Janowitz, and the question of Civilian Control", *Armed forces and society, 23(2), Hiver 1996, pp. 149–178.* And Bernard Boëne, *"Permanence et relativité de la spécificité militaire: examen critique de la littérature existante, esquisse d'une synthèse*", pp. 188–240, dans Bernard Boëne, dir., *La spécificité militaire*, Paris, Armand Colin, 1990. Janowitz Morris, *The Professionnal soldier: A social and Political portrait* (1re éd. 1960), New York, The Free Press, 1971, p. 464.
2. Philippe Contamine (1986) have exactly shown how french patriotism were built with the war of *Cent Years* firtly, and secondly against United Kingdom.
3. Katia Sorin analyze with more details the process of feminisation in the army in France: Katia Sorin, *Femmes en armes, une place introuvable*. Paris, L'Harmattan, 2003.

THE CIVIL–MILITARY GAP AMONG GERMAN FUTURE ELITES

Sabine Collmer and Gerhard Kümmel

1. METHODOLOGY AND SOCIO-DEMOGRAPHIC SAMPLE DESCRIPTION

We surveyed 270 young officers studying at the Bundeswehr University in Munich and 400 civilian students from Potsdam University. Both groups of future elites were from the social sciences, law, economics or computer sciences departments. The questionnaires were distributed to respondents between January and May 2004. All respondents were volunteers. Return rates were 99% for the military sample with 268 questionnaires returned and 25% for the civilian sample with 100 questionnaires returned so that a total of 368 questionnaires were processed.

The data analysis was carried out with the statistical package SPSS, Version 12.0.1 G for Windows. For statistical purposes, responses were often grouped to reflect either a positive, negative or neutral position. According to scale level, a chi-square test of significance or a two-tailed *T*-test was conducted in order to test statistically significant differences between the two groups.

320 respondents were male (256 studying officers, 64 students) and 42 were female (6 studying officers, 36 students). Six persons did not indicate their gender. The age of respondents from the Bundeswehr University varied from 20 to 32 years; the age of respondents from Potsdam University varied

Cultural Differences between the Military and Parent Society in Democratic Countries
Contributions to Conflict Management, Peace Economics and Development, Volume 4, 255–259

ISSN: 1572-8323/doi:10.1016/S1572-8323(07)04013-1

from 19 to 35 years. The mean age was 26. As regards religious affiliation, officer students were more catholic than the civilian students whereas the latter were both more atheistic and religiously more diverse. A military background, i.e. some military family tradition, was largely absent in both groups. With officer students, there was none who indicated that his father had been either a contract or a career soldier, but 2.9% indicated that this was the case for their mothers. By contrast, the father of 3.2% of the civilian students and the mother of 1.1% were either a contract or a career soldier. Yet, 71% of the officer students and 75% of the civilian students, respectively said that there father had ever served in the military, i.e. mostly as a conscript.

2. FINDINGS

The empirical data clearly show that there is some civil–military gap in Germany. This gap is documented and presents statistically significant differences between civilian students and military students along the lines of levels of significance ($p \leq 0.001$ and $p \leq 0.01$, respectively).

The overall picture emerging from these data does not come as a surprise. Although there are areas where the opinions of both groups of future elites overlap, military and civilian students differ significantly on a wide range of issues: values and norms; world views; domestic policy; foreign, security and defense policy, threat perceptions, military policy, role of the armed forces, military operations, etc. The most important of these will be dealt with in the following.

2.1. Norms and World Views

The base line here is the much more pronounced skeptical or pessimistic view of the world and of mankind by officer students. Whereas only close to two-thirds of the civilian students think that *human nature being what it is there will always be war*, more than four-fifths of the military students agree to this item (64 vs. 83%) This is reflected in explicitly traditional orientations and conservative attitudes. In terms of political inclination, the officer students are almost exclusively center-right, with only a few indicating a right-wing political attitude whereas the civilian students, in general, are center-left and leftist. Equally, officer students place much more emphasis than civilian students on values like discipline (97 vs. 81%), self-control

(95 vs. 82%), honor (80 vs. 44%), obedience (72 vs. 43%), patriotism (53 vs. 20%) and traditionalism (53 vs. 37%). Civilian students, by contrast, stress values like spirit/sense of equality (93 vs. 83%), creativity (98 vs. 87%) and generosity (71 vs. 52%). In line with this, officer students attach more relevance than civilian students to the *promotion of patriotism (as) an important aim of citizenship education* (48 vs. 15%), the *primary allegiance (of Germans) to Germany* (82 vs. 39%), the *performance of military service in defense of Germany (as the) strongest indicator of good citizenship* (46 vs. 8%) and to seeing *all Germans (to) be willing to fight for our country* (77 vs. 23%).

2.2. Domestic Policy, Foreign Policy and Threat Perceptions

Given the pattern of the differences in the normative fabric of officer and civilian students just sketched, it is easily understood why officer students give more weight than civilian students to *maintaining order* as the No. 1 goal in domestic policy (50 vs. 27%). Also, *fighting higher prices* is more important to them than to the civilians (13 vs. 7%). By contrast, the latter are more concerned about *giving the people more say in politics* (40 vs. 22%) and *freedom of speech* (26 vs. 16%). This means that, in Ronald Inglehart's terms, officer students are rather materialistic whereas civilian students are rather post-materialistic. This is also reflected in the issue area of foreign policy. Whereas *combating world hunger* and *helping to improve the standard of living in less developed countries* is more important for civilian than for officer students (88 vs. 71% and 81 vs. 58%, respectively) as is *fostering international cooperation to solve common problems* and *preventing and defending human rights in other countries* (95 vs. 85% and 91 vs. 82%, respectively), the latter attach more weight to *maintaining the external security of Germany* and *strengthening regional security alliances such as NATO* (95 vs. 71% and 74 vs. 54%, respectively). Threat perceptions also diverge. Officer students perceive *mass immigration* and *attacks on computer networks* as more likely than civilian students (55 vs. 18% and 78 vs. 63%, respectively) who, by contrast, feel more threatened than officer students by an *accidental nuclear war* and *environmental problems* (24 vs. 10% and 55 vs. 40%, respectively).

2.3. Security Policy and Things Military

In line with what has been detailed above, opinions about and attitudes towards security political issues and things military seem to reflect a collision of two different worlds, as well. This collision seems to resonate with markedly different approaches to and conceptions of the security political worst case, war, and the instrument being employed in such a case, the armed forces. Whereas 58% of the officer students think that *sometimes war is necessary to protect the national interest* only 21% of the civilian students do so. 61% of the latter, but only 12% of the former deem *the military (to be) a necessary evil*. And more than a fifth (21%) of the civilian students, but virtually none of the officer students think that *the military should be abolished*. The diverging viewpoints on the relevance of the armed forces as a security political instrument also come to the fore when compared to other instruments. More than four-fifths of the civilian students (83%), but only 60% of the officer students perceive *the national security of Germany (to) depend more on international trade and a strong domestic economy than on our military strength*. By contrast, 51% of the officer students compared to only 20% of the civilian students argue that *strong armed forces improve our image in the world*. In the same vein, the roles ascribed to the military are different when comparing the two groups of future elites. Whereas 63% of the civilian students want to see the military being employed for *the protection of the environment*, only 32% of the officer students do so. The flip side of the coin is that the acceptance of *peace enforcement* and *combat missions* of the military by officers is much higher than by civilians (peace enforcement: 67 vs. 31%; combat missions: 65 vs. 26%). In addition, *the defense of the country* as a role for the military is approved of by all the officer students compared to 93% of the civilian students. The different valuations of war and the military can also be observed when it comes to providing the military the means for its use: 95% of the officer, but only 25% of the civilian students want to see the defense budget to raise somewhat or considerably. To lower these funds somewhat or considerably is argued by none of the officer, but 35% of the civilian students. Corresponding to this is the fact that civilian students are more sensitive to issues of the democratic civilian control of the military and perceive a more problematic situation here: 9 out of 10 (91%) civilian, but virtually all officer students *rate the political subordination of the military (as) rather or completely realized*. Furthermore, whereas 70% of the officer students agree *that when force is used, military rather than political goals should determine its application*, only 34% of the civilian students do so. A similar pattern, with much less agreement from the civilian side, can be observed when the respondents were asked whether *politicians must give professional autonomy to the military* (84 vs. 40%).

3. DISCUSSION AND CONCLUSION

The empirical data are evidence of an existing civil–military gap among German future elites. Is this reason for concern? Has the German civil–military relations thermometer gone feverish? We would argue that much more research on these issues is necessary and that, based on these preliminary findings, so far there is indeed no cause for massive concern in the German case. One reason is that, as organization sociology tells us, it is quite normal to have some variation and difference between a given subgroup or organization and the larger group or society. The second is that the civil–military gap is not something new in Germany, but has a historical dimension. The third, at last, is that the civil–military gap is, to a certain degree, amenable to interventions by the military and the defense establishment as political actors because (1) it can, to some extent, be traced back to significantly less *interest in defense and security issues* among the civilian students compared to officer students (85 vs. 99%); (2) it is a function of much less civilian *knowledge about the military* (53 vs. 13%) and (3) much more civilian than officer students describe themselves as having a good portion of uncertainty and doubt in their opinions (56 vs. 36%) and much more officer than civilian students see themselves as persons where it is *hard (or even) very hard to change (their) mind* (94 vs. 75%). This suggests that a sound information and public relations policy of the armed forces might be quite influential and decisive. Indeed, we would argue, that in a modern democratic information society it is even absolutely necessary for the military to engage in the public sphere in order to enlist the support of society that is vital to accomplishing its missions. In these times, acceptance and legitimacy of the military and of military operations can only be achieved through engaging in the public discourse and to explain and defend the objectives to be achieved in a certain mission again and again.

THE CULTURAL GAP BETWEEN THE MILITARY AND THE PARENT SOCIETY IN ITALY

Giuseppe Caforio

1. PREMISE

The state of the relations between the armed forces and society in Italy displays some general features. The first is the presence of a very broad-based pacifism that has two different origins which, although quite different from each other and in some ways opposing, often end up by uniting or allying. These two traditions are a Marxist–anarchic, or more generically leftist, one, and a Catholic one that is still very strong in our country. Since the end of the Second World War, the extent of this pacifism, often with a good dose of antimilitarism, has always made relations between the country and its armed forces difficult.

This situation has shown some rather significant changes in the last decade, however. Italy's ever-increasing participation in peace-support operations, which is very extensive in proportion to the commitments of other, comparable countries, has given new popularity to the armed forces, both because of their use in functions more easily reconciled with pacifist ideals and because, finally put to the test, they have demonstrated capabilities and skills that for many have been a revelation. The transition from conscription to voluntary service, although certainly heralding other problems in the

Cultural Differences between the Military and Parent Society in Democratic Countries
Contributions to Conflict Management, Peace Economics and Development, Volume 4, 261–266

ISSN: 1572-8323/doi:10.1016/S1572-8323(07)04014-3

relationship with public opinion, has also allowed the armed forces to shed the unpopularity due to the sacrifices required of male citizens. Added to these aspects is the rapid change of the international situation, which, with the materialising of a significant threat from Islamic fundamentalism, has brought the problem of security[1] to the attention of everyone.

All of the surveys conducted in the last decade, therefore, have recorded an increased level of social acceptance of the armed forces in Italy.

Data from our research allow us to summarize here the main peculiar national characters emerging both for future and present elites.

2. ATTITUDES OF FUTURE ELITES

The university students and the cadets at the military academies display significant basic differences that, as pointed out in previous studies (Caforio, 1998), are likely the result of a different anticipatory socialisation of the two groups examined here.

Beginning with character traits, we note that the Italian future officers exhibit greater determination than their university peers. The cadets' determination is also shown in less fear of being in disagreement with the group they belong to than their university peers. Rather expected and already abundantly pointed out in the literature is the cadets' more politically conservative stance compared to society at large, and therefore in our case compared to their university peers.

On an average the cadets display more confidence in national institutions than their university fellows, except for the media, Parliament, trade unions and political parties: in short, their level of confidence is lower for everything that concerns national politics.

To finish up the analysis on personal values and attitudes, it must be noted that the cadets display greater attachment to their points of reference – the family, Italy, themselves, friends and colleagues – than do the university students.

Among the cadets and the university students the perception of the most important threats, such as terrorism, mass immigration from foreign countries, organised crime and international drug trafficking, largely coincide. The interviewees' attitudes toward the missions assigned to the national armed forces seem rather influenced by value choices. The two groups show agreement as to the most obvious missions: however, the university group shows much lower levels of approval for those missions that involve more typically military activities: participation in peace-enforcement and combat missions. This attitude may be influenced by the strong ideological grip of pacifism. This seems to be confirmed by the sizeable percentage of university students who feel factors other than military force are more important for guaranteeing the country's national security.

On the defence budget, a shared general opinion emerges, although with percentage differences between the two groups, that is more in favour of increasing, rather than reducing, military expenditures. This is a new development with respect to attitudes in the past, that probably derives both from increased visibility of military functions and from an acquired awareness of a larger budget commitment in countries comparable to Italy.

Fundamental democratic principles appear to be embraced fully by the young people in both groups examined, but in judging their concrete realisation in Italy the cadets appear more optimistic on average than their university peers. In addition, there is a full identity of views between the two groups that the armed forces are subordinate to the political power, but politicians must give professional autonomy to the military. On public use of this autonomy the cadets appear more cautious than their university peers, however. They are, in fact, rather doubtful as to the advisability of making public statements by militaries, while the future civilian elites appear oriented toward considering the military like any other professional sector.

Part of the capacity for political control of the armed forces is the level of knowledge that political leaders have of the military aspects of national policy. The interviewees' opinions on this knowledge are not comforting, since nearly half of the sample credits the political world with modest or no knowledge of these aspects. As far as the purpose and function of the armed forces is concerned, both groups agree that the armed forces exist to defend the country and its national interests. However, a good fifth of the university students feel that the military should be abolished and 43% deem it a necessary evil, positions obviously not shared by the cadets.

In any case, although with different majorities, the two groups concur that at times war is necessary to defend the national interests and human nature is such that there will always be wars.

When the officer's educational level is being judged, a large gap exists here between cadets' awareness of receiving a good level of education and a (likely) dearth of knowledge as to the content of this educational process on the part of their university peers.

As to the assessment of the level of information provided by the media on national security, a common critical attitude prevails among all the young people interviewed, but the criticism is stronger among cadets. These data confirm that a different attitude of the two cultures toward the world of information, already evidenced in the past, tends to project itself toward the future as well.

Voluntary military service for women was introduced very recently in Italy; both groups are in agreement that women service should be voluntary. Women's entry into the armed forces being accepted by the majority, there remains the question of the appropriate roles with which they should be entrusted. On this point the two groups' opinions diverge. While a majority of university students feel that women should have access to all roles, including combat, a relative majority of cadets feel they should be excluded from such roles. The conception of women as something "different" from men remains in both groups in Italy, however.

3. ATTITUDES OF PRESENT ELITES – CHANGES OVER TIME

All the interviewed experts pointed out that following the Second World War for a long period there was a strong disconnect between the country and its armed forces. Conversely, in civil society widespread pacifist and antimilitarist attitudes were taking root. All this in the context of a "low-profile" Italian foreign policy in that period, one that certainly did not exalt the role of the armed forces. Until very recently, according to the interviewees, this resulted in a lack of awareness of the armed forces on the part of public opinion, of their tasks, their problems. In such a framework, only striking episodes were brought to the fore in the media. Given that the activity of the Italian military was limited to training, at least until the intervention in Lebanon in 1982, these episodes were mostly negative, such as instances of hazing, training accidents and scandals.

The interviewees point out that the changing international situation and Italy's shift to an active foreign policy, with the resulting deployment in many countries of military contingents radically altered, in the course of the 1990s and the early 2000s, the public's views on the national armed forces. The present remaining causes of these tensions are seen as twofold, one of a cognitive nature, the other ideological. The first derives from the scant knowledge that the public, and politicians in particular, have of the aspects and issues of national security. The ideological cause derives from the continuing strong hold of pacifist and anti-militarist ideologies on the country.

As far as relations with media are concerned, most of the interviewees think that military leaders in Italy have little or no possibility of expressing their views in the media. On the advisability of military leaders dealing with national security issues in the media, some of the interviewees report cases in which affirmations made by the military in the media have caused tension between public opinion and the armed forces. In any event it seems clear that the relationship between the media and the military has been, and perhaps still is, problematic in Italy.

The interviewees are instead unanimous in judging the level of information on national security issues in Italy as meagre and insufficient. According to them, the media are poorly prepared on security issues and still exhibit a propensity for privileging sensational episodes. However, the level of information has improved with respect to the past, also because the armed forces have better equipped themselves for communicating with the public.

The prevalent threat recognised as imminent for Italy by all of the interviewees is, obviously, terrorism. However, for many of them terrorism is correlated with and included within a more detailed set of forms of action, such as mass immigration, the missile threat and politically unstable countries. Not only that, but also the threat constituted by the insecurity produced by terrorism on the part of the population is raised. For most of the interviewees, the mission of the armed forces principally remains the country's defence: this mission can only be carried out in an international dimension, whether it be the EU, NATO or the UN. There is a widely shared view, however, that the prevalent operations should be PSOs, with an adequate development of intelligence activities. The necessary tool for putting the armed forces in the conditions to fulfil the mission entrusted to them is essentially the defence budget: the great majority of the interviewees offer a completely negative assessment on this point.

In Italy, political control over the military is entrusted to Parliament and to the government. It is felt by most of the interviewees to be effective, but some of them complain of a prevalence of governmental control, with a certain shunting aside of Parliament. Besides that, they feel that this control often lacks incisiveness due to the general unpreparedness of politicians on security issues. For the majority of the interviewees, the politico-military decisions suffer from this marginalisation of Parliament. In the relationship between politicians and the top military, the most widely shared view is that it is the politicians who make the choices, without a substantial role of military leaders.

The change that has occurred in civil/military relations in Italy in the last ten years, as it emerges on the whole from the expert survey, is that of a gradual rapprochement and of increased prestige for the military. We have seen in this decade what one interviewee efficaciously called "*a reappropriation of its armed forces by Italian society.*" This is something different from a rapprochement between the two cultures, however: it appears to have occurred for some aspects and not for others.

The two cultures remain distant primarily for what concerns the set of values and attitudes proper to their members. In the face of hedonistic, self-referential, egoistic values, prevalent in civilian culture, military culture preserves the traditional values of personal sacrifice for the community. Also different are the results of the respective educational processes, especially from a cognitive point of view: the interviewees share the view that the public and the elected political leaders, are largely ignorant of the problems and aspects of national security.

What emerges from this analysis, therefore, is the impression that some aspects of the cultural gap regard a necessary peculiarity of military culture with respect to civilian culture (Boene, 1990), while others, constitute a national specificity. Without pretending to be exhaustive, I would include among the latter the marked ignorance on the part of all the "non-military" actors (citizenry, media, politicians) on national security issues, the imperfect dynamics of the decision-making processes for military policy choices, and the lack of balance in political control over the armed forces.

NOTE

1. The theme of security has always been given short shrift in Italy during the "First Republic", whose governments, under the Cold War guarantee of the American nuclear umbrella, limited themselves to maintaining a military instrument that was sufficient for carrying out (at a minimum) the requests of the American ally.

REFERENCES

Boene, B. (1990). How unique should the military be? *European Journal of Sociology*, *31*, 3–59.

Caforio, G. (Ed.) (1998). *The European cadet: Professional socialisation in military academies.* Baden-Baden: Nomos.

THE CIVIL–MILITARY GAP IN THE NETHERLANDS

René Moelker

INTRODUCTION

Civil–military clashes that result from tensions or even a 'gap' between the military organisation and civil society are rather seldom. However, from time to time the headlines of the newspapers report of 'scandals', 'abuses' or 'wrongs' that result from civil–military tensions. Sometimes those wrongs came out in the open after some delay. This happened in respect to a coup-attempt by General Kruls shortly after World War II (Hoogenboezem, 2004). Evaluation of and reappraisal of the war against Indonesian freedom fighters in 1946–1947, euphemistically called 'police actions', led to large-scale public discussions 20 years later. In the 1970s, the Dutch citizens acknowledged that these police actions actually were deeds of war and the legitimacy of this war was intensely discussed as were the war crimes committed during the anti-guerrilla operations (Doorn & Hendrix, 1970). In the 1980s, the soldiers' union published a black book on hazing practises in the armed forces that made it into the headlines. It led to research (Stoppelenburg, 1990) and attempts to stop these practices that often stemmed from the conscripts themselves. Union work and societal forces in favour of democratisation considerably contributed to civilianisation of the armed forces. The one-liner 'as military as necessary, as civilian as possible' became factual accepted policy. In the early 1990s, the suspension of

Cultural Differences between the Military and Parent Society in Democratic Countries
Contributions to Conflict Management, Peace Economics and Development, Volume 4, 267–273

ISSN: 1572-8323/doi:10.1016/S1572-8323(07)04015-5

conscription, the most important decision of defence restructuring, barely raised societal discussion (Joana et al., 2005; Moelker, Olsthoorn, Bos-Bakx, & Soeters, 2005), but the mishap in Srebrenica in 1995 certainly did! Peacekeeping gradually was seen and socially accepted as core business and when it became evident that keeping the peace in Bosnia was not without risks and when genocidal events befell the refugees in Srebrenica, the civil–military gap was clearly revealed and became the main issue of public debate. It led to discussion on the right of freedom of speech for civil servants when armed forces functionaries overtly expressed themselves in the newspapers (Kreemers, 2002). But the humanitarian debacle also led to a parliamentary inquiry (Parlementaire Enquête commissie, 2003) that, in 2003, caused government to fall. Parliamentary decision-making procedures regarding peacekeeping missions have been improved since. Article 100 of the Constitution states that parliament must be informed on peacekeeping operations unless there are very serious considerations not to do so. Government informs parliament by use of the 'toetsingskader' (Moelker, 2004). This is a list of criteria that is used to provide a checklist for informing parliament and to improve the quality of the decision-making. The 'toetsingskader' acknowledges that decision-making is an intertwined and convergent process that improves quality by inputs from civilian stakeholders and civilian and military experts. It enables a priori parliamentary control. A list for use by parliamentarians in other countries is given by Born (2003, p. 125).

Article 97 of the Netherlands' constitution states that government is in supreme command over the armed forces. This means that decisions are a collective responsibility of all ministers in the government. The government is held accountable by parliament, which in extreme cases has the right to send the government home. This constitutional construction is the formal way in which the civil–military gap is bridged. The population elects parliament and in this way the population can be the judge of policies and political balances of power. But parliamentary control is not an accurate reflection of the differences in value orientations, attitudes and opinions of soldiers and citizens. Members of parliament are so called 'elite' and because not many of them have been conscripted they may also be estranged from the armed forces. Furthermore civilian students (the future elite) and military cadets (from which the elite of generals will be recruited) may also differ considerably in matters of civil–military relations, civil–political relations, culture, norm and values.

On an average, clashes between military culture and civil culture happen seldom. There are certainly differences between civilians and the military but these differences normally do not lead to problems. Research into legitimacy of tasks of the military, points at ample societal support for the armed forces (Meulen, 2003), this finding applies especially to peacekeeping tasks, which are the most popular.

PERSONAL VALUES AND ATTITUDES

In the society at large values are considered important, but at the same time they are more and more conscious of the fact that the specific Dutch values, like respect, equal treatment, integrity in general and more specifically integrity of the body, freedom of speech, religion and association, tolerance are vulnerable. It is difficult to pinpoint values and norms because of the highly individualised society. Individualism indeed is a core value that allows freedom of choice and at the same time a degree of value relativism. The differences between cadets and students (cadets are more conservative and the students are more liberal) that are reported in this research would in the larger society not be considered a problem. The moral anchors in a plural society differ in each group and some groups are strongly anchored while others are weak. What is considered a problem, are breaches in integrity, anti-social behaviour, aggression, indecent language, discrimination, etc. When deviancy is within the boundaries demarcated by law, most people find it difficult to react to bothersome and annoying behaviour. Some scholars warn for a moral crisis due to individualism. The citizen feels threatened by anti-social behaviour (Boutelier, de Beer, & van Praag, 2004). The government and the prime minister, who is inspired by Etzioni, takes the discussion on values seriously and issued a research into the matter. The main conclusion was that the Dutch are more bothered by unpleasant behaviour than by disagreement about norms and values (WRR, 2003).

There is much agreement on trust in institutions among cadets and students. The lowest level of trust is confided in the church. On a scale of 0–10, the church scores an average of 4.2. The president is second lowest on the ladder of trust (average 5.4). The media ranks third place. The highest averages for trust are allotted to banks and universities. Main differences relate to professions in uniforms. Cadets trust the police to a higher degree than students do. The largest difference has to do with trust in the military. In other publications (Prast, Mosch, & van Raaij, 2006) comparable findings are reported. The research by Prast et al. departs from a different methodology, but the outcomes among others supports the finding of trust in banks and financial institutions.

Cadets and students are highly attached to family (respectively 9.2 and 8.8). For cadets, attachment to friends comes second than attachment to oneself. For students it is the reverse, attachment to oneself comes second place and to friends third. On average cadets score higher on attachment to country, profession and colleagues than students do, but of course, students do not yet have a job and nationalism is always higher in the military. Attachment to Europe or the global community score lower than 5. Attachment to religious communities is lowest (3.1). Cadets and students do not differ on the above mentioned types of attachment. The general pattern can be interpreted as a typically Dutch petit bourgeois pattern of attachment. The Netherlands is a modern individualised society, which at the same time stresses the importance of family and friends.

SECURITY POLICY AND FOREIGN POLICY AND THE TASKS OF THE MILITARY

Threat perception is influenced by the events happening at a certain moment. The questionnaires were taken, as mentioned, in 2003 before the terrorist attacks on Barcelona and also the events that happened thereafter would, with certainty, have changed the results. Drug trafficking, organised crime and attacks on computer networks are perceived to be the most likely threats to the Netherlands national security by the respondents. After the assassination of movie director Theo van Gogh and the confrontation with Islamic fundamentalism in recent times, 'terrorism' will rank much higher.

Cadets and students both agree with and allot the highest approval to the use of the armed forces in defending the national integrity. The second most popular use of the armed forces is peacekeeping. In the wider society controlling crises and peacekeeping comes before defending the national integrity (Meulen, 2003, p. 64). But these results are difficult to compare because of differences in methodology. However, the support for peace-support operations in the Netherlands is strong.

CIVIL MILITARY RELATIONS

In the period from the 1960s to the late 1980s, civilians were critical of the armed forces. This was related to the general critical attitude towards the nuclear bomb as a weapon of deterrence and the waning legitimacy of the conscript system. Nowadays the new missions of the armed forces are supported. Peacekeeping is not considered as important as public health or education, because of its lesser influence on personal lives (Meulen, 2003, p. 72).

The students and cadets were asked to order 16 professions according to their prestige. Evidently the military officers' profession ranked high among the cadets (second position) and 6th among students. The ranking by the students is comparable to findings in stratification studies (Sixma & Ultee, 1983). In these studies, the officers' profession does not rank among the most prestigious occupations.

GENDER ROLES AND THE MILITARY: IS THERE A GENDER GAP?

Cadets and students were asked to express their views on the question whether or not women should be fully integrated in the armed forces, even in combat roles. The comparison showed that male cadets and male civilian students almost equally favour (or disfavour) integration. Females are much more in favour of integration than the males, but there is a difference between the female cadets and the female students. The female cadets are much more in favour of full integration than the female students. This difference may stem from the fact that female cadets are better informed about the content of the job and maybe they are more supporting the idea that women too can perform well at it (whereas female students are not so sure about this).

But there are differences between the sexes also in the wider society. The Netherlands is a liberal and progressive country with a strong egalitarian ethos. However, the Central Bureau for Statistics concludes that emancipation is stagnating (Portegijs, Boelens, & Keuzekamp, 2002). Only 55 per cent of Dutch women participate on the labour market, meaning that they work at least 12 h in a paid job. At the same time, the Netherlands is number one at working part-time. 70 per cent of the labouring female population is working part-time. Women still conform very much to ascribed and traditional gender roles and choose to remain at home to take care for kids and family. The glass ceiling is not easily broken when women are too much involved in part-time work. Making a career is difficult when working on a part-time basis. That is why the Netherlands is lagging behind regarding the percentage of women working in higher managerial positions.

FORMAT AND SIZE OF THE MILITARY

From time to time the discussion about service to society reoccurs in the media, but on average the students oppose the idea that citizens, be it males or females, should serve their country (averages 2.8 and 2.9). Cadets agree somewhat with the statement that males should enlist in military of civil service (average 2.1). When a general conscription system would be reintroduced, most respondents are in favour of including female draftees. Regarding the recruitment problems, the students are a bit sceptical of the armed forces' capacity to attract motivated and high quality recruits, whereas the cadets adhere to the position that the armed forces are able to attract qualified personnel.

The civilian students are correct in being sceptical about recruitment. Since the Netherlands decided to suspend conscription in 1992 it regularly faces shortages in personnel (Moelker et al., 2005). The last conscript left the armed forces in 1996. During the transformation process the concept of civil service was discussed but public support for this concept was low. The size of the organisation in 1992 was approximately 130,000 personnel but the organisation had to slim down considerably. Reorganisation after reorganisation transformed the armed forces into an expeditionary organisation able to cope well with deployment and peacekeeping assignments. At the same time the armed forces should also be able to function at the high end of the spectre of violence. The resulting all-volunteer force consists of 50,000 military personnel and are supported by a civilian component of 20,000, but the all-volunteer force concept faces serious recruitment problems (especially when there are shortages on the labour market). The armed forces try to recruit more women and minorities to meet with manpower demands and to better mirror the society.

REFERENCES

Born, H. (2003). *Parliamentary oversight of the security sector. Principles, mechanisms and practices*. Lausanne: Inter-Parliamentary Union/Geneva Centre for the Democratic Control of Armed Forces.

Boutelier, H., de Beer, P., & van Praag, C. (2004). Bindingsloos of bandeloos. Normen, waarden en individualisereing. Werkdocument 103, Den Haag: SCP.

Doorn, J. A. A. van., & Hendrix, W. J. (1970). *Ontsporing van geweld: Over het Nederlands/Indisch/Indonesisch conflict*. Rotterdam: Universitaire Pers Rotterdam.

Hoogenboezem, J. (2004). Civil society and control of the military. Paper presented at the ERGOMAS-Conference, Paris, 8–12 December 2004.

Joana, J., Smith, A., Ammendola, T., Genieus, W., Olsthoorn, P., Bos-Bakx, M., Moelker, R., & Soeters, J. (Eds). (2005). *Professionalisation des Armées et Gestion de la Ressource Humaine* (Vol. 70). Paris: Centre d'études en Sciences Sociales de la Défense (C2SD).

Kreemers, B. (2002). *De achterkant van de maan: Haagse schaduwen over Srebrenica*. Amsterdam: Prometeus.

Meulen, J. S. van der (2003). Civiel-militaire betrekkingen. In: R. Moelker & J. Soeters (Eds), *Krijgsmacht en Samenleving*. Amsterdam: Boom.

Moelker, R. (2004). *Democratic Decision-making and deployments : The case of the Netherlands' peacekeepers in Srebrenica and Iraq*. http://www.dcaf.ch/publications/Working_Papers/140.pdf, Geneva: DCAF (Democratic Control Armed Forces) Working Paper, July, 24 pages.

Moelker, R., Olsthoorn, P., Bos-Bakx, M., & Soeters, J. (2005). *From conscription to expeditionary armed forces. Trends in the professionalisation of the Royal Netherlands Armed Forces*. Research Paper FMB 05-70. Breda: HDO/KMA.

Parlementaire Enquête commissie (2003). *Missie Zonder Vrede*. Gravenhage: SDU uitgevers.

Portegijs, W., Boelens, A., & Keuzekamp, S. (2002). *Emancipatiemonitor 2002*. Den Haag: Sociaal en Cultureel Planbureau/Centraal Bureau voor de Statistiek [SCP-publicatie 2002/13 : distinguished policy evaluation-monitoring report by a leading governmental policy research bureau] also published on the internet: http://www.cbs.nl/nl/publicaties/publicaties/maatschappij/leefsituatie/emancipatiemonitor-2002.pdf

Prast, H., Mosch, R., & van Raaij, W.F. (2006) *Vertrouwen, cement van de samenleving en aanjager van de economie*. De Nederlandsche Bank.

Sixma, H., & Ultee, W. (1983). Een beroepsprestigeschaal voor Nederland in de jaren tachtig. *Mens en Maatschappij*, *8*(4), 360–382.

Stoppelenburg (1990) *Geweld in de krijgsmacht: verslag van een onderzoek naar agressief gedrag bij jonge militairen*. Tilburg: Instituut Voor Arbeidsvraagstukken.

WRR (2003). *Waarden, normen en de last van het gedrag*. Amsterdam: Amsterdam University Press.

CIVIL–MILITARY CULTURAL GAP IN ROMANIA

Marian Zulean

The reform of civil–military relations and the establishment of a democratic control of Armed Forces were important concerns for the Romanian transition, after 1989. The main reasons were related with a misperception that the military were supporters of Ceausescu's dictatorship, their involvement in the overthrow of Ceausescu's regime, in 1989, when they could have established a military control of society.

However Romania has no tradition in militarism, except for some short period of time, during the Second World War. In the Middle Ages, the main armies on Romanian territories were the occupation armies of Ottoman, Tsarist or Austro-Hungarian empires. A former colonel, Alexandru Ioan Cuza, was elected "Principe" of Romania, in 1859, and was the one who established the modern Army. Later on, the Constitution of 1923 drew some incipient norms of democratic civilian control of Armed Forces and Romania experienced its golden age of unity and development.

During the Cold War, Romanian military was under the (subjective) civilian control of the Communist Party, with Russian parallel chains of control that lasted till 1958. However, after 1968, both Romanian military and foreign policies became more nationalistic, the main doctrine was the "total war" (struggle of the entire people) and the ideology claimed that the military is the armed branch of the Romanian people, with the recruitment of the officers mostly from the working class and the basis of the army consisted of conscripts.

Cultural Differences between the Military and Parent Society in Democratic Countries
Contributions to Conflict Management, Peace Economics and Development, Volume 4, 275–278

ISSN: 1572-8323/doi:10.1016/S1572-8323(07)04016-7

After the end of the Cold War, although the military supported the overthrow of Ceausescu, the people in the streets and Western institutions asked for building civilian oversight over the Armed Forces. The process required civilians to assume the leadership positions, while military should develop a professional military culture and answer to the political and civil society inquiries. On the other hand, in the last 15 years, the Armed Forces and the Church were the most trustable institutions, in the public opinion polls. Now, as Romania became a NATO member and the public still supported the military, as traditional societies do, it makes sense to investigate the existence of a civil–military cultural gap.

The opportunity was offered by a cross-national European research, that investigated the existence of a cultural gap between the military culture and that of its parent society. Since the main sample consists of 180 civilian students and military cadets in their 1st and 4th years of study is good to know that the Romanian system of education has been changed, after 1997, so the military cadets would pursue only brief military training, during their 4 years of study, but will professionalise in the fifth year of a training course. That would somehow create expectation of convergence of opinions, beliefs and, generally, the culture.

While the first part of the study investigated, through a questionnaire, the values, attitudes, opinions, norms, emotions and feelings of the cadets compared to their civilian peers, the second part was a qualitative analysis of the actual elites and was done in order to get a grip of the evolution of the civil–military culture over time and to use similar indicators as control variables.

The study revealed the existence of many similar views, opinions, beliefs, emotions but also the existence of smaller or higher variance between civilian and military students' views. Although the difference between civilian and military students' confidence in institutions was very slight, besides their own institutions, favoring the church, and voluntary organisations, a reason for concern is the lowest score obtained by the political institutions (parties, parliament or government). The concern becomes more evident when we consider that the political and military leaders do not share the same values as society in the eyes of those surveyed. A slight difference is also revealed on the issues of attachment to the country, patriotism as a personal value and the role of discipline in educating kids.

The most evident differences between civilian and military students views that can illustrate an increasing gap are:

- while the military students are predominantly materialists (in Inglehart's terms), favoring domestic issues and a national orientation, the civilian

peers are predominantly post-materialists, favoring liberalism and the political participation of the public in decision-making;
- military students are stronger supporters of helping less-developed countries (LDCs), preserving the world peace and fighting terrorism than their civilian peers; they also advocate a rise of defense spending and request a greater role for the military in society;
- regarding the public image of the military: while the military students consider it as rather good and they rate it first among 16 professions, the civilian students consider it as not very good, place it in the middle of the list of professions and would like to see the military abolished;
- the attitudes towards conscription and the AVF take the shape of a deep gap. The military students favor a national service, consider that the draft "guarantees an exchange of values" and recommends all citizens some kind of national service, the civilians consider the conscription a loss of time, favor an AVF and do not show esteem for the military profession. However, both civilian and military students consider that an AVF fits better to the new missions of the military (see Table 1).

A deep gap is shown also on possible military missions, where the military students favor "defense of the country", "sending troops abroad", "peacekeeping", "peace-enforcement" more than the civilian students; the findings on the difference related to possible missions are also confirmed by the interviews with the present elites.

Summarising the findings of interview research, it can be said that the actual elites' views were more "convergent" on civil–military tensions, critical but basically did not contradict the future elites' opinions. The recruitment system, income differences, lack of some association rights for the active military, discipline and budget allocation are issues of tensions already mentioned by the students. The majority of the interviewees agree that the military has a positive image in the media and in public. All are very critical of politicians as managers of defense issues. There are many points of view related to the presumptive gap between the politicians and militaries and different perceptions of missions and tasks. As far as the democratic civilian control is concerned the common view was that all norms and mechanisms of control are in place but that there were some diverging points about how the mechanism works and how to improve it.

The final conclusion is that a certain difference between the civilian and military culture exists in Romania, particularly on such issues as the role of patriotism and discipline in education, foreign and security goals, image of the military profession and conscription/national service. However the gap

Table 1. Conscription vs. AVF (in Percent).

	Chi-Square	Civilian Students	Cadets
All male citizens should be required to do some national service	0.001	34	70.7
All (male and female) citizens should be required to do some national	0.024	5.5	21.4
There is a natural link between democracy and conscription	0.016	35.2	48.3
The general military draft should include women too	0.039	14.3	7.8
The draft guarantees a steady exchange of values, opinions and perceptions between society and armed forces	0.000	28.6	65.1
An AVF fits better than conscription the need of new missions	0.10	86.9	92.1
Looking at the whole national economy, conscription causes more costs than an AVF, because of the waste of human resources	0.016	69.3	85.4
I am proud of women and men who serve in the military	0.039	69.3	89.7
The Romanian Armed Forces are attracting high-quality, motivated recruits	0.000	33	64.1

does not seem to become wider, or to represent a fear of a militarisation of society. On the contrary, the institution of democratic civilian control norms and mechanisms, restructuration and professionalisation of the Army to be compatible with NATO forces was considered by some military elites as a risk of civilianisation. A high concern should be placed on the risk of politicians to become considered as not knowledgeable about military matters and not to share the same values as their parent society.

SOME REMARKS ON CIVIL–MILITARY RELATIONS IN POLAND

Adam Kołodziejczyk

1. INTRODUCTION

The issue of civil–military relations in a democratic country officially appeared as a practical problem at the Round Table Accords at the beginning of 1989. From the press information coming at that time, it resulted that the solidarity-favoring independence side (contemporary opposition) demanded the right of influence upon the country defense policy and military supervision. This attitude expressed the feelings of the Polish public (including a significant part of the Polish People's Army professional staff) who negatively assessed the principle of the Polish United Workers' Party (PUWP) leading role over the armed forces.

It is worth mentioning that the defense system of Polish People's Republic (PRL), in an essential part, constituted a segment excluded from the country social and economic natural spheres of life. There existed an isolated, centrally governed sphere of military industry, military commerce and sciences fulfilling only military needs. As a result of the above, the basic element of the national defense system – the armed forces – formed an enclave deprived of natural ties with the radicalized society, being in a way a "socialist fortress" in the socialist state undergoing a legitimacy crisis.

Cultural Differences between the Military and Parent Society in Democratic Countries
Contributions to Conflict Management, Peace Economics and Development, Volume 4, 279–285

ISSN: 1572-8323/doi:10.1016/S1572-8323(07)04017-9

Party guided and supervised, and isolated from the society, the Polish People's Army constituted an essential element in the strategic military system of the Warsaw Treaty Organization. The party domination over the military eliminating any other social factors, both in Poland and in other countries of the former communist block, resulted from the political instructions of the east block doctrine. One of its basic principles was giving the supervision over the armed forces only to military people – generals of exactly oriented ideological and political attitude (Marxist–Leninist outlook on life) with significant achievements in the party's political activity (participation in party conferences and conventions), graduating from military academy in the Soviet Union.

After overthrowing of communism in Poland on June 4, 1989, in the result of the first free elections in 62 years, and after that year's autumn events in Europe initiating the collapse of the communist system, a multiform process of the country political, social and economic transformation was set in motion. The chapter of a single party supervision over the military was closed, and premises appeared allowing for the reorganization of the armed forces in the direction of the patterns existing in the democratic countries.

2. THE HERITAGE AND THE PRESENT DAY IN THE CIVIL–MILITARY RELATIONS IN POLAND

The necessity of educating a group of civilian specialists highly qualified in the field of military science and defense is the most important issue in the present day civil-to-military relations in Poland. The lack of such specialists is explained by some experts as the tradition having roots in the period between the two World Wars, according to which there was a trend that the defense issues remained in the gesture of military professionals. This tradition has not been overcome even after the year 1989, and the state institutions (MoD, National Security Bureau) dealing with these problems are foredoomed to rely mainly upon regular military men (including the retired ones). In this situation, it is very important to answer the following question: Why has not such a staff been created in Poland during the 15 years after the collapse of communism? As it turns out that the post-communist party, the parliamentary formation and the former Polish Presidents were probably in opposition to this solution. In any case, it is a true fact that currently, there is no sufficiently numerous and suitably prepared staff of specialists in the field of military-to-civil relations in Poland.

3. PROBLEMS AND TENSIONS IN THE CIVIL-TO-MILITARY RELATIONS

Generally, we can formulate a thesis that the civil control over the military is too much politically oriented (and even party oriented). Any changes in the political trends and the ministerial reshuffles can be transformed into definite personal changes in the army itself, because the minister is connected with a definite political option. In any way, the model of civil-to-military relations that still exists in Poland is not an optimal one, and it requires far-reaching changes and modifications. The tensions in civil–military relations especially take place and occur on the occasions of promotions to given posts or nominations. The decisions in these matters are still politically oriented. The observations of some "miraculous" careers in the army, particularly in recent times, do not allow anybody to misrepresent the expert's thesis. It is possible to say that in the sphere of these issues, the "patron–customer" agreement, as it was recently described by the sociologists, is more and more evident in the Polish Army.

During the transformation period, there were a few cases of tensions in the civil–military relations. The famous event in Drawsko Pomorskie (1994) is perceived as one of the major tensions in the civil-to-military relations in recent times. Yet, the first expert enumerates other but remote in time examples of tensions. Among the others, some examples include frequent disputes about the control over the army, to which regular soldiers were not the party. In 1992, there was a dispute between the President and Minister Parys concerning the President's right to be directly involved in the military issues, and the latter's conception of expert dealing with the extension of "vetting" on the regular military staff of the Polish Army. In 1994, there was a dispute with Prime Minister Pawlak concerning the appointment of a candidate to the post of the Minister of National Defense. According to the speech of one of the officers (Col. Chwastek), which was delivered in the mass-media in 2001, where the current leadership of MoD, high-ranking generals and personnel management in the Polish Army were subjected to crushing criticism. The officer was fired from the army and legal actions were taken against him before a military court. In the result of the military court's judgment, the officer was relegated from the army and his military rank was reduced. The officer's speech had no political repercussions, and it was not received with open support by regular military staff. The inquiries conducted by WBBS (Military Office for Sociological Research) still showed that a major percentage of the regular soldiers in the Polish Army admitted that the officer was perfectly right in his essential case, but did not approve of the form of his announcement. That is to say, to call a press conference without the consent of his superiors.

4. SOURCES OF TENSIONS IN THE CIVIL–MILITARY RELATIONS

The tensions resulted from imprecise constitutional clauses and were partially associated with the political ambitions and the lack of experience of some politicians. In conjunction with the above mentioned opinion, in the meantime it is worth remarking on the clarity of competence distribution. Even Mr. Szmajdziński, the former Minister of National Defense, gave voice to this situation in one of his TV speeches, in which due to the tension between President Kwaśniewski and Prime Minister Leszek Miller, he stated that he was in an embarrassing situation having two superiors: the Prime Minister as the member of the government and the President, the superior of the armed forces.

The most essential source of tensions is the lack of clarity of the constitutional clauses combined with the lack of clear distribution of competence and subordination of the armed forces to only one center of power. Such a situation obviously favors conflicts "at the top" and in indirectly affects the army's morale both as the National Armed Forces and the participant of the allied defense pact. Other reasons also play certain roles and should not be neglected, but it seems they have a secondary significance in relation to the discussed original legal cause.

Generally, we can seek the reasons of these tensions in the diversity of the opinions prevailing among the politicians and high-ranking military commanders.

5. TENSIONS IN THE CIVIL–MILITARY RELATIONS VERSUS THE ACCOMPLISHMENT OF ITS TASKS BY THE POLISH ARMY

When we questioned whether the tensions in civil–military relations affect the accomplishment of its tasks by the army, answers briefly: such tensions really exist and have a colossal impact upon accomplishment of tasks assigned both to some category of the military officers as well as – indirectly – to the whole army. Tensions are the components of the democratic system and according to the inquiries conducted by WIBS/WBBS, they are presented in many fields of activity at the point of contact of those who make the political decisions and the ones who accomplish the military tasks stemming from these decisions. However, these tensions are not well known to the public opinion due to their secret nature. They only reveal when a certain critical point is exceeded. The above given examples of tensions were of this nature. In Poland, the objective source of tensions is also the army's budget. The jargon of the military circles has been permanently enriched by phrases defining the budgetary condition of the army as a "budget of agony" and a "survival budget".

The basic achievement of the young Polish democracy was that it succeeded in spite of complete dissatisfaction with painful reforms involving the reduction of the army without any evident reaction of the military circles. It might be said that following the "Drawsko experience", high-ranking military officers did not claim the right to defend the army's interests. It is possible that the situation developed this way because of the political consensus on the trends of the reforms in the army. According to these trends, the minor costs of the reforms were borne by the high-ranking military officers. Anyway, when tracing the results of carried out in the recent years military opinion surveys concerning the mood among the regular soldiers holding different posts in the army, it is necessary to say that the dissatisfaction with the reforms in the army was higher among the lower personnel corps in the armed forces.

However, the situation outlined above may be subject to changes because the current political system revealed many structural dysfunctions (party oriented state, scandals on the line of contact of politics and business, crime, corruption in the State administration, high-level of unemployment, crisis of common medical and welfare system and in consequence the lack of feeling of security among the citizens). These types of dysfunctions will not be easy to remove due to unfavorable development of the political situation. The spirit of enterprise of the Poles and the high economic growth are the main advantages, despite unfavorable internal (especially bureaucratic) and external constrains. All these factors affect the awareness of the military environments and the feeling of the sense of duty.

6. KEY-MILITARY MISSIONS OF THE ARMY

The fundamental tasks and missions of the Polish Army are: First, to provide the assurance of territorial defense of the country within the framework of the NATO defense system in case of the attack by a potential adversary. The Polish Army would have to be in a position to resist effectively for as long as it is necessary for the initiation of the allied system of defense. In the present international situation, this task in my opinion has the hypothetical character, but the armed forces must also be prepared in case of unfavorable change of international situation. Second, the Polish Army accomplishes international missions within a framework of the UN, NATO operations or ad hoc coalitions according to the aims established by the State authorities (as the mission in Iraq). The crucial points of these missions are to ensure Polish contribution to the shaping of the international situation and to strengthen Poland's position in the world in accordance with the Polish Government's official standpoint.

7. THE NATURE OF THE ARMY VERSUS THE PRINCIPLES OF A PARLIAMENTARY DEMOCRACY

There are objective contradictions between "the nature of the Army" and the parliamentary principle. It means that the democratic principles cannot be transferred to the structures of the armed forces (orders are not voted on, scientific axioms or methods of conducting operations are not subject of consideration), but it does not mean that this institution should stay in a conflict with the principles of a parliamentary democracy. However, these principles do not relate to the internal structure of the army, but to its dependence on democratically elected State authorities.

We can observe contradictions between the nature of the army and the rules of a parliamentary democracy, but these contradictions could be verbalized in a different way. The essence of the matter is not in the difference of the nature of the army, but in its inscription into the structures of operation of a democratic political and social reality. There can be a number of ways of "installing" the army in the democratic political system. Certainly, the mechanical solutions must not be transferred from other democratic countries, as it sometimes happen in Poland.

8. PUBLIC OPINION VERSUS THE ARMY

Generally the public opinion's attitude toward the army has been good (both before World War II and in the times of Polish People's Republic including the period of the Martial Law) and so it is now. The results of the investigation confirm that the army has high support of the public opinion, but this cordiality results partially from the lack of information on the army as well as the fact of festive contacts between the citizens and the army (for instance during celebrated holidays and national anniversaries with the participation of the army). However, this situation can change when the society notices that the army becomes politically/party oriented. Therefore, it is in the interest of the army to keep beyond the sphere of the political or party games. The democratic civil control over the army assumes that the armed forces are not connected with any political option, they are not involved in any rivalry between any parties, and that the civil national authorities do not introduce the political rules of selection and staff promotions within the army.

THE HISTORICAL BASIS FOR CIVIL–MILITARY RELATIONS IN SLOVENIA

Ljubica Jelušič and Maja Garb

Slovenian society was historically very ambivalent towards the military. In former Yugoslavia (1945–1991) many people understood the military as the socialising agent, the organisation that would help their sons to grow up, and as provider of social assistance in cases of natural catastrophes. The role of defence of the homeland was perceived as legitimate task of the military, but the expectation of foreign military threat was gradually decreasing, especially in 1980s. The prioritisation of national security function of the military has been changed into expectations of more civilianised and liberal armed forces. The Yugoslav policy of active participation in non-alignment movement helped people to believe that they live in a neutral country without foreign enemies. The perception of low military threat in public and on the other side very tough and enemies-searching former Yugoslav military elites caused tensions between Slovenian civil society and Yugoslav military elites. The associations of civil society asked for recognition of conscientious objection, which was not permitted in former Yugoslav military until mid-eighties. Even then, the status of conscientious objectors was given to religious believers only, and they had to serve the military duty within the military, without arms. The citizens' movements asked for use of mother tongue for conscripts in the army, while the military pushed forward one of

Cultural Differences between the Military and Parent Society in Democratic Countries
Contributions to Conflict Management, Peace Economics and Development, Volume 4, 287–291

ISSN: 1572-8323/doi:10.1016/S1572-8323(07)04018-0

the Yugoslav official languages, the Serbian one. In 1991, Slovenian decision to gain independence, caused an armed conflict with former Yugoslav army in June–July 1991, and in 1992, Slovenia was a internationally recognised sovereign state.

In 1991, the new military was formed on the basis of former territorial defence militia units and enjoyed high level of legitimacy. Slovenian public regarded it as the victorious army from clashes with the federal army and was very supportive towards it. Having very negative experiences from the former Yugoslavia with the army that became the instrument of politics against the people, whose security was to provide for, the Slovenian political elite and experts decided to establish very firm and transparent civilian dominance over the armed forces. The defence sector in general, and particularly the military system was put under control of the executive power of the Ministry of Defence, where many civil servants have higher public administration ranks than military equivalents, where military is politically controlled by the political party that rules the Ministry of Defence, and where the military is additionally scrutinised by the media for every single accident. Therefore, Slovenia in its early years was in line with at that time prevalent European trend to civilianise many previously uniformed posts in the Ministry of Defence (Forster, 2005, p. 35). Since Slovenian army was at the beginning of the development, there were very few military officials that would like to work in civilian part of the Ministry of Defence. So, the concept of the new defence sector was civilianisation from the scratch, not just change of uniforms, as happened in many eastern European countries in transition. Forster (2005, pp. 115–116) included Slovenia and Slovenian army into the group of countries that have weakened gatekeeper militaries, which means that the distinctiveness of the armed forces within and as compared to society has been considerably eroded.

We can elaborate further on this thesis, stating that at the beginning of the Slovenian state and the military, the distinctiveness of armed forces as compared to society was only on a symbolic level – uniforms, military vehicles, military barracks, colours, some very civilianised and rational rituals. The majority of personnel derived from civilian jobs – yesterday's low managers became officers, people with civilian professions entered and adapted their civilian experiences to the new equipment, former reservists became new occupational soldiers. At the beginning, their military outlook was very poor, but in social terms, they were very close to the civil society, sharing values, attitudes and expectations of the public, and not those of the newly established armed forces. Within years of professionalisation, there was also a process of re-militarisation going on in the military. We can state, that in 2006, the gap between the military and society is much broader than it was in first stages of the newborn military. Civil society is more excluded from the controlling mechanisms over the military, and politicians sometimes also complain about uncooperativeness of the military. At the other side, when we talk to the military high officials, they also complain about the civilian politics that is entering too much in the military professionalism, and that the professional ability of the politics to control the military is very weak.

In case of Slovenia, civil society power was one of the basic elements of the social system. The non-governmental organisations, some critical media and defence studies experts remained sceptical about majority of defence system activities, although they did not have many opportunities to look inside the army, what is happening to the conscripts, how the NCOs and officers are professionalised. In 2003, when the military compulsory duty was suspended, the military gained even more support and in public opinion polls, it was listed among three or four top country's most trusted institutions, together with the president of the state, "tolar" (Slovenian currency), and EURO as European currency (Politbarometer, 1/2006). The high reputation of the Army remained stable also in times when Slovenian political scene proved to be unable to achieve any kind of compromise regarding Slovenian military participation in Iraq. The Government (probably because of expecting high criticism) in January 2006 decided to deploy soldiers in Iraq without having any kind of discussion in the parliament or in some other security agencies in the country.

In October 2003, the last conscripts left the Slovenian military and it became fully volunteer military force (AVF). The future of civil–military relations is now stemming from a new set of values. Military is becoming like a company for those who need some adventures or short-term job, the contract of at least 5 years is offered. Those, who do not accept the military values, are not going to be forced into its files. Volunteering for military jobs was very high in 2003 and 2004, whereas in 2005 and 2006 the number of applicants decreased.

The military, which entered the full professionalism as still a very patriarchal institution, is exposed to high interest of women to join the army. According to critics and suspicious attitudes of males, the integration of women will be one of the testing points of military culture. Is it able to adapt to the new social group or is it going to change standards in order to stop female influx? In 1991, when Slovenian Army was formed, there were some female soldiers, NCO's and officers, in it. The entrance for women to the military was very open. Such recruitment policy served as a proof that

Slovenian Army is fully different in comparison to the former, in War for Independence defeated Yugoslav Peoples Army, which did not allow women to fill in rank-and-files. The concept of "Women in army" was a clear symbol of military liberalism and openness to the diversification. Very receptive policy towards women has led to nearly 15% of female personnel in the current army. Unfortunately, their influx was not accompanied with appropriate socialisation of male population in the army, and military tended to give women "traditional" women's roles in areas as education, logistics, communication, administration, which limit their promotion opportunities (Jelušič & Malešič, 2003, p. 180). With increasing number of women, the number of problems also increased (for example, unclear policy of sexual harassment and mobbing, equal or adapted standards for both genders, division of sanitary places, military partnerships and marriages, sexual relations and separation of couples, male gentlemanship and female exploitation of male superiors' weak points, the exclusion of deployment of women in peace operations, etc.).

In the years 2002, 2003 and 2004, there were tectonic changes in Slovenian civil–military relations. In 2002, the Government and parliament decided very quickly and without any public debate, to suspend compulsory military service. In one year, in 2003, Slovenian Army changes into full all-volunteer force. Its readiness to change the system of manning was very poor, the inner structure of strata was not transformed from conscript to occupational type of soldiers, the officers did not have time to learn how to deal with privates, but the military stayed quiet and without complains. It accepted the political order and changed the format of units. In 2004, another challenge appeared on the political scene. Slovenia became full member of EU and NATO. Both memberships brought along a variety of new tasks for the military, too.

The broad spectrum of tasks is fulfilled outside the country, which makes civilian dominance over the military more complicated. Sometimes, civil society gets the impression that Slovenian army has many supreme commanders: one in president of the state, another in minister of defence, the third one in minister of foreign affairs (that negotiates the participation in peace support operations), the fourth one in NATO Secretary General and the Fifth (if not more) one in EU's offices. The governmental decision to deploy 11% of the military force in the peace support operations (expected for 2007) all over the world (Bosnia and Herzegovina, Kosovo, Iraq, Lebanon, Sudan, Afghanistan) shows that the military is becoming one of the most important vehicles for foreign policy and will have to operate in multinational military and civilian environment. The high level of military deployment affects the readiness of the soldiers to stay in the army in negative sense. The increase of numbers of soldiers who left the army in 2006 is going to be a new challenge for the military and civilian political elites. They have to find the mechanisms to maintain the soldiers in the military, and have to urgently invent better approaches to the recruitment policy.

REFERENCES

Forster, A. (2005). *Armed forces and society in Europe*. Hampshire, NY: Palgrave MacMillan.

Jelušič, L., & Malešič, M. (2003). "'La Petite Muette' and suspicious controller: Armed forces and society in Slovenia". In: A. Forster, T. Edmunds & A. Cottey (Eds), *Soldiers and societies in postcommunist Europe, legitimacy and change. One Europe or several?* (pp. 169–184). Hampshire, NY: Palgrave MacMillan.

Politbarometer (1/2006). januar 2006 "Javnomnenjske raziskave o odnosu javnosti do aktualnih razmer in dogajanj v Sloveniji", Ljubljana, FDV IDV-CJMMK. (Public Opinion Surveys on public attitudes towards current situation in Slovenia).

CIVIL–MILITARY RELATIONS AND THE EMERGENCE OF A CIVIL–MILITARY GAP IN SOUTH AFRICA

Lindy Heinecken

NEW SECURITY ENVIRONMENT

For almost three decades prior to the end of Cold War, South Africa's defence policy was focused on combating a "so-called" total onslaught on the country. This found the former South African Defence Force (SADF) deployed extensively in neighbouring states to counter an enemy invasion and internally, in support of the police to suppress the rising tide of black resistance against the state's Apartheid policies. With the collapse of communism and the unbanning of the African National Congress (ANC) and South African Communist Party in 1990, the country would witness a fundamental reform of its armed forces, their role and purpose, civil control of the armed forces and in civil–military relations (Nathan, 1994).

Post-Cold War the absence of an external threat led to a total rethink of security. By 1994, after an extensive review process and the creation of the new South African National Defence Force (SANDF), the tasks of the future defence force were defined and ratified in the final Constitution in Section 200 (2): "to defend and protect the republic, its territorial integrity and its people in accordance with the Constitution and the principles of

Cultural Differences between the Military and Parent Society in Democratic Countries
Contributions to Conflict Management, Peace Economics and Development, Volume 4, 293–300

ISSN: 1572-8323/doi:10.1016/S1572-8323(07)04019-2

international law regulating the use of force". Section 201 (2) also makes provision for the President to authorise the employment of the defence force "(a) in co-operation with the police service; (b) in defence of the Republic; or (c) in fulfilment of an international obligation" (Constitution of the Republic of South Africa, 1996).

The first and primary role of the SANDF remained defence against external aggression. However, it was in the execution of its secondary function, "to defend and protect its people in accordance with the Constitution and principles of international law", that the SANDF was most operational. Since the end of the Cold War, the SANDF spent most of its time supporting the South African Police Service (SAPS) in crime prevention operations, borderline control and rendering assistance to other government departments, especially the departments of Health and Agriculture. Efforts to maintain extensive capabilities in both primary and secondary areas eventually resulted in the adoption of a new military strategy configured around three main objectives in 2002, namely, defence against aggression, the promotion of security and supporting the people of South Africa (Department of Defence, 2002a). Coupled to each of these objectives are specific missions prioritised according to risk as envisaged for the next 10 years.

For the immediate future, the Minister of Defence has identified diplomatic drives/initiatives in Africa and regional security in the form of peace missions and post-conflict reconstruction as priorities. Consequently, priority has shifted from support for the people such as borderline control and cooperation with the police, to promoting security in terms of South Africa's foreign policy goals, international and regional peace-support operations and humanitarian aid missions (Department of Defence, 2004). However, within broader society there is some tension over the prioritisation of defence tasks and more specifically, the deployment of the SANDF in countries beyond South Africa's immediate borders, such as Burundi and the Democratic Republic of Congo (DRC). Some feel that the scare resources are better spend on internal security concerns such as crime, drug trafficking, illegal immigration and internal conflict exacerbated by high unemployment and poverty, than by "keeping the peace in Africa" (South African Institute of Race Relations, 2003).

Nonetheless, government has taken a definite decision to remove the armed forces from these internal roles, to hand these tasks over to the police and channel the available "defence" resources to external deployments. Given the country's relative economic and military prowess, it has become obligated for political, strategic and geographic reasons to take the lead in terms of peacekeeping and regional security initiatives. Prior to 1990, South Africa was isolated from the international community due to its Apartheid policies. Now the country has been welcomed back into many international organisations, most notably the United Nations (UN), the Organisation of African Unity (OAU) and the Southern African Development Community (SADC).

DEFENCE IN DEMOCRACY

Besides the challenges the new security environment posed, the SANDF was also compelled to adjust its policies and practices to the imperatives spelt out in the new Constitution of the Republic of South Africa and the Bill of Rights. This marked the beginning of a process of radical transformation, affecting civil control over the armed forces and prompting the need for organisational, cultural and legal reform of its policies and practices. The stresses and strains emanating from these systemic forces evoked new tensions both within the SANDF concerning the impact on military functioning, and on civil–military relations.

As regards civil control, while there was firm executive control over the armed forces before the reforms of 1994, there was little real civilian oversight and no civilian outside of cabinet had any influence over the military since 1967 (Cilliers & Heinecken, 2000). This was to change radically in post-1994. In the new Constitution, Section 204, the Minister of Defence was mandated to exercise control over the SANDF and to be accountable for the entire defence function. A civilian Defence Secretariat was established to formulate the policies, programmes and budgets and to control the execution of the mandate of the defence force. The Secretary of Defence assumed the role of administrative head and accounting officer, as well as being principal departmental adviser to the Minister with regard to defence policy matters within the Department of Defence (DoD). The Chief of the SANDF, previously effectively in command of the Department of Defence, became chiefly responsible for the efficient management, command and administration of the SANDF and its operations (Republic of South Africa, 2003).

As few civilians had any real experience in defence matters, this gave rise to considerable tension between the office of the Secretary of Defence, Chief of the Defence Force and Ministry of Defence. According to a Democratic Alliance (DA) representative in Parliament, the main tensions concern the power, duties and areas of responsibility of the Secretary of Defence and the Chief of the SANDF (Schmidt, 2003). There is also tension between military commanders and the Ministry of Defence. Some believe that politicians are placing undue pressure on the SANDF, without fully understanding the implications of their decisions. Statements include "politicians speak out before the military has been consulted and this is a source of great tension for commanders" (Senior Military Officer, 2003). "Politicians promise things that the military cannot deliver" (Malan, 2003). "Politicians have no idea of the role of the military" and show a "lack of real interest in finding out what is going on" (Anon, 2003).

Decisions made at the political level pertain not only to the deployment of the forces, but also to the internal functioning of the armed forces. Prior to 1993, the South African armed forces were essentially an all-white male conscript force. Post-1994, one of the government's priorities was to restore this racial imbalance and to ensure that the new "all-volunteer" SANDF would be representative of the broader populace of South Africa (Department of Defence, 1998). While many Western armed forces have been obliged to accommodate greater cultural diversity within their ranks due to recruitment deficits, in South Africa this has been driven more by political imperatives than manning problems.

As the years have progressed, the racial profile of the SANDF has changed significantly. Where prior to 1990 the Defence Force was predominately white, now it is predominately black and the SANDF faces problems in recruiting whites, who have become increasingly alienated due to the government's assertive affirmative action policies. Another important observation is the growing dominance of military leadership from the former armed wing of the ANC, Umkhonto we Sizwe (MK). This is an important consideration in terms of civil–military relations and the opposition Democratic Alliance has already warned that the "ANC is slowly but surely taking control over the defence force" (Van Eeden, 2005). Should this affect the apolitical professionalism of the officer corps, it may have disastrous implications for democracy.

Another aspect associated with the cultural and legal transformation of the SANDF is the growing emphasis on the equality of rights as defined in the Bill of Rights in the Constitution. Given the high premium placed on discipline, loyalty and obedience by the military, accommodating changes in policies emanating from these social pressures, particularly in the area of employment equity has not been easy. The South African armed forces in recent years have been obligated to revise their military justice system and to recognise the right of members in uniform to belong to trade unions. Consequently, the entire Defence Act of 1956 has been subject to review and replaced by the new Defence Act, No. 42 of 2002 to ensure that the SANDF is managed in accordance with the Constitution. The military trade unions, most notably the South African National Defence Union (SANDU) has also become increasingly assertive in demanding their "democratic rights" in the field of employee relations.

As regards gender equality, the Constitutional provisions that forbid discrimination on the grounds of race and gender has meant that the SANDF was compelled to issue policy guidelines allowing women to be trained and employed in all ranks and positions, including combat roles. Although most of these women still serve in traditional "female" roles, since 1996 there are women crews in the Infantry, Artillery and the Armoured Corps of the Army, as well as in the Air Force as pilots and in the SA Navy on ships at sea, excluding submarines. Women have benefited from government's initiatives to improve gender representivity in the armed forces and the number of women in uniform has increased from an average of 9% in 1995 to 16.2% by February 2005.

PUBLIC OPINION, THE MEDIA AND THE MILITARY

The armed forces have also begun to enjoy a new-found legitimacy among the broader populace. Prior to the end of the Cold War, the perceived communist threat masked the real threat facing the ruling Nationalist Government – that posed by the growing black consciousness movement and the government's struggle to maintain white supremacy. At the time most of the defence budget, which rose steadily during the 1980s was spend on internal deployment alongside the police. For many blacks the former SADF was seen as a force that suppressed and undermined their human dignity and freedom as citizens, rather than one that protected them.

Today this is no longer the case although public perception of the SANDF remains divided by race. In terms of funding, given the socio-economic challenges facing government, defence receives a relatively low priority and there is little public support for the contrary, given both the lack of understanding and interest in military affairs. A recent survey by the Human Sciences Research Council, for example, showed that the public felt that either too much (32%) or enough (22%) was being spent on defence (Department of Defence, 2002b, p. 58). However, on the entire range of defence issues, the public was indifferent. The fact that over a quarter of the public was uncertain on a range of defence matters, points to a lack of understanding or interest in military affairs, symptomatic of the emergence of a civil–military gap.

With the end of conscription and the withdrawal of troops in internal operations, the SANDF has become an increasingly "faceless organisation". The public knows little about how the SANDF operates, the challenges it faces, how the defence budget is spent and the operations the SANDF is involved in (Department of Defence, 2002b, p. 34). One of the main problems, according to Kent and Malan, is that the SANDF does not have a proactive public information strategy and has chosen to suppress information, rather than providing open and timely information on military matters (Kent & Malan, 2003). Academics confirm that, "there is not enough information on explaining the role and function of the military. People sit with snippets of information and there is no informed or mature debate on military issues" (Liebenberg, 2003). Cilliers (1996, p. 83), for example, contends there is "a knowledge gap in areas of strategic studies, national security and conflict management" not only in South Africa, but Africa in general.

The fact that the SANDF has no proactive public information strategy has meant that media attention has focused on sensational issues – sex scandals, racial tensions, the conflict with the military trade unions and disciplinary problems, rather than the positive contribution the SANDF is making. Therefore, it is not surprising that officers consider the media critical of the military, that public opinion of the military was not very good and that the public viewed their profession negatively. This invariably affects morale, recruitment and retention.

While the Department of Defence holds regular information briefings with the Parliamentary Portfolio committees to inform, advise and to direct operations, there is an apparent lack of credible information to make informed decisions on military matters. Many express the view that the military should be more involved in constructive dialogue with civil society (Cilliers, 1996). However, a policy directive on media liaison issued by the Minister of Defence, Mosiuoa Lekota, in July 2000, centralised all communications with the media, virtually denying commanders the opportunity to communicate directly with the media on any matter unless it passed through the Office of the Minister of Defence (Esterhuyse, 2003). This situation is considered to have created renewed and unnecessary tension between the military and the media (Kent & Malan, 2003).

EMERGENCE OF A CIVIL–MILITARY GAP

In terms of the civil–military gap debate, the first point of contention relates to the function of the armed forces – what the military is trained for (warfighting), what civil society wants from the military (internal/personal security) and what the politicians regard as national and foreign policy priorities (regional security). This has given rise to tensions in terms of funding, defence priorities and relations between political decision makers and the armed forces.

As regard the pressure to accommodate the imperatives enshrined in the Constitution, this has created some degree of "functional tension" within the SANDF, it grapples to accommodate these societal pressures, with little due consideration for the impact they hold for professional competence and efficiency. Exacerbating this is the lack of debate on military affairs within society. The lack of credible information to the public, the negative publicity and growing distance between civil society and the military supports the contention of the emergence of a civil–military gap which is affecting not only information available to the public on military affairs, but informed decision making, necessary to guide the formulation of defence policy and political leadership – something analysts have questioned for sometime (Cilliers, 1996, pp. 93–94).

ACKNOWLEDGMENTS

The author wishes to acknowledge the contributions of Maj. Castro Khwela, Lt. Richard Gueli and Dr. Ariane Neethling for their contributions to earlier versions of the South African Civil–Military GAP project.

REFERENCES

Anon. (2003). Journalist who preferred to remain anonymous from the Mail and Guardian, Interview by Castro Khwela, Cape Town, September 15.

Cilliers, J. (1996). Security and tansition in South Africa. In: L. Diamond & M. F. Plattner (Eds), *Civil-military relations and democracy* (pp. 89–94). Baltimore and London: The Johns Hopkins University Press.

Cilliers, C., & Heinecken, L. (2000). South Africa: Emerging from a time warp. In: C. C. Moskos, J. A. Williams & D. R. Segal (Eds), *The postmodern military: Armed forces after the cold war* (p. 251). New York: Oxford Press.

Constitution of the Republic of South Africa, Act 108 of 1996, Pretoria.

Department of Defence (1998). White paper on defence and defence review. Pretoria: Department of Defence, pp. 122–123.

Department of Defence (2002a). Safeguarding South Africa for a better life for all. *Strategic Plan for FY 2002/03 to 2004/5*, pp. 4–5.

Department of Defence (2002b). Annual report for the financial year 2001/2002. Pretoria.

Department of Defence (2004). Strategic business plan FY2004/05 to FY2006/07, p. 8.

Esterhuyse, A. (2003) The South African armed forces and the media: A difficult marriage. Paper delivered at the XXIXth international congress of history in Bucharest, Romania, 10–16 August 2003.

Kent, V., & Malan, M. (2003). Decisions, decisions: South Africa's foray into regional peace operations. *Institute for Security Studies Occasional Paper*, 72(April), p. 9.

Liebenberg, I. (2003). Lecturer: Department of Sociology, University of South Africa, Interview by Lindy Heinecken, Saldanha, September 5.

Malan, M. (2003). Head Peace Missions Programme, Institute for Security Studies, Interview by Lindy Heinecken, Pretoria, July 9.

Nathan, L. (1994). *The changing of the guard: Armed forces and defence policy in a democratic South Africa*. Pretoria: HSRC Publishers.

Republic of South Africa (2003). Defence Act No. 42 of 2002, 20 February 2003, pp. 16–20.

Schmidt, H. C. (2003). Democratic Alliance, Member of Parliament, Interview by Castro Khwela, Cape Town, September 22.

Senior Military Officer (2003). Interview by Lindy Heinecken, Pretoria, July 11.

South African Institute of Race Relations (2003). *South African race relations survey 2002/2003*. Johannesburg: South African Institute of Race Relations, p. 458

Van Eeden, J. (2005). "ANC 'neem stadig maar seker beheer oor weermag oor", (ANC slowly but surely taken over control of defence force), *Rapport*, 20 Feb 05.

THE DIFFICULTIES FACED BY CIVIL–MILITARY RELATIONS UNDERGOING CONSTANT IMPROVEMENT IN SPAIN SINCE 1975

Rafael Martínez Martínez and
Antonio M. Díaz Fernández

Civil–military relations in contemporary Spain can be traced back to the Civil War period. After three years of bloody fratricide war the victory of the insurgent forces saw the Spanish Republic turned into an authoritarian regime (totalitarian at the beginning) with General Franco at its head. Franco's dictatorship was not a military dictatorship, but rather the dictatorship of a military officer who developed a three-pillar power base upon which he felt secure and whose three sides – the armed forces, the Church and the single fascist party FET-JONS – offered him complete control over society. During the almost 40 years that the authoritarian regime lasted, millions of Spanish men spent part of their lives as conscripts to military service under the orders of predominantly fascist officers and subject to the rule of an oppressive political power. It is not surprising, therefore, that in Spain the armed forces are regarded as one of the pillars of an authoritarian regime rather than, as is the case in other European countries, as those brave

Cultural Differences between the Military and Parent Society in Democratic Countries
Contributions to Conflict Management, Peace Economics and Development, Volume 4, 301–306

ISSN: 1572-8323/doi:10.1016/S1572-8323(07)04020-9

troops who defended democracy against fascism during the Second World War. Civil–military relations in Spain are therefore difficult, and to this day they bear the marks of dictatorship – this despite the fact that since the first governments of the democratic period attempts have been made to improve them.

The first democratic government of Adolfo Suárez faced a number of enormous challenges: (i) creating a constitutional framework to promote peaceful social relations; (ii) economic modernisation; (iii) integration within Europe; (iii) the territorial organisation of power and (iv) military reform. With respect to the armed forces, there was an urgent need for modernisation in order to distance them from political power and transform them into a military administration that was subject, therefore, to civil supremacy; there was also a need to reduce their numbers to more reasonable levels.

Around the mid-1980s – after a military *coup d'etât* (1981) and which time the democratic process had been consolidated after full membership of the European Union was granted in 1986 – Spain's democracy still faced several challenges in the area of security and defence. Although the armed forces had been democratised there remained a large civil–military gap. Members of the Spanish military were not well considered socially, and the profession as a whole was severely discredited.[1] Anti-military feeling and its corollary, the desire to see the end of the armed forces, began to take greater root in the public consciousness but without the old fear of reprisals. This trend was not helped by the enormous presence of US bases and troops on Spanish soil, and the accompanying feeling that sovereignty was being violated. In this context the notable growth in conscientious objection was understandable. However, far from improving civil–military relations the attempt to address this issue through a poorly planned and wide-ranging professionalisation of the armed forces merely created a new problem for the government: the extreme difficulty of finding volunteer soldiers.

By the 1990s, the challenge facing Spain concerned the establishment of its own defence strategy. This strategy involved: (i) increasing its influence and involvement within the defensive structure of NATO and the EU; (ii) strengthening the commitment to peacekeeping operations and (iii) socialising the Spanish people into a culture of defence.

In short, during the last 70 years, every reason adduced above has generated in the Spanish society a strong anti-military feeling that only recently, and very slowly, it has started to be diminished. For these reasons, it is not unusual that survey implemented in April 2004 to future civil and military elites shows a wide gap in this civil–military relationship. In the next pages we will try to explain the main areas of this gap:

(A) The main gap concerns the disparity with respect to the role of the military; whereas cadets prioritise more traditional functions (defence of the country and its interests), university students want the armed forces to be geared toward peace and focused on (i) aid to civil authority and (ii) peacekeeping missions and other non-combat activities.
(B) This dichotomy between traditional armed forces and those geared toward peace role is reproduced when determining the ranking of possible foreign-policy goals. Cadets prioritise goals such as *preventing the spread of weapons of mass destruction*, along with the traditional military role of *maintaining the external security of Spain*. In contrast, university students prioritise not only two foreign-policy goals related to security but also two others with a greater humanitarian component: *combating world hunger* and *promoting and defending human rights in other countries*.
(C) Since the beginning of the democratic period one of the issues that has characterised Spain is its rejection of military spending. This trend could still be observed three decades later although less intensively.[2] 35% of university students already believe that this expenditure is excessive as contrasted with military students who believe right the opposite (76%).
(D) With respect to the personal importance attributed to some of the basic principles of democracy, it is clear that the values embodied by the revolutionary slogan *liberté*, *égalité*, *fraternité* enjoy strong support among both cadets and university students. However, it is a worrying sign that for the future civil elite, military subordination to civil authority and the social integration of military personnel are not regarded as important or considered to have been achieved. Although cadets agree that they have yet to achieve social integration they do consider civil supremacy and social integration to be important goals, and also believe that civil supremacy in politics has been achieved.

Another issue linked to the above and which makes the convergence of opinion difficult is cognitive dissonance among the military. Military personnel believe that Spanish society is anti-patriotic and, furthermore, predict that they will no longer be necessary at some point in the future. However, in recent years the interest aroused in the average citizen by patriotic symbols (flag and national anthem) has grown and such an interest is now shown by a majority of the population; moreover, over half the Spanish people believe that the armed forces will continue to be necessary in the future for defence purposes.

(E) In terms of ideological self-categorisation the difference between both worlds should be pointed out. So, whereas university students have its mean in the centre-left, quite similar to that of the society (4.37); cadets mean grows to centre-right (6.6).

(F) In terms of the four options presented on the Inglehart (1990) scale, university students opt for a more participative society, what Dahl (1999) calls an 'inclusive society'. Cadets, to a similar degree, believe that the next 10 years of government should place an emphasis on maintaining order. It is not surprising that 61% of them believe that what young people need most of all is firm discipline from their parents, while only 31% of young people agree with this. In terms of national politics a new discrepancy arises upon analysing the interrelationship between security and the economy. Over half the students believe that national security depends more on international trade and a strong domestic economy than on military strength, a position that is rejected by cadets.

(G) After their immediate circle, cadets identify with their country more than with their region or native city, a finding which reveals a high degree of institutional commitment. Even their autonomous community, in a State where multi-nationality is a constant feature of political debate,[3] is ranked after Europe. In contrast, university students place their autonomous community and native city after Spain, a finding that indicates a weaker attachment to the country as a whole.

(H) With respect to religion, the process of secularisation that has unfolded in Spain over the last 30 years is clearly reflected among university students. Among cadets the process is less visible as 80% describe themselves as Catholic, although half of them only attend church during the most important festivities and do not attend mass on a regular basis.

(I) There is broad agreement between the military and civilians in terms of the main values they desire for their children and the values they expect in military personnel. They also share a desire for difference between the values that characterise the civilian and military worlds.

(J) The two groups also coincide in the belief that the armed forces are ready to take on a new role other than their traditional defensive one, namely, providing disaster and humanitarian relief abroad, and participating in peacekeeping missions. Cadets support the use of military forces in peacekeeping operations and disaster relief, and this indicates their greater willingness, compared to their commanding officers (Martínez & Díaz, 1999; Martínez, 2000).

(K) Finally, cadets have a distorted view – and something of a victim mentality – with respect to how they believe they are seen by society. While 51% of university students agreed that the armed forces have a poor public image, almost 75% of cadets believed this to be the case. However, it may be that cadets are identifying public image with professional prestige, for the latter is indeed low and both groups view it as such. Thus, the image of the armed forces is not as bad as cadets believe, although the military profession as a whole is held in very low prestige.

Despite the differences briefly reviewed above, the members of these two elite groups whom we have interviewed in depth agree – as the title of the paper attests – that civil–military relations in Spain have improved significantly during 25 years of democracy. Obviously, there is a long way still to go, but much progress has undoubtedly been made.

NOTES

1. The data from the sixteen cases reported here reveal that the social prestige assigned to the military by the future ruling elite is only lower in Switzerland.
2. Recent studies carried out by Spanish Centre for Sociological Research (CIS) number 2234, 2277, 2317 and 2379 shown that 24% of Spaniards considers defence spending is much larger than that in others public areas. The reality is that defence spending fell from 2.38% of GDP to 1.20% between 1982 and 2002.
3. Spain has a number of autonomous or historic communities, such as Catalonia, the Basque Country and Galicia, in which an important percentage of the population has a subjective national identity other than Spanish, these people regarding themselves as preferably or exclusively Catalan, Galician or Basque. In contrast, people from Castile and Leon, Castile and La Mancha, and Madrid usually regard themselves subjectively as Spanish. People from the rest of the country tend to have a dual subjective national identity: they identify themselves with both their autonomous community (Aragonese, Andalusian, etc.) and with Spain.

ACKNOWLEDGMENT

We thank and acknowledge the help of Xavier Coller, Sandra Bermudez, Ignasi Pérez and Jesús Palomar in various stages of the data analysis. We are also grateful to Santiago Delgado and Rut Bermejo for their invaluable assistance with collecting data from their universities. Mercedes Batiste and the IEEE (Spanish Institute of Strategic Studies) once again made a generous and selfless contribution to our research, and took responsibility for conducting the survey in three officer academies.

REFERENCES

Dahl, R. (1999). *La democracia. Una guía para los ciudadanos*. Madrid: Taurus.

Inglehart, R. (1990). *El cambio cultural en las sociedades industriales avanzadas* (XXI ed.). Madrid: CIS/Siglo.

Martínez, R. (2000). La proyección social de las nuevas misiones de las FAS. In: P. Vilanova & R. Martínez (Eds), *Cuadernos del General, no 1 Monograph, Seguridad y Defensa en el siglo XXI*. Madrid: Instituto Universitario General Gutiérrez Mellado.

Martínez, R., & Díaz, A. (1999). El papel del Ejército ante situaciones de grave riesgo, catástrofe y calamidad. Revista Aragonesa de Administración Pública, no 15.

THE SWEDISH ARMED FORCES: RECENT DEVELOPMENTS AND FUTURE STRATEGY

Alise Weibull

INTRODUCTION

Sweden is militarily non-allied and has for centuries relied on its own ability to defend itself. Even "neutrality" has traditionally been associated with Sweden, but with increased international involvement this concept has been eroded more and more. Sweden has about nine million inhabitants, is geographically extensive with a length of about 1,500 kilometres from north to south and is, especially in the northern regions, often sparsely populated. Altogether these conditions have had an influence on the dimensioning and structuring of the armed forces. For example, during the 1950s Sweden had the fourth largest air force in the Western world and as late as at the end of the Cold War Sweden, at least on paper, maintained an impressive number of armed forces (850,000 after mobilisation). However the equipment and training of these forces left much to be desired (Åselius, 2005).

Cultural Differences between the Military and Parent Society in Democratic Countries
Contributions to Conflict Management, Peace Economics and Development, Volume 4, 307–312

ISSN: 1572-8323/doi:10.1016/S1572-8323(07)04021-0

A LONG GOODBYE TO THE COLD WAR

The end of the Cold War and the international developments in subsequent years has resulted in comprehensive reforms of the Swedish Armed Forces. The clear threats that the Soviet Union and the Warsaw Pact posed on Sweden disappeared more or less overnight. The Baltic Sea region is, to a previously unforeseen extent, characterised by stability and close bilateral and multilateral co-operation. However, this is not to say that the profound events around 1989–1990 led to immediate changes in the Swedish Armed Forces. The wording in the Parliament Resolution on Defence was much the same until 1996. Until then, the directions did not contain any explicit commitment to international operations. The aim of the Total Defence was to advance our security-political objectives by way of operations for enhanced stability in our part of the world. Following Sweden's entry into the EU in 1995, the EU has become an important platform for international collaboration on security matters. However, not until 2002 was a standardised military doctrine, which integrated Swedish military thinking into a common Western military discourse, officially authorised. The previously prioritised and guiding task of defending Sweden against an invasion has now changed to the creation of highly competent military and civil defence resources, capable of participating in a broader range of national and international tasks and adaptable to new needs and conditions in the future. The armed forces shall be able to serve at short notice in various crisis regions around the world and be able to deal with the most complex situations and most difficult tasks (Annual exchange of information on defence planning, 2005).

INTERNATIONAL CO-OPERATION

When it comes to traditional peacekeeping missions, Sweden is quite experienced. The first peacekeeping mission was in the Middle East in 1956. Since then Sweden's contribution has been about 80,000 troops in various assignments around the world. Today approximately 1,500 women and men per year are recruited for missions abroad. The international force consists of officers and volunteers who have completed their military service, as well as of civilians with specialist competence in various fields (Swedish Armed Forces, 2005).

A Nordic Battle Group will be offered to the EU from January 2008. The Swedish troop contribution will be around 1,100 personnel and the rest, about 400, will come from Finland, Norway and Estonia. Although this force only represents a small portion of the Swedish Armed Forces capabilities in terms of volume, it will force changes to be made within many areas of the armed forces. For instance a new education system for conscripts will be introduced from 2006. Military service will be divided into three terms, more adjusted to the civilian school terms. The first two terms will be pursued as a conscript (11 months), while the third term is optional and directly focussed on international service. Other changes include contracted soldiers from 2006, new contracts for officers serving abroad and more of joint exercises with the armed forces of other countries.

MILITARY PERSONNEL

The Swedish Armed Forces have only two categories of officers: regular officers and reserve officers. There are no non-commissioned officers. On a voluntary basis all military positions, including combat positions, are open to women.

As mentioned above, Sweden still drafts soldiers for military service. Conscription and the people's will to defend the country were still the main considerations in the defence proposition of 1995/1996. In this proposition it was also argued that: "we will never accept that our conscript defence will be replaced by a professional army" (Proposition, 1995/1996: 12, p. 3). One important argument for keeping conscription has been the size of the country, which underlines the need for a large defence. Another reason is the diversity of recruits, meaning that conscripts provide the organisation with a broad range of knowledge and experience. A third argument is that conscription satisfies a firm belief among the people, with regard to the military (Kuhlmann, 2000; Noll, 2005).

However, the military's need for conscripts is much less than the number actually drafted, and the rest has been planned to strengthen the civilian defence and the home guard. In 2004 approximately 14,000 conscripts (age group 55,000) began their national service in the armed forces. In 2005, the number of conscripts was 8,500.

The manning of the Swedish defence forces after the Cold War has also been commented on in an international report. When four scholars from abroad[1] were committed by the Swedish National Defence College to give their views on the Swedish defence forces in the late 1990s (see Weibull & Kuhlmann, 2000), they concluded that the decline of the mass armed force "is less in evidence in Sweden than in most other Western countries"

(Boëne & Dandeker, 2000, p. 154). Their impression was that Sweden was not culturally ready for an all-voluntary force. At the same time they judged alternative systems as less stable than before and the erosion of their legitimacy a serious possibility. In sum their hypothesis was that Sweden would have an all-voluntary force within 10–15 years. Today, 6 years later, it might be too early to say that they were right in their predictions, but nevertheless the direction is there.

As passed military service is a requirement for application for both officer and military missions abroad, there are concerns that the future recruiting base might prove too small. It has already been claimed that the supply of military personnel has gone from a classification to a recruitment and selection problem. Therefore, the possibility of attracting youth for today's missions and positions is a key question. One goal is that at least 30% of those who serve as conscripts can be recruited for international missions, a goal that must be judged very optimistic. Another more general goal is to increase the interest for serving abroad among young men and women.

When a scholar from the Netherlands recently studied the manning situation in the Swedish Armed Forces he concluded that in practice it boils down to a voluntary army based on draft. Few young people join the forces and those who show a lack of commitment are exempted. Service to the state is no longer self-evident and idealistic (Noll, 2005). These judgements are also confirmed by opinion polls and an advisory committee have recommended that those who serve should be compensated, both economically and in other ways. Opinion polls in 2002 also show that only a slight majority (52%) of the public prefers conscription, and that many (41%) prefer an all-voluntary force.

FROM PEOPLE'S DEFENCE TO A HIGH-TECH DEFENCE

How can one describe the future of the Swedish defence forces? The broader definition of security has led to new tasks for the military. The future command systems will have to provide speed, flexibility and endurance with the emphasis on network based command techniques. The rapid development of information technology is an important factor in the ongoing change. In recent years the term "Revolution in military affairs", has been used to symbolise this change and has also been the object of intensive debate. The development of, what is referred to as, a "network based defence" is the Swedish application of these thoughts. Some researchers mean that this change involves a need to strengthen the training doctrine "Auftragstechnic", and that the current hierarchy, ranks, and other systems for command and control must be questioned (Brehmer & Sundin, 2005). The line of reasoning is that in a network-centric model, there must be self-synchronisation, i.e. some of the responsibility for co-ordination and concentration of strength is moved to the local level. Even if conscripts are not totally excluded from positions in this network-centric world, a change to more professionalised defence forces seems quite plausible.

THE MILITARY TURBULENCE AND THE STUDY OF CIVIL–MILITARY GAP

One important question is how the turbulent situation in the Swedish Defence during the last 10 years influenced the answers given in the study of the civil–military gap referred to in both this and a former volume (Caforio & Kümmel, 2005), and especially the cadets' answers. At the time of the data collection in the spring of 2004 (Weibull, 2005), the situation for these cadets was very shaky. The rumour was already out that it might be meaningless for them to complete their education to become an officer, as a position in the military could not be guaranteed. In reality, the problem of the surplus of officers was solved in a way that the regiment/wing that had sent them to the officer school, were to decide their staying or leaving. In that situation many cadets actually left the school before any decision was made. This turbulent situation, although felt in a diffuse way, might at least in part explain some of the results of the study. For example quite a few cadets and civilian students estimated the image of the military among the public as negative. Among the cadets there was also a tendency toward a reduced feeling of professional identity, motivation and legitimacy, more explicit than found in former studies.

NOTE

1. Bernard Boëne, France; Christopher Dandeker, United Kingdom; Jürgen Kuhlmann, Germany, and Jan van der Meulen, The Netherlands.

REFERENCES

Annual exchange of information on defence planning (2005). *The Kingdom of Sweden. Vienna document 1999*. Stockholm: Försvarsmakten.

Åselius, G. (2005). Swedish strategic culture after 1945. *Cooperation and Conflict: Journal of the Nordic International Studies Association*, *40*(1), 25–44.

Boëne, B., & Dandeker, C. (2000). Armed forces, state and society in Sweden: A view from a wider European perspective. In: A. Weibull & J. Kuhlmann (Eds), *Facing uncertainty. Report no 2. The Swedish military in international perspective* (pp. 59–105). Stockholm: Swedish National Defence College.

Brehmer, B., & Sundin, C. (2005). *Rolf 2010. Overall joint command and control in crises and war*. Stockholm: National Defence College.

Caforio, G., & Kümmel, G. (Eds). (2005). Military missions and their implications reconsidered: The aftermath of September 11th. Amsterdam: Elsevier.

Kuhlmann, J. (2000). Manning defence forces. The issue of conscription. In: A. Weibull & J. Kuhlmann (Eds), *Facing uncertainty. Report no 2. The Swedish military in international perspective* (pp. 59–105). Stockholm: Swedish National Defence College.

Noll, J. E. (2005). *Leadership and institutional reform in consensual democracies. Dutch and Swedish defence organizations after the Cold War*. Göttingen: Cuvillier Verlag.

Proposition 1995/1996:12 *Totalförsvar i förnyelse*. (*Renewing the Total Defence*). Stockholm: The Government.

Swedish Armed Forces (2005). *The facts*. Stockholm: Swedish Armed Forces.

Weibull, A. (2005). Is there a cultural gap in civil–military relations in Sweden. In: G. Caforio & G. Kümmel (Eds), *Military missions and their implications reconsidered: The aftermath of September 11th* (pp. 249–263). Amsterdam: Elsevier.

Weibull, A., & Kuhlmann, J. (Eds). (2000). *Facing uncertainty. Report no 2. The Swedish military in international perspective*. Stockholm: Swedish National Defence College.

THE STRUCTURAL BASIS OF THE SWISS ARMY

Karl W. Haltiner and Tibor Szvircsev Tresch

INTRODUCTION

Switzerland is characterized by the smallness of its territory ($41{,}000\,km^2$) as well as by its considerable ethnic, linguistic, and cultural diversity. This combination of small size and diversity has had a strong influence on Swiss politics and the Swiss militia army. There has always been a pressure to take into consideration many different interests in political decision making. It is not primarily theoretical considerations that have been decisive for the army format (model) and the civil–military relations but rather the political and historical conditions of the founding of the Swiss Federation. These circumstances are the principles of federalism on the one hand and the century-old tradition of the citizen militia in connection with a deeply rooted distrust of military professionalism on the other. In addition, the neutrality of Switzerland plays an important role as well.

THE MILITIA AS A SPECIAL CASE OF CIVIL–MILITARY RELATIONS

Art. 58 (1) of the Swiss constitution states that Switzerland has an army which is organized as a militia. The state is not allowed to establish a

Cultural Differences between the Military and Parent Society in Democratic Countries
Contributions to Conflict Management, Peace Economics and Development, Volume 4, 313–317

ISSN: 1572-8323/doi:10.1016/S1572-8323(07)04022-2

professional army and to have standing troops. Thus Switzerland – together with Israel – represents a special case in history because it is one of the last countries which relies upon conscription and a militia system and which does not keep standing troops (Williams, 2000, p. 267). A militia by definition consists of non-permanent mobilization-based forces. In times of peace it has at its command only a rudimentary framework of personnel. According to Art. 59 (1) of the constitution, every Swiss male has to serve in the army. All Swiss males are drafted at the age of 19. About 40 percent are considered unfit for duty; the remaining part is enlisted. Those men who are unfit for any military service – or under special circumstances for civil service – pay compensation taxes. Women may serve on a voluntary basis. For conscientious objectors an alternative service was introduced in 1996. While today's law allows for a civilian service, it is still the exception to the rule.

The following characteristics of the current Swiss militia system are a consequence of the two constitutional parameters, the prohibition of standing troops and the duty of all Swiss men to do military service:

- Officers and non-commissioned officers are part of the militia. The few professional officers and non-commissioned officers serve as instructors to the militia cadre and are themselves subordinated to the militia primacy.
- A system of annual or biennial refresher courses after a short basic training at the age of 20. Troops are normally mobilized only for training purposes. An uninterrupted service, creating a standby army from which the personnel are later transferred to a reserve force, exists just for a maximum of 15 percent of all recruits.
- Part-time soldiership for most of the male population during a long period of life. After a basic training lasting between 18 and 21 weeks, the male Swiss citizen must perform another 18 or 21 weeks of military services in form of refresher courses lasting between 1 and 3 weeks spread over a period of 14 years.
- The peculiarity of the militia is that it does not constitute a reserve army: during his service, the militiaman remains an active member of a war formation with all the attendant circumstances (personal equipment at home, armament, continuous training).
- A high military participation ratio as a consequence of the extensive interpretation of conscription according to article 59 (1) of the Federal constitution of 1999.

The fact that the militia is still upheld, however, depends on technical, societal, economic, and foreign political prerequisites. These prerequisites shall be discussed in more detail.

The functioning of the militia is directly dependent on voluntary military participation of the civil elite. Anybody embarking on a military career has to do considerably more days of military service than just the mandatory minimum. Diminishing interest in a militia career would lead to losing the specific identity of the civil and military elites which is one of the main pillars of the forces' legitimacy in Switzerland.

The militia's strength is primarily the result of the masses of people under arms. If the military wants to uphold its credibility, it must be possible for volunteers to accept militia tasks and militia leadership positions beside a fulltime civilian profession and thus make use of that very professional knowledge. There are, therefore, limits to the degree of specialization of the personnel, the degree of organizational differentiation, and to a modern military labor division. The extension of military tasks as observed today, the dynamics and the scale of innovations in military technology bring the militia to its limits.

The militia force structure is meant to guarantee a low military presence and thus safeguard the civilian control of the military organization (Haltiner, 2000, p. 141). In this way there is little danger that the state uses the militia for aggressive aims (Klein, 1999, p. 13f).

In comparison with other armed forces, the most salient feature of the Swiss militia is undoubtedly its low degree of professionalization among the military cadre. The officers and non-commissioned officers are conscripts who are willing, on a voluntary basis, to do military service that goes far beyond the mandatory days of service. A militiaman serves 260 days, a lieutenant 600 days, and a colonel more than 1,000 days. The militia system depends on the extent to which sufficient talented young men can be counted on. The law allows for coercion or compulsory service, if necessary, to recruit enough military staff. The 3,205 professional officers and non-commissioned officers and the 1,075 contracted military personnel – for a militia of 220,000 troops – serve as instructors for the militia cadre. Nothing underscores better the primacy of the militia than the fact that professional officers can make career only on the militia-track. They earn their promotions in militia services, in refresher courses of their militia-army formations jointly with their militia-colleagues. Senior positions of command are mainly held by professional officers because it is rather difficult for militia officers to change from a civilian to a full-time military profession at this late time. However, in principle, all positions are open to militia officers.

In terms of their critical mass and their function as instructors, the 3,205 professional military staff do not shape the system. Thus, the ultimate command of the militia army stays after all in civilian hands. Additionally, it must be kept in mind that the members of the Swiss militia army keep their personal weapons at home, which reveals a further aspect of political control. This is correct if the personal ownership of a weapon is considered to be an expression of a citizen's freedom. Today, however, the weapons are kept at home mainly for functional reasons, especially for the acceleration of mobilization.

However, as stated in the theory of social change the attitude toward the military is becoming increasingly indifferent among the Swiss society. Acceptance of the military is still running high and the military is perceived as a necessary evil. On the other hand, the Swiss society is not ready to contribute personally to the military any more (Haltiner, 2003a, p. 6). This may be a reason for an increasingly higher acceptance of a professional army in Switzerland (Haltiner, Wenger, Szvircsev Tresch, & Würmli, 2005).

Whoever wants to become a professional officer in Switzerland follows a so called "in-between model" (Haltiner, 2003b). This educational model is a contractual co-operation between the military school and a public university. The professional officer candidates complete parts of their studies in a military institution; for the other parts they rely on a civilian institution. In the in-between model the courses obviously do not take place in a closed military institution. The academic part of the study program plays an important role. Future professional officers of the Swiss army who do not yet have an academic degree first attend the three-year Bachelor Study Course at ETH Zurich and Swiss Military Academy. The study course leads to the internationally recognized academic degree Bachelor of Arts ETH in public affairs as well as to the Swiss Federal Commission of Professional Officer. Further studies can be undertaken leading to an advanced degree such as a Master's degree or even a Master of Advanced Studies. The admission requirements for the three-year course are: federal or cantonal certificate of higher secondary education or an upper secondary certificate in professional education plus a pre-study course; first lieutenant in the militia army with completion of company commander course or staff course. For the one-year Diploma Course the future officer must have a University degree or equivalent and the rank of a captain. For both study programs the candidate needs a good military record with recommendations, an unblemished police record, and he must have completed the required command experience and be accepted by the Assessment Center for Future Professional Officers. After completion of either of these study programs, the professional officers start work as coaches and trainers and are responsible for a unit or work as class instructors in cadre schools.

REFERENCES

Haltiner, K. W. (2000). Military sociology in Switzerland. In: G. Kümmel & A. D. Prüfert (Eds), *Military sociology. The richness of a discipline* (pp. 140–148). Baden-Baden: Nomos Verlagsgesellschaft.

Haltiner, K. W. (2003a). Spartaner oder Athener? – Die europäische Offiziersberufsausbildung vor neuen Herausforderungen. In: G. Kümmel & S. Collmer (Eds), *Soldat – Militär – Politik – Gesellschaft. Facetten militärbezogener sozialwissenschaftlicher Forschung. Liber amicorum für Paul Klein* (pp. 35–48). Baden-Baden: Nomos Verlagsgesellschaft.

Haltiner, K. W. (2003b). *Die Militarsoziologie als Spiegel gesellschaftlicher und internationaler Umbrüche.* Unpublished paper at the Swiss Military Academy at the ETH, Zurich.

Haltiner, K. W., Wenger, A., Szvircsev Tresch, T., & Würmli, S. (2005). *Sicherheit 2005. Aussen- Sicherheits- und Verteidigungspolitische Meinungsbildung im Trend.* Au/Zürich: Militärakademie an der ETH und Forschungsstelle für Sicherheitspolitik und Konfliktanalyse der ETH Zürich.

Klein, P. (1999). Begriffswelt: Wehrpflicht, Miliz, Massenheer, Freiwilligenarmee, stehendes Heer, u.a.m. In: K. W. Haltiner & A. Kühner (Eds), *Wehrpflicht und Miliz – Ende einer Epoche? Der europäische Streitkräftewandel und die Schweizer Miliz* (pp. 13–18). Baden-Baden: Nomos Verlagsgesellschaft.

Williams, J. A. (2000). The postmodern military reconsidered. In: C. C. Moskos, J. A. Williams & D. R. Segal (Eds), *The postmodern military. Armed forces after the Cold War* (pp. 265–278). New York: Oxford University Press.

A COMPARISON OF CIVIL–MILITARY ATTITUDES: THE CASE OF TURKEY

Bahattin Akşit, Sibel Kalaycıoğlu, Kadir Varoğlu and Mehmet Çakar

1. INTRODUCTION

It is a very challenging attempt to illuminate the structures and processes of the difference between civil and military attitudes in Turkey. The Turkish case is unique in many aspects because while Turkey is a Muslim country, which was founded on the historical tradition of Ottoman Empire, it has been also a secular country with a modern parliamentary system. On the one hand, Turkey had struggled to settle pluralism with the establishment of the Turkish Republic in 1923. Also, the military as an actor has always had a significant and active role in shaping the political culture in Turkey (Cizre, 1997). This study aims to understand the level of current gap between the civil–military cultures in Turkey. The main source of data for this study has been the data of European Research Group on Military and Society (ERGOMAS) project called "Cultural Dimensions of Civil–Military Relations in Democratic Societies" which was conducted on both the future elites consisting of civil and military college/university students and interviews from current elites. Turkish part of the data was conducted by the present team using questions from the ERGOMAS Project.

Cultural Differences between the Military and Parent Society in Democratic Countries
Contributions to Conflict Management, Peace Economics and Development, Volume 4, 319–325

ISSN: 1572-8323/doi:10.1016/S1572-8323(07)04023-4

2. A BRIEF HISTORICAL EVALUATION AND CURRENT STRUCTURE OF MILITARY

Turkish history shows many developments that emphasize the duality and interdependence of civil–military cultures. For example, Hale (1996) maintains that Turkish military heritage has three determinants. First had been the military's identification with the state in the rising period of the Ottoman Empire. Second was military's undertaking of the reforms in 19th century. Third had been military's withdrawal to barracks and involvement in politics only in times of threats to state security. As emphasized by various writers, the major cause of post-independence war period after 1923 seems to be connected with the reality that the Turkish military bureaucratic class became the most powerful political group in the Republican state. Also, Karabelias (1999, p. 131) stressed this point as "*Ottoman officer corps' tradition, knowledge and experiences from past domestic and external struggles had passed on to the army of the Republic*".

While modern Turkish military with pro-western values has been characterized as one of the constitutive agents in the formation of the republican, reformist, secularist and democratic attempts, it had been unavoidably involved in politics (Momayezi, 1998). In the long run, one of the reasons for the weakness of a civil–political culture in Turkey has been the effect of getting used to Turkish military's political intervention culture. One possible cause and outcome of this contradictory democracy culture has been the lack of politicians' control over the military. But the paradox is that after all the coups in 1960, 1971 and 1980; the military has not rejected democracy (Narli, 2000). After the 1980 coup, military involvements in politics were transformed into a more indirect form. As a result, it is possible to say that the military has been conscious of the need to avoid excessive arbitrariness (Demirel, 2005, p. 254). Later, the civilian control over the nature of relationships has accelerated with Turkey's EU membership process. For instance, European Commission Progress Report (2005, pp. 12–15) for Turkey has emphasized that further changes have been introduced over the last year in order to align civilian control of the military with practice in EU member states and Turkey has made good progress in reforming civil–military relations since 2002.

Historically, the Turkish Military Service system has always been a mixed system with a minority of core professionals and a majority of non-professionals. Today, the Turkish Armed Forces (TAF) is composed of four

Table 1. Professionals and Conscripts (May 2004).

Service	Professionals[a] (% of total service)	Conscripts[b] (% of total service)
Army	16.7	83.3
Navy	50.5	49.5
Air Force	54.4	45.6
Gendarmerie	18.7	81.3

[a]Professionals include, commissioned officers, non-commissioned officers, specialists, and civilians (officials and workers).
[b]Non-professionals include conscripted reserve officers, and long and short-term conscripts (subject to 15 or 6 months of service).

sister services: Army, Navy, Air Force and Gendarmerie. The distribution of the personnel is shown on Table 1.

3. ATTITUDES OF FUTURE AND CURRENT ELITES

3.1. Demographic Profile

The Turkish sample (252 in total) consisted of two groups of students: 97 cadets from the military academy and 155 civilian students. The civilian respondents were students of economics, public administration and political science, management, sociology and psychology departments, and 142 of the respondents were male.

In the sample, the male respondents were 56.1% and female 42.7%, no female among the cadets except one. Among 155 students 106 were female. All cadets were born between 1973 and 1980 while majority of the students were born between 1980 and 1986, hence cadets were slightly elder than the students. Students were mainly selected from the Economics and Political Science Departments of Middle East Technical University. In terms of the years of education, cadets were selected only from 1st and 4th year whereas the students include 2nd and 3rd years.

In terms of the family origins of both cadets and students, it can be said that fathers of the cadets were mostly from skilled working class occupations whereas fathers of the students were from middle class with professional, teaching and managing occupations. Mothers of cadets are mostly housewives while almost half the students reported teaching, nursing, clerical and some managerial occupations for their mothers, which was a higher rate for Turkey where women's labor force participation is about 25%.

3.2. Personal Values

The preferred qualities of education for their children by both cadets and students showed minor differences. In values which referred to the perception of authority like responsibility, self-control, orderliness, found high approval among both groups except obedience which was more important for the cadets than the students. Also, they agreed on values like honor and honesty as most important which may be accepted as representing a general view of Turkish society. The strong belief in honor, mostly family honor, has been emphasized also by some studies made in Turkey (Rittersberger-Tulıç & Kalaycıoğlu, 1999). Honesty, on the other hand, has been one of the major arguments recently in Turkish public opinion after many allegations of corruption. It is interesting that both groups also agreed on values, which emphasized open-mindedness, initiative, spirit of equality and tolerance which may be said to represent the youth values against a rather repressive traditional culture in Turkey. Hence, almost half in both groups found traditionalism as unimportant. Besides values of patriotism and comradeship were rated very important again by both groups, though slightly higher for the cadets.

University students seemed to be more religious than the cadets. One possible reason for this would be the impact of the rationalist and modernist education tradition of the TAF (Uyar & Varoğlu, 2004). There was also a significant difference between the cadets and students in terms of their political attitudes. While students showed more leftist position with 48.3%, cadets' political position was mostly in the center-left with 42.2%. The differences between cadets and students became wider with the calculation of the Inglehart index (1977). The cadets had more materialistic and masculine values while students showed a more post-materialistic and mixed value preferences.

For years, in the public opinion polls, TAF had been rated as the most trustworthy institution. This study also revealed a similar picture. In terms of confidence in various institutions the first three were military, presidency of the republic and universities for both groups. Only the order was changing slightly, while cadets rated the highest confidence in the military and the students rated universities; while cadets rated presidency, students rated the military with the second highest confidence. The lowest confidence was accorded to media institutions and to organized political parties. It was also found that high confidence level was in concordance with the level of knowledge about the rated institution.

There were also significant differences between cadets and students in terms of their attachments. While the military elites showed significantly more attachment to the country and their profession/colleagues, students manifested more attachment to themselves. However, attachment to family and friends were highest in both groups. This shows the importance of primordial ties in Turkey. Hence, we can talk about a contradiction experienced by the youth between high attachment to their families but on the other hand a wish to escape from traditionalism. Also attachments to friends and comradeship have to be evaluated together.

3.3. Security Policy

In terms of threats to national security both cadets and students rated terrorism and organized crime as the most likely ones. The two groups were different in items like environmental problems, proliferation of weapons of mass destruction, an accidental nuclear war and a military attack by a foreign state. Cadets see these more unlikely compared to students. The respondents' attitudes towards the use of the national armed forces were apparently related to the perceived threat such as terrorism, but they exhibit differences that seemed influenced by their value orientations and knowledge level. Both groups gave priority to defending country, fighting terrorism and participating in peacekeeping missions.

Another point was the considerable percentage of civilian demand to raise the defense budget up to 38.9% compared to 25% of the cadets. Surprisingly, 37% of cadets showed a tendency in favor of reducing the defense budget while it was 24.2% for the university students.

3.4. Democratic Control

In Turkey, the democratic control of the military has been in the agenda of society for a long time, especially in the process of EU membership. One of the main issues among the requirements of EU from Turkey has the subordination of the military to the political leadership. In this study, 48.4% of cadets believed that subordination of the military to political leadership was achieved while this percentage was 37.6% for students. Another attitude difference was the civilians' disagreement of subordinating the military profession to political leadership. While 49.7% of students disagreed with the statement of military profession was subordinate to political leadership, 37.7% of cadets showed the same disagreement.

3.5. Public Image of the Military

In the present study there seemed to be a high-level of positive evaluation of the public image of the military by both groups. There was a significant difference ($p < .001$) between cadets and civilians in terms of the ratings of the image of the military profession by the public. *T*-test measures showed that cadets with $M = 2.78$ had more positive image than civilians with $M = 3.77$ (1 being very positive). Similarly, there was a significant difference between ($p < .001$) the groups in their ratings of the military officer education (cadets $M = 3.15$ vs. civilians $M = 4.04$, 1 being very positive) indicating that cadets rated it more positively than civilians. Also, 60% of the whole sample found mass media depictions of the military as supportive.

3.6. Gender Aspects

It is hard to say that there has been integration of women into TAF. Rather, there had been discriminatory hiring practices, which had been very low in admittance percentage. Women were admitted in the TAF only as officers. They had not been employed as NCOs or enlisted personnel except for Gendarmerie. In the findings it is also very interesting to find that among the students, the majority of whom were female, only about one-third accepts the optional integration of women into armed forces even in combat roles. Majority of students and cadets accept optional integration of women in non-combat roles. Also, both students and cadets say no to compulsory integration of women in a considerable majority. Hence, soldiering is still accepted as a male role among the youth.

4. CONCLUSION

Two points are important to understand TAF and civil–military relations in Turkey. First is, the historical roots and different roles of the armed forces and the conscription system. Second factor is, the change process of transition because of internal and external factors like perceptions of threat, technological developments and societal and environmental changes.

As it is argued in expert interviews and supported by the various public opinion surveys, there is a perception of incompetency towards politicians in Turkey. When this perception is attributed to the historical role of military in politics, the traditional role of armed forces has been reproduced in Turkish society.

There is no intention of TAF to alter into all-volunteer force in the short run because of threat perceptions. On the other hand, the civilian authorities consider that evaluation about continuing conscript system as a need of the country and perceive this as a kind of expert opinion.

Also, there is a big consensus about primordial ties and comradeship even if they are coming from different class backgrounds. It was interesting to see the cadets agreeing to the reduction of the military budget more than the students. Also, the similarity between two groups in terms of democratic values was an indicator of an acceptance of tolerance and flexibility rising among the youth culture.

REFERENCES

Cizre, U. (1997). The anatomy of the Turkish military's political autonomy. *Comparative Politics*, *29*(2), 151–166.

Demirel, T. (2005). Lessons of military regimes and democracy: The Turkish case in a comparative perspective. *Armed Forces & Society*, *31*(2), 245–271.

European Commission Progress Report for Turkey (2005). Brussels. http://europa.eu.int/comm/enlargement/turkey/docs.htm

Hale, W. (1996). *Türkiye'de Ordu ve Siyaset*. Istanbul: Hil Yayınları.

Inglehart, R. (1977). *The silent revolution: Changing values and political styles among Western publics*. Princeton: Princeton University Press.

Karabelias, G. (1999). The evolution of civil–military relations in post-war Turkey, 1980–95. *Middle Eastern Studies*, *35*(4), 130–151.

Momayezi, N. (1998). Civil–military relations in Turkey. *International Journal on World Peace*, *15*(3), 3–28.

Narli, N. (2000). Civil–military relations in Turkey. *Turkish Studies*, *1*(1), 107–127.

Rittersberger-Tiliç, H., & Kalaycioğlu, S. (1999). Legitimation and re-production of domestic violence in Turkish families. *Zeitschrift für Türkeistudien*, *2*, 225–241.

Uyar, M., & Varoğlu, K. (2004). *In search of modernity and rationality: The case of Turkish military academy*. Unpublished paper presented in RC01 meeting, 7–9 July 2004, Ankara.

CONCLUSION: COMPARISON OF CURRENT AND FUTURE ELITES

Giuseppe Caforio

1. INTRODUCTION

The expert survey, carried out in the manner described in Part I of this volume (in Chapter 2), enables us to get a look, through the opinions of a set of top leaders and opinion makers, at the perception of the cultural gap between society and armed forces felt by current elites, as well as to gain insights into the trends over time.

Unlike what is commonly done in the quantitative analysis (see Part II of the book), it seems appropriate here, in the qualitative analysis, to start out from what the individual national realities reveal, and later to attempt a few operations of synthesis that transcend those realities.

The data of the expert survey will then be compared in this final chapter with those that emerged from the survey of future elites, to glean elements for a general summary and evaluation on the cultural gap.

Since the questions that we asked ourselves and that interest us essentially regard four aspects of the cultural differences between the military and its parent society,[1] the treatment that follows will be subdivided according to those same aspects, namely: the existence, nature of cultural differences and their trend, country by country; what shapes this gap; the gap and civil–military relations; the change over time, i.e., a comparison of present and future elites. Besides that, looking at the empirical results, I judged it to be

Cultural Differences between the Military and Parent Society in Democratic Countries
Contributions to Conflict Management, Peace Economics and Development, Volume 4, 327–352

ISSN: 1572-8323/doi:10.1016/S1572-8323(07)04025-8

significant to insert a short paragraph on the different perceptions of cultural differences according to the roles of the present elites of our sample.

2. SURVEY OF CURRENT ELITES

2.1. The Cultural Differences and their Trend

The cultural differences between armed forces and society in the individual countries were investigated through a survey on the past tensions perceived by the studied current elites, on the present tensions, and on those that they identify as the principal causes of these tensions.

Starting out, as stated, from a survey on the national dimensions of these differences as reported by the current elites (see Matrix 1), we see that in several countries (France, Italy, Romania, Slovenia and Spain) it is the abandonment of conscription and the transition to an all-volunteer force that is considered to be at the origin of past tensions, tensions that in many cases are still present. This is indeed an epoch-making passage, as I have had occasion to point out also elsewhere,[2] for all the European countries, where for nearly two centuries conscription represented an instrument of amalgamation and exchange between civil and military society and achieved a social representativeness in the latter that today, with its abandonment, tends to be greatly diluted.

In other countries, however, such as Sweden and Germany, it is a process of transformation of the armed forces that is indicated as the origin of tensions, while in South Africa the use of the armed forces in internal security tasks is pointed to as the cause of tensions in the past.

In a few countries, past social tensions caused by a significant politico-social passage from one regime to another are cited: such is the case of Spain, after the fall of Francoism, of Slovenia, following its recently acquired independence and of the ex-communist countries (Bulgaria, Poland and Romania). In Turkey it was the interventionism of the military in political life – structural in the country's situation – that created past tensions. In Switzerland, the past tensions refer to the normal conflict between politicians and military leaders regarding the budget, military procurement and related scandals.

Getting to the present, we find a decrease in tensions almost everywhere: an absence of significant current tensions is indicated by the French, Italian, Polish, Slovenian, Spanish and Swiss interviewees. In the same and in other countries the existence of minor tensions today is indicated in spheres that

Matrix 1. The Nature of the Gap and its Trend: National Dimensions (Checklist Matrix)[a].

	Bulgaria	France	Germany	Italy	Poland	Romania[b]
Past tensions	Transition to democratic AF; soldiers abroad in PSOs	Transition from conscription to all-volunteer; Algerian war; nuclear power; draft	Rearmament; NATO deployment of cruise missiles; budget; peace movements	Separateness of the military; AF perceived as necessary evil; military values different from civil society	Officer promotions; disputes over control of the Army	Downsizing of military's status; conscription
Present tensions	Modernisation projects; personnel reduction; missions and tasks of AF	Budget; growing individualism; end of conscription	Conscription; military missions abroad; integration of women; military base closures; budget; civil–military cooperation; internal use of AF	Military budget; no tensions; a kind of psychological drag effect	No tensions; budget; different opinions	Conscription; budget; discharged military personnel; fewer tensions
Causes of tensions	Soviet-type mindset of generals; different vision between MoD and GS; lack of legislative norms	Army lacks social function	Costs; international change; downsizing of military; pacifism; lack of public debate	Lack of information; ideological positions; pacifism	Imprecise constitutional clauses; inexperienced politicians; dispute politicians/commanders	Different culture; lack of communication

Matrix 1. *(Continued)*

	Slovenia	South Africa	Spain	Sweden	Switzerland	Turkey
Past tensions	Transition from conscription; duplication of tasks in MoD	Use of AF for internal reasons	Past atmosphere of occupation forces; transition	Reform in the AF; distrust between military and communist wing	Engines purchase; scandals	Cyprus; Higher Education Council (YOK); military interventions
Present tensions	No tensions; status of the military	Between military and politicians	Promised modernisation has never taken place; no tension between military and society	Force transformation Shrinking AF; scandals; cultural clashes in international co-operation	No tensions; budget; manpower competition; missions	Secularism Islamism; YOK; EU membership process; decrease of tensions in latest period
Causes of tensions	Rapidity of changes	Budget; missions (PSOs); cultural differences; unrealistic expectations by politicians	Rapid change; absence of nation culture; modernisation has not taken place; pacifism	Misuse of taxpayers money; changing missions; a smaller AF but the same costs	International situation; uncertain missions; professionalisation	Educational differences; military elites; politicians not prepared

[a]More than one response is frequently indicated in the individual boxes of the matrix, often in contradiction with each other: this occurs because among the interviewed experts there are majority opinions (the first answer) and minority views (the following ones).
[b]Conscription will be abolished in 2007.

constitute the normal dialectic between the two cultures: the military budget, modernisation of the armed forces, the status of military personnel. In some countries where significant downsizing of the military has occurred, such as the former communist countries, Sweden and Germany, continuing tension due to the effects of this cutback is registered.

The chief cause of this positive trend in civil–military relations is identified by a majority of the interviewed experts in the increased visibility of the work of the armed forces and in the greater sharing of objectives between the two spheres, civil and military, that peace support operations (PSOs) produced. Added to this, in the last few years, seems to be an increased perception of threat in the surveyed countries that makes the need for a military be felt with greater force and social consensus. In some countries, finally, such as France and Italy, the professionalisation of the armed forces is also felt to have acted in a positive sense.

A particular case is represented by Turkey, where a revival of Islamism and its greater political appeal seem to call into question the secularism of the Kemalist tradition, particularly dear to the military.

The causes of the tensions between the two spheres, according to the opinions expressed by the interviewed sample, can be classified into structural causes and contingent causes. The structural causes indicated are essentially of two types: a different culture and a different mindset between the civilian and military worlds in general (a cause reported in Bulgaria, France, Italy, Romania, South Africa and Spain) and, descending from the former, conflict between the political leadership and the military leadership, for the most part ascribed to politicians being poorly versed in national security issues (Bulgaria, Poland, Romania, South Africa and Turkey).

The contingent local causes range from ideological issues, like the presence of strong pacifist/antimilitarist (Germany, Italy, Spain, Sweden) or religious (Turkey) fringes, to legislative deficiencies (Bulgaria, Poland), to a lack of public information (Italy, Romania), to military procurement scandals (Sweden), to the particular case of Switzerland, where a profoundly altered international situation poses important questions both for the country's foreign policy stance and for the mission of its armed forces.

Generally speaking, from the empirical findings we can say that cultural differences exist – with different nuances country by country – but the common trend is towards a decrease.

2.2. What Shapes the Gap

The character of the gap existing between the two cultures was examined by asking the interviewees questions chiefly on the following six aspects of it: trusting the military, consequences of officers' expressed opinions, opportunity for military leaders to express their opinions on security issues in the media, citizens' knowledge in security matters, the media's attitude towards the military and citizens' attitude towards the military (see Matrix 2).

The experts' trust in their national armed forces is declared to be high in all the surveyed countries with the exception of South Africa; this trust is also declared to be on the rise with respect to the past, presumably for the reasons indicated in the preceding section.

For South Africa, the interviewees point to reasons of both operational capacity – "The state of readiness of the armed forces is currently poor and undesirable", responds one of the interviewees – and to politico-military choices that have alienated the armed forces from the population. Another interviewee states: "With the withdrawal of the commandos (rural protection units), the gap between the military and society will widen, as normal civilians will have less and less contact with the military", and further, "Its reputation is still low, since its popularity has gone down".

The interviewees display interesting opinions on the relationship between officers and the media. A datum common to various countries is that officers have little or no possibility of expressing their views and assessments on their country's external security policy through the media, either due to a law that prevents it (Bulgaria, Romania, Slovenia, Spain) or to a concrete practical difficulty in doing so (Italy, South Africa), even if the experts of some countries (France) declare that the possibilities are greater today than in the past. Significantly, France is precisely the country where the theory of the army as the *Grande Muette* was born.

But there is also a group of countries where this possibility and freedom is considered to exist: these are Sweden and Switzerland, and also Turkey, where an officer who intervenes in the media does so in the name of the military establishment, however, as spokesman. Contrasting assessments on the possibility of military leaders expressing their opinions in the media are presented by the various German interviewees.

Where expressed, these opinions appear to have had negative consequences in some countries: extreme in Poland – up to expulsion of the officer – more moderate, but still dissuasive, in Germany, Italy, Spain and Turkey. In several countries (Bulgaria, France, Romania, South Africa, Sweden and

Matrix 2. What Shapes the Gap: National Dimensions (Checklist Matrix)[a].

	Bulgaria	France	Germany	Italy	Poland	Romania[b]
Trusting the military	High, but something of a myth	Good; better due to professionalisation; trust in the military system	The more the Bundeswehr became engaged in military missions abroad, the more its prestige grew; high	Much more than in the past	NA	High level; higher than in the past
Conse-quence of opinions	NA	NA	Yes. See the recent case of Gen. Günzel	Negatives but of instrumentalisa-tion by the media	Fired from the Army	NA
Opportunity to express opinion	No chance for the military	More than in the past	Citizen in uniform allows for a critical soldier; balanced; restraints; no freedom of speech	Do not really have this possibility	NA	Internal regulations prevent or prohibit
Citizens' knowledge	Lack of information and knowledge	Communication is growing; more informed	Information available; too little; deficient	Poorly informed	Lack of information	Low, military does not communicate
Media's attitude	Positive, but sometimes looking for "military scandals"	Better than in the past; cautious	Good; negative; critical, open; more positive; not dealt with as necessary; objective, adequate; better than in the past; a certain disinterest	Not against today; journalists lack preparation; relationship not good between military and media	Contribute to civilian control; critical and positive	Critical but positive
Citizens' attitude	Traditionally positive but military not of great importance in their lives	Positive image due to peace missions and to professionalisation; no interest but confidence	Good; between neutral and positive; better than in the past; positive; societal disinterest	Very positive attitudes due to large participation in PSOs	Is and was good	Positive and more than in the past

Matrix 2. *(Continued)*

	Slovenia	South Africa	Spain	Sweden	Switzerland	Turkey
Trusting the military	Better reputation than in the past	Distrust	New pride from participation in PSOs	High	NA	High trust
Consequence of opinions	Rarely	NA	There were problems	NA	NA	In some cases
Opportunity to express opinion	Clearly limited; they need authorisation	No freedom of speech; officers not able to	Limitations; self-censure	Yes	Officers were and are normally allowed	Formally free, but officers always express the Army's official point of view
Citizens' knowledge	Knowledge is not good; more than in the past	Very little is known; other fields are more important	There is mutual ignorance; they are not interested	Defence is a fairly peripheral matter	Not very much; not very interested	Lack of knowledge; soldiers are not open to the public
Media's attitude	Work of media is positive; little expertise in security affairs	Balanced, but often sensational; relationship between media and military disastrous	During the transition media and the military were antagonistic; no professionals	Not as interested; few specialised in defence; media coverage is decreasing	Critical but positive; very few competent	Press used the civil military tensions for their headlines; few prepared journalists
Citizens' attitude	Positive; much higher than it was	Still positive but decreasing; some doubts about PSOs	Wrong because of ignorance; not very interested	People don't think that defence is a sufficiently interesting and important issue	Positive but "yes, but without me"	Very positive

[a]More than one response is frequently indicated in the individual boxes of the matrix, often in contradiction with each other; this occurs because among the interviewed experts there are majority opinions (the first answer) and minority views (the following ones).
[b]Conscription will be abolished in 2007.

Switzerland) the interviewed experts avoided expressing themselves on this aspect.

The attitude of the media is never considered prejudicially hostile to the military; in many countries (Germany, Poland, Romania, Slovenia and Switzerland) the experts consider it critical, but positive. For the experts of Bulgaria, Italy, South Africa and Turkey, journalists have the defect of often being on the lookout for sensationalism.

Where the experts of nearly all the countries are in agreement is in denouncing a lack of preparation of the media on military issues and the presence of few journalists specialised in the sector. In some countries (Italy and South Africa) a difficult relationship ("disastrous", for a South African expert) between the media and the military is reported.

The understanding that citizens have of their country's external security issues is of course closely linked to the level of information provided by the media: thus, opinion is generalised among the interviewed experts regarding a lack of information of their fellow citizens, to which a lack of interest in these issues on their part often contributes. This view is explicitly stated by the interviewees of France ("no interest but confidence"), South Africa, Spain, Sweden, Switzerland and Turkey, but can be read between the lines of the affirmations by the experts of other countries as well.

Despite this, the attitude of citizens toward their armed forces is generally considered to be positive, with the sole exception of Spain. Another datum that is quite widespread is the view that this attitude is better today than in the past (France, Germany, Italy, Romania, Slovenia), an improvement to which the positive participation in PSOs seems to have contributed, significantly in some countries (Italy, for example).

2.3. The Gap and Civil–Military Relations

For concrete application of a research like ours, it appears essential to examine what the actual state of relations between the military and its parent society is. This section does this by examining six fundamental aspects of these relations. Starting with the perception of threats to national security and the resulting priorities given to the various types of mission to assign to the armed forces, we then examine opinions on the instrument that the country gives the armed forces to accomplish these missions, the defence budget. And finally, the delicate relationship between the political and military worlds is examined, through democratic control of the armed forces and the decision-making process with regard to military security.

The principal threat to military security, perceived in common by the interviewed elites, is terrorism: the sole exception here is South Africa, whose top leaders and opinion makers do not seem to perceive particular threats to the country's security, and, in part, Switzerland, where a sensation of non-threat prevails among the interviewed experts but with a minority that still fear an involvement in terrorist attacks. Next to appear are individual fears on the part of various countries: as summarised in Matrix 3, the Italian experts see a strong threat from mass immigration, the Spanish ones from drug trafficking and international crime, the Swedish and Turkish ones traditional military threats from nearby countries (Russia for the former, more than one neighbour for the latter). In some countries, unfortunately, the interviewers did not collect (or did not get) answers on this item.

A comparison of these data with the opinions on threats expressed by the general public in the countries of this survey that were also included in the contemporary Eurobarometer (Spring 2004) sees substantially coinciding positions between elites and public opinion, but with the public displaying greater sensitivity to the issue of mass immigration.

Having delineated the threat, the priority of the missions to assign to one's national armed forces takes different and more complex forms than a simple response to the perceived threats, also because according to some interviewees (in Spain, for example) the main perceived threat, terrorism, is not a matter chiefly for the armed forces but for other institutions. From the standpoint of missions, therefore, the responses can be seen as revealing two basic orientations characterising two groups of countries: a first group in which the interviewed experts indicate, with various national nuances, a range of missions that more or less coincides with those that fall under the MOOTW label, in a dimension of international co-operation. These countries include Bulgaria, Germany, Italy, Poland, Romania, Slovenia, South Africa and Spain. In a second group of countries (Sweden and Switzerland), traditions of neutrality make it more difficult, in today's radically changed international context, to define the missions of their armed forces with the same clarity as before: as one Swedish interviewee efficaciously puts it, "The military is in search of a mission". However, previous deployments of the Swedish armed forces in peacekeeping missions seem to make reorienting the military function easier for this country, according to the interviewed experts.

Turkey, finally, is a case apart. Here the interviewed experts still see as prevalent the traditional function of the armed forces, i.e., armed defence of the republic against internal and external enemies, a mission that agrees well with the perception of a military threat from neighbouring countries.

Matrix 3. The Gap and Civil–Military Relations: National Dimensions (Checklist Matrix)[a].

	Bulgaria	France	Germany	Italy	Poland	Romania[b]
Major threats	International terrorism	NA	Terrorism	Mass immigration; international terrorism; Islamic fundamentalism	NA	Terrorism
Missions	Different approach military and civilians on the main mission	NA	Crisis reaction; peacekeeping; defence of NATO; fighting terrorism, also within country; Petersberg Tasks	In terms of European security; all missions; PSOs	Country's external security; international missions in a framework of the UN, NATO operations or ad hoc coalitions	For politicians, PSOs, disasters, etc; for military, defend the country
Budget	Very high, but not properly used	The military always asks for a larger budget than politicians give	Severe strains on the military budget; scarce; scarce; deficient	Too low; too strict; ridiculous; inadequate	"Agony budget" and "survival budget"	Different opinions, from partially satisfied to insufficient
Political control	High enough but not in public interest	Good; fully democratic; efficient	Through Parliament, executive, media; enough; self-control; too little control	OK but political leaders are not aware of the security issues	Internal control; political supremacy	Very well regulated civilian control; army controls itself
Political–military decisions	Very little real dialogue	Politicians decide and the military leader executes	Made by civilians, not by soldiers	Decisions are taken by politicians; lack of involvement of any military	Militaries an advisory function only	Politicians have the supremacy
Decision-making	Military leaders should be more involved	The military should have a real place in political decision-making	Revision of decision-making procedure needed; mutual trust and respect	Parliament not involved enough; politicians have their own goals	Militaries not involved in decision-making	Military leaders participate in debate but do not take part in making decisions

Matrix 3. (*Continued*)

	Slovenia	South Africa	Spain	Sweden	Switzerland	Turkey
Major threats	NA	No perceived threats	Terrorism, drugs, international criminal networks	Fear and suspicion of Russia still permeates the Swedish population	No real threats; "eastern foe" image has disappeared, and terrorism has become a real threat	Terrorism and ethnic discrimination; some military perceive external threat by neighbours
Missions	Fulfilling the NATO alliance tasks; all missions	Peace missions and OOTW; peace and stability on the continent; crime, trafficking in drugs and women	New missions; peace missions; humanitarian aid	Political sphere has lots of expectations of AF; the military is in search of a mission	Federal Councillors avoid decisions on army's role because it would be politically difficult; Switzerland has been in an identity crisis	Protect the republic from internal and external threats
Budget	NA	Budget constraints; no training for troops	Society is against military budget	Industry took half of defence budget, very little for training soldiers	Citizens push for a reduction; this can have severe consequences	No particular problems
Political control	Military internal; government; not enough involvement of civil society	Internal control; not much interaction between the two	Civil supremacy is perfectly assumed	No problems in that regard	Swiss army is controlled in a very democratic and transparent way	Military controls itself; no real parliamentary control
Political military decisions	By politicians	Politicians do not know the state of the military	Mixed organisms; military consider politicians aliens	Politicians and military in total agreement	Militia concept allows a mixing of political and military responsibilities	Politicians are insufficient and unqualified compared to soldiers
Decision-making	Military is not involved enough	Politicians often speak out before the military has been consulted	Military leaders only as consultants	NA	Parliament has a very strong position	Soldiers are more dominant in the decision-making processes

[a]More than one response is frequently indicated in the individual boxes of the matrix, often in contradiction with each other: this occurs because among the interviewed experts there are majority opinions (the first answer) and minority views (the following ones).
[b]Conscription will be abolished in 2007.

From the point of view of the means that each country allocates to accomplish the assigned missions, here, too, various groupings of countries must be distinguished. A first, more numerous group is made up of countries whose elites feel the military budget is inadequate: the range here goes from the extreme cases of Poland ("agony budget") and Italy (where all the experts deem it inadequate) to those of Germany, Romania, South Africa, Spain and Sweden, who express themselves more generically in terms of "budget constraints". In other countries, such as Bulgaria and Turkey, the defence budget is considered adequate, although according to some Bulgarian interviewees it does not appear to be "properly used" (an issue also raised by the Swedish experts, who complain that too small a share is destined to the actual training of troops). The French experts limit themselves to registering a disagreement between the military and political leadership as to the adequacy of defence funds, without taking an explicit position. It is interesting to note here that in some countries (Spain and Switzerland), according to the interviewees, there is strong pressure from public opinion for a reduction of military expenditures.

Political control appears to be ensured in all the examined countries, according to the interviewees' responses, although with a few differences in the ways it is exercised. In several countries the experts lay emphasis on internal control of the military, founded on professionalisation in the sense indicated by Huntington (Huntington, 1957), i.e., on a professionalisation whose code includes a detachment of the military from politics and a strict division of spheres of competence between politicians and the military leadership. This appears to be the position of most of the German, Polish, Romanian, Slovenian, South African and Turkish experts. In the other countries political control is ensured by the political organisms designed for this under the various constitutions; in some, however, an incompetence of politicians on security issues is lamented that negatively impacts the exercise of this control. This situation is pointed to by the interviewees of Italy, South Africa and Turkey.

Politico-military decisions are formally taken by the political leadership everywhere, but with different degrees of involvement of the military brass in the decision-making process. Here we go from the case of Turkey, where, according to the experts, the military leaders are dominant in decision-making (also due to the incompetence of politicians) to those of Bulgaria, Germany, Italy and Poland, where the involvement of the military leadership is considered marginal and insufficient by the experts, with intermediate positions like that of France, where greater involvement of military leaders is merely a wish, and the ideal one of Sweden, where "politicians and militaries act in total agreement".

2.4. Analysis of the Gap According to Roles

It seems interesting, also for the purposes of a later comparison between the results of the expert surveys reported here and those of the survey conducted among future elites described in Part II of this volume, to examine the responses of the interviewees according to the roles they play in the national context.

These roles are grouped here into the following five basic categories: politicians, scientists, managers, military and journalists.

The question this section wants to answer is whether the opinions and attitudes of the individual categories, independently of home country, differ from each other, and if so, how.

Referring the reader for a detailed examination, albeit of synthesis, to Matrix 4, we note that it is the military leaders who characterise themselves most significantly with respect to the other four categories of top leaders. They appear to be the only ones still strongly tied to defence of the national territory as the primary mission of the armed forces, and indicate politicians' incompetence as the principal cause of tension between civilians and military (a view seconded by the scientists), sharing only with journalists the opportunity/necessity of greater involvement on their part in making political decisions that regard national security. For what concerns the effectiveness of political control of the armed forces, they are the only ones not to express any reservations; instead, many affirm that it is excessive.

The interviewed politicians see the armed forces chiefly as an instrument for all emergencies, with a marginal interest toward the more typically military ones. Not by chance, the prevalent choice for the missions to assign is MOOTW, although accompanied by a hope for greater flexibility. With regard to politico-military decisions they naturally reaffirm their supremacy, while as cause of tension between the two spheres they point to ideological differences (the primacy of ideology is perhaps rather to be expected for a politician), but they also acknowledge little understanding of military issues on the part of the public, as well as the resulting educational and cultural differences. Even in this characterisation, however, the politicians are less distant from the military leaders than the other categories included in the research.

Matrix 4. The Civil–Military Cultural Gap: Role-Ordered Matrix.

	Causes of tensions	Media's attitudes	Citizens' attitudes	Missions	Political control	Polit./mil. decisions
Politicians $N =$	Ideologies; citizens' poor knowledge; abandoning conscription; educational differences	Neutral to positive; journalists lack preparation; according to the politics	Positive, improving with PSOs; not very interested	MOOTW; all missions	Assured; internal control; Parliament lacking	The military participate in debate but do not take part in making the decision; military decides
Scientists $N =$	Cultural gap; budget; abandoning conscription; educational differences	Not competent; supportive	Positive; not interested; yes but without me	Identity crises; PSOs	Limited control by Parliament; internal; government	Politicians; lack of competence of politicians
Managers $N =$	Cultural gap; budget; reforms; international changes	Negative and sensationalist; balanced; a positive attitude today	Positive due to PSOs; lack of information	MOOTW; politicians more flexible	Parliament is not fully playing its role; efficient	Under pressure of different lobbies; politicians take the final decisions
Military $N =$	Incompetence of politicians; scandals and media; shrinking AF; changing tasks; missions; budget	Sensational; no professionals; neutral; not interested; they try to manipulate and provoke the army	Positive but mainly emotional; need for communication	Territorial defence; all missions; PSOs as opportunity	Totally assumed, maybe even too well; internal control	Politicians are "waterproof" to military's needs; military should have more chances to express opinions; military decides
Journalists $N =$	Ideological reasons; scandals; lack of interest; citizens' bad experiences	Journalists disappeared when the threat disappeared; few specialised; military not open; neutral	Detached because of ignorance; there is nothing to defend ourselves against; positive	Peacekeeping and humanitarian; all missions	Parliament still has much to control; transparency in the military is a myth; internal control	Politicians make decisions; military should be more involved; poor preparation of politicians

The priority of assigning MOOTW to the armed forces is also shared by the managers and, although with greater emphasis on PSOs, by the scientists and journalists, while the ideological, educational and cultural differences cited by the politicians as the main cause of civil–military tensions are shared by scientists, journalists and also managers. And finally, regarding political control of the armed forces, the politicians share with the other categories the view that, although a sufficiently sound control system exists everywhere, parliamentary control in particular often appears to be only formal.

The managers differentiate themselves from the other groups for an interpretation of decision-making in political–military matters as strongly influenced by the various lobbies.

The scientists share with the managers the cultural gap and budget issues as causes of tension between the civilian and military sectors, and in decision-making see a general incompetence of politicians on national defence problems.

The journalists, finally, ascribe the public's scant understanding of national defence issues, also indicated by the politicians, to lack of interest in them. According to this category, lack of understanding is one of the causes of tension between the two spheres, along with scandals within the military and, as already mentioned, ideological differences.

An analysis by topic shows agreement by all categories on the poor preparation of journalists on national security aspects and on a dearth of specialised journalists; according to the journalists themselves this derives from a decline in the threat, which produces a muted public interest in these issues.

Lastly, all the categories agree in considering the public's attitude toward the national armed forces as generally positive, with some reservations on the part of the journalists, who also see citizens as detached due to little understanding in this regard.

3. COMPARISON OF FUTURE AND PRESENT ELITES

The comparison between the two studied elites can be made only in very general terms here, for two fundamental reasons. The first is that the survey on the future elites, as described in detail in Part I of this volume, was a quantitative analysis, conducted on a fairly broad and representative sample of the investigated universe, while the survey on the present elites was carried out by means of interviews – and therefore the analysis of the results was qualitative – and the chosen sample was much more limited.

The second reason is that the survey topics were not exactly the same: in particular, the future elites were not asked to express their opinions regarding the existence of a gap and its causes and consequences (for obvious reasons). It follows that in the comparisons below, everything treated in Section 2.1 of this chapter will be absent.

Starting therefore from "What Shapes the Gap" (Matrix 5), we note in general that in the data obtained from the current elites a historical dimension is present that does not appear in the survey conducted on cadets and university students. The current top leaders interviewed are able to throw two important evolutionary aspects of the examined items into relief. The first is the phenomenon of a recent growth in trust in the military and its prevalent cause (increased participation in PSOs). The second is the often negative historical consequences for officers who have expressed personal opinions in the media. Perhaps also for this reason one registers a first difference of opinions between the two examined elites: while the young people are mostly favourable to freedom of expression for the military, like for other citizens, the current elites appear to be more cautious and more divided about espousing this view.

Understanding of national defence issues constitutes another moment of differentiation: while a majority of the future elites declare that they have good grasp of these issues, the current leaders and opinion makers feel that citizens in general have little understanding of them, and that politicians themselves are lacking in preparation on this subject. The public's limited

Matrix 5. What Shapes the Gap: Comparison of Future and Present Elites.

	Present elites	Future elites
Trusting the Military	Very high trust, higher than in the past: good impact of participation in PSOs	Very high trust
Opportunity of Officers to Express Opinion	Very few chances to do it in most countries. Bad consequences for expressed opinions; divided as to opportunity	Majority is in favour
Citizens' Knowledge	Citizens have scant knowledge	Elites show good knowledge
Media's Attitude	Often sensationalist; journalists lack specific preparation; public not very interested	Balanced; not good media coverage
Citizens' Attitude	Positive, but often not very interested	Mostly positive

understanding on security issues appears to be confirmed, at least in Europe, by the data of the recent Eurobarometers (2003 and 2004); one can therefore say that the future elites in general (not only the military ones) seem to be significantly better informed on these topics than average citizens in the respective countries.

On the attitude of the media, the future elites complain of insufficient coverage of military issues; the present elites agree, but they also indicate the causes (sensationalism of the media, poorly prepared journalists, little interest on the part of readers).

Citizens' attitudes toward their armed forces are deemed positive by both samples, confirming the common datum in the opinion polls of the examined countries, but the current elites also register a growing public disinterest in the military which is more marked in some countries.

Differences of opinion between the two groups are also noted in regard to threat perception and the priority for assigning missions to the national armed forces (Matrix 6). The present elites feel the terrorist threat more strongly and, for some countries, also the threat posed by mass immigration.

The opinions on defence funding are quite similar. Interestingly, both the current elites and the future ones feel the necessity/advisability of spending more on defence in the examined countries. This is an attitude that seems to clash with an opposing one of the citizens, who in many countries, as declared by the current leaders interviewed, press for a reduction in such

Matrix 6. The Gap and Civil-Military Relations: Comparison of Future and Present Elites.

	Present elites	Future elites
Major threats	Terrorism; mass immigration; drug trafficking; crime in some countries only	Crime; drug trafficking; terrorism; war over vital raw materials
Missions	MOOTW; PSOs; national defence	Country defence; civil disasters; PSOs; fight terrorism; proliferation
Budget	Too low; public opinion wants further reductions	It should grow (64%); it should stay as it is (20%)
Political control	Generally realised; greater role of parliament desired	Necessary and fully realised
Political–military decisions	Made by politicians; military leadership not involved enough; lack of preparation among politicians	No political influence of the military; politicians have too little knowledge of security issues

expenditures. Here the gap seems to be between elites as a whole, both present and future, and public opinion in general.

Political control of the armed forces is judged to be well achieved by both groups examined, with more caution on the part of the current leaders, who often invoke a more significant role on the part of national parliaments.

On political–military decisions, no one questions the pre-eminent role of the political actors, but their specific preparation is considered poor by both of the examined samples. The current elites also often call for greater involvement of the military leadership in decision-making.

In evaluating the general picture of the comparison between current elites and future elites, a couple of considerations of some interest once again emerge.

The first is that, despite the differences in attitudes and opinions registered here between the current civilian and military leaders (see Section 2.4 of this chapter), there is much greater agreement of responses among them than is registered between cadets and university students. Apparently, at the start of the career, professional roles are lived in much more clear-cut and conflicting ways.

A second consideration – which is, at bottom, a specification of the first – is that taking as a whole the opinions expressed at the two levels, future elites and current elites, we see the disappearance of certain extreme aspects in the latter that were proper to a sizeable minority of the university students. None of the interviewed experts cast doubt, for example, on the necessity of national armed forces, on their professionalism (albeit with different accents) or the need for adequate budget appropriations. Interesting in this regard is the affirmation of one Italian interviewee (a journalist), politically positioned on the left, who declared: "I, who was an antimilitarist in the past, saw in Bosnia what it means for a country not to have an army and I think my country has to have armed forces and I want it to have them".

4. CONCLUSIONS

In order to present a synthetic framework, in Matrix 7 I have tried to summarise the main aspects of the present and future elites on the key themes of the research: the trend of the gap is absent for the reason given in the previous section.

This matrix does not require any further comment, I believe.

Matrix 7. Civil–Military Cultural Gap: Conceptual Matrix.

	Nature of the Gap	What Shapes the Gap	Civil-Military Relations
Present elites	Fewer differences between civilians and military (opinions on missions, involvement in decision-making, incompetence of politicians); very few extreme antimilitary positions	High trust in the military; good attitude of citizens but lack of interest; some doubts on the opportunity for officers to express their views in the media; media are neutral but journalists lack preparation in security	Political control generally assured, some absence of parliaments; lack of knowledge by politicians; budget is too low; main missions PSOs and MOOTW in general
Future elites[a]	Rather strong differences between cadets and univ. students (opinions on nation, role of armed forces, citizen state relations, collective interests, media perception, military training perception); some percentages (15–20%) of extreme antimilitary positions among univ. students	Elites have good knowledge and trust in the military; citizens have a good attitude towards AF; officers should be allowed to express their opinions in the media; media attitude is seen differently, but media coverage is scarce	Political control is important and largely assured; politicians have modest knowledge of military affairs; defence budget should grow; main military missions are defending the country, civil disasters, PSOs, fighting terrorism, proliferation

[a]It must be considered that the patterns and the intensity of a gap potential vary along the 13 countries, sometimes even considerably.

4.1. Present and Future Elites

Attempting to draw a few more general conclusions, it must be said that cultural differences between civilian and military respondents appears to be more present in the young than among the current elites: it probably attenuates with experience and with the broadening of individuals' political and social vision with advancing age. Reasons for considering it a generational change do not emerge: indeed, the trend, with the expanded deployment of armed forces in PSOs, toward greater public appreciation of the military and its function in most of the examined countries can lead one to believe that when today's future elites become active elites the shift will be towards even greater uniformity of opinions and judgements between military and civilians than today and in the past.

The different vision between the two elites with regard to a kind of democratic normalisation of the military profession also appears significant: the future elites seem to consider the officer a citizen like anyone else, with the same rights of public expression (through the media) and sharing the same values and democratic conceptions, points on which the present elites display a more conservative attitude.

Albeit with the cited differences, certain points of agreement present in both elites, current and future, appear interesting: in particular, the opinion regarding insufficient preparation of politicians, and also of journalists, on security issues, and perhaps as a consequence, ignorance of the public on these topics. There also appears to be agreement on the necessity of adapting the military budget to the actual security requirements in the various countries: on this theme there seems to be present a gap between the public opinion of the examined countries and the surveyed elites as a whole.

4.2. Civil and Military Culture

Finally, examining the surveyed elites as a whole, we see the main differences that emerge between the two cultures, civilian and military.

A first group of these differences is present, and will likely remain also in the future, that appear to be inherent to the particular mission of the military. They mainly stem from the more in-depth analysis made on the future elites and are chiefly centred on the following traits that characterise military culture:

1. Primacy of the community over the individual and less emphasis on individual rights and interests: this is perhaps the biggest contrast between the dominant individualistic culture that reigns in postmodern democratic societies[3] and the culture of solidarity prevalent in the military subculture.
2. A major trust in State institutions: a probable consequence of the primacy of the community;
3. The greater emphasis laid by the military on missions with a more strictly military content over missions to provide aid and/or restore internal order and peacekeeping missions. It should be pointed out here that the emphasis placed on these roles appears to be aimed at preserving that warrior culture that military leaders deem necessary for military effectiveness, even in tasks other than warfighting.[4]

4. Greater pessimism as to the entity and likelihood of national security threats, which seems to be an integral part of the culture of those who have concrete responsibility for that security.
5. The necessity of recognising and respecting a professional and ethical autonomy of the military.

These are aspects that, in agreement with the prevalent literature already cited (see Chapter 1), it would be a mistake to want to do away with if one does not wish the military to lose its ability to perform its specific function.[5]

A second group of cultural differences emerges from the present research which do not appear to be closely tied to military effectiveness. It seems desirable to at least mitigate them with a view to better civil–military collaboration, increasingly necessary in the face of today's diversified threats. They can be summarised as follows:

1. A different perception of national security issues and aspects between the political class and military professionals. Two principal causes of this difference emerge from the research: one, natural to every professional sector, is constituted by the overestimation that the military professional makes of his function; the second is represented by the general lack of preparation of politicians on these issues. This is an assessment that, although with differing intensities, is made both by members of the military and by civilians, both by the present elites and by the future ones.
2. A decision-making process with regard to military issues that is often seen as unsatisfactory by numerous interviewees. In particular, the military elites (and not only them) complain of not being involved enough in this process; the civilians complain of little involvement of national parliaments both in the decision-making process and in political control of the armed forces. The causes of this situation are ascribed to poor decision-making practices by many governments and/or national legislative deficiencies.
3. Mutual distrust between the media and the military (more towards the latter than the former). The media feel that military leaders always want to hide something, the military leaders feel that the media are only out for a scoop, to highlight scandals or create them, without making any contribution to discussion of the basic problems of security. The causes of this distrust that emerge from the research are, for the military, a certain closure to or, at least, a preoccupation towards the media, for the media, poor preparation of journalists and a lack of genuine interest in military security issues.

4. General lack of understanding and, often, disinterest of the public in military security issues. The causes are multiple: the situation is undoubtedly influenced by the postmodern position of advanced democratic societies, where individualism is pushed to the extreme and prevails over the spirit of community, but the incompetence of politicians and the cited shortcomings of the media also contribute, and are indicated as causes of the public's ignorance by many interviewees.

As can be seen, it is a matter of general political problems, certainly national but more or less common to all the examined countries, problems that cannot be solved by the military institution itself but which require wide-ranging political planning. Nevertheless, they must be tackled by governments and national parliaments, particularly in the momentous and delicate passage from conscription to volunteer military service.

4.3. America and Europe

One last aspect to deal with in these concluding notes regards the comparison between the results of the present research and the American research of Feaver and Kohn (see Feaver & Kohn, 2001), which provided the idea and the stimulus for it. The assumed data in fact enable us to make a comparison, even if sketchy,[6] of the cultural gap in non-American advanced democracies with the gap registered in the U.S.

Taking up again the list of the most significant results of the TISS report, already evidenced in Chapter 1, concordances and discordances with the results of our research can be seen for each of them.

The principal data of the TISS survey were therefore the following:

1. Our first finding was that there are many "gaps" to be explored, reflecting multiple dimensions and between different segments of the military and civilian populations.
2. The gap between the U.S. military and civilian society is growing.
3. As we leave the 20th century, the number of people who have served in the military or have other personal connections with the military is declining. This "experience gap" is an artefact of the shrinking all-volunteer force.
4. The elite military is fairly critical about the quality of leadership in the political institutions.
5. The elite military possess a pervasive hostility towards the media.

6. Military (and the mass military) have more trust and confidence in government institutions than civilians.
7. On social values, elite military officers diverge from both elite and mass civilians.
8. By a very large margin (76%), elite military officers oppose gays and lesbians openly serving in the military. But a majority of civilian elites (55%) and the mass public (57%) support gays and lesbians openly serving.
9. The civilian population, both elite and especially mass, has very little understanding of civil–military relations and civilian control of the military.
10. The popular media through fiction and film reinforces a diverse set of stereotypes about the military and civilian society.

The research inside the non-American democracies included in our sample shows, on the same points, the following results:

1) The existence of various gaps (due to the existence of subcultures), in addition to the one between civilian culture and military culture, is confirmed also in the countries of our sample, including:
   a) The gender gap (see Chapter 9, Part II). Indeed, as the authors of that chapter point out, the adoption of an all-volunteer force in several of the countries examined here over the last 15 years has produced recruitment problems everywhere that have led to greater reliance on recruitment of women. In the process, women become a focus of attention. The research data lead us to conclude on this topic that there is not only a civil–military gap concerning the integration of women into the armed forces. Rather, there is a gender gap and a gap between specific countries.
   b) The gap between the nations studied here. As already mentioned in the preceding point, "The variance between the 13 countries included in our survey is mostly larger than the one between civil and military students when it comes to the basic value dimensions" (see Chapter 3, Part II).
   c) The gap between university students of different faculties. For example, those attending political science faculties display, in almost all of the countries, political and opinion positions (attitude toward the media, see Chapter 5, Part II) that significantly differentiate them from the students of the other examined faculties.
2) A growing gap between civil and military culture is not found in the countries we surveyed. If anything, the last decade has registered an

opposing trend and the opinion of the interviewed experts is that this trend will last, at least in the medium term.

3) The experience gap[7] also exists in the countries studied by us and appears to be a direct consequence of the general passage from conscription to all-volunteer forces and, even where this has not yet occurred, of significant downsizing of the armed services. The decline in the number of people who have served in the military appears to be general in all postmodern countries.
4) Also in the countries of our sample the military elite (but not only) appears to be critical of the political leadership, but limited to military security issues.
5) Not exactly a hostility but a distrust of the media by the military exists in the countries studied by us as well. The trend of this gap appears to be declining, however (see Chapter 5, Part II, for the future elites, and this chapter for the present elites).
6) The greater trust that military place in state institutions is general to all the examined countries: it probably constitutes an identifying feature of military culture.
7) The divergence on social values found by the TISS research for the U.S. does not have a general correspondent in the studied countries; on this point national subjectivities prevail.
8) The problem was not posed to our interviewees.
9) A lack of understanding of the issues and aspects of military security among national civilian populations emerges in our survey also and appears to be general; this is not so for the theme of political control of the armed forces, where the elites interviewed by us display good understanding and precise opinions.
10) The analysis that we performed on the perception of the media does not allow a comparison on stereotypes.

In short, the existence of various cultural differences, such as an experience gap of the civilian population, and also of the political class, appears to be general also in the countries included in our survey. Some characteristics already encountered in the American military elite, such as a particular trust in government institutions, a certain distrust of the media and a critical attitude towards politicians' ability to manage military security, are present in the military elites of our sample and are probably structural.

What appears to be clearly opposing is the trend found for the civil–military gap – on the rise in the U.S., probably diminishing in the countries that we surveyed. This aspect appears to be particularly important in view of the datum, already cited, that emerged from our research: the presence in the existing cultural gap of aspects that do not appear to be necessitated by or necessary to military effectiveness and which it thus appears desirable to at least mitigate with a view to better civil–military collaboration.

NOTES

1. A fifth aspect, mentioned in Chapter 1, the national dimensions of the gap, has been also dealt with in Chapter 10 of this book.
2. See "The Cultural Gap between the Military and Parent Society in Italy", in Caforio and Kümmel (2005, pp. 127–150).
3. Also concurring is Anthony Forster (2006), who, referring to the thought of Christopher Dandeker, points to today's (p. 7) "changed societal context in which the supporting framework for core military values is increasingly challenged by a more individualistic, egalitarian and litigious society...".
4. Various authors express themselves on this: for example, Anthony Forster (2006), reporting the words of Charles Guthrie (p. 217): "Capabilities based on war-fighting will give us the ability to contribute to other types of operations – the reverse is not true."
5. "Armed forces will to a degree always have some differences from society, since they carry a distinctive duty to discharge the lethal use of force within prescribed circumstances," writes Forster (2006, p. 129), referring to the ideas of Christopher Dandeker.
6. The research conducted by us used different methodologies from the U.S. study, just as both the investigated universes and the chosen samples are different. However, the fact that the topic is identical and that many questions of the administered questionnaire are similar make comparison possible.
7. As we wrote in Chapter 1: as we leave the 20th century, the number of people have served in the military or have other personal connections with the military is declining. This "experience gap" is an artifact of the shrinking all-volunteer force.

REFERENCES

Caforio, G., & Kümmel, G. (Eds). (2005). *Military missions and their implications reconsidered: The aftermath of September 11th*. Amsterdam: Elsevier.

Feaver, P. D., & Kohn, R. H. (Eds). (2001). *Soldiers and civilians: The civil–military gap and American national security*. Cambridge: MIT Press.

Forster, A. (2006). *Armed forces and society in Europe*. New York Houndmills: Palgrave Macmillan.

Huntington, S. (1957). *The soldier and the state*. Cambridge: Harvard University Press.

NOTE ON CONTRIBUTORS

Bahattin Akşit, BA (1968), METU; MA (1971) and PhD (1975) University of Chicago. Dr. Akşit, Professor in the Department of Sociology, Middle East Technical University, conducts research in the following areas: Psycho-social aspects of disaster management; Community participation and volunteer associations; Rural structural transformations, Social change and cleavage in towns and cities; Sociology of religion and secularism; Sociology of Middle East and Central Asia; Army and conflict resolution. Recent publications are: (1) Karanci, N., Akşit, B. and Dirik, G. (2005). Impact of a community disaster awareness training program in Turkey, *Social Behavior and Personality: An International Journal*, 33(3); (2) Akşit, B., Karanci, N. and Gunduz-Hosgör, A. (2001), *Turkey, working street children in three metropolitan cities*, International Labour Organization; (3) Akşit, B. (1993). Studies in rural transformation in Turkey. In: P. Stirling (Ed.), *Culture and the economy: Changes in Turkish villages*. Cambridgeshire: The Eothen Press; (4) Akşit, B. (1991). Islamic education in Turkey: Medrese reform in late Ottoman times and Imam-hatip schools. In: R. Tapper (Ed.), *Islam in modern Turkey: Religion politics and literature in a secular state*. London: I B Tauris and University of London.

Axel Augé, Philosophy Doctor (PhD). Ecole de Saint-Cyr Coëtquidan (France), Centre de recherche de Coëtquidan (CREC). Teaching, first Sociology of military and civil organisation, second State, army and society in Saint-Cyr military College. Sociologist, especially on military sociology in south countries (Africa) and on social network in small group and student's military sociability.

Giuseppe Caforio is retired general of the Italian Army. He is president of the Research Committee 01 "Armed Forces and Conflict Resolution" of the ISA, vice-president of the Italian Interuniversity Centre of Historical and Military Studies, founding member and coordinator of a working group of the ERGOMAS, as well as member of several other institutes of research.

He is also an outside consultant of the governmental Italian Centre of Strategic and Military Studies. He has a Strategic Sciences degree, a Law degree, a Political Science degree and a Master in Communication Science. Publications: more than 120 monographs, articles and research papers in the field of the sociology of the military and different aspects of civil–military relations published in eight different languages. His recent main publications include: *The sociology of the military*, (1998); (Ed.) *The flexible officer. Professional education and military operation other than war: A cross-national analysis*, 2001; (Ed.) *Handbook of the sociology of the military*, 2003; (Ed.) *Social sciences and the military*, 2006.

Mehmet Çakar was born in 1976, Turkey. He graduated from Faculty of Economics and Administrative Sciences, Baskent University, Ankara, Turkey in 2001. Later in 2004 he got MSc in Political Science from Middle East Technical University. He is currently a doctorate candidate and research assistant at the same university, Management and Organisation programme and MA candidate in Sociology, Hacettepe University, Ankara. His academic and intellectual interests were mainly on the topics of organisational sociology and civil–military relations.

Sabine Collmer, born in Stuttgart, Germany, studied Sociology, Psychology and Anthropology at the University of Munich and earned a doctoral degree (Dr Phil) in 1995 from Technical University Munich. Her professional background covers research at the Institute for Social Research of the Bundeswehr (SOWI) (1991–1995), science management at Technical University Berlin (1995–1998) and Assistant Professor at the University of the German Armed Forces in Munich (1999–2005). Since 2000, she is the acting vice-president of the working group on armed forces and social sciences (AMS) in Germany. She currently holds the position of Director of Research at the George C. Marshall European Centre for Security Studies in Garmisch-Partenkirchen, Germany. She has published widely on civil–military relations and new forms of warfare.

Antonio M. Díaz Fernández holds a doctorate in Political Science and Administration from the University of Barcelona and completed his university degree in Law and Political Science. He also holds a Masters in Commerce and Legislation awarded by the Barcelona College of Lawyers and in Peace, Security and Defence awarded by the University Institute "General

Gutiérrez Mellado" of Madrid. He has won prizes in 1997 and 2003 from the Spanish Ministry of Defence for his research into security and has held professorships at the universities of Barcelona and of San Salvador. He is currently the director of a research project on cooperation between European intelligence services. He is Professor of the University Institute "General Gutiérrez Mellado" in Madrid (Spain) and Rey Juan Carlos University where he teaches and carries out research into the intelligence services. He is also Professor of Political Science at the University of Burgos. His most recent publication on the Spanish intelligence services is "Historia de una transicion" (The history of a transition) Alianza Editorial, Madrid (2005).

Maja Garb, PhD in Defence Science. Works at the Faculty of Social Sciences, University of Ljubljana, Slovenia, as Assistant Professor and research fellow. Fields of current research interest: military professionalism, demobilisation and social reintegration of military personnel, the personnel aspects of peace operations, military leadership, cultural dimensions of civil–military relations and post-conflict reconstruction.

Karl W. Haltiner is Professor of Sociology and Head of Military Sociology at the Military Academy at the Swiss Federal Institute of Technology (ETH) in Zurich, Switzerland. His current research is on the relations of armed forces and society. He focuses mainly on the democratic control of the military and on the effects of social changes on the armed forces and the officer profession in Europe. He directs the annual trend study *Swiss Public Opinion and Security Policy*. His recent books include *The European armed forces in transition* (edited with Franz Kernic & Paul Klein, 2005) and *Civil–military relations in Europe* (edited with H. Born, M. Caparini, & J. Kuhlmann, 2006).

Lindy Heinecken was formerly Deputy Director of the Centre for Military Studies (CEMIS) at the South African Military Academy. She now serves as Professor of Sociology at Stellenbosch University. She has contributed to numerous books in the field of military sociology and has published widely on subjects such as the management of diversity within armed forces, civil–military relations, military unionism and HIV/AIDS and security. Her most recent publication is a book edited together with Richard Bartle titled *Military unionism in the post Cold War era: A future reality*.

Ljubica Jelušič is Professor for military sociology, theories of war, peace studies and anthropology of war at the Faculty of Social Sciences, University of Ljubljana. She is teaching at the Senior Officer Course and General Staff Course of the Slovenian Army. Her main research interests and led projects are: Slovenian army in peace operations, defense restructuring and conversion, human resources management in the military and democratic control over the armed forces. Some of the published books: *Military legitimacy* (Ljubljana, 1997), *Sexism in the military uniform* (Ed. Ljubljana, 2003), *Peace operations and the role of Slovenia* (Ed. Ljubljana, 2005).

Sibel Kalaycıoğlu (Associate Professor), Department of Sociology, Middle East Technical University, Ankara, Turkey. PhD from University of Kent at Canterbury. Her interest areas are: social stratification and mobility, sociology of migration, political sociology, relationship and conflict between state and civil society, citizenship, political participation, sociology of work and industry, social deviance, sociology of development, sociology of coexistence and conflict. Her publications include: Rittersberger-Tılıç, H. and Kalaycıoğlu, S. (1998). Nation-state and the individual: Alternative strategies of consent from below, *Asian and African Studies, Slovak Academy of Sciences*, 7(1), 69–80, Slovakia; Rittersberger-Tılıç, H. and Kalaycıoğlu, S. (1999). Legitimation and re-production of domestic violence in Turkish families, *Zeitschrift für Türkeistudien*, 2, 225–241; Kalaycıoğlu, S. and Rittersberger-Tılıç, H. (2000). Intergenerational solidarity networks of instrumental and cultural transfers within migrant families: A sample from Turkey, *Ageing and Society*, Cambridge University Press, Vol. 20, pp. 523–542.

Adam Kołodziejczyk, Polish Military retired Colonel, graduated High Military School in Poznań (1975, Social Sciences). He received MA in Philosophy at the University of Adam Mickiewicz in Poznań (1976). He was the lecturer of Sociology at High Officer School in Piła. In 1985, received his PhD at the Military Political Academy in Warsaw. Director Military Institute for Sociological Research (1990–1999) and Military Office for Sociological Research (1999–2003). Vice-president of First Private University for Business and Administration in Warsaw (2004–2006). Member of Polish Sociological Association and International Sociological Association (RC 01) and ERGOMAS. He is currently the director of Institute of the Sociology in High School of the Personnel Management in Warsaw. Coordinator of several national research projects in the field of social sciences and participant in international research projects (e.g. ERGOMAS, SOWI).

Gerhard Kümmel (1964), DrPhil, Study of Political Science, Sociology and History at the Philipps University Marburg (1985–1991); Dissertation scholarship of the Friedrich-Naumann-Foundation (1991–1994); Research scholarship of the German Historical Institute, Washington, DC (1992); Post-doctorate scholarship of the German Research Foundation (DFG) (1995–1997); J. William Fulbright Dissertation Award of the Fulbright-Commission (1996); Lecturer of the German Academic Exchange Service (DAAD) at the University of Victoria, Canada (Winter term, 1997); Senior researcher at the Bundeswehr Institute for Social Research (SOWI) since September 1997; President of the German Working Group Armed Forces and Society (AMS); Vice-president of Research Committee 01: Armed Forces and Conflict Resolution within the International Sociological Association (ISA-RC 01). Fields of interest: Security Politics and Military Sociology. Current projects: The Integration of Women into the Bundeswehr and The Postheroic Society. Recent publication in English: *Military missions and their implications reconsidered: The aftermath of September 11th* (co-edited with G. Caforio), Amsterdam: Elsevier, 2005.

Rafael Martínez Martínez is doctor in Laws (University of Zaragoza) and Professor of Political Science at the University of Barcelona. He has been research fellow at Pau et Païs de l'Adour University (France), Fondation Nationale des Sciènces Politiques (Paris, France) and the Department of Political Science at Yale University (USA). He has taught at the following universities: Pau and Lyon (France), Católica (Uruguay), Centroamericana (El Salvador), Zaragoza, UNED and Barcelona (Spain). He has received several prizes, among them the National Prize of Research given by the Ministry of Defence (2002). His areas of research are: security and defence, electoral systems, government and political parties.

René Moelker (Rotterdam, 1960) is Associate Professor of Sociology at the Netherlands Defense Academy. He holds a PhD from the Erasmus University, Rotterdam (1992). His work in military sociology concentrates on the sociology of military families, military technology, military profession, military education, conflict in Chechnya and media. His latest book (2006) together with Ulrich vom Hagen and Joseph Soeters reports on military cooperation between German and Dutch soldiers. His latest project is an editorial one regarding Norbert Elias' work on military sociology which is to be published in 2007 as *The genesis of the naval profession* (UCD Press).

Marina Nuciari is Professor of Sociology at University of Torino (Italy), Department of Social Sciences and Professor of Military Sociology at the Faculty of Strategic Studies, Italian Army Military Academy. She is a founding member of ERGOMAS and was its chairperson from 1992 to 1996. She is also member of several other research institutes, such as, the Inter-University Seminar on Armed Forces and Society (since 1993), the Associazione Italiana di Sociologia (AIS); Board member of the Research Committee 01 of the International Sociological Association. She is author of many volumes and articles in the fields of general sociology, military sociology and cross-cultural research.

Tibor Szvircsev Tresch is a military sociologist and is an assistant at the Military Academy at the ETH in Zurich. He studied Sociology, Political Science, and Criminology at the University of Zurich. He earned a doctor's degree in Sociology at the University of Zurich in 2005. The topic of his thesis focuses on the ongoing transformation process in Europe's armed forces from conscription to all volunteer forces. Since April 2002 he has been a teaching and research assistant at the Military Academy at the ETH Zurich, Lectureship Military Sociology. He lectured also at the ETH Zurich and the University Zurich in military sociology. From August 2006 until July 2007 he has an assignment to the NATO Defense College in Rome as a Senior Research Fellow. He is actually interested in the question of the cooperation between armed forces in PSO regarding the topic of military cultures.

Demet Varoğlu, born in Ankara, Turkey, is an Associate Professor of Organizational Behavior. She had her BSc in Business Administration and MBA from Middle East Technical University, and received her PhD in General Management from School of Political Sciences, Ankara University. While she was working on her dissertation, she spent 16 months (between August 1990 and December 1991) in Ottawa, Canada, and besides working on her dissertation she also taught Organizational Behavior at the University of Ottawa. She retired after working for more than 20 years at the Department of Business Administration at METU. Currently, she teaches Introduction to Management, Human Resource Management, and Negotiation at TOBB University of Economics and Technology. She has publications on employee and managerial behavior, conflict management, political behavior in organizations and women in armed forces. Her main research interests are gender and political issues in organizations besides various forms of discrimination in organizations.

Kadir Varoğlu (retired Colonel) was born in 1958. He worked as officer in the Turkish Armed Forces, chaired Systems Management Department and established Institute of Defence Sciences at the Turkish Military Academy. After retiring, he started to work for Başkent University in Ankara and now chairing Department of Management. He has books and articles published on leadership, negotiation, cross-cultural studies in international management and strategic management.

Claude Weber has a PhD in Social Sciences (Ethnology) from the Marc Bloch University in Strasbourg (France). He is Senior Lecturer in Sociology and Chief of the Sociology Department at the French Military Academy St-Cyr in Coëtquidan. He teaches Military Sociology, Sociology of the Military Action, Management of All Volunteers Forces, Relations between Military and Media and Management of Intercultural Relationships. Member of the Military Sociology Laboratory in St-Cyr Coëtquidan and the Anthropology and Sociology Laboratory from the University of Rennes, he is presently conducting research about one battalion of cadets in St-Cyr (immersion) and about the management of the cultural diversity during operations in the French Army.

Alise Weibull is a researcher at the Swedish National Defence College, Department of Leadership and Management. Within the department she is responsible for a research area named "Organisation and profession". Dr. Weibull is, since the beginning of the 1990s, a member of the European Research Group on Military and Society (ERGOMAS) and is also a member of the Inter-University Seminar on Armed Forces and Society (IUS) and Research Committee 01, Armed Forces and Conflict Resolution of the International Sociological Association (ISA). Much of her recent writings have been concerned with understanding military challenges in international missions. A new ERGOMAS working group named "High reliability organisations in a network centric world" is under formation with Weibull as the coordinator.

Yantsislav Yanakiev. 1995, PhD in Sociology from Institute of Sociology, Bulgarian Academy of Sciences, Sofia (Thesis: *Quantification of Categorical Survey's Data: Application of Optimal Scaling Methods*); 1982, Naval Academy, Varna (MSc, Military Science); chief of "Systems Analyses" Department and senior researcher at Defence Advanced Research Institute, G. S. Rakovski Defence and Staff College, Sofia. Key research interests: Sociology of the military (changing patterns of military organisation; the new military missions and the challenges of the military professionalism; public opinion and security policy; international military cooperation in the post-Cold War period; the military and the young generation; minority and gender issues in the military). Publications: more than 50 monographs, articles and research papers in the field of the sociology of the military and different aspects of civil–military relations published in Bulgarian, English and Russian languages.

Marian Zulean holds a PhD in (Military) Sociology. He is currently adviser with the National Security Department, Office of the Romanian President and Associate Professor at the University of Bucharest and SNSPA. He teaches policy analysis, international security and civil–military relations. He is a member of the IUS, RC 01 of ISA and ERGOMAS. His main fields of interests are military sociology, civil–military relations, security sector reform, NATO transformation, international affairs and global public policy. Among his latest publications: The military in post-communist countries in transition, in: G. Caforio (Ed.), *Social sciences and the military*, Routledge, 2006; Civil–military cultural gap in Romania, in: G. Caforio and G. Kummel (Eds), *Military missions and their implications reconsidered: The aftermath of September 11th*, Elsevier, 2005; Reforming the security sectors in SEE: Lessons learned and their relevance for a wider Black Sea area policy. *Connections*, Vol. III, No. 4, December 2004.

INDEX

www.ingramcontent.com/pod-product-compliance
Ingram Content Group UK Ltd.
Pitfield, Milton Keynes, MK11 3LW, UK
UKHW020845290926
15470UKWH00004B/1571

9 780444 530240